CU00663752

SELF-HARM: LONGER-TERM MANAGEMENT

National Clinical Guideline Number 133

National Collaborating Centre for Mental Health
commissioned by the

**National Institute for Health &
Clinical Excellence**

published by
**The British Psychological Society and The Royal College of
Psychiatrists**

British Library Cataloguing-in-Publication Data

A catalogue record for this book is available from the British Library.

ISBN-: 978-1-908020-41-3

Printed in Great Britain by Stanley L. Hunt (Printers) Ltd.

Additional material: data CD-Rom created by Pix18 (www.pix18.co.uk)

developed by	National Collaborating Centre for Mental Health
	The Royal College of Psychiatrists
	4th Floor, Standon House
	21 Mansell Street
	London
	E1 8AA
	www.nccmh.org.uk

commissioned by National Institute for Health and Clinical Excellence
MidCity Place, 71 High Holborn
London
WCIV 6NA
www.nice.org.uk

published by The British Psychological Society
St Andrews House
48 Princess Road East
Leicester
LE1 7DR
www.bps.org.uk

The British Psychological Society

and

The Royal College of Psychiatrists
17 Belgrave Square
London
SW1X 8PG
www.rcpsych.ac.uk

RC PSYCH
ROYAL COLLEGE OF
PSYCHIATRISTS

CONTENTS

Contents

GUIDELINE DEVELOPMENT GROUP MEMBERS

Professor Navneet Kapur (Chair)
Professor of Psychiatry and Population Health, University of Manchester
Honorary Consultant Psychiatrist, Manchester Mental Health and Social Care Trust

Professor Tim Kendall (Facilitator, Guideline Development Group)
Director, National Collaborating Centre for Mental Health (NCCMH)
Medical Director, Sheffield Health and Social Care Trust
Consultant Adult Psychiatrist

Mr Benedict Anigbogu
Health Economist (from October 2010), NCCMH

Mr Gareth Allen
Representing Service User and Carer Interests

Mr Simon Baston
Lead Nurse Liaison Psychiatry, Sheffield Health and Social Care NHS Foundation Trust

Ms Henna Bhatti
Research Assistant, NCCMH

Dr Andrew Briggs
Head of Child and Adolescent Psychotherapy, Kent & Medway NHS and Social
Care Partnership Trust

Professor Stephen Briggs
Consultant Social Worker, Tavistock and Portman NHS Foundation Trust
Professor of Social Work, University Of East London

Mr Anthony Cox
Knowledge Manager, PAPYRUS Prevention of Young Suicide (until March 2011)
Representing Service User and Carer Interests

Ms Melissa Chan
Systematic Reviewer, NCCMH

Mr Matthew Dyer
Health Economist (until September 2010), NCCMH

Dr Jonathan Evans
Consultant Senior Lecturer, University of Bristol

Guideline development group members

Dr Paul Gill
Consultant in Liaison Psychiatry, Sheffield Health and Social Care Trust
Chair, Faculty of Liaison Psychiatry, Royal College of Psychiatrists

Ms Naomi Glover
Research Assistant, NCCMH

Ms Marie Halton
Research Assistant, NCCMH

Ms Kate Hunt
Lead Professional Consultant Clinical Psychologist, Acute & Crisis Services,
Sussex Partnership NHS Foundation Trust

Dr Suzanne Kearney
General Practitioner (GP)

Ms Katherine Leggett
Project Manager, NCCMH

Mr Nick Meader
Systematic Reviewer (until October 2010), NCCMH

Professor Rory O'Connor
Professor of Psychology, University of Stirling

Mr Richard Pacitti
Chief Executive, Mind in Croydon
Representing Service User and Carer Interests

Ms Sarah Stockton
Senior Information Scientist, NCCMH

Dr Michaela Swales
Consultant Clinical Psychologist, North Wales Adolescent Service & Senior
Lecturer, School of Psychology, Bangor University

Dr Clare Taylor
Senior Editor, NCCMH

Dr Alison Wood
Consultant in Adolescent Psychiatry, Cheshire and Mersey Regional Tier 4
Adolescent Service

ACKNOWLEDGEMENTS

The Guideline Development Group would like to thank:
Professor Keith Hawton, and the many authors who provided data for the Cochrane Review included in this guideline.
Ms Nuala Ernest, Assistant Editor, NCCMH
Ms Melinda Smith, Research Assistant, NCCMH

1   PREFACE

This guideline has been developed to advise on the long-term management of self-harm and follows on from *Self-harm: the Short-Term Physical and Psychological Management and Secondary Prevention of Self-harm in Primary and Secondary Care* (NICE, 2004a). The short-term management guideline includes guidance for the treatment of self-harm within the first 48 hours of an incident. The current guideline is concerned with the longer-term psychological treatment of both single and recurrent episodes of self-harm, and does not include recommendations for the physical treatment of self-harm or for psychosocial management in emergency departments (these can be found in NICE, 2004a).

The guideline recommendations have been developed by a multidisciplinary team of healthcare professionals, people who self-harm, their carers and guideline methodologists after careful consideration of the best available evidence. It is intended that the guideline will be useful to clinicians and service commissioners in providing and planning high-quality care for people who self-harm while also emphasising the importance of the experience of care for people who self-harm and their carers (see Appendix 1 for more details on the scope of the guideline).

Although the evidence base is rapidly expanding, there are a number of major gaps and future revisions of this guideline will incorporate new scientific evidence as it develops. The guideline makes a number of research recommendations specifically to address gaps in the evidence base. In the meantime, it is hoped that the guideline will assist clinicians, people who self-harm and their carers by identifying the merits of particular treatment approaches where the evidence from research and clinical experience exists.

1.1   NATIONAL CLINICAL GUIDELINES

1.1.1   What are clinical guidelines?

Clinical guidelines are 'systematically developed statements that assist clinicians and patients in making decisions about appropriate treatment for specific conditions' (Mann, 1996). They are derived from the best available research evidence, using predetermined and systematic methods to identify and evaluate the evidence relating to the specific condition in question. Where evidence is lacking, the guidelines incorporate statements and recommendations based upon the consensus statements developed by the Guideline Development Group (GDG).

Clinical guidelines are intended to improve the process and outcomes of healthcare in a number of different ways. They can:

● provide up-to-date evidence-based recommendations for the management of conditions and disorders by healthcare professionals

- be used as the basis to set standards to assess the practice of healthcare professionals
- form the basis for education and training of healthcare professionals
- assist people who self-harm and their carers in making informed decisions about their treatment and care
- improve communication between healthcare professionals, people who self-harm and their carers
- help identify priority areas for further research.

1.1.2   Uses and limitation of clinical guidelines

Guidelines are not a substitute for professional knowledge and clinical judgement. They can be limited in their usefulness and applicability by a number of different factors: the availability of high-quality research evidence, the quality of the methodology used in the development of the guideline, the generalisability of research findings and the uniqueness of individuals who self-harm.

Although the quality of research in this field is variable, the methodology used here reflects current international understanding on the appropriate practice for guideline development (Appraisal of Guidelines for Research and Evaluation Instrument [AGREE]; www.agreetrust.org; AGREE Collaboration, 2003), ensuring the collection and selection of the best research evidence available and the systematic generation of treatment recommendations applicable to the majority of people who self-harm. However, there will always be some people and situations for which clinical guideline recommendations are not readily applicable. This guideline does not, therefore, override the individual responsibility of healthcare professionals to make appropriate decisions in the circumstances of the individual, in consultation with the person who self-harms and/or their carer.

In addition to the clinical evidence, cost-effectiveness information, where available, is taken into account in the generation of statements and recommendations of the clinical guidelines. While national guidelines are concerned with clinical and cost effectiveness, issues of affordability and implementation costs are to be determined by the National Health Service (NHS).

In using guidelines, it is important to remember that the absence of empirical evidence for the effectiveness of a particular intervention is not the same as evidence for ineffectiveness. In addition, and of particular relevance in mental health, evidence-based treatments are often delivered within the context of an overall treatment programme including a range of activities, the purpose of which may be to help engage the person and provide an appropriate context for the delivery of specific interventions. It is important to maintain and enhance the service context in which these interventions are delivered, otherwise the specific benefits of effective interventions will be lost. Indeed, the importance of organising care in order to support and encourage a good therapeutic relationship is at times as important as the specific treatments offered.

1.1.3 Why develop national guidelines?

The National Institute for Health and Clinical Excellence (NICE) was established as a Special Health Authority for England and Wales in 1999, with a remit to provide a single source of authoritative and reliable guidance for service-users, professionals and the public. NICE guidance aims to improve standards of care, diminish unacceptable variations in the provision and quality of care across the NHS, and ensure that the health service is person centred. All guidance is developed in a transparent and collaborative manner, using the best available evidence and involving all relevant stakeholders.

NICE generates guidance in a number of different ways, three of which are relevant here. First, national guidance is produced by the Technology Appraisal Committee to give robust advice about a particular treatment, intervention, procedure or other health technology. Second, NICE commissions public health intervention guidance focused on types of activity (interventions) that help to reduce people's risk of developing a disease or condition or help to promote or maintain a healthy lifestyle. Third, NICE commissions the production of national clinical guidelines focused upon the overall treatment and management of a specific condition. To enable this latter development, NICE has established four National Collaborating Centres in conjunction with a range of professional organisations involved in healthcare.

1.1.4 The National Collaborating Centre for Mental Health

This guideline has been commissioned by NICE and developed within the National Collaborating Centre for Mental Health (NCCMH). The NCCMH is a collaboration of the professional organisations involved in the field of mental health, national service-user and carer organisations, a number of academic institutions and NICE. The NCCMH is funded by NICE and is led by a partnership between the Royal College of Psychiatrists and the British Psychological Society's Centre for Outcomes Research and Effectiveness, based at University College London.

1.1.5 From national guidelines to local protocols

Once a national guideline has been published and disseminated, local healthcare groups will be expected to produce a plan and identify resources for implementation, along with appropriate timetables. Subsequently, a multidisciplinary group involving commissioners of healthcare, primary care and specialist mental health professionals, service-users and carers should undertake the translation of the implementation plan into local protocols, taking into account both the recommendations set out in this guideline and the priorities set in the National Service Framework for Mental Health (Department of Health, 1999) and related documentation. The nature and pace of the local plan will reflect local healthcare needs and the nature of existing services; full implementation may take a considerable time, especially where substantial training needs are identified.

1.1.6   Auditing the implementation of guidelines

This guideline identifies key areas of clinical practice and service delivery for local and national audit. Although the generation of audit standards is an important and necessary step in the implementation of this guidance, a more broadly based implementation strategy will be developed. Nevertheless, it should be noted that the Care Quality Commission will monitor the extent to which Primary Care Trusts, trusts responsible for mental health and social care, and Health Authorities have implemented these guidelines.

1.2   THE SELF-HARM: LONGER-TERM MANAGEMENT GUIDELINE

1.2.1   Who has developed this guideline?

The GDG was convened by the NCCMH and supported by funding from NICE. The GDG included one service user and two carer representatives, and professionals from psychiatry, clinical psychology, general practice, nursing and social care.

Staff from the NCCMH provided leadership and support throughout the process of guideline development, undertaking systematic searches, information retrieval, appraisal and systematic review of the evidence. Members of the GDG received training in the process of guideline development from NCCMH staff, and the service user and carers received training and support from the NICE Patient and Public Involvement Programme. The NICE Guidelines Technical Adviser provided advice and assistance regarding aspects of the guideline development process.

All GDG members made formal declarations of interest at the outset, which were updated at every GDG meeting. The GDG met 13 times throughout the process of guideline development. It met as a whole, but key topics were led by a national expert in the relevant topic. The GDG was supported by the NCCMH technical team, with additional expert advice from special advisers where needed. The group oversaw the production and synthesis of research evidence before presentation. All statements and recommendations in this guideline have been generated and agreed by the whole GDG.

1.2.2   For whom is this guideline intended?

This guideline will be relevant for adults and young people who self-harm.

The guideline covers the care provided by primary, community, secondary, tertiary and other healthcare professionals who have direct contact with, and make decisions concerning the care of, adults and young people who self-harm.

The guideline will also be relevant to the work, but will not cover the practice, of those in:
- occupational health services
- social services
- the independent sector.

1.2.3   Specific aims of this guideline

The guideline makes recommendations for the longer-term management of self-harm. It aims to:
- evaluate the role of specific psychological, psychosocial and pharmacological interventions in the longer-term treatment of self-harm
- evaluate the role of psychological and psychosocial interventions in combination with pharmacological interventions in the longer-term treatment of self-harm
- evaluate the role of specific service-level interventions for people who self-harm
- integrate the above to provide best-practice advice on the longer-term care of individuals who self-harm
- promote the implementation of best clinical practice through the development of recommendations tailored to the requirements of the NHS in England and Wales.

1.2.4   The structure of this guideline

The guideline is divided into chapters, each covering a set of related topics. The first three chapters provide a summary of the clinical practice and research recommendations, and a general introduction to guidelines and to the methods used to develop them. Chapter 4 to Chapter 9 provide the evidence that underpins the recommendations about the longer-term treatment and management of self-harm.

Each evidence chapter begins with a general introduction to the topic that sets the recommendations in context. Depending on the nature of the evidence, narrative syntheses or meta-analyses were conducted, and the structure of the chapters varies accordingly. Where appropriate, details about current practice, the evidence base and any research limitations are provided. Where meta-analyses were conducted, information is given about both the interventions included and the studies considered for review. Clinical summaries are then used to summarise the evidence presented. Finally, recommendations related to each topic are presented at the end of each chapter. On the CD-ROM, full details about the included studies utilised in the meta-analysis can be found in Appendix 15 together with a list of excluded studies and risk of bias tables where available. Where meta-analyses were conducted, the data are presented using forest plots in Appendix 16 and GRADE evidence profiles can be found in Appendix 17 (see Text Box 1 for details). Narratively synthesised studies that were not meta-analysed are listed in the References.

1.2.5   Evidence for children and young people

There is not a separate chapter relating to children and young people as issues for this group have been addressed throughout the guideline. These can be found in the following sections: 4.4.4 to 4.4.10; 5.3; 6.2.9 to 6.2.11; 6.2.16; 6.2.18; 6.3.7; 6.3.8; 6.5.1; 7.2.7 to 7.2.8; 9.2.3; 9.4; and 9.5.

Text Box 1: Appendices on CD-ROM

Search strategies for the identification of clinical studies	Appendix 9
Search strategies for the identification of health economic evidence	Appendix 12
Clinical study characteristics tables	Appendix 15
Clinical evidence forest plots and toxicity data	Appendix 16
GRADE evidence profiles	Appendix 17

In the event that amendments or minor updates need to be made to the guideline, please check the NCCMH website (nccmh.org.uk), where these will be listed and a corrected PDF file available to download.

2   INTRODUCTION TO SELF-HARM

2.1   THE BEHAVIOUR

2.1.1   Terminology

The term self-harm is used in this guideline to refer to any act of self-poisoning or self-injury carried out by an individual irrespective of motivation (Hawton *et al.*, 2003a). This commonly involves self-poisoning with medication or self-injury by cutting. There are a number of important exclusions that this term is not intended to cover. These include harm to the self arising from excessive consumption of alcohol or recreational drugs, mismanagement of physical health conditions, body piercing or starvation arising from anorexia nervosa. In the past, various other terms have been used including 'parasuicide' and 'attempted suicide' (Kreitman, 1977), the latter to describe self-harm in which the primary motivation is to end life. However, it became evident that motivation is complex and does not fall neatly into such categories. Terms such as 'non fatal deliberate self-harm' (Morgan *et al.*, 1975) were preferred because they avoided making inferences about the motivation behind the behaviour. However, the word 'deliberate' is no longer preferred because it can be considered judgemental and it has been argued that the extent to which the behaviour is 'deliberate' or 'intentional' is not always clear – those who harm themselves during a dissociative state often describe diminished or absent awareness of their actions at these times.

2.1.2   How common is self-harm?

Population estimates of the prevalence of self-harm in the community vary considerably. One cross-national study of 17 countries found that an average of 2.7% of people reported a previous episode of self-harm, but with considerable variation between 0.5% in Italy and 5% in the US (Nock *et al.*, 2008). This variation may well reflect a person's willingness to report self-harm. In the UK, an adult psychiatric morbidity survey collected self-reported data on 'attempted suicide' and 'self-harm' (McManus *et al.*, 2009), according to whether or not the person reported that they had intended to take their life. Overall 5.6% reported lifetime suicide attempts (6.9% of women and 4.3% of men) with 0.7% reporting this had occurred in the last year. Self-reported lifetime history of self-harm (without lethal intent) was slightly less common: 4.9% overall (5.4% of women and 4.4% of men). Self-harm can occur at any age but is most common in young people[1].

---

[1]In this guideline, children and young people are defined as people aged 8 to 17 years, inclusive.

In Meltzer and colleagues' survey (2001) of 12,529 children and young people aged 5 to 15 years, 1.3% had tried to harm themselves. Data in this survey was collected from parental interviews; when information is obtained directly from young people, rates are considerably higher. Hawton and colleagues (2002) conducted a questionnaire survey of 6,020 Year 11 pupils in the Oxford area. They reported that 13.2% of young people responding had self-harmed at some point in their lives, 6.9% in the previous year. Only 12.6% of those who had harmed themselves had presented to hospital, the vast majority of acts of self-harm being 'invisible' to professionals. Although rates of self-harm vary between countries (Madge *et al.*, 2008), research in England, Canada and Australia between 2002 and 2005 indicated that the lifetime rate of self-harm in schools was 12 to 15% (De Leo & Heller, 2004; Ross & Heath, 2002). In contrast, only approximately 5% of all episodes of self-harm occur in people over the age of 65 (Dennis *et al.*, 1997; Draper, 1996).

Much of the detailed epidemiological study of self-harm has been based in hospital settings and suggests self-harm might account for over 200,000 hospital attendances in England every year (Hawton *et al.*, 2007). Recent data from Oxford, Manchester and Derby suggested that rates of hospital presentation for self-harm varied at between 400 and 550 per 100,000 per year for women and between 300 and 400 per 100,000 per year for men (Bergen *et al.*, 2010a). Rates fell by between 8 and 21% over an 8-year period (from 2000 to 2007), with a more pronounced fall in men.

2.1.3   Methods of self-harm

Methods of self-harm can be divided into two broad groups: self-poisoning and self-injury. Although statistically there may be different motivations and intentions behind the method chosen (Sutton, 2007), there is a variety of individual and practical reasons that spans both groups. Assumptions cannot be made about motivation and intent based on the chosen method of self-harm and, indeed, there is good evidence that people often switch methods of self-harm (Lilley *et al.*, 2008a)

Studies of attendance at emergency departments following self-harm show that approximately 80% of people have taken an overdose of prescribed or over-the-counter medication (Horrocks *et al.*, 2003), most commonly analgesics or antidepressants. A small percentage of overdoses are of illicit drugs or other substances (for example, household substances or plant material). However, these figures can be misleading because people who self-poison are more likely to seek help than those who self-injure (Hawton *et al.*, 2002; Meltzer *et al.*, 2002). General population studies have shown that self-injury may be more common than self-poisoning (Hawton *et al.*, 2002; Meltzer *et al.*, 2001).

Of those who self-injure, cutting is the most common method (Hawton *et al.*, 2002; Horrocks *et al.*, 2003). Less common methods include burning, hanging, stabbing, swallowing or inserting objects, shooting, drowning, and jumping from heights or in front of vehicles.

2.1.4 Outcomes: repetition and suicide

Approximately one in five people who attend an emergency department following self-harm will harm themselves again in the following year (Bergen *et al.*, 2010a); a small minority of people will do so repeatedly. The frequency with which some of the latter group self-harm means that they are over-represented among those who present at an emergency department or receive psychiatric care. There is no good evidence to support the widely-voiced opinion that people who harm themselves repeatedly, particularly by cutting, are less likely to die by suicide than those who harm themselves in other ways. Indeed one hospital-based study suggested that self-cutting increased suicide risk (Cooper *et al.*, 2005). Repetition of self-harm may occur quickly with up to one in ten repeat episodes occurring within 5 days of the index attempt (Kapur *et al.*, 2005).

The suicide rate in the general population varies across countries. In the UK in 2009, the suicide rate per 100,000 was 3.0 for females and 10.9 for males (World Health Organization, 2011). Following an act of self-harm, the rate of suicide increases to between 50 and 100 times the rate of suicide in the general population (Hawton *et al.*, 2003a; Owens *et al.*, 2002). Men who self-harm are more than twice as likely to die by suicide as women and the risk increases greatly with age for both genders (Hawton *et al.*, 2003b). It has been estimated that one quarter of all people who die by suicide would have attended an emergency department in the previous year (Gairin *et al.*, 2003). In a large long-term study of over 20 years, Runeson and colleagues (2010) found that certain methods of self-harm were associated with increased suicide risk. Hanging, strangulation and suffocation were associated with a six-fold increased risk of future successful suicide compared with self-poisoning (Runeson *et al.*, 2010).

2.1.5 Why do people self-harm?

Self-harm does not often simply follow the wish to die. Those who self-harm may do so to communicate with others or influence them to secure help or care. They may self-harm to obtain relief from a particular emotional state or overwhelming situation (Hjelmeland *et al.*, 2002).

One particular intention or motive might predominate or all might coexist. This means that a person who self-harms repeatedly might not always do so for the same reason each time, or by the same method (Horrocks *et al.*, 2003). Assumptions about intent, therefore, should not be made on the basis of a previous pattern of self-harm; each act must be assessed separately to determine the motivation behind it. Failure to do this can result in the meaning of the act being misunderstood and an interpretation that the service user finds judgemental or dismissive. This will inevitably lead to a breakdown in the therapeutic relationship, as well as making it less likely that appropriate help will be offered at times when a person is at high risk of suicide.

Consistent with these differences in intention and motive, people who self-harm might have very different expectations about how health services should respond and what constitutes a good outcome. In particular, people who harm themselves as a way of relieving distress (through cutting, for example) might be compelled to do this as a coping strategy to prevent suicide. They are likely to continue to need to do this until they receive appropriate and sufficient psychotherapeutic interventions and support.

2.1.6 Motives for self-harm in young people

The Child and Adolescent Self-Harm in Europe (CASE) (Hawton & Rodham, 2006) study is the largest and most extensive study of self-harm in 15- to 16-year-olds in the community. The original study comprised seven countries including England; a modified version recently covered Scotland (O'Connor *et al.*, 2009a). The method of self-harm most commonly reported in these studies was self-cutting.

Consistent with the clinical studies, the young people endorsed psychological pain motives more frequently than other motives. 'Wanting to get relief from a terrible state of mind', 'wanting to die', 'wanting to punish oneself' and 'wanting to show how desperate one was feeling' are the top four motives endorsed by young people across Europe (Hawton & Rodham, 2006; Madge *et al.*, 2008; O'Connor *et al.*, 2009a).

2.1.7 The meaning of self-harm

It can be difficult for people to understand how an apparently self-destructive act such as self-harm can serve a positive purpose or have meaning for people.

Following a qualitative study of 76 women, Arnold (1995) argued that self-harm 'had evolved as a way of coping with unbearable feelings engendered by painful life experience.' For the women who took part in the study, it served a range of purposes including relief of feelings, self-punishment, regaining control and communicating to others. Arnold (1995) suggests that:

> *successful approaches to helping someone overcome self-injury need to examine fully the purposes served for an individual and the alternatives which may need to be in place before they can leave self-injury behind.*

Babiker and Arnold (1997) expand on the functions and meanings of self-harm thus: functions concerned with coping and surviving, functions concerned with the self, functions concerned with dealing with one's experience, functions concerned with self-punishment and sacrifice, and functions concerning relationships with others. Other models that explore the meaning of self-harm and may be useful to promote understanding in clinicians include 'the eight Cs of self-injury' (Sutton, 2007):

- coping and crisis intervention
- calming and comforting
- control
- cleansing
- confirmation of existence

- creating comfortable numbness
- chastisement
- communication.

2.1.8   Factors that are associated with self-harm

Demographics, socioeconomic factors and life events
Self-harm is more common in the young with the incidence peaking between the ages of 15 and 19 years in females and 20 and 24 years in males. Self-harm occurs in all sections of the population but is more common among people who are disadvantaged in socioeconomic terms and among those who are single or divorced, live alone, are single parents or have a severe lack of social support (Meltzer *et al.*, 2002).

Life events are strongly associated with self-harm in two ways. First, there is a strong relationship between the likelihood of self-harm and the number and type of adverse events that a person reports having experienced during the course of his/her life. These include victimisation and, in particular, sexual abuse (Meltzer *et al.*, 2002; O'Connor *et al.*, 2009b). Second, life events, particularly relationship problems, can precipitate an act of self-harm (Haw & Hawton, 2008; O'Connor *et al.*, 2010). Many people who self-harm have a physical illness at the time and a substantial proportion of them report this as the factor that precipitated the act (De Leo *et al.*, 1999).

Some evidence suggests that a family history of self-harm may be a risk factor for repetition of self-harm. A large-scale cross-sectional study with over 6,000 participants conducted among young people in England (Hawton *et al.*, 2002) reported that self-harm in family members was a risk factor for both males and females. Although this was based on students' self-reports resulting in possible ascertainment bias, this finding suggests there is an intergenerational transmission of risk, one explanation for which is genetic susceptibility. This hypothesis is supported by a large twin study with 5,995 participants based in Australia, which found that history of self-harm in a co-twin was strongly predictive of self-harm in monozygotic twin pairs but not in dizygotic twin pairs, suggesting that the heritability of suicidal thoughts and behaviours was in the region of 45% (Statham *et al.*, 1998).

The association between self-harm and mental disorder
Most people who attend an emergency department following an act of self-harm will meet criteria for one or more psychiatric diagnoses at the time they are assessed (Haw *et al.*, 2001). More than two thirds would be diagnosed as having depression although within 12 to 16 months two thirds of these will no longer fulfil diagnostic criteria for depression.

People diagnosed as having certain types of mental disorder are much more likely to self-harm (Skegg, 2005). For this group, the recognition and treatment of these disorders can be an important component of care. In one survey of a sample of the British population, people with current symptoms of a mental disorder were up to 20 times more likely to report having harmed themselves in the past (Meltzer *et al.*, 2002). The association was particularly strong for those diagnosed as having phobic and psychotic disorders. People diagnosed as having schizophrenia are most at risk and approximately half of this group will have harmed themselves at some time.

Certain psychological characteristics are more common among people who self-harm, including impulsivity, poor problem solving, hopelessness, impaired positive future thinking/goal re-engagement, high levels of self-criticism and perfectionism (Brezo *et al.*, 2005; MacLeod *et al.*, 1997; O'Connor *et al.*, 2009b; Slee *et al.*, 2008). Also, people who self-harm more often have interpersonal difficulties. It is possible to apply diagnostic criteria to these characteristics. This explains why nearly half of those who present to an emergency department meet criteria for having a personality disorder (Haw *et al.*, 2001). However, there are problems with doing this because:

- The diagnostic label tends to divert attention from helping the person to overcome their problems and can even lead to the person being denied help (National Institute for Mental Health in England, 2003).
- Some people who self-harm suggest that the label 'personality disorder' can lead to damaging stigmatisation by care workers (Babiker & Arnold, 1997; Pembroke, 1994). Moreover, this stigma may prevent those who self-harm from seeking help (Fortune *et al.*, 2008).

The association between self-harm and alcohol and drug use

Approximately half of people who attend an emergency department following self-harm will have consumed alcohol immediately preceding or as part of the self-harm episode (Horrocks *et al.*, 2003; Merrill *et al.*, 1992). For many, this is a factor that complicates immediate management either by impairing judgement and capacity, or by adding to the toxic effects of ingested substances. Approximately one quarter of those who self-harm will have a diagnosis of harmful use of alcohol (Haw *et al.*, 2001). Men are more likely to drink before an episode of self-harm than women (Hawton *et al.*, 2003b) and are more likely to be misusing drugs or alcohol, as well as to have higher rates of several risk factors for suicide (Taylor *et al.*, 1999). Substance misuse is associated with hospital admission for self-harm in inpatients discharged from psychiatric care (Gunnell *et al.*, 2008).

The association between self-harm and child abuse and domestic violence

Child sexual abuse is known to be associated with self-harm (Fliege *et al.*, 2009; Hawton *et al.*, 2002; Meltzer *et al.*, 2002), especially among people who repeatedly self-harm, as well as a range of mental health problems particularly in teenage years and adulthood for females, and for looked-after children (Meltzer *et al.*, 2002). Physical abuse is also implicated in self-harm (Glassman *et al.*, 2007; O'Connor *et al.*, 2009a). Those who experienced bullying in childhood are at increased risk of future self-harm even after adjustment for the co-occurrence of other risks such as abuse (Meltzer *et al.*, 2011). Experience of domestic violence (intimate partner violence) is a significant risk factor for self-harm. Compared with controls, in a retrospective cohort study, people suffering from domestic violence were more likely to present with self-harm than controls (Boyle *et al.*, 2006). It is suggested that healthcare professionals explore whether self-harm is an issue when there is evidence of domestic violence (Sansone *et al.*, 2007).

It is important to note that socioeconomic factors such as unemployment and poverty, childhood experiences of abuse, and experiences of domestic violence are all associated with a wide range of mental disorders, as well as self-harm. How these experiences and factors interact needs to be explored and better understood.

The association between sexual orientation and self-harm
Growing evidence supports an association between sexual orientation and self-harm in men and women (O'Connor *et al.*, 2009b; Skegg *et al.*, 2003). In a recent systematic review and meta-analysis (including data from 214,344 heterosexual and 11,971 non-heterosexual people), lesbian, gay and bisexual people were at a heightened risk of self-harm compared with heterosexual people (King *et al.*, 2008). The evidence for this association thus far is strongest for young people.

2.1.9   Special groups

Young people
The rate of self-harm is low in early childhood but increases rapidly with the onset of teenage years (Hawton *et al.*, 2002). Hawton and Rodham (2006) conducted a school-based survey of 6,000 young people in Year 11 (aged 15 and 16 years) in Oxfordshire, Northamptonshire and Birmingham. The percentage of participants from the survey who reported having deliberately tried to harm themselves at some point in their lives was 13.2%, with 8.6% in the last year. Rates were higher in girls than boys both for lifetime (20.2 versus 7%) and for previous year (13.4 versus 4.4%). This anonymous survey also examined the factors associated with self-harm, coping strategies used and access to services (Hawton & Rodham, 2006). Self-harm is clearly related to interpersonal difficulties: younger teenagers describe family problems and older teenagers cite partner issues (Hawton *et al.*, 2003a). Little is known about the problem of self-harm in younger children; however, there appears to be a difference in the female to male ratio with increasing age, from 8:1 females to males in 10- to 14-year-olds through 3.1:1 in 15- to 19-year-olds, to 1.6:1 in 20- to 24-year-olds (Hawton & Harriss, 2008a). One study found an overall self-harm rate of 29 per 100,000 (ages 10 to 19 years) (Clarke *et al.*, 2000). An Oxford study comparing trends in self-harm between 1985 and 1995 found that the largest rise was in 15- to 24-year-old males (+194.1%) (Hawton *et al.*, 1997).

Asian women
Husain and colleagues (2006) concluded that South Asian women are at an increased risk of self-harm. The demographic characteristics, precipitating factors and recent clinical management are different in South Asian compared with white women. South Asian women may be more likely to self-harm between the ages of 16 and 24 years than white women. South Asian women are less likely to attend the accident and emergency (A&E) department with a repeat episode of self-harm. Across all age groups, the rates of self-harm are lower in South Asian men compared with South Asian women. However, a more recent cohort study of 20,574 individuals from three

UK centres found no increased risk in this group, instead reporting an elevated risk in young black women (Cooper *et al.*, 2010).

Older people
Hawton and Harriss (2006) studied 730 people who were 60 years or older and had presented to hospital following self-harm. The authors found very high suicidal intent among this group and, at follow-up over 20 years, very high suicide rates (4.5%). Dennis and colleagues (2005) studied older people with depression, finding that two thirds had significant suicidal intent. Older people with depression who self-harmed were more likely to have a poorly integrated social network; loneliness and lack of support from services were identified as important factors in determining suicidal behaviour in older adults.

Lamprecht and colleagues (2005) examined self-harm in older people presenting to acute hospital services over 3 years. More males (56%) than females (26%) who presented with self-harm were married. The observations suggested an increase in self-harm in men, and marriage may no longer be a protective factor among older men.

Dennis and colleagues (2007) confirmed their previous finding that the majority of older people who harmed themselves had high suicidal intent and a high proportion (69%) were depressed. Individuals were frequently living alone with an isolated lifestyle and poor physical health. Barr and colleagues (2004) described four characteristics that have been shown to be associated with increased vulnerability in older people who self-harm: increased suicidal intent, physical illness, mental illness and social isolation.

People with a learning disability
Some genetic conditions associated with learning disability increase the likelihood that the individual with that condition will exhibit self-injurious behaviour (Gates, 2003). Wisely and colleagues (2002) identified that endogenous opioids produce a morphine-like effect that can account for the development of some forms of self-harm.

James and Warner (2005) argue that self-harm represents a significant yet poorly theorised area of concern with respect to women who have learning disabilities, particularly in the context of secure service provision. Their self-harm is meaningful and consideration should be given to how they understand and manage their experiences, cognitions and emotions.

2.1.10   Service provision for self-harm

There are no accurate figures for the number of presentations to emergency departments, but extrapolated from registers held at centres in the UK there are around 200,000 attendances in England annually (Hawton *et al.*, 2003b). One hallmark of service provision for self-harm has been its variability, which has been consistent over time (Bennewith *et al.*, 2004; Blake & Mitchell, 1978; Kapur *et al.*, 1998). Studies have also suggested under provision with respect to self-harm services. In one study of 32 general hospitals in England, only just over half of episodes resulted in a specialist psychosocial assessment and the range was 36 to 82%. There was also considerable variation in psychiatric admission (overall 9.5%; range 2.5 to 23.8%), and mental health follow-up (overall 51%; range 35 to 82%) (Bennewith *et al.*, 2004). Possible reasons for poor services include limited resources, a lack of an evidence base for treatments, and the unpopularity of this group of service users among some clinical staff (Kapur *et al.*, 1999).

2.1.11   Professional attitudes to self-harm and service users' experience

People who self-harm often describe experiencing negative responses from staff in mental health services and emergency departments. This may be linked to professionals' lack of understanding of the behaviour (Arnold, 1995):

> *Professionals are often terrified by self-injury. Their normal empathy with others' distress and their confidence and ability to help often desert them when faced with someone who persistently hurts themselves. This problem reflects a serious and widespread lack of understanding of self-injury, which results in great inconsistency and inadequacies in services.*

As part of writing NICE Clinical Guideline 16, *Self-harm: the Short-term Physical and Psychological Management and Secondary Prevention of Self-harm in Primary and Secondary Care* (NICE, 2004a; NCCMH, 2004), a series of focus groups were held with service users to establish their experience of professionals' attitude to self-harm. Service users mentioned approaches that they had found helpful and supportive, but also mentioned less positive responses.

Ramon and colleagues (1975) found that the lethality of self-harm is also an influencing factor on nursing and medical staff's attitudes towards self-harm, with sympathy and lethality being positively correlated. This finding was mirrored in a US study (Ansel & McGee, 1971) and an Australian study (Bailey, 1994), both of which found that positive attitudes were more likely to be displayed towards clearly suicidal or despairing patients.

2.2   TREATMENT AND MANAGEMENT IN THE NATIONAL HEALTH SERVICE

2.2.1   Detection, recognition and referral in primary care

Available figures suggest that up to 6.6% (Meltzer *et al.*, 2002) of individuals seen in primary care may have a history of self-harm that may not be identified during the consultation. Some of the factors contributing to this include the narrow time constraints upon consultation time, which may not facilitate the development of a confiding relationship/atmosphere in which thoughts/acts of self-harm may be disclosed. Additionally, interactions with members of the primary care team will usually be task related and there is not a culture of routinely asking about self-harm, unless there are features suggesting this. Many healthcare professionals are not educated in risk factors for self-harm and may miss opportunities to detect it. Research interventions in primary care for those who have self-harmed have been made possible by proactive invitation of service users known to self-harm (Bennewith *et al.*, 2002).

Young people who self-harm frequently come to the attention of school teachers and young people's health advisors. Whilst these staff often receive training in how to handle a young person disclosing that they self-harm, this aspect of work causes concern among staff who often request further training from local healthcare professionals. In some areas, schools – supported by child and adolescent mental health services (CAMHS) staff – provide universal interventions focused on the development of emotional literacy and coping skills, in an endeavour to decrease the likelihood of self-harm.

2.2.2   Assessment

Assessment should encompass both an assessment of risk and the wider context and needs of the service user. Assessment is intended to determine the type and intensity of future input required by the service user. One of the main challenges in assessment of risk post-self-harm is that there are no risk assessments that can accurately determine the likely risk of repetition. All measures are likely to class too many people at high risk of repetition and possible future death and to misclassify some people as low risk when in fact they are at high risk (Department of Health, 2007). Consequently, *Self-Harm: the Short-term Physical and Psychological Management and Secondary Prevention of Self-harm in Primary and Secondary Care* (NICE, 2004a) recommends that healthcare professionals do not use risk assessments alone to decide not to offer follow-up. Subsequent to assessment, the assessing clinician may recommend no follow-up, follow-up in primary care, referral to a community mental health team (CMHT) or crisis resolution and home treatment team, referral for psychological treatment or a recommendation for inpatient admission. In some areas psychiatric liaison teams may offer brief time limited follow-up (1 to 4 weeks) before discharge or referral on to the CMHT.

Young people
Young people, especially those under 16 years old, on presentation at emergency departments are likely to be admitted to the paediatric ward to await assessment by CAMHS prior to discharge. In some areas 17- to 18-year-olds may receive similar treatment, in others they may receive assessment under the protocol used for the treatment of adults. In other respects, their treatment will resemble that of adults; firstly addressing any medical issues before moving onto risk and psychosocial assessment. The outcomes following assessment will vary. Some young people will refuse further input from CAMHS, in part because the self-harm act and the response from the system may have resulted in at least a temporary resolution of the difficulties precipitating the behaviour. Others will accept an offer of further assessment or therapy, which is usually family-centred, although non-attendance at follow-up is a common problem with young people (Piacentini *et al.*, 1995). A small proportion of young people may remain highly suicidal and need admission directly (within 24 hours) to

inpatient psychiatric treatment in Tier 4, but this is often delayed. Depending upon the assessment of the relevant factors contributing to the episode of self-harm, some young people may be referred to Social Services under the Children Act (Her Majesty's Stationary Office [HMSO],1989 and 2004).

Assessment in secondary care services

Assessment for adults most commonly occurs in the context of the CMHT and will focus more broadly on the range of presenting problems of the service user. The team, as part of this initial assessment, will also conduct a risk assessment and are likely to develop an initial safety plan with the service user and/or carer. As part of the assessment, the team will consider the relationship between the self-harm and the other presenting problems of the service user. In some circumstances the team may not address a service user's self-harm actively as part of the treatment plan if it is believed that this is a result of a particular psychiatric diagnosis, for example depression. Rather, the focus will be on the primary psychiatric diagnosis. In other circumstances where the self-harm is potentially highly lethal, management of self-harm may form the centre of the treatment plan and service users may receive treatments that focus directly on reducing self-harm. These different treatment options and evidence relating to them will be discussed further in Chapter 7.

Whilst significant numbers of young people who self-harm may be managed by staff in Tier 1 (teachers, social workers and GPs), many young people who self-harm are referred for assessment to the Tier 3 CAMHS team. Young people who self-harm will receive an assessment of their wider presenting problems as well as an assessment of self-harm, encompassing an assessment of risk. Subsequent to this assessment, young people are likely to be offered a range of interventions that may or may not focus specifically on the self-harm.

2.2.3   Pharmacological treatments

Pharmacological treatments do not play a direct role in the management of self-harm; however, they have a significant indirect part to play in the management of associated conditions. Depression, anxiety disorders and schizophrenia are associated with a higher risk of self-harm, and the pharmacological treatment of these conditions is documented in their respective guidelines (NICE, 2009a, 2005b and c, 2011a and 2009b, respectively). There have been reports linking lithium treatment with a reduction in suicidal behaviour (Cipriani *et al.*, 2005). Other coexisting conditions that may increase the risk of self-harm, such as chronic pain, may also lend themselves to pharmacological treatment (NICE, 2009c).

2.2.4   Psychological treatments

Self-harm is associated with a wide variety of psychiatric diagnoses and psychological problems. Psychological treatments offered to service users who self-harm differ to the extent to which self-harm is an explicit goal of the treatment. In routine clinical practice service users will receive a wide range of psychological interventions that may or may not focus primarily on their self-harm. Addressing self-harm may occur in series or in parallel with other interventions the service user is receiving. Treatments for self-harm are discussed in Chapter 7.

2.2.5   Harm reduction

For many service users a consideration of a 'harm-reduction approach' may be indicated. Whilst the concept and use of a 'harm-reduction' approach has been well established in relation to substance and alcohol misuse, the use of such an approach in relation to self-harm has been the focus of much controversy. It raises a number of complex and often inter-related clinical, ethical and legal issues, and requires careful consideration of a number factors, including: the meaning and function of self-harm for the individual; the importance of supporting the service user to achieve their own goals and retain their autonomy, dignity and responsibility wherever possible; the need to balance the risks associated with a harm reduction approach versus the risks associated with a 'preventative approach'; and the application of potentially relevant legalisation (HMSO, 1983, 1989, 2004, 2005 and 2007a). Further discussion of this issue can be found in Chapter 7.

2.2.6   Risk and recovery

Following the publication of *Our Health, Our Care, Our Say* (Department of Health, 2006), choice and control are now considered critical components in the development of health and social care policy and practice. It is a policy that supports a 'recovery-oriented' approach, which aims to empower people to live a meaningful and purposeful life and promotes self-management (Shepherd *et al.*, 2008).

Essentially, there is a need to ensure that any risk management plans are 'defensible' rather than 'defensive'. The concept of 'positive risk' taking is highly relevant. This is an approach that both balances the service user's quality of life and safety needs of the service user, family, carers and public and considers the 'potential benefits and harms of choosing one course of action over another' (Morgan, 2004; Morgan, 2007).

2.2.7   Partnerships with other sectors

Individuals who self-harm may be involved with social care agencies and the voluntary sector in addition to involvement with healthcare services. In some areas staff from multiple agencies may work together to provide specific treatments or social care interventions particularly to support service users with long-standing histories of self-harm.

2.2.8   Looked-after children

Looked-after children and adolescents may demonstrate far higher levels of psychiatric diagnoses than children in the general population (Meltzer *et al.*, 2001; Dimigen, 1999). Children are taken into state care for many reasons, the main being physical and sexual abuse by parents and/or associates. These traumatic experiences often lead to long-term psychiatric conditions and thus mental ill health. Interventions for this group of young people may be complex and might include securing longer-term placements.

2.2.9   Training

The majority of professionals working in secondary care will have received training in the assessment and management of risk associated with self-harm and suicidal behaviours. Despite this, clinicians frequently report high levels of anxiety around working with service users who self-harm and concern about working with high levels of risk. The 'Better Services for People who Self-Harm' project (Royal College of Psychiatrists, 2007) surveyed staff in ambulance services, emergency departments and mental health services regarding their need for training about self-harm. All groups of staff reported a need for further training with ambulance staff indicating the greatest need, but even many staff in mental health services felt under-trained in this area. Training in how to treat factors associated with high risk is less widely available and practitioners may rely on safety plans that focus on decreasing access to the means to self-harm and distraction or other crisis skills. Such strategies may help service users manage a short-term crisis but are unlikely to resolve more substantive issues leading to self-harm.

There is a range of training programmes developed for training healthcare professionals who work with people who self-harm, which are reviewed in Chapter 5.

2.3   ECONOMIC COSTS OF SELF-HARM

In addition to the physical and mental impact of self-harm on service users as well as their families and carers, self-harm imposes a significant economic cost both on the health sector and society in general. To date, no formal attempt has been made to quantify the total economic cost of self-harm within the UK. Because self-harm is associated with a range of mental disorders rather than a diagnosis, it is difficult to determine resource use and costs attributable directly to self-harm rather than any underlying cause (Sinclair *et al.*, 2010a). However, it is clear that the assessment and management of self-harm incurs significant NHS resources, with 101,670 emergency department attendances recorded in 2008/09 due to self-harm (NHS Information Centre, 2009). This is probably a considerable underestimate – extrapolating from a study of three hospitals, Hawton and colleagues (2007) estimated there were 220,000 episodes dealt with by hospitals in England each year. Previously published studies have focused on the immediate costs of self-harm management rather than the wider costs involved in the longer-term management of self-harm (Sinclair *et al.*, 2006).

A recent UK-based study retrospectively collected healthcare resource use from a cohort of people who self-harm recruited from a general hospital following an episode of self-harm (Sinclair *et al.*, 2010a). The results of the study showed that a cumulative increase in the number of self-harm episodes was correlated with increased healthcare and social services costs within a 6-month period, particularly for service users who experienced five or more self-harm episodes. There was significantly more use of psychotropic medication and psychiatric care in those who harmed themselves five times or more during the 6-month study period. Care for service users with five or more episodes was characterised by high resource use of psychiatric services in the first 7 years after their first episode. Overall, total healthcare and social service costs were £3,524 (2004/05 prices) more per 6-month period for service users who self-harmed on five or more occasions compared with single episode service users. Within the year following the first ever episode of self-harm, inpatient and outpatient psychiatric services accounted for 69% and social services accounted for 19% of total costs. The results of the study highlighted a cumulative effect on healthcare costs, with increasing episodes of self-harm, particularly for service users with five or more episodes.

Byford and colleagues (2009) estimated the long-term costs, over 6 years, of a cohort of young people who participated in an RCT following an episode of self-poisoning. Lifetime and current (6-month) costs were calculated and compared with general population controls to explore costs incurred by the UK general public sector. Resource-use data included inpatient and day-patient services for psychiatric reasons, pregnancy or child birth, foster or residential care, supported accommodation, special education, prison and criminal justice, and social security benefits. Over the longer-term follow-up, the self-poisoning group used substantially more public sector resources in terms of special education, foster care, residential care or other supported accommodation, and social security benefits. They also spent more time in prison or police custody and had a number of hospital attendances for psychiatric reasons, in comparison with the general population control group. Lifetime differences in the costs of key services were large and statistically significant. The self-poisoning group incurred significantly more costs per year in terms of psychiatric hospital contacts, supported accommodation, special education and social security benefits. In total, the self-poisoning group cost over £1,500 per year compared with only £65 per year in the control group (mean difference £1,440; p < 0.001).

The indirect costs of self-harm in terms of lost productivity, days lost from work, as well as costs to families and carers are unknown but are likely to be substantial given its prevalence within the UK. Ensuring the efficient use of available healthcare resources will maximise the health benefits for people who self-harm and can potentially reduce costs to the UK healthcare system and society in the long term.

3   METHODS USED TO DEVELOP THIS GUIDELINE

3.1   OVERVIEW

The development of this guideline drew upon methods outlined by NICE (further information is available in *The Guidelines Manual* [NICE, 2009d]). A team of health professionals, lay representatives and technical experts known as the Guideline Development Group (GDG), with support from the NCCMH staff, undertook the development of a patient-centred, evidence-based guideline. There are six basic steps in the process of developing a guideline:

1. Define the scope, which sets the parameters of the guideline and provides a focus and steer for the development work.
2. Define review questions considered important for practitioners and service users.
3. Develop criteria for evidence searching and search for evidence.
4. Design validated protocols for systematic review and apply to evidence recovered by search.
5. Synthesise and (meta-) analyse data retrieved, guided by the review questions, and produce GRADE evidence profiles and summaries.
6. Answer review questions with evidence-based recommendations for clinical practice.

The clinical practice recommendations made by the GDG are therefore derived from the most up-to-date and robust evidence base for the clinical and cost effectiveness of the treatments and services used in the longer-term management of self-harm. In addition, to ensure a service user and carer focus, the concerns of service users and carers regarding health and social care have been highlighted and addressed by recommendations agreed by the whole GDG.

3.2   THE SCOPE

Guideline topics are selected by the Department of Health and the Welsh Assembly Government, which identify the main areas to be covered by the guideline in a specific remit (see *The Guidelines Manual* [NICE, 2009d] for further information). The NCCMH developed a scope for the guideline based on the remit. The purpose of the scope is to:

- provide an overview of what the guideline will include and exclude
- identify the key aspects of care that must be included
- set the boundaries of the development work and provide a clear framework to enable work to stay within the priorities agreed by NICE and the National Collaborating Centre, and the remit from the Department of Health/Welsh Assembly Government
- inform the development of the review questions and search strategy

- inform professionals and the public about expected content of the guideline
- keep the guideline to a reasonable size to ensure that its development can be carried out within the allocated period.

An initial draft of the scope was sent to registered stakeholders who had agreed to attend a scoping workshop. The workshop was used to:

- obtain feedback on the selected key clinical issues
- identify which patient or population subgroups should be specified (if any)
- seek views on the composition of the GDG
- encourage applications for GDG membership.

The draft scope was subject to consultation with registered stakeholders over a 4-week period. During the consultation period, the scope was posted on the NICE website (www.nice.org.uk). Comments were invited from stakeholder organisations and the Guideline Review Panel. Further information about the Guideline Review Panel can also be found on the NICE website. The NCCMH and NICE reviewed the scope in light of comments received, and the revised scope was signed off by the Guideline Review Panel.

3.3   THE GUIDELINE DEVELOPMENT GROUP

The GDG consisted of: professionals in psychiatry, clinical psychology, nursing, social work and general practice; academic experts in psychiatry and psychology; and a service user, carer representatives and representatives from service user organisations. The carer perspective was provided through topic group discussion with carers. The service user topic group meetings were coordinated between staff from NCCMH, the service user and the carer representatives. The guideline development process was supported by staff from the NCCMH, who undertook the clinical and health economics literature searches, reviewed and presented the evidence to the GDG, managed the process and contributed to drafting the guideline.

3.3.1   Guideline Development Group meetings

Thirteen GDG meetings were held between November 2009 and June 2010. During each day-long GDG meeting, in a plenary session, review questions and clinical and economic evidence were reviewed and assessed, and recommendations formulated. At each meeting, all GDG members declared any potential conflicts of interest, and service user and carer concerns were routinely discussed as part of a standing agenda.

3.3.2   Service users and carers

Individuals with direct experience of services gave an integral service-user focus to the GDG and the guideline. The GDG included a service user and representatives of a national service user group. They contributed as full GDG members to writing the review questions, helping to ensure that the evidence addressed their views and preferences, highlighting sensitive issues and terminology relevant to the guideline, and bringing service-user research to the attention of the GDG. In drafting the guideline, they contributed to writing the guideline's introduction and Chapter 4, and identified recommendations from the service user and carer perspective.

3.3.3 Special advisors

Special advisors, who had specific expertise in one or more aspects of treatment and management relevant to the guideline, assisted the GDG, commenting on specific aspects of the developing guideline and making presentations to the GDG. Appendix 3 lists those who agreed to act as special advisors.

3.3.4 National and international experts

National and international experts in the area under review were identified through the literature search and through the experience of the GDG members. These experts were contacted to recommend unpublished or soon-to-be published studies, to ensure that up-to-date evidence was included in the development of the guideline. They informed the group about completed trials at the pre-publication stage, systematic reviews in the process of being published, studies relating to the cost effectiveness of treatment and trial data if the GDG could be provided with full access to the complete trial report. Appendix 6 lists researchers who were contacted.

3.4 REVIEW QUESTIONS

Review (clinical) questions were used to guide the identification and interrogation of the evidence base relevant to the topic of the guideline. Before the first GDG meeting, an analytic framework (see Appendix 7) was prepared by NCCMH staff based on the scope and an overview of existing guidelines, and was discussed with the guideline Chair. The framework was used to provide a structure from which the review questions were drafted. Both the analytic framework and the draft review questions were then discussed by the GDG at the first few meetings and amended as necessary. Where appropriate, the framework and questions were refined once the evidence had been searched and, where necessary, sub-questions were generated. Questions submitted by stakeholders were also discussed by the GDG and the rationale for not including any questions was recorded in the minutes. The final list of review questions can be found in Appendix 8.

For questions about interventions, the PICO (patient, intervention, comparison and outcome) framework was used (see Table 1).

For questions that were not related to effectiveness (intervention studies), a different question format was used. Please see the question formats in the review protocols (Appendix 8).

Table 1: Features of a well-formulated question on effectiveness intervention – the PICO guide

Patients/population	Which patients or population of patients are we interested in? How can they be best described? Are there subgroups that need to be considered?
Intervention	Which intervention, treatment or approach should be used?
Comparison	What is/are the main alternative/s to compare with the intervention?
Outcome	What is really important for the patient? Which outcomes should be considered: intermediate or short-term measures; mortality; morbidity and treatment complications; rates of relapse; late morbidity and readmission; return to work, physical and social functioning and other measures such as quality of life; general health status?

Table 2: Best study design to answer each type of question

Type of question	Best primary study design
Effectiveness or other impact of an intervention	Randomised controlled trial (RCT); other studies that may be considered in the absence of RCTs are the following: internally/externally controlled before-and-after trial, interrupted time-series
Accuracy of information (for example, risk factor, test, prediction rule)	Comparing the information against a valid gold standard in a randomised trial or inception cohort study
Rates (of disease, patient experience, rare side effects)	Prospective cohort, registry, cross-sectional study

To help facilitate the literature review, a note was made of the best study design type to answer each question. There are four main types of review question of relevance to NICE guidelines. These are listed in Table 2. For each type of question, the best primary study design varies, where 'best' is interpreted as 'least likely to give misleading answers to the question'.

However, in all cases, a well-conducted systematic review (of the appropriate type of study) is likely to always yield a better answer than a single study.

Deciding on the best design type to answer a specific review question does not mean that studies of different design types addressing the same question were discarded.

3.5   SYSTEMATIC CLINICAL LITERATURE REVIEW

The aim of the clinical literature review was to systematically identify and synthesise relevant evidence from the literature in order to answer the specific review questions developed by the GDG. Thus, clinical practice recommendations are evidence-based, where possible, and if evidence is not available informal consensus methods are used (see Section 3.5.6) and the need for future research is specified.

3.5.1   Methodology

A stepwise hierarchical approach was taken to locating and presenting evidence to the GDG. The NCCMH developed this process based on methods set out by NICE (*The Guidelines Manual* [NICE, 2009d]), and after considering recommendations from a range of other sources. These included:
- BMJ (*British Medical Journal*) *Clinical Evidence*
- Clinical Policy and Practice Program of the New South Wales Department of Health (Australia)
- The Cochrane Collaboration
- Grading of Recommendations: Assessment, Development and Evaluation (GRADE) Working Group (2004)
- New Zealand Guidelines Group
- NHS Centre for Reviews and Dissemination (CRD)
- Oxford Centre for Evidence-Based Medicine
- Oxford Systematic Review Development Programme
- Scottish Intercollegiate Guidelines Network
- United States Agency for Healthcare Research and Quality.

3.5.2   The review process

Scoping searches
A broad preliminary search of the literature was undertaken in July 2009 to obtain an overview of the issues likely to be covered by the scope, and to help define key areas. Searches were restricted to clinical guidelines, health technology assessment (HTA) reports, key systematic reviews and RCTs, and conducted in the following databases and websites:
- BMJ *Clinical Evidence*
- Canadian Medical Association Infobase (Canadian guidelines)
- Clinical Policy and Practice Program of the New South Wales Department of Health (Australia)
- Clinical Practice Guidelines (Australian Guidelines)
- Cochrane Central Register of Controlled Trials (CENTRAL)
- Cochrane Database of Abstracts of Reviews of Effects
- Cochrane Database of Systematic Reviews (CDSR)

- Excerpta Medical Database (EMBASE)
- Guidelines International Network
- Health Evidence Bulletin Wales
- Health Management Information Consortium (HMIC)
- HTA database (technology assessments)
- Medical Literature Analysis and Retrieval System Online (MEDLINE)/MEDLINE in Process
- National Health and Medical Research Council
- National Library for Health Guidelines Finder
- New Zealand Guidelines Group
- NHS CRD
- OmniMedicalSearch
- Scottish Intercollegiate Guidelines Network
- Turning Research Into Practice
- United States Agency for Healthcare Research and Quality
- Websites of NICE and the National Institute for Health Research HTA Programme for guidelines and HTAs in development.

Existing NICE guidelines were updated where necessary. Other relevant guidelines were assessed for quality using the AGREE instrument (AGREE Collaboration, 2003). The evidence base underlying high-quality existing guidelines was utilised and updated as appropriate. Further information about this process can be found in The Guidelines Manual (NICE, 2009d).

Systematic literature searches

After the scope was finalised, a systematic search strategy was developed to locate all the relevant evidence. Searches were conducted in the following databases:

- Cumulative Index to Nursing and Allied Health Literature (CINAHL)
- EMBASE
- MEDLINE/MEDLINE In-Process
- Cochrane Database of Abstracts of Reviews of Effects
- CDSR
- CENTRAL
- HTA database
- Health Management Information Consortium
- International Bibliography of the Social Sciences
- American Psychiatric Association Psychological Information Database (PsycINFO)
- PsycEXTRA (see under PsycNET in abbreviations)
- PsycBOOKS (see under PsycNET in abbreviations)

The search strategies were initially developed for MEDLINE before being translated for use in other databases/interfaces. Strategies were built up through a number of trial searches, and discussions of the results of the searches with the review team and GDG, to ensure that all possible relevant search terms were covered. To assure comprehensive coverage, search terms for self-harm were kept purposely broad to help counter dissimilarities in database indexing practices and imprecise reporting of study populations by authors in the titles and abstracts of records.

Methods used to develop this guideline

Reference manager

Citations from each search were downloaded into Reference Manager (a software product for managing references and formatting bibliographies) and duplicates removed. Records were then screened against the inclusion criteria of the reviews before being quality appraised (see below). The unfiltered search results were saved and retained for future potential re-analysis to help keep the process both replicable and transparent.

Search filters

To aid retrieval of relevant and sound evidence, study design filters were, where appropriate, used to limit searches to systematic reviews, RCTs and observational studies. The systematic review and RCT filters are adaptations of pre-tested strategies designed by the CRD and the Health Information Research Unit of McMaster University, Ontario. The observational study filter was developed in-house. The filters, which comprise a combination of controlled vocabulary and free-text retrieval methods, maximise sensitivity (or recall) to ensure that as many potentially relevant records as possible are retrieved from a search.

Date and language restrictions

Systematic database searches were initially conducted in March 2010 up to the most recent searchable date. Search updates were generated on a 6-monthly basis, with the final re-runs carried out in January 2011 ahead of the guideline consultation. After this point, studies were only included if they were judged by the GDG to be exceptional (for example, if the evidence was likely to change a recommendation).

Although no language restrictions were applied at the searching stage, foreign language studies were not requested or reviewed unless they were of particular importance to a review question. Date restrictions were applied to searches for systematic reviews and updates of published reviews only (see Appendix 9). No date restrictions were imposed for the remainder of the searches.

Other search methods

Other search methods involved were: (1) scanning the reference lists of all eligible publications (systematic reviews, stakeholder evidence and included studies) for more published reports and citations of unpublished research; (2) sending lists of studies meeting the inclusion criteria to subject experts (identified through searches and the GDG) and asking them to check the lists for completeness, and to provide information of any published or unpublished research for consideration (see Appendix 6); (3) checking the tables of contents of key journals for studies that might have been missed by the database and reference list searches; (4) tracking key studies in the Science Citation Index (prospectively) over time for further useful references.

Full details of the search strategies and filters used for the systematic review of clinical evidence are provided in Appendix 9.

Study selection and quality assessment

All primary-level studies included after the first scan of citations were acquired in full and re-evaluated for eligibility at the time when they were being entered into the study information database. More specific eligibility criteria were developed for each review question and are described in the relevant clinical evidence chapters. Eligible systematic reviews and primary-level studies were critically appraised for methodological quality (see Appendix 11 for quality checklist templates). The eligibility of each study was confirmed by at least one member of the GDG.

For some review questions, it was necessary to prioritise the evidence with respect to the UK context (that is, external validity). To make this process explicit, the GDG took into account the following factors when assessing the evidence:

- **participant factors** (for example, gender, age and ethnicity)
- **provider factors** (for example, model fidelity, the conditions under which the intervention was performed and the availability of experienced staff to undertake the procedure)
- **cultural factors** (for example, differences in standard care and differences in the welfare system).

It was the responsibility of the GDG to decide which prioritisation factors were relevant to each review question in light of the UK context and then decide how they should modify their recommendations.

Unpublished evidence

The GDG used a number of criteria when deciding whether or not to accept unpublished data. First, the evidence must have been accompanied by a trial report containing sufficient detail to properly assess the quality of the data. Second, the evidence must have been submitted with the understanding that data from the study and a summary of the study's characteristics would be published in the full guideline. Therefore, the GDG did not accept evidence submitted as commercial in confidence. However, the GDG recognised that unpublished evidence submitted by investigators might later be retracted by those investigators if the inclusion of such data would jeopardise publication of their research.

3.5.3   Data extraction

Study characteristics and outcome data were extracted from all eligible studies that met the minimum quality criteria and were meta-analysed, using a bespoke database and Review Manager 5.0.25 (Cochrane Collaboration, 2011) and/or Word-based forms (see Appendix 11 for quality checklist templates).

In most circumstances, for a given outcome (continuous and dichotomous) where more than 50% of the number randomised to any group were lost to follow-up, the data were excluded from the analysis (except for the outcome 'leaving the study early', in which case the denominator was the number randomised). Where possible, dichotomous efficacy outcomes were calculated on an intention-to-treat (ITT) basis (that is, a 'once-randomised-always-analyse' basis). Where there was good evidence that those participants who ceased to engage in the study were likely to have an unfavourable outcome, early withdrawals were included in both the numerator and denominator. Adverse effects were entered into Review Manager as reported by the study authors because it is usually not possible to determine whether early withdrawals had an unfavourable outcome. Where there was limited data for a particular review, the 50% rule was not applied. In these circumstances the evidence was downgraded due to the risk of bias.

Where some of the studies failed to report standard deviations (SDs) (for a continuous outcome) and where an estimate of the variance could not be computed from other reported data or obtained from the study author, the following approach was taken[2].

When the number of studies with missing SDs was less than one third and when the total number of studies was at least ten, the pooled SD was imputed (calculated from all the other studies in the same meta-analysis that used the same version of the outcome measure). In this case, the appropriateness of the imputation was made by comparing the standardised mean differences (SMDs) of those trials that had reported SDs against the hypothetical SMDs of the same trials based on the imputed SDs. If they converged, the meta-analytical results were considered to be reliable.

When the conditions above could not be met, SDs were taken from another related systematic review (if available). In this case, the results were considered to be less reliable.

The meta-analysis of survival data was based on log hazard ratios and standard errors. Because individual patient data were not available in included studies, hazard ratios and standard errors calculated from a Cox proportional hazard model were extracted. Where necessary, standard errors were calculated from confidence intervals (CIs) or p-values according to standard formulae (see the Cochrane *Handbook for Systematic Reviews of Interventions*, version 5.0.2, Higgins *et al.*, 2009). Data were summarised using the generic inverse variance method using Review Manager.

Consultation with another reviewer or members of the GDG was used to overcome difficulties with coding. Data from studies included in existing systematic reviews were extracted independently by one reviewer and cross-checked with the existing data set. Where possible, two independent reviewers extracted data from new studies. Where double data extraction was not possible, data extracted by one reviewer was checked by the second reviewer. Disagreements were resolved through discussion. Where consensus could not be reached, a third reviewer or GDG members resolved the disagreement. Masked assessment (that is, blind to the journal from which the article comes, the authors, the institution and the magnitude of the effect) was not used because it is unclear that doing so reduces bias (Berlin, 2001; Jadad *et al.*, 1996).

3.5.4   Synthesising the evidence

Meta-analysis
Where possible, meta-analysis was used to synthesise the evidence using Review Manager. If necessary, reanalyses of the data or sub-analyses were used to answer review questions not addressed in the original studies or reviews.

---

[2]Based on the approach suggested by Furukawa and colleagues (2006).

Dichotomous outcomes were analysed as relative risks (RR) with the associated 95% CI (for an example, see Figure 1). A relative risk (also called a risk ratio) is the ratio of the treatment event rate to the control event rate. An RR of 1 indicates no difference between treatment and control. In Figure 1, the overall RR of 0.73 indicates that the event rate (that is, non-remission rate) associated with intervention A is approximately three quarters of that with the control intervention or, in other words, the RR reduction is 27%.

The CI shows a range of values within which there is 95% confidence that the true effect will lie. If the effect size has a CI that does not cross the 'line of no effect', then the effect is commonly interpreted as being statistically significant.

Continuous outcomes were analysed using the mean difference, or SMD when different measures were used in different studies to estimate the same underlying effect (for an example, see Figure 2). If reported by study authors, ITT data, using a valid method for imputation of missing data, were preferred over data only from people who completed the study.

Heterogeneity

To check for consistency of effects among studies, both the I^2 statistic and the chi-squared test of heterogeneity, as well as a visual inspection of the forest plots were used. The I^2 statistic describes the proportion of total variation in study estimates that is due to heterogeneity (Higgins & Thompson, 2002). The I^2 statistic was interpreted in the follow way based on Higgins and Green (2009):

● 0 to 40%: might not be important
● 30 to 60%: may represent moderate heterogeneity

Figure 1: Example of a forest plot displaying dichotomous data

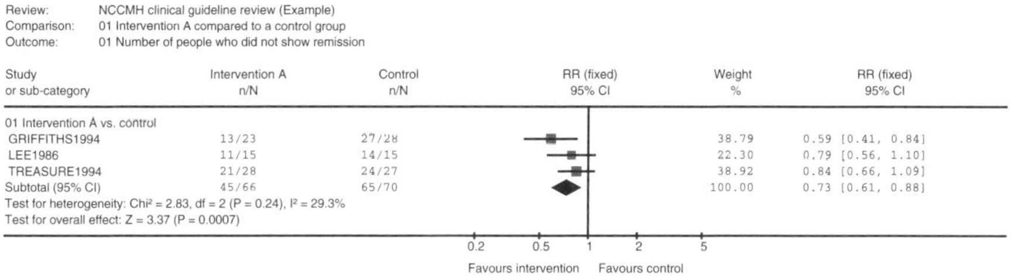

Figure 2: Example of a forest plot displaying continuous data

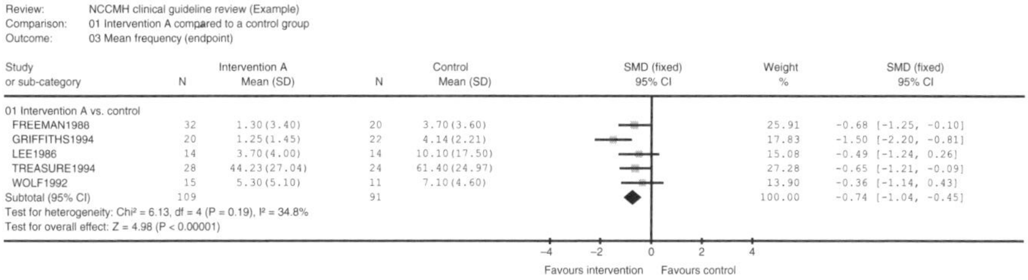

- 50 to 90%: may represent substantial heterogeneity
- 75 to 100%: considerable heterogeneity.

Two factors were used to make a judgement about importance of the observed value of I^2: first, the magnitude and direction of effects, and second, the strength of evidence for heterogeneity (for example, p-value from the chi-squared test or CI for I^2).

Publication bias

Where there was sufficient data, the intention was to use funnel plots to explore the possibility of publication bias. Asymmetry of the plot would be taken to indicate possible publication bias and investigated further.

Where necessary, an estimate of the proportion of eligible data that were missing (because some studies did not include all relevant outcomes) was calculated for each analysis.

3.5.5   Presenting the data to the Guideline Development Group

Study characteristics tables and, where appropriate, forest plots that had been generated with Review Manager were presented to the GDG.

Where meta-analysis was not appropriate and/or possible, the reported results from each primary-level study were included in the study characteristics table and, where appropriate, in a narrative synthesis. Details of studies that were meta-analysed can be found in study characteristics tables in Appendix 15; studies that were only narratively reviewed can be found in the References.

Evidence profile tables

A GRADE[3] evidence profile was used to summarise both the quality of the evidence and the results of the evidence synthesis (see Table 3 for an example of an evidence profile). The GRADE approach is based on a sequential assessment of the quality of evidence, followed by judgment about the balance between desirable and undesirable effects, and subsequent decision about the strength of a recommendation.

For each outcome, quality may be reduced depending on the following factors:

- **study design** (randomised trial, observational study, or any other evidence)
- **limitations** (based on the quality of individual studies)
- **inconsistency** (see Section 3.5.4 for how consistency was assessed)
- **indirectness** (that is, how closely the outcome measures, interventions and participants match those of interest)
- **imprecision** (based on the CI around the effect size).

For observational studies, the quality may be increased if there is a large effect, plausible confounding would have changed the effect, or there is evidence of a dose–response gradient (details would be provided under the other considerations column). Each evidence profile also included a summary of the findings: number of patients included in each group, an estimate of the magnitude of the effect and the overall quality of the evidence for each outcome.

---

[3]For further information about GRADE, see www.gradeworkinggroup.org.

Table 3: Example of GRADE evidence profile

| | Quality assessment | | | | | | No. of patients | | Summary of findings | | |
| | | | | | | | | | Effect | | |
No. of studies	Design	Limitations	Inconsistency	Indirectness	Imprecision	Other	Intervention	Control	Relative risk (95% CI)	Absolute	Quality
Outcome 1											
6	Randomised trials	No serious limitations	No serious inconsistency	No serious indirectness	Very serious[1,2]	None	8/191	7/150	RR 0.94 (0.39 to 2.23)	0 fewer per 100 (from 3 fewer to 6 more)	⊕⊕OO LOW
Outcome 2											
3	Randomised trials	No serious limitations	No serious inconsistency	No serious indirectness	No serious imprecision	None	120/600	220/450	RR 0.39 (0.23 to 0.65)	30 fewer per 100 (from 17 fewer to 38 fewer)	⊕⊕⊕⊕ HIGH
Outcome 3											
3	Randomised trials	No serious limitations	Serious inconsistency[3]	No serious indirectness	Very serious[1,2]	None	83	81	–	MD –3.51 (–11.51 to 4.49)	⊕OOO VERY LOW
Outcome 4											
3	Randomised trials	No serious limitations	No serious inconsistency	No serious indirectness	Serious[1]	None	88	93	–	SMD –0.26 (–0.50 to –0.03)	⊕⊕⊕O MODERATE
Outcome 5											
4	Randomised trials	No serious limitations	No serious inconsistency	No serious indirectness	Very serious	None	109	114	–	SMD –0.13 (–0.6 to 0.34)	⊕⊕OO LOW

[1] Optimal information size not met.
[2] The CI includes both (1) no effect and (2) appreciable benefit or appreciable harm.
[3] Considerable heterogeneity.

3.5.6   Method used to answer a review question in the absence of appropriately designed, high-quality research

In the absence of appropriately designed, high-quality research or where the GDG were of the opinion (on the basis of previous searches or their knowledge of the literature) that there was unlikely to be such evidence, an informal consensus process was adopted. This process focused on those questions that the GDG considered a priority.

Informal consensus

The starting point for the process of informal consensus was that a member of the GDG identified, with help from the systematic reviewer, a narrative synthesis or key study that most directly addressed the review question. Where this was not possible, a brief review of the recent literature was initiated. These were then used as a basis for beginning an iterative process to identify lower levels of evidence relevant to the review question and to lead to written statements for the guideline. The process involved a number of steps:

1. A description of what is known about the issues concerning the clinical question was written by one of the GDG members.
2. Evidence from the existing studies was then presented in narrative form to the GDG and further comments were sought about the evidence and its perceived relevance to the review question.
3. Based on the feedback from the GDG, additional information was sought and added to the information collected. This included studies that did not directly address the review question but were thought to contain relevant data.
4. A summary of statements that directly addressed the review question were then developed.
5. Following this, on occasion and as deemed appropriate by the development group, the report was then sent to appointed experts outside of the GDG for peer review and comment. The information from this process was then fed back to the GDG for further discussion of the statements
6. Recommendations were then developed and could also be sent for further external peer review.
7. After this final stage of comment, the statements and recommendations were again reviewed and agreed upon by the GDG.

3.5.7   Forming the clinical summaries and recommendations

Once the GRADE evidence profiles relating to a particular review question were completed, summary evidence tables were developed (these tables are presented in the evidence chapters). Finally, the systematic reviewer in conjunction with the GDG produced a clinical evidence summary.

After the GRADE profiles and clinical summaries were presented to the GDG, the associated recommendations were drafted. In making recommendations, the GDG took into account the trade-off between the benefits and downsides of treatment as well as other important factors, such as economic considerations, social value judgements[4], the requirements to prevent discrimination and to promote equality[5], and the group's awareness of practical issues (Eccles *et al.*, 1998; NICE, 2009d).

Finally, to show clearly how the GDG moved from the evidence to the recommendations, each chapter has a section called 'from evidence to recommendations'. Underpinning this section is the concept of the 'strength' of a recommendation (Schunemann *et al.*, 2003). This takes into account the quality of the evidence but is conceptually different. Some recommendations are 'strong' in that the GDG believes that the vast majority of healthcare professionals and service users would choose a particular intervention if they considered the evidence in the same way that the GDG has. This is generally the case if the benefits clearly outweigh the harms for most people and the intervention is likely to be cost effective. However, there is often a closer balance between benefits and harms, and some service users would not choose an intervention whereas others would. This may happen, for example, if some service users are particularly averse to some side effect and others are not. In these circumstances the recommendation is generally weaker, although it may be possible to make stronger recommendations about specific groups of service users. The strength of each recommendation is reflected in the wording of the recommendation, rather than by using labels or symbols.

Where the GDG identified areas in which there are uncertainties or where robust evidence was lacking, they developed research recommendations. Those that were identified as 'high-priority' were included in the NICE version of the guideline.

3.6   HEALTH ECONOMICS METHODS

The aim of the health economics was to contribute to the guideline's development by providing evidence on the cost effectiveness of interventions for the longer-term management of self-harm covered in the guideline. This was achieved by:

● systematic literature review of existing economic evidence

● decision-analytic economic modelling.

Systematic reviews of economic literature were conducted in all areas covered in the guideline. Economic modelling was undertaken in areas with likely major resource implications, where the current extent of uncertainty over cost effectiveness was significant and economic analysis was expected to reduce this uncertainty, in accordance with *The Guidelines Manual* (NICE, 2009d). Prioritisation of areas for economic modelling was a joint decision between the Health Economist and the GDG. The rationale for prioritising review questions for economic modelling was set out in an economic plan agreed between NICE, the GDG, the health economist and

---

[4]See NICE's Social Value Judgements: Principles for the Development of NICE Guidance (NICE, 2008): www.nice.org.uk/aboutnice/howwework/socialvaluejudgements/socialvaluejudgements.jsp.
[5]See NICE's equality scheme: www.nice.org.uk/aboutnice/howwework/NICEEqualityScheme.jsp.

the other members of the technical team. The economic question selected as a key issue addressed by economic modelling was:

- Cost-effectiveness of psychological intervention and treatment as usual for prevention of self-harm repetition among people who self-harm.

In addition, literature on the health-related quality of life (HRQoL) of people who self-harm was systematically searched to identify studies reporting appropriate utility scores that could be utilised in a cost-utility analysis.

The rest of this section describes the methods adopted in the systematic literature review of economic studies. Methods employed in economic modelling are described in the respective sections of the guideline.

3.6.1   Search strategy for economic evidence

Scoping searches

A broad preliminary search of the literature was undertaken in July 2009 to obtain an overview of the issues likely to be covered by the scope, and help define key areas. Searches were restricted to economic studies and HTA reports, and conducted in the following databases:

- EMBASE
- MEDLINE/MEDLINE In-Process
- HTA database (technology assessments)
- NHS Economic Evaluation Database

Any relevant economic evidence arising from the clinical scoping searches was also made available to the health economist during the same period.

Systematic literature searches

After the scope was finalised, a systematic search strategy was developed to locate all the relevant evidence. Searches were restricted to economic evidence (including full and partial economic evaluations) and HTA reports, and conducted in the following databases:

- CINAHL
- EconLit
- EMBASE
- MEDLINE/MEDLINE In-Process
- PsycINFO
- HTA database (technology assessments)
- NHS Economic Evaluation Database

Any relevant economic evidence arising from the clinical searches was also made available to the health economist during the same period.

The search strategies were initially developed for MEDLINE before being translated for use in other databases/interfaces. Strategies were built up through a number of trial searches, and discussions of the results of the searches with the review team and GDG, to ensure that all possible relevant search terms were covered. To assure comprehensive coverage, search terms for self-harm were kept purposely broad to help counter dissimilarities in database indexing practices, and imprecise reporting of study populations by authors in the titles and abstracts of records.

Reference Manager
Citations from each search were downloaded into Reference Manager (a software product for managing references and formatting bibliographies) and duplicates removed. Records were then screened against the inclusion criteria of the reviews before being quality appraised. The unfiltered search results were saved and retained for future potential re-analysis to help keep the process both replicable and transparent.

Search filters
The search filter for health economics is an adaptation of a pre-tested strategy filter designed by the CRD (CRD, 2007). The search filter is designed to retrieve records of economic evidence (including full and partial economic evaluations) from the vast amount of literature indexed to major medical databases such as MEDLINE. The filter, which comprises a combination of controlled vocabulary and free-text retrieval methods, maximises sensitivity (or recall) to ensure that as many potentially relevant records as possible are retrieved from a search. Full details of the filter are provided in Appendix 12.

Date and language restrictions
Systematic database searches were initially conducted in March 2010 up to the most recent searchable date. Search updates were generated on a 6-monthly basis, with the final re-runs carried out in January 2011 ahead of the guideline consultation. After this point, studies were included only if they were judged by the GDG to be exceptional (for example, the evidence was likely to change a recommendation).

Although no language restrictions were applied at the searching stage, foreign language studies were not requested or reviewed unless they were of particular importance to an area under review. All of the searches were restricted to research published from 1995 onwards in order to obtain data relevant to current healthcare settings and costs.

Other search methods
Other search methods involved scanning the reference lists of all eligible publications (systematic reviews, stakeholder evidence, and included studies from the economic and clinical reviews) to identify further studies for consideration.

Full details of the search strategies and filter used for the systematic review of health economic evidence are provided in Appendix 12.

3.6.2   Inclusion criteria for economic studies

The following inclusion criteria were applied to select studies identified by the economic searches for further consideration:

- Only studies from Organisation for Economic Co-operation and Development countries were included, because the aim of the review was to identify economic information transferable to the UK context.
- Selection criteria based on types of clinical conditions and patients as well as interventions assessed were identical to the clinical literature review.
- Studies were included provided that sufficient details regarding methods and results were available to enable the methodological quality of the study to be assessed, and provided that the study's data and results were extractable. Poster presentations of abstracts were excluded.
- Full economic evaluations that compared two or more relevant options and considered both costs and consequences were included in the review.
- Economic studies were included if they used clinical effectiveness data from an RCT, a prospective cohort study or a systematic review and meta-analysis of clinical studies. Studies that had a mirror-image or other retrospective design were excluded from the review.
- Studies were included only if the examined interventions were clearly described. This involved the dosage and route of administration, and the duration of treatment in the case of pharmacological treatments, and the types of health professionals involved, as well as the frequency and duration of treatment in the case of psychological interventions. Evaluations in which medications were treated as a class were excluded from further consideration.
- Studies that adopted a very narrow perspective, ignoring major categories of costs to the NHS, were excluded; for example studies that estimated exclusively drug acquisition costs or hospitalisation costs were considered non-informative to the guideline development process.

3.6.3   Applicability and quality criteria for economic studies

All economic studies eligible for inclusion were appraised for their applicability and quality using the methodology checklist for economic evaluations recommended by NICE (NICE, 2009d), which is shown in Appendix 13 of this guideline. The methodology checklist for economic evaluations was also applied to the economic models developed specifically for this guideline. All studies that fully or partially met the applicability and quality criteria described in the methodology checklist were considered during the guideline development process, along with the results of the economic modelling conducted specifically for this guideline.

3.6.4   Presentation of economic evidence

The economic evidence considered in the guideline is provided in the respective evidence chapters, following presentation of the relevant clinical evidence. The references to included studies and the respective evidence tables with the study characteristics and results are provided in Appendix 14. Methods and results of economic modelling undertaken alongside the guideline development process are presented in the relevant evidence chapters. Characteristics and results of all economic studies considered during the guideline development process (including modelling studies conducted for this guideline) are summarised in economic evidence profiles accompanying respective GRADE clinical evidence profiles in Appendix 17.

3.6.5   Results of the systematic search of economic literature

The titles of all studies identified by the systematic search of the literature were screened for their relevance to the topic (that is, economic issues and information on HRQoL in people who self-harm). References that were clearly not relevant were excluded first. The abstracts of all potentially relevant studies (12 references) were then assessed against the inclusion criteria for economic evaluations by the health economist. Full texts of the studies potentially meeting the inclusion criteria (including those for which eligibility was not clear from the abstract) were obtained. Studies that did not meet the inclusion criteria, were duplicates, were secondary publications of one study, or had been updated in more recent publications were subsequently excluded. Finally, two economic studies that fully or partially met the applicability and quality criteria were considered at formulation of the guideline recommendations.

3.7   STAKEHOLDER CONTRIBUTIONS

Professionals, service users, and companies have contributed to and commented on the guideline at key stages in its development. Stakeholders for this guideline include:

- service users and carer stakeholders: national patient and carer organisations that represent the interests of people whose care will be covered by the guideline
- local patient and carer organisations: but only if there is no relevant national organisation
- professional stakeholders' national organisations: that represent the healthcare professionals who provide the services described in the guideline
- commercial stakeholders: companies that manufacture drugs or devices used in treatment of the condition covered by the guideline and whose interests may be significantly affected by the guideline
- providers and commissioners of health services in England and Wales
- statutory organisations: including the Department of Health, the Welsh Assembly Government, NHS Quality Improvement Scotland, the Healthcare Commission and the National Patient Safety Agency
- research organisations that have carried out nationally recognised research in the area.

NICE clinical guidelines are produced for the NHS in England and Wales, so a 'national' organisation is defined as one that represents England and/or Wales or has a commercial interest in England and/or Wales.

Stakeholders have been involved in the guideline's development at the following points:

- commenting on the initial scope of the guideline and attending a scoping workshop held by NICE
- contributing possible review questions and lists of evidence to the GDG
- commenting on the draft of the guideline
- highlighting factual errors in the pre-publication check.

3.8   VALIDATION OF THE GUIDELINE

Registered stakeholders had an opportunity to comment on the draft guideline, which was posted on the NICE website during the consultation period. Following the consultation, all comments from stakeholders and others were responded to and the guideline updated as appropriate. The Guideline Review Panel also reviewed the guideline and checked that stakeholders' comments had been addressed.

Following the consultation period, the GDG finalised the recommendations and the NCCMH produced the final documents. These were then submitted to NICE for the pre-publication check where stakeholders were given the opportunity to highlight factual errors. Any errors were corrected by the NCCMH, then the guideline was formally approved by NICE and issued as guidance to the NHS in England and Wales.

4   EXPERIENCE OF CARE

4.1   INTRODUCTION

This chapter provides an overview of the experience of people who self-harm including different age groups such as young people and adults, and special groups such as those with mild learning disabilities, males or those with borderline personality disorder, and their families/carers.

The first section comprises first-hand personal accounts written by people who self-harm and families/carers, which provide an understanding of self-harm, accessing services, having treatment and caring for someone who self-harms. It should be noted that these accounts are not representative of the experiences of all people who self-harm and therefore can only ever be illustrative. For instance, the personal accounts are all written by adults who self-harm and most of them used the method of cutting.

The second section of the chapter includes a review of the qualitative literature which provides a basis for the recommendations, found at the end of the final section.

4.2   PERSONAL ACCOUNTS—PEOPLE WHO SELF-HARM

4.2.1   Introduction

The writers of the personal accounts from people who self-harm were contacted through representatives on the GDG and through various agencies that had access to people who self-harm. The people who were approached to write the accounts were asked to consider a number of questions when composing their narratives. These included:

- When did you first seek help for self-harm and whom did you contact? (Please describe this first contact.)
- What helped or did not help you gain access to services? Did a friend or family member help you gain access to these services?
- Do you think that any life experiences led to the onset of the problem? If so, please describe if you feel able to do so.
- In what ways has the self-harm affected your everyday life (such as education, employment and making relationships) and the lives of those close to you?
- What possible treatments were discussed with you?
- What treatment(s) did you receive? Please describe any drug treatment and/or psychological therapy.
- Was the treatment(s) helpful? (Please describe what worked for you and what didn't work for you.)
- How would you describe your relationship with your practitioner(s) (for example, your GP, psychologist or other)

- Did you use any other approaches to help your self-harm in addition to those provided by NHS services, for example private treatment? If so please describe what was helpful and not helpful.
- Do you have any language support needs, including needing help with reading or speaking English? If so, did this have an impact on your understanding of the self-harm or on receiving treatment?
- Did you attend a support group and was this helpful? Did family and friends close to you or people in your community help and support you?
- How has the nature of the problem changed over time?
- How do you feel now?
- If your self-harm has improved, do you use any strategies to help you to stay well? If so, please describe these strategies.

Each author signed a consent form allowing the account to be reproduced in this guideline. Four personal accounts from people who self-harm(ed) were received in total.

4.2.2   Personal account A

I started to harm myself when I was 10 years old. I don't remember what was happening in my life at the time, but I know I always felt alone, like I didn't fit in or belong. On paper, I had the perfect family: a Mum and Dad, and a younger sister on whom I doted. Yet feelings of pain and struggle began to surface from an early age, when I was too young to have the words to describe what I was feeling. These feelings became increasingly pronounced and at 13 my self-destruction escalated. I began to harm myself more and more severely, either cutting or burning myself and with little regard for the long-term consequences of my actions. Despite people around me having some inclination about what was happening to me, no one intervened, and my difficulties continued, shrouded in a secrecy that allowed them to get worse.

As I headed towards adulthood, self-harm was still a part of my life on a daily basis. This got much worse in my twenties, when I no longer lived at home, and where I had the freedom and independence for the self-harm to worsen both in frequency and severity. I had always cut myself, but somehow the superficial cuts of my youth no longer satisfied the growing self-loathing and despair that I felt as an adult. The cuts got deeper, and more frequent; they migrated to other areas of my body that could be well concealed, and when this no longer provided the same level of relief, I began to self-poison. I had turned to a range of substances to poison myself with, ranging from significant and life threatening amounts of paracetamol, to other painkilling medication, iron tablets, and psychiatric medication. On one occasion I used weed killer to poison myself. Both cutting and poisoning myself had escalated to the point where they warranted medical intervention. I ended up sitting in an A&E [accident and emergency] department like so many others, wondering what was going to happen to me, or what people would think, nursing cuts so deep and painful that I would need stitching. The overdosing and self-poisoning required countless hospital admissions to undo the damage to myself. Some of these acts were direct attempts upon my life, and others were in the absence of care over whether I lived or died; I no longer cared. All I wanted was peace inside from the constant struggle and torment.

There were times when I attended A&E voluntarily, but there were other times when I was taken there by ambulance after becoming unwell or after collapse. This aspect of my self-destruction was painful for those who witnessed it. Although I tried to keep my self-harm private, sometimes I was so unwell that other people in my life needed to know.

Some friends watched me do these things to myself, tormented and frightened by what was going to happen to me. These relationships waned. People could no longer invest in an attachment to someone who didn't have the will to live anymore. A couple of friends, in particular, attempted to advocate on my behalf to services, to let them know that I needed help and support. It was so hard for me to ask for help, because I believed that I deserved none, and when people did offer their help I was suspicious of it. It was hard for me that people needed to intervene, and it was even harder because it was only when there was a chorus of voices seeking help that there was any action from services.

I feared statutory services and I didn't want to go to a doctor as I felt so ashamed. Instead, I looked for help in the voluntary sector and attended a support group for women who self-harmed. Here I began to focus solely upon myself as a self-harmer. I was exposed to the harming of others, and this made my harming much worse during this time. In my experience, support groups are unhelpful unless they are well moderated; for me it was an arena in which competitive urges towards self-destruction could rise. Due to this I ended up in A&E countless times for treatment for the cuts and for overdosing.

My GP became aware of my problems, and I was seen by a psychiatrist, and a CPN [community psychiatric nurse]. The self-harm was so severe that I was deemed too high a risk for psychotherapy.

I was prescribed medication (Seroxat) that only worsened my condition, as I entered a world where all I could think about was self-harm. I soon became an inpatient because of the level of risk I posed to myself. Ultimately therapy was offered by an astounding therapist who, with my CPN, recognised that unless some intervention was offered, it was likely that I might end up completing suicide. Self-harm, suicidality and suicide became a messed-up continuum that I found very difficult to pick apart.

The CPN and therapist worked collaboratively to try and keep me safe. They were on hand to support me in managing my distress and learn to accept help and support and begin to articulate my struggles instead of turning them inwards. Their hard work was matched by my own. At first, the self-harm continued to escalate – the more I talked about everything that hurt, the more I ruminated upon self-destruction. But they persisted, and I persisted. The progress I made was in tiny steps, first just increasing my awareness of why I was self-harming. Countless times I had been asked 'why I was doing this' but I am not sure I really knew. I just responded to my distress in a physical way, and to begin to do things differently, I had to at first understand the motivation behind the harm.

No one had ever really talked about what my options were for treatment. In fact the opposite: I have a range of really damaging experiences such as being called a 'time waster', or being treated by CPNs as someone who was not willing to engage, and written off as an 'expected suicide' by the local crisis intervention team. This couldn't be it for me. I was told each time I was in hospital that I 'had to be' assessed, and that my level of risk meant that people were going to step in and tell me what to do. I never really had a choice, except to choose to take a gamble on those kind individuals who were, by chance, involved in my life, and to learn to get better.

My relationships with the therapist and my CPN were absolutely crucial to me overcoming the self-harm, as was my relationship with two GPs, who collectively gave me the skills to save my own life. Without their dedication, compassion and commitment I doubt I would be here writing these words for you to read. I was receiving CBT [cognitive behavioural therapy], and soon that and all the support helped me to recognise that the self-harm was only but a symptom of a damaged sense of self and distress that had been rampaging out of control since I was a child.

Over the years I was prescribed a number of other medications, including oxazepam, chlorpromazine, mirtazapine, quetiapine, lorazepam, temazepam and carbamazepine. I needed none of these – what I needed was someone to hear me and help me, and with patience and care, to explore and overcome these difficulties. Medicating a problem like this was only ever going to be a temporary measure, a prop. I ended up taking three or four medications at any one time, and I should never have been medicated to this level – all it did was perpetuate feelings of dissociation and lack of control.

There were many life experiences that contributed to my self-harm and distress and medication was not going to remedy these. Mainly these were related to a sense of autonomy and worth, with a range of invalidating experiences leading me to feel as though I had no right to my emotional experience, and therefore no recourse to expressing or exploring these strains naturally. Everything that I encountered in an emotional way was subsequently subjugated, and an internal process of dismissing my real feelings became second nature. These feelings then popped up somewhere else, where self-harm was used to manage them. Getting better involved re-learning and relating to my emotion, validating my experiences, and developing greater skills at emotional management and regulation.

For a long time I was isolated beyond measure, almost living two lives. I ended up withdrawing from almost all social activity, and gave up my well-paid job because I could no longer sustain the life that I was trying to live. For years I was out of work, with very little else happening in my life except for distress, despair, self-harm and sleeplessness.

Getting better was a long road. When the 2004 NICE self-harm guideline was being developed, I was one of the individuals interviewed and my account of my experiences was used in the guidance. To be able to sit here and write from a different perspective as recovered, as another guideline on self-harm is developed, is an interesting exercise. I now work as a therapist. I know that there was very little access to services when I needed it the most. I was repeatedly met with judgement or contempt from those others involved in my care who never took the time to get to know me, the person behind the harm. So I now run a service, which was established out of direct experience of the lack of services for those who self-harm.

The distress that I experience now I relate to in a more managed way – I understand myself so much more and accept that there are times when I will struggle more than others. I also know that no matter what – there is no going back for me. Self-harm is a thing of my past. I have learnt a new way of being, and I believe faithfully that this can happen for other people if we develop and deliver appropriate and needs-led services that are dedicated to meeting people in their distress and helping them to move through this at their own pace.

4.2.3 Personal account B

Disgust. Shame. The look of pity. Intrigue. Fear. These are views I have experienced, and unfortunately become accustomed to, as a 28-year-old woman with scars covering my arms. I have not self-harmed for just over 3 years now, but the scars are still on my arms and shall remain there for life.

When I first spoke to someone (a teacher) about my self-harm urges, I was only 14 or 15 years old. She was fantastic and offered me the school counsellor's services. As I got older and life circumstances took a hold of me, the self-harm in the form of cutting, gradually grew worse.

At the age of about 21, I started attending A&E to be stitched back together. There were times when, unfortunately, the experience at A&E itself left me feeling worthless. There could be one fantastic triage nurse or doctor but their care would be undermined by another nurse, doctor or receptionist whose care or attitude would be cold or their frustration towards me for causing damage to my own body would show. I think there were times when the fact that I am of South-Asian origin, living in a city with a high Asian population, led to pre-judgements being made of me. Doctors assumed that the reason why I had self-harmed was due to a cultural conflict. They did not wait or ask; if they had done so they would have found it was actually due to growing up in an abusive home, and having a child out of wedlock might have been a factor, although this was by no means the foundation of my problems.

It is difficult to remember exactly how I felt during the periods of cutting as it is like I was a totally different person to who I am now. I do recall being at a loss, angry and frustrated – I was scared. The fear of hurting others, especially my daughter was very real and this led me to justify my cutting; I was not hurting anyone else, thereby it was all OK. During the time I cut, there was no pain; looking back now it shocks me that I did this to myself. After cutting, however, the pain was excruciating: small cuts stung, big cuts really hurt. But practicalities took over first: how was I going to dress them? Did I need to go to hospital? What was I going to tell my daughter? I did regret the cuts I made because they were not really stating my case for sanity, however they accomplished something – they helped me through an immensely difficult period of my life.

The care and treatment that I have received has been mixed and difficult to label as 'good' or 'bad'. Within each service there are individuals who shine through. It is the triage nurse who took the extra moment to tell me that I should not worry about my daughter and placed a hand gently and reassuringly on my shoulder. It is the doctor who when stitching me up did not rush and make me feel as if I had committed a sin, but instead spoke to me and informed me of the psychiatric liaison team who were available. It is the CPN who comes every day and calls in between visits, listens to what I have to say and does not just fill out the care plan. It is the members of the home treatment team who will take a few minutes out to sit down and not simply check that I am taking my medication. It is the psychiatric consultant who puts away all his notes and lets me explain what is going on in my head without assuming he knows my problems. It is the psychotherapist who does not rush me and allows me to talk or remain silent.

I have had input from GPs, A&E staff, psychiatric unit staff, mental health nurses, CPNs and the home treatment team. Alongside all these individuals I have also been fortunate to have had the support of some of the best counsellors and psychotherapists I could ever wish to meet. All of these people working together, with not just one another but also with me, has, in my opinion, led to my recovery. My own circumstances were made more bearable and workable when services worked together: my therapist understanding the impact the medication I was taking was having on my mood helped me in therapy as I could make sense of my mood swings; my key worker in the housing project knowing the impact the medication was having upon my ability to care for my daughter also helped as it meant social services were not unnecessarily brought into the situation.

My family have found it difficult to understand my self-harm as well as my bipolar disorder (which was diagnosed around 2004); maybe it is a cultural issue or maybe it is just simply too distressing for them to acknowledge. My friends have taken the time to learn about self-harm and understand that removing all sharp objects only benefits their conscience, and in reality put me at risk because I was more likely to not 'safe self-harm'.

I have a beautiful 9-year-old daughter who is now aware of the story behind my scars. It was not easy explaining self-harm to her, but I knew it was such a big part of me; I needed to tell her because I could not hide it. I wish that everyone could take a leaf out of the innocent book of a child's mind. It is so simple; there is no judgement, just honest questions and accepting responses. She still saw me as 'Mum', but 'Mum who got very sad at times and hurt herself'. Unfortunately there were those who thought I posed a risk to my daughter due to my self-harm, but thankfully they soon realised this was not the case.

People constantly ask how it is that I have managed to stay 'well' for so long and not self-harm. The true answer is that I do not have a definitive answer. I can only say that I know that therapy really played a major part in my life. The ability to finally have an opportunity to open up that locked box of terrible memories to someone in a safe and supportive environment had a profound impact upon me. Don't get me wrong, it was scary and there were times when therapy itself led to self-harm episodes, but without those terribly tough sessions, I hate to think what my life would be like now. Would I still be self-harming to the degree that I was? Medication, as much as I hate it, also played its part, but only once I began to understand what the tablets were for and how different ones benefited, or, hindered me. Getting the right combination enabled me to be rested (zopiclone), less agitated (lorazepam) and keep my mood stable (lithium/antidepressants). This in combination with therapy, in combination with supportive professionals, is what has enabled me to now be 'well', a better mother, and a full time student at university studying for, ironically, a psychology degree! I am now in control.

4.2.4   Personal account C[6]

The first time I self-harmed was when I was 15 years old. I was taking GCEs and CSEs at school. There was a lot of pressure from my parents as I was going to be the first person in their family to go to college and become a teacher. My grandmother had wanted to teach but poverty intervened and at 14 she was a servant in a big house, my mother had a fantasy of teaching but lacked the intellect so it was pretty clear that I was there to fulfil their dreams. I didn't want to become a teacher; I wanted to learn what I wanted to be. I wanted to leave home and see strange things. I wanted to stop living safely and take some risks. I wanted to go out when it was cold without wearing a scarf or cross the road without being that careful. I wanted to drink, take drugs and meet the kind of men I wasn't supposed to.

A few weeks before my exams began, having missed the mocks due to illness, I felt as though I was shattering into a thousand pieces. No matter what I did to try and rebuild myself it was the wrong thing. My mother hectored me in to revising to get the results she needed. It was made clear that when I qualified I'd still live in the same town and that I would be expected to support my parents financially. I'd been supporting them emotionally, being their surrogate parents since I was 12 and it was just too much. I later learned that it was when I was around 15 years old that I began to experience bipolar disorder for the first time and that makes a lot of sense. My parents didn't notice, except for the odd moment, that I was under a great deal of stress and then they wrote me off as being difficult. I've spent my whole life being difficult.

I found myself out in the dark one night, walking around terraced streets that were too narrow by the day and by the night narrower still so I had to turn my anorectic body sideways to make my way through without banging my bony elbows on the doors as I passed by. It wasn't the best neighbourhood in the world. We had a poly, a town centre and a red light district all within a few hundred yards. Across the main road was the area that even the residents didn't go to at night. At the top of the road was a school in a few acres of ground where my brother's friend had found a hanging body one morning. Not the sort of place you should let your kids roam around after dark.

I heard a noise behind me and began to run as fast as my barely strung together body would take me, tripping in the dark knee first on to a pile of glass. The noise

[6]Reproduced with permission from: http://weirdsid.wordpress.com/ (accessed February 2011).

behind me was in my head. My school trousers were ruined, my hands were filthy, I was crying but I felt relieved. The nagging and shouting love-in I got when I returned home was spectacular. What was I doing out? Well actually nobody had realised that I wasn't there so I always felt that it was a pretty redundant question. Much emphasis was laid upon how much the family relied upon me and how I had to stop being so dramatic and pass my exams. The relief that I'd felt earlier quickly disappeared.

Adding to the pressure was the fact that I'd formed a relationship with someone older from school. I was 15 and he was 18. He was pressuring me into having sex with him; my mother was pressuring me to marry him. I was staying with him because he was joining the army and I thought it would be an escape from the family that held me so tightly against my will. I felt kidnapped in my own home. Life was a mess.

I passed the exams and left school. I didn't go onto further education I went out to work. My family was furious especially as one of the jobs I took was in a factory. It suited me well and the money was fantastic and the accidental injuries were frequent. I still have the faded scars on my hands, each one a moment of misery blissfully relieved.

I had no idea until I was in my mid forties why I really did what I did. A consultant psychiatrist was doing a study on self-harm and asked me to be part of the study. There was a recorded session with a researcher and I described my experiences of what I did, how it felt, what the outcome was. Even now as I'm typing this I feel the scars on my arm twitching. That's usually a sign that something is stressful and that harm could be on the way. I had to stop wearing earrings because I always felt tempted to pull them out the hard way when I felt my scars twitch.

I sat in a room in a psychiatric outpatients department. A lovely room with a plant in that I tended each time I went. As the researcher settled herself and set up the recording equipment I had my chat with the plant, watered it, washed its leaves, wasted some time until I had to sit down and begin to talk. I wanted to talk but, like all of these experiences, sometimes you learn truths about yourself that you'd rather you didn't.

We talked of when I harmed and the ritual. Had there been any time when I hadn't followed this pattern of harming. Surprisingly yes, a ten-year gap during the time I was conscientiously drinking England dry. Yet another form of self-harm.

We talked of why I harmed and the outcome and this is why I can never say that I will stop harming myself. I feel pressure building up inside me when I have mood swings. I have violent moods swings. They're sudden, massive physical attacks that my mind wreaks on my body. I have no control over them but I can gain relief from them. I am a fully inflated balloon waiting to explode loudly. The self-harm is a strip of sellotape over the balloon and a pin piercing the balloon through the sellotape. The balloon deflates slowly, easily, painlessly, and comfortably. It leaves me exhausted, ravaged, a mess of tears, laughter, sadness and joy. It leaves me alive because without it I would surely kill myself.

As I harm I get a hit. A legal shot of a drug I never used in my hedonistic days as an abuser. That's probably the truest reason why I won't stop harming.

I've tried to stop. I've tried drawing on myself and holding ice and all of the other things that don't come close to stopping me want to die. I have formulated a way of harming safely with the knowledge and consent of my GP and my consultant. It's not ideal but it keeps me alive and scarred as opposed to dead and without a mark.

4.2.5   Personal account D

I first suffered from depression in my late teens and early twenties, after what I had always assumed was the usual teenage angst and drama became more serious. I became withdrawn from my friends and family, and had negative thoughts about myself and those around me. I believed that I was worthless, and I assumed everyone else agreed. At some point – I don't remember the first time – I started cutting myself. I used a razor blade to carve increasingly deep and angry wounds into my arms.

It was at this point that my parents decisively intervened, and involved our GP. I was prescribed antidepressants and referred to a specialist. As this was the mid 1990s, and I was still very new to the terminology of mental health disorders, I don't remember exactly what drugs I took. I visited the psychiatric department of my local hospital as a regular outpatient, and I finally found a person to whom I felt I could really talk. At the time, I didn't really care what qualifications she had – I just knew that, for the first time, I felt that I was managing the problem, and not being managed by it.

With the support of my family, my health improved, and I went on to university – a year older than my peers but more confident in my ability to deal with the stresses and pressures of life. In later years, I was able to identify what I saw as early warnings of a relapse, and manage the symptoms before I lost control.

Fifteen years later, however, in my mid-thirties, I became depressed again. Now with a wife and child, and all the responsibilities that entails, I found that my working environment caused severe anxiety and I quickly lost my ability to manage the symptoms. Eventually, I began cutting myself whilst at work.

It's difficult to say definitively why I cut myself. There was certainly an element of release involved – immediately after cutting, I would feel better, less anxious, and so that feeling of relief became an incentive to cut again. I also believe I wanted to create a physical manifestation of the emotional turmoil – a physical wound is so much more visible and obvious. However, there's a clear paradox here because I didn't want anyone else to see the wounds. Perhaps I was creating this physical evidence to convince myself that there was something wrong.

I went to see my GP seeking some medication that I naïvely believed would magically make the problem disappear. I was prescribed an antidepressant (mirtazapine), and my doctor also took time to ask me how I felt during the periods of depression and anxiety, and how I felt when I was self-harming. She asked what I thought might be causing the problems. Although I didn't have the answers, I appreciated the questions being asked.

I am usually a self-confident and self-reliant person and therefore I found it very difficult to ask for help – it felt like I was exposing myself. Although I had no previous relationship with my GP, she was patient, understanding and sympathetic. As my treatment continued, I found my fortnightly consultations with her to be a useful barometer of my progress.

Initially, I withdrew from my 'normal' life – I stopped working and spent little time with my family, preferring my own company. I would try to read, but found I could only concentrate for short periods of time before my thoughts would wander. During this time I continued to cut myself when I felt particularly worthless.

After several weeks, I was assessed by the local mental health team and referred to a group CBT course. This was a classroom-based course with around eight other service users. I found this of limited use, as I was so anxious at the prospect of joining the group, I found it difficult to concentrate on the content. Also, I had no relationship or rapport with the chap who was delivering the content, so I found what he was saying did not carry much weight.

A friend gave me a book produced by the National Self Harm Network about 'safe cutting'. This was useful because, as silly as this might sound, I didn't want to do any serious damage to myself. Although there were times when I felt suicidal, these were very different from the times I cut myself. When I was cutting myself, the motivation was certainly not to end my life, but to hurt myself – to damage myself.

Later on, I was seen by an occupational therapist. These sessions were one to one and focused specifically on my own recovery. Straight away this was more useful and as I built a rapport with the therapist, I found myself participating more with the process. Each week we would agree clear targets and goals – go to the shops three times, speak to my parents, spend time with my son – then we would review those goals the following week. This follow-up was crucial as it allowed me to see what progress I was making – it's all too easy to just see the bad side of things.

It's fairly obvious that group CBT is far cheaper to provide than the one-to-one therapy. However, in my opinion, it doesn't deliver anywhere near the value it should. I shouldn't speak for other members of the group, but the atmosphere within the room was tense and agitated – I'm not sure that anyone was learning much.

As, gradually, I started to feel better, I tried to analyse what had made the difference – I think it's probably an element of everything – the drugs, the various therapies, the GP consultations, the natural cycle of my mental health. The local mental health team invited me to join a reading club (bibliotherapy). We read short stories and novels, and discussed them as a group. We had all been suffering from mental health conditions, but the group wasn't about that – it was about the books. I found this to be a really useful exercise. It helped me get back into the social habits I had lost whilst I had been ill. The timing was important – I wouldn't have been able to participate in the group unless I had already gone through the therapies I had had up to that point.

4.3 PERSONAL ACCOUNTS—CARERS

4.3.1 Introduction

The methods used for obtaining the carers' accounts were the same as outlined in Section 4.2.1, but the questions included:
- In what way do you care for someone with self-harm?
- How long have you been a carer of someone with self-harm?
- In what ways has being a carer affected your everyday life (such as schooling, employment and making relationships) and the lives of those close to you?
- How involved are/were you in the treatment plans of the person with self-harm?

- Were you offered support by the person's practitioners (for example, their GP, psychologist, or other)?
- How would you describe your relationship with the person's practitioner(s)?
- Have you and your family been offered help or received assessment/treatment by a healthcare professional?
- Did you attend a support group and was this helpful?
- Did any people close to you help and support you in your role as a carer?

4.3.2   Carer account A

My son died in April 2010, so I have written this account from my point of view as his mother and carer. My mother, who suffered from depression and anxiety, also self-harmed and took her life in June of the same year after many previous attempts. I would like to understand what drove them to such desperate methods because neither of them had any particularly awful life events, in fact, generally speaking, the opposite would be the case. But what was going on in their minds must have negated the positive aspects of their lives.

My son began self-harming when he was 13 when we were living in Germany as part of the MOD [Ministry of Defence]. My son wrote a suicide note and took an overdose of over-the-counter pain relief drugs with alcohol. Before this event, he had had an argument with a friend about some money he was owed, and I had been a little cross with him because he had taken some things that belonged to his brother. He was taken to a German hospital and when he left the hospital we were told that he should see a child psychologist immediately but the only one available as part of the MOD services was an educational psychologist. He saw this professional for about a year. The main diagnosis was anxiety, and he was given relaxation tapes and taught exercises to control this. The psychologist thought that he would probably try to end his life again, so we were obviously terribly worried about this.

At the age of 25 my son attempted suicide again. We were still living in Germany and he was taken to hospital and put under close scrutiny. He had been depressed and was taking medication for this. By this time he had a serious alcohol problem and had experienced withdrawal seizures. He stayed in the unit for about 5 months. The quality of care was very good; he had therapy and self-help, although the language was a bit of a barrier as my son did not speak fluent German. He was prescribed citalopram. After leaving hospital he was assigned to a CBT therapist and saw her every week until we left Germany about 3 months later.

We left Germany to live in the UK and my son registered with a local GP, taking a copy of the therapist's notes with him. We also asked for his hospital notes to be transferred to the practice, but this didn't happen for several months. He was put on a waiting list for counselling and no copy was taken of the therapist's letter. His prescription was changed to venlafaxine, which was the same medication that my mother was taking.

Two months later, he was admitted to A&E, after cutting his wrist and taking an overdose of antidepressants, painkillers and iron tablets (he had previously had a bad accident and broken his leg, so he had a lot of pills prescribed for pain). He was put on a ward in a general hospital. I asked what would happen and was told he would probably be sent home after seeing a psychiatrist. I asked to speak to a doctor on the ward so I could make him aware of my son's history, which was arranged and my son then saw a psychiatrist. My son told the psychiatrist that he would not be safe if he went home, and he was admitted to a psychiatric hospital. He was diagnosed with severe depression and treated with high doses of antidepressants. He stayed there for 5 months and was then transferred to the crisis team. He was on a waiting list for CBT and he had about eight sessions of this about 3 months after he left hospital.

My son rarely talked about self-harming – when we asked him about the various injuries he had, he would say they were accidental, and it is possible that some of them were, as he was still having withdrawal fits from trying to regulate his alcohol intake. He lived alone, so many of these were not witnessed. His CPN thought that the fits he was having were psychogenic; his psychiatrist seemed convinced the problem was alcohol addiction. His notes show that he did talk about hurting himself to his CPN – describing it as 'giving himself a good battering'. There is nothing in his notes to say that self-harming was discussed or explored.

My son often talked about feelings of emptiness and said that was why he drank. Drinking seemed to put him in touch with his emotions but in an exaggerated way so that he often became very tearful and upset. When he was sober he was often quite distant and withdrawn.

My son had always been a quiet child, he was generally very passive, although would have quite severe mood swings, which in early childhood were tantrums and later on would show themselves in outbursts of frustration such as breaking things in his house or hitting himself. He had usually been drinking when he lashed out at himself. He was quite insightful about this and had ways of calming himself such as taking a bath, or using a punch ball. He found dealing with change, such as starting school, very difficult, and because we moved around a lot in Germany he had many changes to deal with. Break ups with a girlfriend usually led to self-harm incidents. He often described himself as worthless and compared himself with his brothers, both of whom were getting on well with their lives, settled with jobs and girlfriends/wives. He had considerable artistic talent, and all of his peers really liked him and thought him very good company, but he didn't seem to be aware of this and thought people didn't like him and were laughing or talking about him behind his back.

My son didn't have a job for the last 3 years of his life. He didn't like to be criticised in any way, and inevitably this could happen if he was employed. So he didn't try to get a job. The drink problem led to several break ups with girlfriends and also to losing respect of his peers. My son was quite naïve – he was taken advantage of by others who borrowed money and didn't pay it back.

About 5 months before he died, my son began talking to me about his self-harm; he said the cuts to his face were so that he didn't do something worse and he talked about how he was planning to end his life and how he proposed to do it. I told the CPN, who advised me to go to my son's GP. The GP said there was nothing that could be done until my son decided he wanted to stop drinking.

My son very rarely saw his named GP; he told me that he didn't understand his problems, and he chose to see more sympathetic doctors from the practice. One of these was very helpful and guided my son to the addiction team, and also re-referred him back to the CMHT.

After his re-referral to the CMHT in April 2009, there was no care plan, I asked why and was told it was because he was with the wellbeing and access team, and they didn't do care plans. I found out later that this team would only normally see a client on about three or four occasions, but my son saw his CPN 37 times.

Once my son accessed the addiction service, things seems to improve quite a bit. The counsellor was aware of dual diagnosis, which his CPN seemed to not be aware of, and she seemed to have a lot of insight into my son's personality. There seems to have been a proper plan for his treatment, and I think he was taken seriously, instead of just a 'drunk'.

There was a plan to refer my son for dialectical behaviour therapy as one of the possible diagnoses was severe emotional personality disorder. The referral process started in September 2009, but he was not actually referred until the week before he died in the following April. There was quite a long waiting list so he wouldn't have accessed the therapy for quite a while.

He only ever saw his psychiatrist when I had made an urgent request – the last time was in February 2010 after he was talking openly about suicide to his addiction counsellor and to me, and because he was physically ill, having lost about 20 kg in weight. The first risk assessment in my son's file, since his re-referral, appears on this date.

My son did see a private counsellor but I don't know if he discussed self-harm issues with her. He also had contact with a Rethink volunteer and met a few times with them. There was a proposal to go to an art class with support, but my son never acted upon it.

I was offered carer support – but what I really needed was to be clear about my position as a carer and what I could do to help, and what not to do. Once my son had accessed the secondary mental health services, I was relieved because I thought I could take a 'back seat' and let the professionals help him. But this didn't seem to happen. He had lots of help in getting benefits, but there didn't seem to be any overall plan. I was largely excluded from his treatment – there was no discussion about his care plan and although I think my son didn't mind me knowing about his treatment, there was never any formal acknowledgement of this. My son hadn't signed any of his care plans and the section about discussion with carers all had ticks in the 'No' boxes.

I had very little faith in the psychiatrist or the CPN, when I asked at the emergency meeting why there was no care plan or a risk assessment, I was told that I was making the situation worse. But the addiction counsellor seemed to have a real understanding of the link between mental illness and substance misuse, and she seemed to have a very good relationship with my son, he was more open and honest with her than with the other agencies. She had also discussed issues of confidentiality with him and I felt when I talked with her that the boundaries were clear and this was a relief because I didn't want to feel disloyal or as though I was prying into his life. I knew that anything she said to me was with his permission.

I was not offered help by a healthcare professional. I attended a voluntary group with carers who had adult children with similar problems. My family were also supportive.

4.4 REVIEW OF THE QUALITATIVE LITERATURE

4.4.1 Introduction

A systematic search for published reviews of relevant qualitative studies of people who self-harm was undertaken. The aim of the review was to explore the experience of care for people who self-harm, the experiences of carers who care for people who self-harm, and of healthcare professionals who work with people who self-harm.

4.4.2 Evidence search

Reviews were sought of qualitative studies that used relevant first-hand experiences of people who self-harm and families/carers. For more information about the databases searched see Table 4.

4.4.3 Studies considered[7]

At the scoping stage, two recent systematic reviews were found and these were modified in two ways. Firstly, only studies that were relevant to the long-term management of people who self-harm were included (for example, studies that focused exclusively

Table 4: Databases searched and inclusion/exclusion criteria for clinical evidence.

Electronic databases	CINAHL, EMBASE, HMIC, International Bibliography of the Social Sciences, MEDLINE, PsycBOOKS, PsycEXTRA, PsycINFO
Date searched	2006 to 25 January 2011
Study design	Systematic reviews of qualitative studies, qualitative studies, observational studies
Population	Individuals who self-harm by any method
Outcomes	None specified – any narrative description of service user experience of self-harm

---

[7]Here and elsewhere in the guideline, each study considered for review is referred to by a study ID in capital letter (primary author and date of publication, except where a study is in press or only submitted for publication, then a date is not used).

on experience of care in general hospital emergency department settings were excluded) and secondly, the reviews were updated to include studies published through to January 2011.

The first systematic review explored the experience of self-harm and treatment from the perspective of people who self-harm (Taylor *et al.*, 2009). This review involved undertaking a search between 1950 and June 2006 and included a total of 31 studies. Of these, a total of 21 studies were included and narratively reviewed for the purpose of this guideline and ten studies were excluded because they focused on shorter- rather than longer-term management. The quantitative studies were not subject to meta-analysis due to the lack of studies providing similar data. They were used instead to provide evidence about the general experiences of a larger population of service users, with the qualitative data used to add depth to the understanding of self-harm through the description of specific experiences.

Since the review (Taylor *et al.*, 2009) only included studies published before 2007, an updated search was conducted to capture more recent studies relating to service user, healthcare professional and carer experience. A total of 2,269 references were identified by the electronic search. Of these references, 2,201 were excluded at the screening stage on the basis of reading the title and/or abstract. The remaining 68 references were assessed for eligibility on the basis of the full text. Overall, 36 qualitative studies and quantitative studies met these inclusion criteria. Thirty-two studies were considered for the review but they did not meet the inclusion criteria so were excluded. The most common reasons for exclusion were: the study focused only on shorter-term medical or psychological management of self-harm rather than longer-term management; the study did not allude to either the experience of self-harm or treatment, or the experience of carers or healthcare professionals; non-English articles or dissertations, and studies in which experiences of services or reasons for self-harm differ (for example, developing countries).

The second systematic review carried out by SAUNDERS2011 (Saunders *et al.* 2011) examined attitudes of healthcare professionals and knowledge regarding people who self-harm, and is reviewed below. However, only findings relating to longer-term management were included. Studies were excluded where, in the judgement of the reviewers and the GDG, there was limited relevance to UK health settings.

Further to this, there were three additional studies HUBAND2004 [Huband & Tantam, 2004], REECE2005 [Reece, 2005], TAYLOR2003 [Taylor, 2003] that were included on the basis of cross-checking an existing literature review (Bosman & Meijel, 2008) that met the inclusion criteria and a further four studies HOPKINS2002 [Hopkins, 2002], JEFFERY2002 [Jeffery & Warm, 2002], MACKAY2005 [Mackay & Barrowclough, 2005], O'DONOVAN2007 [O'Donovan, 2007] were included after cross-checking a recent literature review carried out by McHale and Felton (2010). These were all qualitative studies that examined the experience of self-harm from the perspective of service users or healthcare professionals.

Further information about both included and excluded studies can be found in Appendix 15a.

4.4.4   Service user experience of self-harm

While reviewing each study, key findings that were relevant to the service user experience of self-harm were extracted and summarised into a study characteristics table (Appendix 15a). There were 27 studies (ADLER2007 [Adler & Adler, 2007], ARNOLD1995 [Arnold, 1995], BAKER2008 [Baker & Fortune, 2008], BURGESS1998 [Burgess *et al.*, 1998], BYWATERS2002 [Bywaters & Rolfe, 2002], CAMGAN1994 [Camgan *et al.*, 1994], CRAIGEN2009 [Craigen & Foster, 2009], CROCKWELL1995 [Crockwell & Burford, 1995], CURTIS2006 [Curtis, 2006], DORER1999 [Dorer *et al.*, 1999], FISH2008 [Fish & Duperouzel, 2008], HARRIS2000 [Harris, 2000], HORNE2009 [Horne & Csipke, 2009], HUBAND2004, HUME2007 [Hume & Platt, 2007], KOKALIARI2008 [Kokaliari & Berzoff, 2008], KOOL2009 [Kool *et al.*, 2009], LESNIAK2010 [Lesniak, 2010], LEWIS2010 [Lewis & Darcy, 2010], MOYER2007 [Moyer & Nelson, 2007], POLK2009 [Polk & Liss, 2009], RAY2007 [Ray, 2007], REECE2005, RUSSELL2010 [Russell *et al.*, 2010], SCHOPPMANN2007 [Schoppmann *et al.*, 2007], SHAW2006 [Shaw, 2006], SINCLAIR2005 [Sinclair & Green, 2005]) that fell under the category of service user experience of self-harm.

The review team listed the themes that emerged from the analysis of these main findings, and these were presented to the GDG and used to structure this chapter. The findings that emerged under the heading of 'service user experience of self-harm' were:
- underlying reasons for engaging in self-harm behaviour (for example, traumatic life events, psychiatric illness, a coping strategy and cultural factors)
- coexisting destructive behaviours
- physical and psychological consequences of self-harm
- stigma and misconceptions about self-harm
- stopping self-harm and recovery
- alternative coping strategies.

These findings appeared in both populations of adults and young people; however, because these populations may differ in their experiences the findings for young people were reported separately.

In addition to these different age groups, there were two subgroups for which the experience of self-harm may have differed and so these were also reported separately. These included people who self-harm with mild/moderate learning disabilities and males who self-harm.

Reasons behind self-harm
The motivations or underlying reasons for self-harm were commonly reported in the literature. Overall, the majority of studies found that self-harm was linked to traumatic life events, difficulties in interpersonal relationships and experiences of isolation or rejection (ADLER2007, ARNOLD1995, BYWATERS2002, CROCKWELL1995, CURTIS2006, HARRIS2000, HORNE2009, KOOL2009, LESNIAK2010, RAY2007, SCHOPPMANN2007). However, it should be noted that many of these studies referred to self-injury as opposed to self-poisoning. There were only four studies that looked at the reasons behind self-poisoning (BURGESS1998, CROCKWELL1995, DORER1999, SINCLAIR2005).

CROCKWELL1995 interviewed women who had engaged in multiple suicide attempts by overdose in Canada and were among the first to examine the underlying reasons behind self-harm. They revealed that overall participants had experienced significant life events such as strained or absent relationships with parents, being bullied at school and physical, sexual or emotional abuse. These life experiences were linked by participants to their self-harm.

In line with these findings, both HARRIS2000 and BYWATERS2002 conducted studies in the UK that also found that the majority of service users' accounts were strongly characterised by traumatic life events or chronic life problems, including physical and sexual abuse in childhood, and the death of a family member; again, all of the participants explicitly linked their self-harm in some way to such experiences. The above findings were replicated in more recent studies carried out in New Zealand (CURTIS2006) and the US (LESNIAK2010), thus strengthening the findings reported here. In fact, many participants in the study carried out by CURTIS2006 spoke explicitly of feeling powerless or out of control in some aspect of their lives, often as a direct result of abuse. Likewise, in the study carried out by Lesniak (2010) all of the participants experienced some form of childhood trauma such as emotional, verbal or physical abuse. They felt ill-equipped to deal with these traumatic events and felt they received no parental support or guidance to help them.

In contrast, in a study carried out by ADLER2007 in the US on females who self-harm it was found that many of the participants did not come from a background of physical or sexual abuse and in fact many had unremarkable childhoods. One female noted:

I've got no history of abuse, and my recollections of my childhood are happy, so why do I self injure? Who knows?

ARNOLD1995 conducted semi-structured interviews (n = 26) and written questionnaires (n = 50) with women who had a history of self-injury, to provide some insight into the act of self-injury, and found that many of the childhood experiences that women felt had led them to self-injure were similar to those reported by other researchers. However, sexual abuse, although common, was less prevalent than many authors reported.

Other common precipitants of self-harm were ruptures in interpersonal relationships and experiences of isolation, loss, abandonment and rejection (ADLER2007, CROCKWELL1995, HORNE2009, KOOL2009, LESNIAK2010, RAY2007, SCHOPPMANN2007). For many respondents, the lack of connection or, conversely, the existence of a very close connection provided a reason to self-harm (KOOL2009). One participant (RAY2007) explains how difficulties in her relationship with her mother were a significant stressor and perhaps triggered her self-harm:

We were extremely close when I was in high school because that's all I had. She was all I had... When I was going through all this stuff, I mean really, really bad depression, my mother was just like, 'I don't want to deal with it'... she was like, 'I'm stepping out'... so I mean I lost the number one person I had in my life.

Many participants voiced some form of abandonment such as neglect, bereavement, fear of being alone or feeling disconnected from those around them (LESNIAK2010). For others, experiences of breakups, fights or other forms of rejection led them to self-harm (ADLER2007). Romantic traumas were a more significant factor cited by males (ADLER2007). Others mentioned that they engaged in self-harm to feel alive or relieve themselves of dissociation (LEWIS2010, POLK2009, SCHOPPMANN2007); in doing so, the visual and tactile perception of blood following self-injury played an important role. To feel dampness and warmth meant to be able to perceive one's own body, and that meant that the state of alienation had ended and one was 'whole' again (SCHOPPMANN2007). Moreover, the results suggested that young adults who indicated that they self-harm to manage tension and dissociation also had a stronger intent to self-harm again – at least within the next 3 months. These individuals also indicated that self-harm produced an effect that was congruent with the reason set they endorsed (that is, tension or dissociation reduction). Thus self-harm may be reinforcing because the goals associated with its reasons are achieved and therefore produce a desired outcome (for example, escape from a psychological state). This may partially explain why these individuals report more past self-harm and a stronger intent to self-harm again (LEWIS2010). Moreover, this reason was used in conjunction with other reasons such as venting emotion or striving for control, indicating that people may harm themselves for different reasons on different occasions (POLK2009).

Other reasons reported for self-harm included school stress, over-commitment in extracurricular activities, self-punishment and a driving sense of perfectionism (ADLER2007, ARNOLD1995, KOKALIARI2008, POLK2009). Another frequent reason for engaging in self-harm was to provide a form of '*self-punishment*' for not meeting expectations of others or themselves (POLK2009). One individual (KOKALIARI2008) wrote:

> *I hate who I am. I hate who I was. I hate what I am becoming. If I can work to kill that, even if only to hurt it, I will accomplish my goal. I feel deserving of punishment for my wrongdoings and if that punishment doesn't come from anywhere else, it will come from me.*

Perfection was also related to body image, where self-harm offered control over the body:

> *Eating disorders are just another form of self-injury, and all these are based on control, and you know, at that point, I could control my body, and so appear perfect.*

Above all, self-harm functioned as a coping mechanism for dealing with intense emotions and an opportunity to regain some control over a person's life (ARNOLD1995, BYWATERS2002, HARRIS2000, HORNE2009, HUBAND2004, HUME2007, LESNIAK2010, LEWIS2010, POLK2009, RAY2007). For example, one individual (POLK2009) claimed:

It was a coping mechanism. Everything would build up inside me until I needed some way to release it. Cutting was that release.

Similarly, in a study carried out by RAY2007 on US students, self-harm was described a method of tension release (that is, '*letting the pain out*') or a means of regaining a sense of control. The tendency to doubt their ability to cope with emotional issues, as well as perceptions of being far more sensitive than others was also highlighted. For instance, one service user stated:

I feel things more strongly than most people... or at least the bad emotions much more powerfully than the average person.

Correspondingly, in a study carried out by HUBAND2004 on women's subjective experience prior to self-harm, the majority of women recalled self-wounding due to an emotional state that intensified over time. Many women consistently spoke to the efficacy and immediacy of self-harm in relieving emotional pain (HUBAND2004, KOKALIARI2008, RAY2007):

It is definitely a quick fix... Welcome to McDonald's society, right where we came from, fast food, anything into a sugar high and then it drops!

Furthermore, the effect of self-harm was described as more powerful than other methods of emotional release, including using a punching bag, writing in a journal and talking to others (RAY2007). On the other hand, many interviewees described their experience with self-harm in a manner that suggested it was primarily utilised as a means of avoiding fully processing emotions (RAY2007).

Others engaged in self-harm to regain a sense of control over their lives (ARNOLD1995, POLK2009). Many indicated feeling out of control before the self-harm and that subsequent self-harm led them to feel in control of something in their lives even if it was just their pain. For example, one participant (POLK2009) reported:

I self-injure for a feeling of control. If I lose control of a situation, I cut to make myself feel that I still have the power to handle the situation.

In contrast, many others viewed self-harm as a consequence of their psychiatric illness and the 'trigger' for accessing help (SINCLAIR2005). Self-harm was a means to get support and attention, because of frustration about not receiving support for their illness (HARRIS2000). They also reported sometimes feeling a strong desire to be admitted, to escape the overwhelming and often uncontrollable emotions leading to self-harm (HARRIS2000). Many of the women acknowledged experiencing significant depressive episodes, with self-harm seen as a symptom of their depression as well as an attempt to relieve depression (RAY2007, SINCLAIR2005).

In another study carried out by POLK2009 in the US, self-harm was used by participants as a means to keep from killing themselves or hurting others. However, it should be noted that only one participant indicated that she used self-harm to keep from hurting others.

The influence of cultural factors on self-harm was also highlighted. In particular, participants suggested that the promotion of an individualistic culture can lead to members of that society being more likely to deal with their feelings alone (KOKALIARI2008):

> *I am wondering if it says something about our culture's need to deal with some-thing on your own as opposed to deal with something with other people or with healthy means ... You can't rely on other people to help you, and sort of like an independent self-sufficient mentality is pretty widespread.*

Attempts to justify the behaviour as sanctioned by popular culture and as a behaviour that is practised by numerous other women also emerged (RAY2007).

Coexisting destructive behaviours
Other destructive behaviours tended to co-occur with self-harm, including drug and alcohol misuse, over-sleeping and eating-disordered behaviour (ARNOLD1995, HUBAND2004, RAY2007, SINCLAIR2005). ARNOLD1995 found that most women who took part in the study engaged in various other sorts of self-harm in addition to inflicting injuries on themselves. Most notable was the high occurrence of eating disorders, while overdosing and misuse of alcohol and drugs were also common. Moreover, there were numerous other ways in which women saw themselves as engaging in self-harm. These included overwork, over-exercising, staying in abusive relationships, unnecessary and repeated risk-taking and smoking.

In another study carried out by RAY2007 one participant touched on the notion that certain types of self-harm behaviours may be interchangeable. In discussing the relationship between purging and cutting she admitted she was seeking the same objective in both behaviours, specifically a release through pain. Similarly, SINCLAIR2005 discovered that co-occurring alcohol misuse dominated for four participants and for these people abstaining from alcohol was key to the resolution of their self-harm. Looking back, they attributed their use of alcohol to an attempt to escape from difficult emotions, but now saw it as precipitating a vicious cycle of low self-esteem and self-loathing. Moreover, refraining from drinking led to an increase in self-pride and individuality, and an immediate end to their acts of self-harm that had required hospital admission. Finally, sleep – or overdose of medication to induce sleep – was cited as an additional alternative release to self-harm (HUBAND2004).

Consequences of self-harm: psychological and physical
Many studies reported the physical and psychological consequences in the aftermath of a self-harm episode. In general, the women expressed mixed feelings about self-harm (RAY2007). They spoke of the manner in which self-harm brought relief to their suffering and offered them a sense of satisfaction and empowerment. At the same time, many alluded to internalised feelings of guilt and shame after an episode of self-harm (HUBAND2004, LESNIAK2010, MOYER2007, RAY2007). In particular,

concern about disappointing or hurting others through self-harm were frequently expressed (RAY2007). They also articulated apprehension about hiding evidence of their injuries and the consequences of others discovering them (for example, having to go back to therapy and losing a job). Moreover, many of the women made comments suggesting that they were dissociated at the time of their self-wounding, for example describing numbness at the time of the wound and of feeling like the cut was to '*another person's arm ... not really mine*' (HUBAND2004). In a recent study carried out by GORDON2010 (Gordon *et al.* 2010), 106 participants with a history of self-harm completed questionnaires about their emotional reactions during their most recent self-harm episode. They found that people with more frequent self-harm episodes felt more soothed, relieved, calmer and attentive following their most recent self-harm episode, suggesting that self-harm may become more reinforcing with reoccurrence.

Along with the psychological impact of self-harm, the physical consequences of self-harm were also apparent in the service user literature. One of the most prominent physical consequences of engaging in self-harm was the sensation of physical pain. HORNE2009 examined the experience of pain sensation in adults and young people who self-harm. Some experienced no pain at all and the remainder felt a reduced level of pain. Others explained that there was a certain pain threshold they needed to reach before they could reconnect with themselves again. The issue of pain was addressed in another study carried out by POLK2009 wherein 16.8% reported no pain, 47.7% little pain, 32.3% some pain and 3.2% reported a great amount of pain during self-harm. In a recent study carried out by GORDON2010, it was found that greater frequency of past self-harm episodes led to more intense feelings of physical pain during their most recent episode.

Stigma and misconceptions about self-harm
Another common finding that surfaced from the service user literature was the mixed reactions of others to their self-harm and the stigma and misconceptions about self-harm. Other people's reactions to their self-harm varied, with some women reporting fairly supportive responses while others received quite negative reactions. To a certain extent, others' reactions seemed to determine if the women would continue to be open about their self-harm and potentially if they would seek help for this behaviour (RAY2007). In a study carried out by BAKER2008, family, friends and wider society including medical and mental health services were often explicitly characterised as judgmental and lacking understanding. Moreover, DORER1999 revealed that the most commonly perceived reaction of others was distress – generally expressed by parents and often associated with concern. The second most common response, which was largely articulated by parents, was anger. Many young people also reported being ignored, whilst others felt that people around them had been overprotective since the overdose. One of the most common responses of peers was to think that the overdose was a 'stupid' action. On the other hand, BURGESS1998 discovered that reactions of significant others to the young people following the overdose were largely favourable with more people responding with understanding and wishing to help than responding with anger. Overall, mothers appeared to be more sympathetic than fathers.

Experience of care

Participants also spoke about various misconceptions about self-harm. The first misconception that was addressed in the literature was that people self-harm to gain attention from others or as a cry for help. The majority of participants expressed strong reactions toward individuals who self-harm *'for attention.'* They spoke of the need to distinguish between, for lack of a better term, 'true' versus 'false self-injurers' (RAY2007). Many of the women expressed anger or annoyance toward people who showed off their injuries or harmed themselves in obvious ways. Conversely, one participant (RAY2007) offered a more sympathetic approach to people who harm themselves for this reason:

> *If this person is doing it for attention they obviously need it. Someone who is going to take it to that extreme has a lot of problems and they just need someone to care. Don't be mean about it. They need help.*

Some women stressed additional misconceptions about self-harm. One participant criticised the tendency to oversimplify the behaviour by attributing it to a single reason, and emphasised the need to recognise the multitude of factors that can simultaneously contribute to this behaviour. Another participant expressed frustration that so much of what is available to read about self-harm focuses on those who have been sexually abused and stated she does not feel this material applies to her. The women discredited stereotypical images of the 'self-injurer' and emphasised the fact that 'normal', productive people engage in this behaviour (RAY2007).

Experience of recovery
An additional key topic to come out of the service user experiences was that of ending self-harm and the process of recovery. In a US study (ADLER2007), the majority of people who had self-harmed for a long period had no intention of ever stopping. Others wanted to quit, but recognised its benefits as a coping mechanism and a means of self-expression. Yet for a small minority, their self-harm subsided after many years, either through therapy or with the help of online peer support and education. Many of these people remained in online communications, helping others, as a way of maintaining their abstinence. KOOL2009 explored people's experiences and motivations for stopping self-harming in a sample of inpatients from a psychiatric intensive treatment centre. All respondents indicated that learning how to cope with their 'inner selves' and others was an important skill to reduce and stop self-harm. The analysis demonstrated that the process of stopping self-harm can be divided into several phases such as: connecting and setting limits; the heightening of self-esteem; gaining an understanding of the self and increasing their sense of autonomy; the use of alternative strategies; and preventing relapse. The first phase of connecting and setting limits provided a sense of safety that allowed service users to reach out more to others and themselves and to feel their emotions, such as pain and sadness. The second phase entailed the heightening of self-esteem with a further deepening of contact with the self. Respondents indicated that their self-esteem increased because they could see and feel that they were recognised by carers and

family and friends as full human beings, with all their faults and imperfections. One of the respondents to KOOL2009 stated:

> *The carers told me they did not disapprove of me as a person, but because of what I did. For me this meant there was nothing wrong with my character, my personality. When I came out of isolation, they saw me as me and I could just start again with a clean slate.*

This growing sense of self-esteem allowed service users to discover their own strengths and creative talents, which in turn contributed to a more positive self-image. By putting these talents to use, they succeeded in expressing their emotions in ways other than self-harm. In the third phase service users learned to understand themselves, which allowed them to realise that they could control their own lives. Respondents learned to know themselves better and began to understand their own behaviour.

The fourth phase was one of increasing the service user's sense of autonomy. They felt that they gradually became better able to make independent decisions about their lives and act upon those decisions, and thus take responsibility for their own behaviour. In this phase, contact with others changed: because of their growing sense of autonomy, the respondents chose who they wanted to forge a connection with and who they did not. They also determined the content and limitations of their contacts with others. As one of the respondents (KOOL2009) expressed:

> *I got control of my life because I realised I could make choices, I could and was allowed to want things for myself and, more importantly, I could stop things.*

The fifth stage entailed implementing alternative strategies to cope with emotional distress and urges to self-injure and asking for help (KOOL2009). Finally, the sixth phase focused on preventing relapse. Even if they had not engaged in self-harm for a long time, the risk of relapse continued to exist for many. All respondents indicated that they still found it very difficult at certain moments, especially in situations of increasing tension, not to injure themselves (KOOL2009).

An additional US study (SHAW2006) examined how female college students stopped self-injuring and the role (if any) of professional treatment in this process. Not all participants expressed an explicit desire to stop or made a conscious decision to stop. Whether women expressed a desire to stop or not, they all stopped cutting when the psychological symptoms giving rise to self-harm, such as alienation or extreme anxiety, discontinued or reduced in number or intensity. Furthermore, all of the women spoke of the importance of self-initiative or taking control of their lives as essential in their journeys toward stopping (SHAW2006). It appears that the women's self-harm diminished as increasing involvement in life pursuits – such as intellectual interests, career goals and enlarged social networks – gained prominence in their lives. Relational ties and support from parents, peers and romantic partners were also of vital significance in helping to stop self-injuring. Participants frequently expressed a desire to satisfy or not concern others as important motivations to stop self-injuring (SHAW2006). For others, disclosure was used as a means of reinforcing their commitment to stopping self-injuring and a means of accessing professional treatment. Fear of being labelled 'crazy' was a frequently-cited deterrent, as well as fear that the behaviour might become increasingly entrenched and out of control. Moreover, the longer women abstained from self-injuring, the easier they found it to resist urges to hurt themselves (SHAW2006).

Alternative coping strategies
Alternative coping strategies played an important role in preventing relapse after stopping self-harm. For instance, in a study carried out by KOOL2009 almost all participants still felt the urge to self-injure at certain moments and had developed specific strategies to respond to these moments. One respondent said:

> *It is still a daily struggle, but I am taking on the challenge every day. I am like: I know what I am doing this for and it is worth it.*

The respondents identified the following strategies: (a) expressing emotions directly, (b) physical exercise, (c) creative activities and (d) establishing a connection with others. It was important that these alternative activities should control precisely those emotions for which self-harm was previously adopted as a controlling strategy. For example, a respondent who tried to control her aggressive impulses through self-harm indicated that 'blowing against a piece of fluff' or pulling on a rubber band hardly had any effect. However, she could vent her aggression in an acceptable manner by kicking a cushion (KOOL2009).

Similarly, in another study carried out by SCHOPPMANN2007 in Germany, participants engaged in many alternative strategies to end feelings of alienation such as jogging, physical labour, listening to loud music and forms of expression that did not require verbal communication, for example painting. However, all participants stated that self-harm was the most effective way to end the agonising experience of alienation.

> *I think jogging would give me the same relief but cutting is easier and acts much faster and that is what I want in these moments – a prompt relief.*

On the other hand, it is important to note that the use of alternative coping strategies was not always found to be helpful and some believed that alternatives were only temporary solutions (CRAIGEN2009):

> *There were periods where I managed to assuage the need to self-injure by picking up another healthy or acceptable behaviour, at the urging of a counsellor... if that makes sense. It didn't really last too long because they were terribly simplistic behaviours that were sort of short-term answers.*

Young people's experience of self-harm
A study carried out on several US students (MOYER2007) unveiled some important findings in relation to the origins of self-harm in young people. Most learned

of self-harm from their friends; they had asked a friend about it or had a friend recommend self-harm to them. The expectations and mental stress placed on these young people often became overwhelming, leaving them feeling as though there was no escape – with the exception of self-harm (MOYER2007). DORER1999 found that participants had varying reasons for overdosing. The majority of participants reported that when they took the overdose they wanted to die. Other reasons for overdosing were to escape from painful feelings, to communicate how bad they felt, or for hospital admission to escape difficult family situations. This supports the idea that the motivation behind self-harm is unique to the individual and is fluctuant in nature.

Regarding the consequences of self-harm, some young people reported that relationships within their family had improved and others felt that it had led them to develop better coping skills (DORER1999). An earlier study by BURGESS1998 found that most young people felt that overall the overdose and its aftermath had resulted in improvements in their lives; whereas others felt that it had made things worse for them. When asked how they felt in the aftermath of the self-harm behaviour, many reported feeling ashamed about what they had done. However, almost half of the participants felt that they would probably or definitely take an overdose again in similar circumstances.

In a study carried out by SINCLAIR2005, young people with a history of self-harm who no longer harmed themselves talked about their experiences in terms of lack of control over their lives and their uncertainty within their family relationships. Specifically, the core finding that emerged from these young people's experience of stopping self-harm was '*the resolution of adolescent chaos*'. For these participants, the defining difference that led them to stop their self-harm was the resolution of their lack of control within the family structure. Family life was recounted as not only chaotic but also also failing to provide any validation of their experiences at the time. For many of the young people interviewed, the sense of autonomy and independence achieved after breaking away from their family allowed them to separate themselves from their unpredictable family environments, providing them with a sense of purpose and responsibility. This gave them enough control to manage their responses to distress in a less self-destructive way (SINCLAIR2005).

Experience of self-harm in people with mild to moderate learning disabilities
FISH2008 examined the experiences of people with mild to moderate learning disabilities who self-harm. The common finding throughout the interviews was healthcare professional/service user relationships (both negative and positive aspects) and the way they affected individuals' ability to cope with stress, emotion and urge to self-harm. Service users reported that healthcare professionals could make them feel that they did not care when they were slow to respond to their distress, were dismissive of their personal problems or were perceived to be uncaring (FISH2008):

> *I feel that nobody cares, and when you talk to them, it's 'Oh, wait a minute'. And when the minute comes it's, like, 'I've not got a minute now, I'm doing this now'*

> or 'I'm doing that now'. In the end you just go in your room and do [self-injure], instead of saying I feel like doing it …

Service users also identified a lack of control over their treatment as a negative aspect of the relationship:

> … I wanted to go to a meeting that's discussing my future or what possibly could happen in my future. And they said no, clients are not allowed. I think that's badly wrong …

Conversely, service users reported that when healthcare professionals spent time with them one-to-one, demonstrated a caring attitude and, most importantly, recognised their individuality, this had a positive effect.

Service users and some healthcare professionals agreed that self-injuring should be allowed. Service users viewed it as a right and also explained that it was futile to attempt to stop self-harm behaviour:

> I think as a self-harmer you should be entitled to what you do to your body as long as it's hurting no-one else's but your own. I feel that I should be entitled to cut up as much as want and when I want. I do feel there are too many people laying the law down as far as I'm concerned as my self-harming.

The feeling of being punished was also highlighted by service users. They explained that this lowered their self-esteem and, as a consequence, made them more likely to self-harm:

> Well when I've cut up in the past there's your punishment of putting you on a level three for a few months until things get better. That's what they've always done with me. They punish me by putting me on a higher supervision level, increase my supervision level to level three. I'd feel bad, they didn't trust me, once I'd cut. I'm alright, I wouldn't do it again cos I feel better.

Experience of self-harm in males
Only two studies examined the experience of self-harm in males (RUSSELL2010, TAYLOR2003). With regard to reasons behind self-harm, they were similar to those provided by women, with early childhood experiences such as neglect and abuse, experiences of rejection in adulthood, and as a coping strategy and alternative communication method being frequently reported (TAYLOR2003).

As with women, guilt and shame were frequent emotions expressed by the men interviewed with one man stating that he felt '*very ashamed*' of his self-harm and another that he was '*punishing myself*' for it. As well as limiting the degree to which men seek support for their self-harm, this shame may perpetuate the problem by damaging their self-esteem further (TAYLOR2003).

RUSSELL2010 examined the experience of self-harm in four males and found the inability to maintain satisfaction or contentment was a central theme portrayed by all participants. One participant (RUSSELL2010) illustrates the potency of this issue in the following statement:

> *Like you were supposed to enjoy a party or you're supposed to enjoy a holiday. At the time you do, but underneath, you didn't, 'cause I always end up in hospital afterwards. My brothers said, oh you're supposed to enjoy it, it's been paid for and that, so I did, but I didn't, 'cause I used to destruct, but I couldn't . . . . I couldn't . . . separate them, happiness and sadness, erm, so I was out there enjoying it, I was enjoying it, but it wasn't lasting, it was like it was a short term thing. . .*

All participants talked about the differences between men's self-harm and women's, as if men's was somehow more real:

> *I think a lot of men do it, whereas a lot of women do it for sympathy, a lot of men do it out of anger and upset and . . . .*

Likewise, in a study carried out by TAYLOR2003 the differences between men and women who self-harm was also a prominent theme. Firstly, men tended to injure themselves more severely than women and had less concern about bodily scars. They were more likely to engage in public and violent self-harm, such as punching themselves or a wall or breaking bones.

The concept of masculinity and the misconception that men should be powerful and should conceal their weakness was another prominent theme (RUSSELL2010, TAYLOR2003). Many of the interviewees felt that the expectation that men are '*stronger*' and '*able to cope*' was a particular issue for men who self-harm. One participant in particular felt that '*to be seen as a man, you have to be seen as not weak*' (TAYLOR2003). Whilst they may try to conceal these feelings, they are likely to find expression in some way. As a result they may resort to self-harm as an expression of their underlying emotions (TAYLOR2003).

4.4.5   Access and barriers to services

In the review of the literature, several findings emerged under the broad heading of 'access and barriers to services' for people who self-harm, including stigma and negative attitudes of healthcare professionals; barriers to help-seeking behaviour were also examined. There were 14 studies in which the themes of access and barriers to treatment were apparent (BOLGER2004 [Bolger *et al*., 2004], BROPHY2006 [Brophy, 2006], BURGESS1998, BYWATERS2002, CAMGAN1994, DOWER2000 [Dower *et al*., 2000], HARRIS2000, HOOD2006 [Hood, 2006], HORROCKS2005 [Horrocks *et al*., 2005], KREITMAN1973 [Kreitman & Chowdhury, 1973], NADA-RAJA2003 [Nada-Raja *et al*., 2003], RAY2007, RISSANEN2009 [Rissanen *et al*., 2009], SCHOPPMANN2007).

Experience of care

Accessibility

Three studies reported findings that were relevant to the accessibility of services (BOLGER2004, BURGESS1998, BYWATERS2002). Several participants felt it was essential that services be as accessible as possible by being staffed 24 hours a day, providing walk-in services and minimal waiting times for appointments (BYWATERS2002). Furthermore, several respondents interviewed explained that they wished they had known about the types of support services available to them before they self-harmed. For instance, many study participants were unaware of local services that provide support to individuals who self-harm (BYWATERS2002). Finally, it was also suggested that services offer alternatives to clinical support such as having nurses working in the community who can treat self-inflicted wounds (BYWATERS2002).

Young people's experience of accessibility to services

Young people, in particular, had a variety of suggestions about how services could be made more accessible for young people who self-harm. It was suggested that services be centrally located. Walk-in services and telephone access as well as decreased waiting time for appointments were recommended. Others wished that prior to taking the overdose they had access to the type of professional help that they had subsequently received (BURGESS1998).

Barriers to treatment

Six studies reported findings that were relevant to barriers to treatment (BROPHY2006, CAMGAN1994, DOWER2000, HARRIS2000, HOOD2006, HORROCKS2005). CAMGAN1994 revealed many problematic issues with regard to communication with professionals. Specifically, inadequate sharing of information by healthcare professionals with service users was perceived as an important problem. Most respondents stated that there was a need for better understanding and more assistance by nurses regarding individual difficulties with problem solving. HARRIS2000 found that participants often felt that they were maltreated because their injuries were self-inflicted.

Other important barriers to treatment were highlighted by HARRIS2000. Firstly, some service users said treatment rooms did not provide privacy, either due to the location of treatment, for example in a waiting room, or lack of respect given by healthcare professionals, for example 'showing off' service users to other members of staff. Finally, some people felt that their need for help was not acknowledged, particularly after no aftercare was arranged. Many said they were not given the opportunity to play an active role in their treatment. In particular, service users perceived that treatments had often been given or forced upon them without any information as to why this was being done. Some respondents explained they had received contact numbers for services at hospital but upon ringing, no one was there to answer their call. Likewise, service users often felt a lack of rapport between themselves and healthcare professionals and a general lack of support (HORROCKS2005).

Young people's experience of barriers to treatment

In a UK-based study on young people who self-harm (BROPHY2006) some respondents who had previously presented to hospital due to a self-harm episode felt ostracised by healthcare professionals who, it was felt, were *act[ing] as if to say "not you again"'*. One study (DOWER2000) provided some insight into the reasons behind early termination of follow-up care. Some felt they had received as much benefit from treatment as possible, were uncomfortable with the professional providing care or the location of the care, or the care they received was deemed unhelpful. Other young people reported that psychiatrists were often unavailable for continued care because they were too busy or had left the service during the young person's treatment period (HOOD2006).

Help-seeking: attitudes towards and barriers

Five studies looked at attitudes and behaviour with regard to help seeking for self-harm in adult populations (HUNTER [Hunter & Cooper, unpublished], KREITMAN1973, NADA-RAJA2003, RAY2007, SCHOPPMANN2007). KREITMAN1973 recruited individuals attending hospital for the first time after a suicide attempt in Edinburgh and carried out individual, semi-structured, face-to-face interviews to investigate attitudes to help-seeking after completion of formal psychiatric examination. Most of the participants were in favour of seeking help, with the most 'acceptable' form of help being specialist services followed by 'anyone available', 'no one' and, lastly, relatives. However, a quarter of participants maintained that seeking help for personal problems was not an acceptable form of behaviour. It must be noted, however, that this study was carried out in the 1970s and the attitudes towards help-seeking and services may have changed since then, placing limitations on the generalisability of the findings reported.

A cohort study carried out on individuals who self-harm in New Zealand examined help-seeking via semi-structured interviews with young adults (NADA-RAJA2003). The main reasons given for seeking help were psychological aspects related to self-harm, specifically for self-harm or for an injury relating to self-harm behaviour (NADA-RAJA2003). Moreover, among the small percentage of services users that did seek help (only 8%), approximately one third reported attitudinal barriers when seeking help from professionals. In a study carried out by HUNTER, participants' lack of continuity of aftercare impacted negatively on their attitudes towards future help-seeking and towards themselves.

Stigma also emerged as an important barrier to seeking help and disclosing to others about their self-harm (RAY2007). While all women reported trying to hide the fact of their self-harm, some alluded to the hidden wish that others would acknowledge their distress and care enough to reach out to them in a supportive and accepting manner. The women appeared quite inhibited in their ability to reach out to others for fear that others would not understand and for fear that they would be labelled as attention seekers. Some spoke of a lack of parental understanding in response to their distress. Others expressed the desire to protect their loved ones from their pain (RAY2007).

Finally, for those who did not seek help, attitudinal barriers such as thinking that they should be strong enough to handle the problem on their own, that the problem would resolve itself and that no one could help, or being too embarrassed to discuss it with anyone, were factors. Confidence and trust were also important conditions for seeking and accepting help (SCHOPPMANN2007). The participants said that they would not ask strangers for help or support (for example, an unknown nurse during a night/weekend shift) because for them strangers were equivalent to someone who could not do anything and someone from whom help was not to be expected.

Young people's experience of help seeking

Only one study (in Finland) examined the experience of help-seeking and barriers to reaching out for support in young people (RISSANEN2009). Three main categories emerged from the analysis: the helpers, factors contributing to help and help-hindering factors. From the viewpoint of young people, any person who knew about their self-harm could be a helper, while adults were felt to be duty-bound to intervene. According to the young people in this study who self-harmed, there was an insufficient reliable presence of parents at home. They also felt that school and healthcare personnel could have done more to intervene. Factors that enabled help-seeking were: becoming conscious of being in need of help; knowledge of self-harm as a phenomena; knowledge of the available help for self-harm; a caring environment; and, finally, support from friends, peers and parents. Other helpful factors were: practical intervention for common problems for young people; early intervention; learning to discuss self-harm, emotions and difficult experiences with someone; and demonstrating genuine care for the young person.

Factors hindering help-seeking were the following: lack of awareness of being in need of help, an inability to seek help, emotional factors, lack of awareness of self-harm or a lack of awareness of the help available for self-harm. Additional unhelpful factors were unresponsiveness to self-harm, underestimating or overstating the meaning of self-mutilation, remaining silent about self-harm, negative emotional reactions of adults or over expectations of the capability of young people to fend for themselves. Knowledge of self-harm as a phenomenon seems to be very important. It emerged in different forms in all three main categories. In fact, knowing facts about self-harm or its existence seems to be a prerequisite for a young person who self-harms to become conscious of the need for help and then to seek help (RISSANEN2009).

Overall, several participants pointed out the importance of accessibility of services especially for young people and the need for inclusion in planning of their treatment. Common barriers to accessing treatment or engaging fully in treatment were stigma, communication difficulties, negative attitudes of healthcare professionals and privacy issues.

4.4.6 Experience of treatment for self-harm

In this review common findings emerged under the broad heading of 'experience of treatment for self-harm', including experience of psychosocial assessment, experience of psychiatric services, experience of constant observation, experience of psychological treatment and experience of medication.

Experiences of psychosocial assessment

Four studies investigated the views of service users with regard to psychosocial assessment (CROCKWELL1995, HORROCKS2005, HUNTER, WHITEHEAD2002 [Whitehead, 2002]). From these four studies it was clear that not all service users received a psychosocial assessment while in hospital, and, for those service users that did, their experience varied across studies.

Service users' insights and anticipation of the psychosocial assessment, and the way in which they interpreted healthcare professionals' management of their assessment, had a large impact on their appraisal of the assessment (CROCKWELL1995, HUNTER). Participants had a more positive experience of assessment when they were given information about it beforehand (CROCKWELL1995). Moreover, the relational aspect of assessment was a key determining factor in service users' appraisal of assessment, highlighting the importance of the therapeutic relationship in the provision of care (HUNTER). Participants experienced assessment positively when it involved a beneficial, hopeful engagement with healthcare professionals and when it involved the restoration of hope or the possibility of change in their circumstances (HUNTER, WHITEHEAD2002). Another important aspect of assessment was the opportunity to talk to someone (HUNTER), with the majority of participants finding this a valuable experience. However, not all participants felt they were given adequate opportunity and it was not always evaluated as a positive experience. Despite this, most participants expressed a desire to speak to someone about their problems, which gave them an opportunity to start thinking about the reasons behind their self-harm.

Conversely, assessment was experienced negatively when the participant felt devalued by the assessor, was treated in a judgemental manner or they felt they were not understood. Similarly, service users who reported being disappointed with their psychosocial management found fault primarily with their lack of involvement in decisions or when the assessor did not give them sufficient time to talk during the assessment (WHITEHEAD2002):

> *OK. The first interview was just 'so tell us what happened' and he wrote it up and said 'um hm, um hm' and wrote notes and he didn't look at me but he was nodding and looking at the other guy. And they looked at each other and exchanged nods. It was very factual like 'So what did you take?' and 'What happened at the house?' Um, you know I felt like saying 'I can understand English, doctor'. It was just very factual. They filled out their little form and that was it.*

Likewise, in the study carried out by HUNTER another negative aspect of assessment seemed to be the experience of not being understood, or when healthcare professionals did not seem interested or genuinely engaged in trying to understand the individual reasons behind their self-harm. Furthermore, when participants experienced assessment as invalidating and when assessment seemed to lead nowhere and offer no hope for change it was experienced negatively and could compound the participant's initial feelings of hopelessness, powerlessness and low self-worth. This study showed that assessments may not have the same salience and importance for users and professionals because assessments are just one single moment in a person's life that is likely to be filled with ongoing difficulties.

Experiences of psychiatric services

Eight studies examined experiences of psychiatric services (ARNOLD1995, BROPHY2006, BYWATERS2002, CARDELL1999 [Cardell & Pitula, 1999], DORER1999, HUME2007, PITULA1996 [Pitula & Cardell 1996], TAYLOR2003). Individuals admitted to psychiatric wards had mixed reactions to their care. The admission to a psychiatric ward was often described as frightening and led to a sense of diminished control over their lives (HUME2007). One 34-year-old male said:

> *I speak positively about it now, but back at the time it was terrible. Locked wards, psychopaths; they used straightjackets and straps.*

Moreover, service users often felt a lack of rapport between themselves and healthcare professionals (ARNOLD1995). One participant described a psychiatrist as '*cold, clinical, [and] impersonal*' (ARNOLD1995). In a study carried out by TAYLOR2003 several of the male participants had experienced negative incidences with psychiatrists. Comments included '*I don't see them unless I absolutely have to*' and '*I made a firm decision not to ever see him again*'. The only positive assessment of support from a psychiatrist was a man who said of his second psychiatrist:

> *She seems to generally care about my wellbeing. I value her opinion and she is quite nice.*

Service users also explained that while on a psychiatric ward they sometimes felt the need to act in exaggerated ways, and even self-harm, to get the attention of staff (BYWATERS2002).

Only two studies (both from adult populations in the US) looked at the experience of constant observation whilst on a psychiatric ward (CARDELL1999, PITULA1996). In the study carried out by PITULA1996 on suicidal inpatients, service users' initial responses to constant observation ranged from discomfort to surprise or anger. On the other hand, study participants reported feeling safe because of the physical presence of observers who could prevent them from responding to self-destructive impulses. Participants reported that the lack of personal privacy was the most distressing aspect of constant observation and service users said that constant observation became almost intolerable after 30 to 36 hours.

In a more recent study carried out by CARDELL1999, the majority of participants expressed positive feelings toward the observers, particularly when they perceived them as friendly and willing to help. Moreover, a significant proportion of service users reported that their dysphoria, anxiety, and suicidal thoughts were decreased by observers who were optimistic, who provided distraction with activities and conversation and who gave emotional support (CARDELL1999). Furthermore, the participants experienced uncomfortable and at times distressing feelings relating to observers' attitudes or behaviour, such as a lack of empathy, a lack of acknowledgement, failure to provide information about constant observation, lack of privacy or personal space and a feeling of confinement. It is clear from these two studies that the positive attitude of healthcare professionals (including empathy and an acknowledgment of the person as a unique individual), providing information about the function of constant observation and an effort to combat privacy issues are essential in improving service user experience of constant observation. However, it should be noted that this study was carried out in the US and the implementation and experiences of constant observation may differ in the UK, thus limiting the generalisability of the findings reported above.

Young people's experience of treatment

A UK study reported findings concerning management of young people on a psychiatric ward (BROPHY2006), where confiscation by staff of objects that could be used to self-harm increased their feelings of a lack of control and contributed to the desire to self-harm again. Another study carried out on young people and adults (BYWATERS2002) echoed these findings in that most felt they were merely being watched and did not receive any sort of therapy for their self-harm. Several young people who presented at hospital after a self-harm episode (HOOD2006) said they experienced a sense of relief upon being provided with aftercare at a community mental health service. Some women communicated a fear of being on a mixed ward while some older young people had negative experiences of being placed on adult wards. However, this was a very small sample size of only ten participants of whom five were female.

In contrast to the negative attitudes reported above, DORER1999 found that the majority of young people rated their contact with child and young people's psychiatric services as positive or very positive. However, almost one third of young people rated their stay as negative or very negative. In relation to the benefits of psychiatric consultation, both studies established that the opportunity of '*talking through problems in detail with another person*' was an important aspect. Despite this positive experience, some service users disliked having to tell their story to several different staff members (DORER1999).

Experience of psychological treatment

Seven studies examined the experience of psychological treatment for those who self-harm (BURGESS1998, BYWATERS2002, CRAIGEN2009, CROCKWELL1995, HOOD2006, HUBAND2004, HUME2007).

HUME2007 found that service users' experiences of therapeutic interventions were strikingly diverse. There was a clear preference for specialist community-based interventions that focus on the provision of immediate aftercare and an acknowledgement that the management of self-harm may not necessarily involve its prevention. In a study carried out by BYWATERS2002 many participants welcomed the opportunity to discuss problems associated with their self-harm with a mental health professional. The drawbacks of psychological treatment were few from the participant's perspective; however, common disadvantages reported were the retelling of their story and opening up to reveal their emotions especially to a stranger. Others were frightened that telling someone their problems would intensify their distress or bring back memories they were trying to repress. Some respondents (BYWATERS2002) appreciated psychological therapy, presumably in a group setting, because it put them in touch with other people like them:

> *The fact that you talk to other people and there were other people who felt exactly the same as you, no matter what state they were in, no matter what part of life they came from, there were people that felt like you. It felt good to feel that you weren't on your own.*

Conversely, in a study carried out by CROCKWELL1995 the stigma associated with an appointment with a psychologist or psychiatrist for some participants was too much to bear and caused individuals to miss their appointments.

> *I hated it. Couldn't stand the psychiatrist... Just thought 'I must be crazy' that's all that came into my head. That's what I thought: 'if you see one of them, you're crazy'.*

CRAIGEN2009 examined the counselling experiences of ten young adult women with a history of self-injurious behaviour. For those interviewed, the most helpful counsellor behaviours were respectful listening, understanding and acting as a friend. Furthermore, the women also discussed behaviours that they viewed to be unhelpful, which included counsellors who failed to demonstrate understanding and counsellors who forced uninvited ideas upon them.

Many of the participants noted that simply talking during sessions was helpful. Almost without exception, the participants considered no-harm contracts ineffective (CRAIGEN2009):

> *I won't make a promise unless I can keep it. Or, I try not to. I need to feel a deep sense of obligation to that person and that particular cause to make that promise. So that wouldn't have worked for me.*

Another alluded to the potential dangers of using no-harm contracts. She suggested that counsellors need to provide service users with new improved coping skills before making them stop using their old coping skills. In terms of the focus of treatment, participants did not like counsellors putting too much emphasis on the self-injurious behaviour. Rather, they reflected about the value of counselling that targeted the underlying issues. Asked what they would tell counsellors working with college-aged women who self-injure, most of the women emphasised that it was important for the counsellor to be nonjudgmental. One said:

> *I think the bottom line is to just try not to alienate them further. Because there is already the knowledge that what you are doing is very bizarre and not normal, and you need to be careful of inadvertently stigmatizing them further.*

An additional study carried out by HUBAND2004 found that psychotherapy or counselling was generally experienced as helpful. However, several participants reported '*drifting off*' and '*losing the plot*' in their therapy sessions, or complained about their therapist enduring silences during which they found it hard to remain focused.

Young people's experience of treatment
BURGESS1998 found that most young people appreciated short-term therapy, mostly on an individual basis. Both young people and their parents appreciated '*talking to someone on the outside*' with whom the family had '*no emotional attachment*' (HOOD2006). However, some young people felt that talking did not make a difference to the way they felt:

> *I've talked and stuff and I still don't really feel a hell of a lot better... Cause you know sometimes even just talking about it doesn't really help, sometimes just a hug or something would be cool, more helpful than sitting here talking about it... The talking and things didn't really help me too much. I don't feel that it changes anything... It just seems to scare a person, that's about it.*

Several participants described situations in which they felt that their therapist did not understand them. These feelings hindered the resolution of the young person's problems:

> *I mean there's lots I'd like to have happen in terms of, like, client and counsellor relationship.... I really still don't feel she quite understands me... I just feel like a lot of times what I say isn't, it feels like it's not valid*

Other participants explained that their relationship with their therapist made them feel '*acknowledged*', '*heard*', '*cared for*', '*reassured*', '*supported*' and '*understood*' (HOOD2006). A positive relationship between service user and therapist was often associated with perceived positive outcomes by the service user.

Overall, the experience of psychological therapy was mostly positive in nature; however, there were some drawbacks such as the stigma associated with receiving therapy and retelling of their story.

Experience of medication
Four studies examined service user experience of medication (HOOD2006, KOOL2009, SHAW2006, SMITH2002 [Smith 2002]). HOOD2006 examined the perspective of young people recruited from community mental health centres in New Zealand with regard to their feelings about medication, and established that views were mixed. The majority (n = 6; 60%) of young people interviewed were prescribed antidepressants as part of their management. Some service users reported (HOOD2006) that medication helped them cope with their underlying problems; however, not all participants had a positive attitude towards medication especially at the beginning:

> *I absolutely hated taking my medication when I first started a couple of years ago. Then it became part of my life and a part of being able to live so I just don't get all down about things... I don't know how it works but I mean I know the*

> *medication's always an option for me now so if things start to get bad and stay bad then it's here.*

Some young people felt that the medication did not work for them and had many undesirable side effects.

> *[B]eing on medication I didn't deal with things or just had trouble with my memory for a while. I didn't know what day of the week it was... I just had no idea where I was or what was happening...*

In another study carried out on adults (SMITH2002) in the UK a more negative view of medication was observed with service users reporting that they felt that medication was seen as a means of shutting them up. Similarly, in a study carried out in the Netherlands (KOOL2009), many participants felt that their emotions were subdued by the medication and as a result they lost their sense of connection with themselves and others. On the other hand, some participants found medications effective in addressing symptoms such as anxiety (KOOL2009, SHAW2006).

4.4.7   Engagement with services and suggestions for service improvement

Aftercare for self-harm can include treatment by a wide range of professionals: psychologists, psychiatrists, social workers, nurses, community services and GPs. Seventeen studies reported findings that were relevant to engagement with services and suggestions for service improvement (ARNOLD1995, BOLGER2004, BROPHY2006, BURGESS1998, BYWATERS2002, CAMGAN1994, CROCKWELL1995, DOWER2000, HOOD2006, HUBAND2004, RAY2007, REECE2005, SCHOPPMANN2007, SHAW2006, SINCLAIR2005, SMITH2002, WHITEHEAD2002).

Common suggestions for service improvement included enhanced continuity of care and specialised training and education on self-harm, along with the provision of better information about self-harm for service users and carers (ARNOLD1995, BYWATERS2002, CAMGAN1994, DOWER2000, HORROCKS2005, WHITEHEAD2002). The importance of tact and respect for service users' individuality was another aspect of care that people expressed as necessary for service improvement (CAMGAN1994, WHITEHEAD2002). What emerged from these studies was that an important factor in determining whether a person's experience of services was helpful was the attitude and approach of the professionals involved. Most of the service users' frustration and discontent with services was caused by the negative or flippant attitudes of healthcare professionals, whether this was expressed in terms of disapproval, disinterest or failure to provide any real help.

Where people felt positive and satisfied with services, this was usually due to the compassionate support offered (ARNOLD1995). Likewise, BYWATERS2002 found that, overall, service users were more satisfied with their treatment when they felt that the professional was genuinely concerned about them, respected them and did not try to belittle them. Moreover, service users said they wanted healthcare professionals to give them more responsibility for their own management (BYWATERS2002, WHITEHEAD2002). Specifically, the need for clinicians to understand the problem individuals faced rather than focusing on their physical disfigurements was a frequent plea (BYWATERS2002):

> *Look at the individual, not the harm. Look at the person beyond the scars. Scars aren't important. It's the person that did them that's important.*

Several service users felt that hospital staff failed to address the underlying issues and did not have sufficient knowledge about or training in caring for people who self-harm (ARNOLD1995). Many service users suggested that more information should be provided to them about self-harm and its prevalence. In particular, information on how common self-harm is would be helpful. One participant (ARNOLD1995) felt this was important to reduce the shame and stigma associated with self-harm:

> *I used to feel abnormal and weird as I thought I was the only person to do this. Information could have helped reduce the shame and isolation this caused me.*

Women in another study carried out by REECE2005 expressed a need to be accepted and to be listened to. In particular, they articulated a desire for healthcare professionals to *'reach out'* to them as individuals and give them an opportunity to express their *'inner torment'* and pain. More recently, Horrocks and colleagues (2005) found that many service users experienced long delays before receiving any aftercare treatment and this led to many feeling disoriented or abandoned. Participants from this study also underlined the importance of professionals focusing on their underlying issues rather than the self-harm itself:

> *It would have been better if someone had understood – the psychological side of it they didn't seem bothered about, they should not have put me down for what I did but tried to talk to me about it and help me.*

In a German study (SCHOPPMANN2007) participants conveyed the importance of personal relationships and confidence in the intervening person, especially if physical contact is involved.

> *If there would be someone with whom I have no trusting relation I would of course not allow a touch, I would not say a word, I would not show a feeling. Nothing! Only someone I trust.*

Similarly, in a study carried out by HUBAND2004 the women reported on a number of management strategies and their helpfulness. 'Having a long-term relationship with one key worker' and 'expressing feelings about the past' were rated overall as the most helpful methods of managing their self-wounding. On the other hand, 'being taught relaxation techniques' was experienced as the least helpful. Indeed, many reported that relaxation actually had the potential to make their self-harm worse, but they had been unable to convince healthcare professionals that this was so. A Canadian study conducted by CROCKWELL1995 on women who had engaged in multiple suicide attempts by overdose established that some participants were satis-fied with their aftercare management because they were given the opportunity to talk about the issues that contributed to their self-harm episode. However, some respon-dents (CROCKWELL1995) said that they felt they were not given a sufficient amount of time for their appointments:

> *[W]hen I left he gave me a prescription for anti-depressants so we hadn't talked, he didn't once say it's OK or give me any bit of feedback. He just wrote me out a prescription. I'd say I was only in there about 15 minutes, 20 at the most, and he wrote me out a prescription for antidepressants and sent me on my way.*

Similar to women, many men prioritised the opportunity to talk about their self-harm and to feel understood by healthcare professionals (TAYLOR2003). In contrast, some service users explained that the lack of opportunity to become involved in discussions about their care made them 'feel disrespected'. One man in particular commented that his team worker had:

> *never asked questions like you've asked me... [s/he] never asks me about self-harm, even after times I've done it.*

This had left him feeling that his self-harm was '*not taken seriously*', which increased his anger and propensity to self-harm again (TAYLOR2003).

In a study carried out by RAY2007 the importance of professionals taking self-harm seriously and acknowledging the depths of the person's pain was highlighted. In particular, the women expressed a preference for practitioners who were direct, proactive and genuine. For most women, negative experiences with therapy appeared to stem from perceptions of therapists as judgmental, unable to relate and lacking in knowledge about self-harm (RAY2007).

Issues of power and control were important in relationships with counsellors and therapists. Effective therapeutic relationships seemed to be characterised by an equal partnership, with participation in the process of therapy such as choosing when and how to disclose abuse (CURTIS2006). Similarly, the confiscation of objects that could be used to self-harm in many cases contributed to a sense of lack of control and an increased desire to self-harm in the future (SMITH2002).

In another study (HUME2007) participants were often provided with the contact telephone numbers of helping organisations in place of, or in addition to, a referral. Although the majority of participants made use of these numbers, some explained they felt uncomfortable initiating their own aftercare by telephoning these organisa-tions. Moreover, several participants in this study were anxious to impress on their friends, family and, in some cases, professionals the importance of managing self-harm rather than its prevention.

Furthermore, the desire or willingness to engage with a service or source of support for self-harm was not uniform. It was reported that those who were unwilling to engage with treatment were more likely to have been harming themselves over a long period. Similarly, service users who reported a longer commitment to a particular intervention tended to recount feeling satisfied with this service. In contrast, experience of a large number of different interventions was associated with less commitment to, or perseverance with, a particular intervention (HUME2007).

Young people's experiences of engagement with service and suggestions for improvement
There were many suggestions by young people for improving engagement and service delivery. Firstly, the importance of having services that are informal and staffed by people with experience of mental disorders was raised as an important issue (BOLGER2004). Moreover, in studies of young people conducted in the UK (BURGESS1998, BROPHY2006, SINCLAIR2005), Ireland (BOLGER2004) and New Zealand (HOOD2006), the opportunity to talk was an important aspect contributing to their positive experience of aftercare. In particular, young people hoped that healthcare professionals would (BROPHY2006):

> ...*listen and respond in a natural way – showing concern and wanting to support you.*

However, not all participants welcomed the opportunity. Like adults, the need for young people's inclusion in the planning of their treatment was highlighted as an important issue for aftercare (BOLGER2004). Over half of the participants could think of other types of help that they would have liked to have received but had not. These included admission to hospital, individual rather than family appointments and specific help with school problems. Furthermore, respect for the young person and the opportunity to build trusting relationships with professionals were important aspects identified as a major factor in their receptiveness to an intervention (CROCKWELL1995, SINCLAIR2005). These needs were expressed by one individual as follows (CROCKWELL1995):

> *Listen to what they're saying, believe in them and make them feel like you're there for them. I know one thing. I really wanted people to be there for me; if they were, it would have made me feel a lot better. I'd say it would help other people too. And don't take it lightly, that's another thing. Some people just take it lightly and go 'that's another one of those teenage phases they're going through' or something like this but it's not. It's real!*

In a US study conducted on female college students (SHAW2006), core aspects of treatment that women described as helpful in their passage toward stopping self-harm included an empathic relationship with a professional who sees strengths beyond diagnostic labels and provides an opportunity to discuss self-injuring behaviour. In addition to the relational features, women also welcomed the helpfulness of pragmatic interventions such as verbal plans for dealing with urges to self-injure and concrete methods of managing emotions. Many of the participants expressed a desire to make sense of their self-harm and explore the logic of their behaviour, but felt that this was lacking in their interventions (SHAW2006).

4.4.8   Social support

Eight studies investigated the needs, benefits and drawbacks of social support, which includes web-based support or information (BAKER2008), support from family or friends (BOLGER2004, HOOD2006), community support groups (CORCORAN2007 [Corcoran *et al.*, 2007]) and support from other people who self-harm (HUME2007) in helping to cope with self-harm behaviour. Overall, participants emphasised the importance of social support in dealing with their self-harm. In particular, many service users expressed a desire for mutual support and shared understanding from others who have harmed themselves (HUME2007).

Feelings of isolation and alienation were common among service users (CAMGAN1994, HUME2007, RAY2007, SCHOPPMANN2007). The notion of being alone surfaced as a significant stressor with self-harm emerging as an antidote and a reaction to loneliness (RAY2007). One interviewee (SCHOPPMANN2007) spoke about how there was no one she could relate to and no one she could trust:

> *I think I felt deserted from everybody. Here you are and nobody is there for me. I couldn't talk to anybody.*

For many service users, isolation and being alone led to feelings of increased restlessness, fear, and anxiety. Self-harm helped to deal with these feelings and to get some relief (SCHOPPMANN2007):

> *I think when I am outside I have social contacts and when I am here, left on my own, perhaps it is the fear of being alone, yes, to be able to stand this, to feel that there is someone, that I am not alone, to feel myself perhaps.*

CORCORAN2007 examined the role of support groups in women's management of their self-harm and possible associated difficulties. Belonging emerged as one of the primary feelings experienced, creating a sense of acceptance and feeling welcome, particularly valued by new members. Belonging was fostered by the anonymous and voluntary nature of the group. Acceptance of differences encouraged participants to express themselves openly and contributed to the development of self-acceptance.

> *...if I can't accept myself as someone who self-injures or maybe I will get to a stage of someone who has self-injured, you know I've got physical scars, ...how am I going to expect the rest of the world to?*

Sharing experiences emerged as a valued aspect of group-membership, which involved a sense of '*genuine empathy*' derived from all participants having self-harm in common. Participants often realised that, contrary to previously held beliefs, their experiences were shared by many others, which increased feelings of self-acceptance, thereby reducing feelings of isolation and subsequent desire to self-injure arising from such feelings. Despite this, many participants felt that the depth of sharing could be compromised by the low frequency and time restraints of meetings, sometimes preventing deeper exploration of issues. 'Autonomy' emerged as important, primarily in the group being 'led and run by the participants themselves':

> *... it's power sharing ... we're equal ... we are ... a group of women ... tackling painful issues ... that we have had to deal with ... so we are strong women,... we don't feel strong all the time but we are equal,... and the empathy, you couldn't get it ... from ... mental health professionals..., there is a power difference.*

'Positive feeling' emerged as a common experience and led to improved mood and light-heartedness, particularly in relation to their self-harm:

> *We have a laugh... it's not all serious and sometimes I think it can be really healthy to just have a laugh... not take it all too seriously which... [is] hard to do if you're on your own or with people who are worried.*

Participants expressed numerous individual changes resulting from group-membership, the most common being increased self-confidence/self-esteem. Moreover, many participants credited group-membership with reduced self-harm. Other changes attributed to group-membership included development of clearer thinking, tapping into inner strengths, discovery of new talents and the ability to do things they had previously been unable to do:

> *There have been days when I've felt like self-harming and thought I don't want to go to the group, and I've gone and I have come away and I've not wanted to self-harm because it has given me a chance to express myself instead.*

A study conducted in the UK examined the impact of self-harm related websites as a form of support for young adults who self-harm (BAKER2008). All participants wrote about understanding and empathy when they described what benefit they derived from using the self-harm and suicide websites. By understanding others online, it is possible that website users may feel helpful and useful, and several participants gave this as an important reason for using the sites. Another theme that arose from the websites was that they were regarded as if they were communities. Participants stated that they provided emotional support, valuable information and advice, and, most importantly, friendship (BAKER2008). These websites were an important coping strategy for those who self-harm with a number of participants stating that their use of self-harm and suicide websites served the same function. Interacting with fellow users was reported as a preferable alternative to self-harm and suicidal behaviours. For some participants, this led to a reduction in the frequency of these behaviours. Participants also wrote about the sites as contributing to their recovery. One reported that the sites had facilitated change '*better than any therapy*':

> *Since using the boards to tell people how I felt and stuff I definitely think the frequency of my s/h [self-harm] has decreased a lot. I know that if I feel I need to do it I can go on the boards or on msn and someone will be there who I can talk to, and get my feelings out as well as being a way to distract myself.*

Young people's experiences of family support
In a study investigating young people, carried out by BOLGER2004, most of the respondents stated that their relationship with their parents and other family members was '*good*' or '*improved*' since the self-harm incident. The majority of the respondents mentioned '*having someone to talk to*' as being of benefit to young people in distress. In the HOOD2006 study of young people and their parents in New Zealand, the young people were usually less enthusiastic about parental involvement in their treatment. Conversely, parents valued their involvement in their child's treatment decisions. However, most young people did acknowledge that having a therapist to mediate allowed them to talk to their parents about issues that they felt they could not raise on their own.

4.4.9   Carer experiences

Seven studies (BYRNE2008 [Byrne *et al.*, 2008], BYWATERS2002, HOOD2006, LINDGREN2010 [Lindgren *et al.*, 2010], MCDONALD2007 [McDonald *et al.*, 2007], OLDERSHAW2008 [Oldershaw *et al.*, 2008], RISSANEN2009) were found that could be categorised under the heading of 'carer experiences'. The review team extracted common findings that emerged from the analysis of the carer perspectives such as the process of discovery, the psychological impact of self-harm, the understanding of the meaning of self-harm, support needs, parental views on treatment, the effects of self-harm on parenting and family life, and the role of carers or parents in their child's recovery and treatment.

First, the process of discovery of self-harm was commonly captured from the carer's perspective. OLDERSHAW2008 found that for many parents, the process was gradual. At the beginning, many parents had a suspicion about their child's behaviour, often spotting injuries. However, they accepted implausible explanations in the hope that the situation would improve without any further intervention. For the majority of cases, formal verification of their child's self-harm was often carried out by schools or other outside organisations in collaboration with the young person. However, despite their initial concerns, many parents reacted to this news by 'brushing it under the carpet' because they felt that the situation would repair itself. Furthermore, the behaviour of outside organisations, such as schools or GPs, was suggested by parents as a key factor in the timing of accessing help. In particular, their attitudes and their willingness to discuss self-harm and give information influenced parental behaviour in the interval between disclosure and referral:

> *The teacher at the school actually was really quite good. She actually gave me a lot of the background for self-harm, why girls self-harm ... she seemed to be quite clued up and in fact it was her that, she was the one that explained to me, a lot of it to me, because I had no idea what it was, what it meant ... I don't feel as though I was floundering as much as I think I would have if I hadn't had her advice.*

All parents from this study advised others in a similar situation to seek help sooner than they had done (OLDERSHAW2008).

Another finding that emerged was the psychological impact of self-harm on parents. Many parents described strong and lasting emotional reactions to their child's behaviour, including shock, disappointment, helplessness, guilt and fear, a persistent feeling of sadness and a sense of loss (OLDERSHAW2008). One of the most prominent psychological reactions, however, was feeling guilt and shame (BYRNE2008, HOOD2006, LINDGREN2010, MCDONALD2007, OLDERSHAW2008). In particular, a feeling of helplessness in discovering or preventing their child's self-harm led to increased guilt and shame. Specifically, they felt guilty that their child was unhappy or hurting to such an extent that they would even consider self-harm (MCDONALD2007). In response to their children's expressed unhappiness, the mothers questioned their relationships with their children and felt that they may have failed them. This caused deep feelings of blame (MCDONALD2007):

> *It was like, what have I done?... You tend to blame yourself ... I wasn't watching, I wasn't caring enough, I wasn't showing enough love, I wasn't giving enough praise.*

Interestingly, these emotional reactions are also mirrored in the accounts of healthcare professionals and service users themselves, increasing confidence in the findings.

Many parents 'searched for a reason' for their child's self-harm behaviour. Many felt that circumstances or life events in their own lives, such as marriage breakdowns or losing family members, had caused their child to self-harm. As a consequence, they blamed themselves for its occurrence (MCDONALD2007). Another source of guilt for these mothers stemmed from their need to be far more vigilant of their children after the self-harm was discovered. The mothers reported, among other things, having read their child's journals and emails as well as listening in to private conversations, in order to supervise their child's activities more thoroughly (MCDONALD2007). One mother commented:

> *It means that you are constantly aware, watching them for any signs ... which is terrible. You feel like you are sneaking around all the time.*

Public stigma also led to strong psychological reactions such as a sense of failure, worry, isolation and fear (BYRNE2008, BYWATERS2002, HOOD2006). For instance, HOOD2006 established that in some cases parents were uncomfortable with their child's referral to aftercare because it increased their feelings of failure and they were worried about the stigma attached to it. Interestingly, fathers in this study were found to worry more than mothers about stigmatisation (HOOD2006). Many felt that better information for the general public was also called for to help alleviate some of the stigmatisation faced by individuals who self-harm (BYWATERS2002). Mirroring findings of past studies, a recent study carried out by BYRNE2008 on the needs of parents and carers found that the discovery of self-harm was associated with stigma, which exacerbated feelings of isolation and despair:

> *... go around trying to cover up, not discussing it in front of family or friends. The biggest thing is the isolation, terror and fear ... it's a very harsh journey.*

The majority of mothers interviewed felt they could not talk to anyone about their child's self-harm because they were aware of the stigmatised nature of self-harm and feared the judgement of others (MCDONALD2007). This fear further contributed to the shame they experienced. Finally, self-harm episodes elicited intense anxiety because many feared the risk of repetition while their child waited for appropriate treatment (BYRNE2008). Parents also described feelings of anger and frustration, and sometimes this anger was directed at their child whose behaviour was disrupting their entire family (BYRNE2008).

A third finding from the carer literature was the parents' understanding of repetitive self-harm behaviour and factors relating to it. OLDERSHAW2008 was the first to investigate parental views of the meaning of their child's self-harm behaviour and the causal factors. They found that parents were sensitive to the behaviour and deeply affected by their experience; however, almost all parents said that their child gave them little or no explanation for their self-harm. Many of the parents felt that from the outside their child appeared to be alright, but internally they were suffering (RISSANEN2009):

> *I knew she had problems of some kind, but her problems were bigger and more serious that I could ever imagine and they could not be seen from the outside.*

When asked if they had any personal opinions on the causes, common causal factors acknowledged by parents were emotional difficulties, situational difficulties such as bullying, and personality factors such as a lack of self-esteem. Most parents recognised that self-harm served a purpose in the young person's life, such as coping with negative emotions or as a means of providing control (OLDERSHAW2008):

> *I can understand that it's some way of you having some sort of control over your pain, over your life, because you feel totally out of control when you're feeling so depressed or vulnerable or whatever.*

Carers gave similar causal factors for engaging in self-harm as professionals and service users themselves, thus strengthening these findings. Yet beyond an intellectual understanding, many parents felt they could not come to terms with their child's self-harm behaviour and understated its significance. Most parents struggled to accept self-harm and recognised the numerous 'typical' teenage behaviours that their child could alternatively have engaged in and felt regret that their child had 'opted' to self-harm. Ultimately, parents felt that they could not fully understand or empathise with self-harm:

> *I find that hard to empathise with because it just wouldn't be my way of dealing with it, erm but I can intellectually understand it.*

An additional finding from the carer literature was the need for support and information about self-harm. Above all, carers expressed the need for support, information about suicidal behaviour in young people, skills for parenting and advice on managing further incidences (BYRNE2008, BYWATERS2002, RISSANEN2009). Furthermore, advice on how to prevent, or manage further episodes was seen as priority for parents and carers (BYRNE2008). The opportunity to avail themselves of support and to share similar circumstances was believed to be extremely important in managing the impact of self-harm (BYRNE2008, OLDERSHAW2008):

> *It would be a relief to be able to talk to someone else who has gone through it. Knowing other people having the same situation really does help. The relief of knowing I'm not the only one.*

Another finding that emerged from the carer literature was their views of services and treatments. Firstly, many parents were divided on their feelings about medication. Specifically, concerns about the side effects, withdrawal effects, changing medication and the long-term effects of medication were frequent worries for parents (HOOD2006). Conversely, some parents were happy that their child was on medication because they saw the beneficial nature of the antidepressants.

Like service users, the majority of the parents felt that services failed to provide their children and themselves as parents with adequate or appropriate support. In particular, the lack of a clear care pathway for 16- to 18-year-olds was highlighted. Akin to service users' views, carers highlighted the lack of continuity of care and specifically the long duration spent waiting for CAMHS appointments (BYRNE2008, HOOD2006). LINDGREN2010 examined parents' experiences of their daughters' professional care in Sweden, and caregivers at all levels of outpatient and inpatient care for children, young people and adults in psychiatric, acute and emergency care, and primary healthcare. The experiences were mixed in nature. With regard to negative experiences, they reported feeling invisible due to feeling that they were not being listened to, seen or taken into account, and being excluded from participating in their daughters' care. On the other hand, parents also experienced feelings of peace and of being comforted, listened to and taken seriously in some meetings with some professionals. Moreover, professionals who showed compassion and an honest willingness to help were experienced as genuine, reliable and helpful, which made them feel valued, validated them as valuable people in their daughters' lives and allowed parents to see some hope for their daughters. Some parents said they found young people's psychiatrists were often unavailable for continued care because they were too busy or had left the service during the young person's treatment period (HOOD2006).

In a recent study carried out by RISSANEN2009 knowledge of self-harm among healthcare professionals was identified by parents as a helpful factor enabling them to approach self-harm in a professional way. Service users also highlighted the importance of knowledge of self-harm in healthcare professionals, and professionals themselves who were more knowledgeable reported feeling more able to treat people who self-harm. According to the parental descriptions, self-help was useful in many ways but was insufficient on its own (RISSANEN2009). Parents also described additional factors that were of help in the relationship between healthcare professionals and young people who self-injure. These helpful factors included trustworthiness, professionals skills, genuine caring, respecting individuality, sensitivity, speaking about self-harm and the reasons for it, co-operation with the whole family and effective communication between nursing units. In addition, parents recognised unhelpful factors such as a disinterested attitude, avoiding discussion of self-harm, reproaching or denouncing parents for their child's self-harm and doubting the honesty of parents when talking about the self-harm. Again, the helpful and unhelpful factors reported by parents reflect those of the service users themselves and in some cases healthcare professionals' views (for example the value of communication), increasing confidence in the findings reported.

A further finding of importance was the effect of self-harm on parenting and family life. It appeared that self-harm resulted in both negative and positive changes in these areas. With regard to negative changes, self-harm was seen to disrupt family dynamics and impede family functioning (BYRNE2008). Many parents reported 'walking on eggshells' around the young people, nervous of triggering an episode of self-harm (OLDERSHAW2008). This impacted on their parenting style and ability to set limits and maintain boundaries. Several parents (OLDERSHAW2008) found that they were now constantly aware of what the young person was doing, both discreetly watching them from a distance, and providing increased overt attention and care-giving:

> *It was like looking after a baby again ... I was hiding the knives, I was hiding any pills ... I was knocking on her door every 5 minutes.*

Many parents felt that they had to deny their own needs and make changes to or limit their lifestyle as a direct result of the self-harm. They found difficulties in balancing parenting and meeting the needs of other children, which heightened the psychological impact of self-harm by increasing parental burden, pressure and stress. Many of the mothers in this study felt guilt regarding their diminishing role within the family – as a wife, mother and core of the family (OLDERSHAW2008). Dealing with their child's self-harm often took them away from their usual roles at work and home, causing them to feel guilty because they believed that they were not meeting the expectations of themselves or others. Four of the mothers interviewed also considered that the extra time, energy and attention spent on a child who self-harms meant that they had neglected the mothering of their other children (MCDONALD2007).

However, parents did feel that self-harm had resulted in some positive changes to family life by strengthening the parent–child relationship (OLDERSHAW2008):

It's actually helped me break down some of those barriers because she's always coming up for cuddles now and actually I don't reject her anymore, and I think that's because I want to and I can. So that's … I think that's a really positive thing.

Finally, carers highlighted the different roles that they played in their child's struggle with their self-harm behaviour and in their recovery. In the study carried out by RISSANEN2009, the parents felt that they played a significant role in their child's self-harm including intervening in the act of self-injuring, giving support for obtaining professional help, showing they cared, and discussing the self-harm behaviour and factors associated with it. They wished to help their child express their feelings more appropriately and develop adaptive coping strategies. On the other hand, many of the parents questioned their competencies at disciplining, boundary-setting and re-establishing healthy relationships with their child. Specifically, parents felt that '*active disciplining*' could run the risk of self-harm recurrence and were left disempowered by self-harm. Problems in communication with young people and the incapacity of parents to help were identified as help-hindering factors in this relationship. On the other hand, helpful factors identified by parents were parental interaction with the young people, including showing care and awareness, ensuring professional help and interaction of the parents with each other. In reference to parental involvement in treatment, HOOD2006 found that young people were usually less enthusiastic about parental involvement while parents were often very happy to have the opportunity to be involved in their child's therapy.

4.4.10　Healthcare professionals' attitudes, knowledge and experience

Fourteen primary studies (COOKE2009 [Cooke & James, 2009], DUPER-OUZEL2008 [Duperouzel & Fish, 2008], GIBB2010 [Gibb *et al.*, 2010], KIBLER2009 [Kibler, 2009], LONG2010 [Long & Jenkins, 2010], REDLEY2010 [Redley, 2010], REECE2005 [Reece, 2005], ROBERTS-DOBIE2007 [Roberts-Dobie & Donatelle, 2007], SIMM2008 [Simm *et al.*, 2008], SMITH2002, THOMPSON2008 [Thompson *et al.*, 2008], TRELOAR2008A [Treloar & Lewis, 2008a], WHEAT-LEY2009 [Wheatley & Austin-Payne, 2009], WHITLOCK2009 [Whitlock *et al.*, 2009]) were found that were categorised under the broad heading of 'healthcare professionals' attitudes, knowledge and experience'. There were a further two reviews identified that fell into this category (McHale & Felton, 2010; SAUNDERS2011). When reviewing the literature, there were a number of themes, such as: the identification of self-harm; healthcare professionals' knowledge and understanding of self-harm and its causes; the attitudes towards self-harm behaviour; psychological impact of self-harm on healthcare professionals; views on treatment and services; views on harm minimisation strategies; and training needs and experiences.

Experience of care

Identification of self-harm
Three studies reported findings related to 'identification of self-harm' (COOKE2009, ROBERTS-DOBIE2007, SIMM2008). For school nurses from a primary care trust, identification of self-harm most commonly occurred when staff were approached by friends of service users and other staff members (COOKE2009). It was a rare occurrence for the school nurses to be approached by children and young people who self-harmed, with only one school nurse having identified self-harm behaviour this way. Similarly, in a US study conducted by ROBERTS-DOBIE2007 on school counsellors, the most common methods of discovery were being informed by a fellow student (67%), a classroom teacher (65%), being approached by the person who self-harms (51%) or the counsellor personally recognising the symptoms (48%). These findings highlight the need for all school employees and peers to be educated about self-harm because they are the primary sources for identification of self-harm. Importantly, in a study conducted on head teachers of primary schools in the UK (SIMM2008) participants noted that the busy nature of school life and demands on time might hide self-harm behaviours from some staff.

Knowledge of self-harm and its causes
There were five studies that explored the topic of knowledge of self-harm and its causes (COOKE2009, DUPEROUZEL2007, KIBLER2009, SIMM2008, THOMPSON2008). In SIMM2008, head teachers of primary schools expressed uncertainty as to what constituted self-harm and what did not. Some participants felt that if the child did not intend to hurt themselves, the behaviour did not qualify as self-harm. Others felt that intentionality did not matter in this way. Finally, some participants felt that self-harm had to be repeated behaviour while others considered that behaviour could count as self-harm even if it only happened once. In another study, school nurses' knowledge of self-harm methods was broad, but commonly focused on 'superficial self-harm' rather than more lethal methods (COOKE2009).

Understanding of the underlying reasons for self-harm
Regarding the underlying reasons for self-harm (DUPEROUZEL2007), healthcare professionals understood that self-harm was an important coping mechanism and a means of control. This was a common underlying reason quoted by service users themselves, thus strengthening the findings reported. Furthermore, the majority (83%) of US school counsellors were also aware that it was best to be direct with students about stopping the self-injurious behaviour and most participants (80%) also believed it was beneficial to educate students about how and why students self-injure (KIBLER2009). Ultimately, in a study conducted on experienced community psychiatric nurses (THOMPSON2008) the importance of understanding service users in order to have more empathy was highlighted.

Another recent study by REDLEY2010 examined clinicians' understanding of self-harm by overdose and their experience of psychosocial assessment. Many saw the act as an impulsive one in the face of adverse life events and influenced by drugs or alcohol. On the contrary, a person's motivation or reasons for taking an overdose are given minimal clinical importance. The authors suggest a number of reasons for this. First, paying greater attention to a person's reasons and motivations may lead to provocation if the clinician does not understand, endorse or agree with the person's motivations. Second, some of the interviews suggested that being intimate with details of people's lives, in order to better understand their reasons for taking an overdose, is not commensurate with the professional role considered necessary to work with them.

LONG2010 recently examined counsellor's perceptions of self-harm and their view of the role of the therapeutic relationship when working with this group. The counsellors concurred that the therapeutic relationship is central when working with people who self-harm. In particular, they recognised the need for time, a safe and confidential environment, non-judgemental support, unconditional positive regard, empathy, equality and sensitivity as important factors in establishing a rapport and a trusting therapeutic relationship. The findings indicate that the therapeutic relationship for self-harm is vital, complex, long-term and multi-dimensional. Observational skills, listening, identifying personal history, supervision, risk assessment and being person-centred were all identified by counsellors as crucial at the beginning of therapy. Two counsellors commented on the use of no-suicide contracts and both agreed that they were detrimental rather than beneficial, in that they 'protect the counsellor rather than the client' and because it takes away a coping mechanism or 'crutch' for dealing with difficult issues. When discussing the ending of the therapeutic relationship, teaching coping strategies and teaching service users to identify triggers for their self-harm and safer self-harm were described as possible options. Many of the counsellors conceded that the ending of therapy was a difficult task and this should be addressed in training.

Attitudes to self-harm
Sixteen studies examined attitudes of healthcare professionals about self-harm and these were predominantly negative in nature (COOKE2009, GIBB2010, HOPKINS2002, JEFFERY2002, KIBLER2009, MACKAY2005 [Mackay & Barrowclough, 2005], McHale and Felton [2010], O'DONOVAN2007, REDLEY2010, REECE2005, SAUNDERS2011, SMITH2002, THOMPSON2008, TRELOAR2008A, WHEATLEY2009, WHITLOCK2009). Some of the negative attitudes addressed by the literature (for example, that self-harm is a means of seeking attention) were quoted as common misconceptions in the perspectives of service users reported above (REECE2005).

A number of studies exposed that many healthcare professionals felt that people who self-harm were labelled as '*attention seeking*' (COOKE2009, KIBLER2009, McHale and Felton [2010], REECE2005, SAUNDERS2011, SMITH2002). For instance, in one study carried out by KIBLER2009 when US counsellors were asked whether most students who self-injure want attention, approximately equal numbers agreed and disagreed with this statement. Also, in the systematic review carried out by SAUNDERS2011 a number of studies indicated an over-representation of attention-seeking as a motive for self-harm. This was found to be less common in psychiatric staff compared with general hospital staff. When asked the reasons why it was felt that people who self-harm were viewed negatively, healthcare professionals frequently cited (SMITH2002):

[a] general fear of working with these people and I think the fear is born out of not quite knowing what to do with them, and due to the blame culture professionals

have lost confidence in themselves and therefore empathy towards other human beings suffering.

Moreover, some healthcare professionals expressed that those who used superficial methods of self-harm were doing so to gain attention, whereas, those engaged in more 'serious' self-harm had different motives (COOKE2009):

I think there are two groups: those that say they're self-harming, and it's ... probably only superficial scratching or whatever and I wonder if it's more attention-seeking or frustration or anything else. And then you get what I call your serious self-harmers that are really abusing or hurting themselves.

On the other hand, not all studies highlighted negative attitudes towards individuals who self-harm. The literature review carried out by SAUNDERS2011 identifies two studies where sympathy was reported by at least 40% of healthcare professionals (Friedman *et al.*, 2006; Pallikkathayil & Morgan, 1988). Moreover, in a study carried out by GIBB2010, there were some positive attitudes including 73% of healthcare professionals stating that they could empathise with a person who has self-harmed and 71% believing that their contact was helpful to people who self-harm.

There are a number of factors that may promote negative attitudes, such as the busy nature of the ward, service users being seen as an obstacle to the ward and challenging behaviour. For instance, in a study carried out by HOPKINS2002 the above factors were highlighted when observing two medical wards and interviewing two healthcare professionals from each ward. In particular, the service users were seen as blocking beds because their needs meant beds were occupied for longer than expected. These service users were deemed to have challenging behaviours because they had different requirements than medical patients. While the study had a small sample (only four participants) to draw these conclusions from, they were supported by the additional observations made (HOPKINS2002). In fact, many healthcare professionals feel that people who self-injure are a difficult group to work with, and this may partially explain the prominence of negative attitudes (GIBB2010, SMITH2002, THOMPSON2008, WHITLOCK2009).

One explanation for this is that self-harm is often comorbid with many other challenging clinical presentations such as bipolar disorder, and depressive and anxiety disorders, disordered eating, and a history of trauma and abuse (WHITLOCK2009). Other possible explanations include the perceived addictive nature of the behaviour and uncertainty about how to best treat or manage self-injurious behaviour (WHITLOCK2009). Finally in a study by GIBB2010, healthcare professionals indicated that their greatest difficulties in working with people who self-harm included repetitive self-harm, frustrating and difficult behaviour, communication difficulties, lack of knowledge about mental illness, a lack of effective interventions and time pressure.

A study carried out by WHEATLEY2009 on nurses provides some additional insight into why they viewed people who self-harm more negatively than other patients. Interestingly, they found that nurses who reported feeling more negative about people who self-harm reported more worry about working with this group.

Furthermore, there were non-significant trends suggesting that nurses who reported feeling more effective in their work with people who self-harm reported less negativity and worry about working with this group, although this was not necessarily the case for female nurses. A study carried out by GIBB2010 found that negative attitudes were significantly associated with higher levels of burnout, through high emotional exhaustion and low personal accomplishment. Finally, unqualified nursing staff reported more negativity and worry in working with people who self-harm than qualified nurses, suggesting that knowledge and education plays an important role in attitudes towards self-harm (WHEATLEY2009).

The literature review carried out by SAUNDERS2011 highlighted a number of additional characteristics that play an important role in influencing attitudes such as job role and gender. For example, within general hospital staff, those who were closer to the frontline were increasingly likely to hold negative viewpoints about and behave negatively towards people who self-harm. Furthermore, negative attitudes towards people who self-harm were more prevalent in doctors compared with nurses. Where this was not found the majority of the studies had a participant population which included psychiatric staff. One study found that psychiatrists had a more positive attitude towards self-harm compared with their colleagues of other specialities, and the same effect was found in non-medical psychiatric staff and their colleagues (TRELOAR2008A). This indicates that psychiatric training and experience goes some way to moderating the effect of job role on healthcare professionals' attitudes. In line with this, exposure of psychiatric staff to people who self-harm was found to improve healthcare professionals' attitudes. Nevertheless, the opposite effect was found in general hospital staff. Another potentially moderating effect, identified by the review, was the influence of gender on attitudes. Three studies found that the attitudes of male staff towards self-harm were significantly more negative compared with those of female staff. However, authors do highlight that the strong gender-role association, with the tendency for men to be doctors and women to be nurses, make results from these studies difficult to interpret.

In a study carried out by O'DONOVAN2007, an additional area influencing negative attitudes was the impact of health professionals' views of the differences between their expected and actual roles. In semi-structured interviews O'DONOVAN2007 revealed that healthcare professionals felt the focus of their role was prescribing medication rather than developing therapeutic relationships within acute mental health wards. This prevents people from being able to address the reasons for their self-harm and developing alternative coping strategies.

Another justification for negative attitudes portrayed by healthcare professionals is the lack of training and education provided to them in the area of self-harm. A literature review of the factors affecting attitudes to self-harm (McHale & Felton, 2010) found that a lack of education was the primary rationale for negative attitudes, which were prevalent in 18 out of the 19 studies reviewed. Additionally, a recent study carried out by TRELOAR2008A on professional attitudes of mental health clinicians and emergency room staff highlighted the importance of training and education on healthcare professionals' attitudes. They found that mental health clinicians had a significantly more positive attitude towards service users with bipolar disorder who self-harmed compared with clinicians working in emergency medicine. Another significant finding was that the female clinicians across both mental health and emergency medicine service settings had more positive attitudes towards patients with borderline personality disorder, although this difference was not significant when controlling for other factors. However, factors such as the frequency of contact with patients with borderline personality disorder, level of university training completed, and years of clinical experience held by the clinicians across mental health and emergency medicine were not associated with attitude ratings towards such patients. As predicted, clinicians across the mental health and emergency department service settings who had attended prior training specifically in the area of borderline personality disorder demonstrated significantly more positive attitudes towards working with this patient group (TRELOAR2008A).

As well as healthcare professionals' characteristics, the varying characteristics of people who self-harm were also identified as moderating factors on healthcare professionals' attitudes (SAUNDERS2011). For example, negative attitudes were more likely to be expressed towards people who repeatedly self-harm. Negative attitudes are also linked to the professional's perceptions of service users' control of self-harm. MACKAY2005 asked questions about attitudes within four hypothetical situations offering different control and stability features. The findings indicated that where the problems specified leading to self-harm were within the control of the service user then elevated disapproval was shown. This may imply that feelings of incompetence lead to negative attitudes (HOPKINS2002, MACKAY2005, O'DONOVAN2007, PATTERSON2007 [Patterson *et al.*, 2007], SMITH2002). Service users presenting frequently at hospital challenge healthcare professionals and their ability to cope with such situations. This could affect their confidence, which further contributes towards negativity (McHale & Felton, 2007). Ramon and colleagues (1975) found that the lethality of self-harm is also an influencing factor on nursing and medical staff's attitudes towards self-harm, with sympathy and lethality being positively correlated. This finding was mirrored in a US study (Ansel & McGee, 1971) and an Australian study (Bailey, 1994), both of which found that positive attitudes were more likely to be displayed towards clearly suicidal or despairing patients. Furthermore, SAUNDERS2011 found that healthcare professionals felt more hostility towards people who self-harm than those with a physical illness. This was attributed to distinctions that professionals make between legitimate and illegitimate needs, with self-harm being considered illegitimate compared with physical illness and, therefore, less worthy of care.

The emotional impact on healthcare professionals who work with people who self-harm

The literature also highlighted the emotional and psychological impact that working with people who self-harm can have on healthcare professionals (DUPEROUZEL2007, REECE2005, REDLEY2010, THOMPSON2008). Similar to carers' experiences, self-harm elicited strong emotional reactions in healthcare professionals. Many participants talked about how frustrating and hopeless the work could be, which was linked to service users not getting better or relapsing (THOMPSON2008), or when service users continued to self-harm following attempts to talk about their behaviour (DUPEROUZEL2007):

> *I suppose it's just like beating your head against a brick wall. You still trying to, you're trying to help her and sort her through and sort her life out and she basically just throws it back in your face. That's how it seems; she's throwing it back in your face.*

The sense of nurse helplessness in dealing with self-harm was a common feature of the nurses' interviews in one study (REECE2005). However, the way in which this helplessness was managed varied, with some expressing feelings of frustration and others expressing feelings of distress. In particular, many of the male nurses conveyed distress and powerful emotional reactions in response to self-harm incidents (REECE2005). Participants also felt inadequate and this was mainly attributed to a lack of resources, lack of time and a feeling of futility (COOKE2009). For others, there was anger towards patients for being 'manipulative'. Furthermore, some participants felt that seeing the physical effects of patients' self-harm was distressing and shocking, and at times they felt disgusted (THOMPSON2008). However, despite the challenging nature of working with people who self-harm, most participants also felt that '*It can be very rewarding*' (THOMPSON2008). Both service users' and carers' feelings of guilt and blame were key concerns for healthcare professionals. They explained that when someone self-harms, they feel personal guilt alongside an institutional pressure and blame culture (DUPEROUZEL2007):

> *If we did allow self-harm and something went wrong we'd be dead meat, for want of a better word. It could be said as negligent.*

With the exception of one participant they all talked about the fear of being blamed for their actions if a patient dies: '*Am I gonna have to account for what I have done?*' Feeling responsible was exacerbated by time pressures, having limited resources and feeling unsupported by other statutory services (THOMPSON2008). Therefore, not surprisingly, all participants except for one found working with this patient group '*very anxiety provoking*' and on occasion described this anxiety as spilling over into their personal lives (THOMPSON2008). Interestingly, service users demonstrated an awareness of this blame-culture but felt it was unfair to hold healthcare professionals responsible for their self-injurious behaviour (DUPEROUZEL2007). Despite most healthcare professionals feeling personally responsible for helping service users get better, there was a clear recognition that '*It's about putting the responsibility back to them*'. The service user should be seen to have ultimate responsibility for their behaviour and nurses felt it was important to work collaboratively with them.

Healthcare professionals' experiences of services and treatments for people who self-harm

An additional finding that emerged from the healthcare professional literature was their experiences of services and treatments available for people who self-harm

(COOKE2009, SMITH2002, WHITLOCK2009). With regard to services available, healthcare professionals explained that other priorities prevented them from giving service users time and space to explore their self-harm (SMITH2002). COOKE2009 discovered that many of the nurses were uncomfortable with referrals, particularly because it involved balancing a breach of confidentiality with a duty of care. They were also uncomfortable with the threshold of specialist services because this often resulted in them having to deal with situations they did not feel equipped to handle. Uncertainty about how to best treat the behaviour was common, with only 28.3% of respondents saying that they knew enough to treat people who had self-injured effectively and three quarters agreeing that this is a subject about which they need more information (WHITLOCK2009). The majority of practitioners reported using CBT or dialectical behaviour therapy (DBT) treatment approaches and the majority reported that these treatments are only sometimes effective (WHITLOCK2009). Moreover, many reported having changed their approach to treatment over time, typically in favour of DBT (WHITLOCK2009). Acquisition of coping mechanisms, improvement of life circumstances and enhanced ability to reflect on the underlying causes of distress were identified as the most common reasons for self-harm cessation following treatment (WHITLOCK2009). Furthermore, healthcare professionals making assumptions and being too focused on the physical manifestations, rather than the associated psychological complexities, of self-harm was another central issue (COOKE2009). In particular, alternative strategies in place of the self-harm behaviour were seen as *'futile'* by some healthcare professionals:

> *I feel silly telling them alternative strategies ... like to hold an ice cube. They seem futile and I feel like I lose credibility ... It seems inadequate – how could it help?*

Similar to both carers and service users, healthcare professionals expressed a need for continual support and additional training (GIBB2010, SMITH2002, THOMPSON2008). Experienced community psychiatric nurses all described the importance of supervision and informal support (THOMPSON2008). Most participants felt that they could rely on their colleagues for reassurance and advice. However, there was also a sense that because the team was extremely busy that they would not want to burden others, so they may not seek support as often as needed (THOMPSON2008). In relation to support for service users, healthcare professionals agreed that peer group support is beneficial because *'to know that other people have had similar experiences can be really helpful'* (SMITH2002). Further suggestions for improvement, as identified in by the SAUNDERS2011 literature review and by a study conducted by GIBB2010, included further training and an increase in resources such as advice, support, facilities, staff levels, faster assessment and greater flexibility with patient allocations. Healthcare professionals identified a specific training need with regard to taking a psychosocial history of people who self-harm and referring them on to psychiatric services. Healthcare professionals also felt that separating the facilities for people with physical health problems and people who self-harm would be beneficial because of the differing needs of the two groups.

Views on harm minimisation

Three studies also captured staff views on harm minimisation strategies (DUPEROUZEL2007, REECE2005, THOMPSON2008) (see Chapter 7 for more information on harm minimisation). Some healthcare professionals felt that self-injuring should be permitted because it reduced the risk of more dangerous behaviours (DUPEROUZEL2007):

> *I don't have a problem with it. I would let them cut as long as it was done, you know what I mean, where there is less risk of infection. Because, to me, if she'd been allowed to cut she wouldn't have started swallowing. She wouldn't have started doing the inserting things like that. Which to me is more life threatening than cutting.*

Many nurses expressed a desire for the service users to stop self-harm, but some knew that realistically they, as nurses, could not stop it from happening, only attempt to contain it (REECE2005). In a study performed on experienced community psychiatric nurses, all talked about the need to minimise and '*contain risk*' and that their role was not necessarily about helping a patient to stop self-harm (THOMPSON2008):

> *I don't actually see it as my aim to stop somebody kind of self-harming. I perhaps see it as maybe acknowledging well that's kind of the way that they're functioning. Maybe we can look at reducing this and making that behaviour as kind of safe as possible.*

O'DONOVAN'S2007 interviews also raised the area of risk management including the removal of property and one-to-one observations. Nurses acknowledged the need to ensure the safety of service users. However, they felt the measures taken were inappropriate and were contravening people's rights. This conflict results in healthcare professionals feeling uncomfortable with the roles that they are required to work within for service user safety.

Views on training and education

Another finding arising from the literature was the need for training and education in issues relating to self-harm (COOKE2009, DUPEROUZEL2007, ROBERTS-DOBIE2007, SIMM2008, SMITH2002, WHEATLEY2009). The majority of healthcare professionals believed that they were able to do their job adequately; however, to provide better care they suggested that they needed additional training (SMITH2002). Likewise, in a study carried out by COOKE2009 the need for training in self-harm was raised as an important issue among the school nurses, with a number of participants feeling ill-equipped to deal with self-harm issues in an appropriate way. Similarly, in a study carried out by DUPEROUZEL2007 service users and healthcare professionals highlighted the need for more staff training in order to understand the behaviour and methods of caring for people who self-harm. It was felt that better understanding would, in turn, improve communication because service users often felt that healthcare professionals avoided discussing self-harm behaviour with them, despite the value that service users placed on this interaction. Mirroring the views of service users themselves, healthcare professionals also felt that communication about self-harm was difficult, and this was attributed to a lack of confidence, something which training could address (DUPEROUZEL2007):

> *Training should include lots and lots of different ideas why people – why and what research tell us what causes people to self-harm, because I don't think that it is very well understood. And I also think that we should have training in how to deal with it. And when it is happening there and then, rather than, not just going off your instincts but following what other people are doing.*

All healthcare professionals expressed a desire for general mental health and self-harm training and, particularly, practical tips on management of self-harm (COOKE2009). Moreover, it was felt to be of importance to look at healthcare professionals' thoughts and feelings surrounding the topic of self-harm (SMITH2002). Supervision was also thought to be essential, as was peer group support and working as a team (SMITH2002). Other training suggestions included increasing knowledge levels especially with regard to alternative strategies and general awareness of self-harm, practical tips for managing young people who self-harm, information regarding organisations who deal with self-harm issues, counselling, and learning about different types of self-harm (COOKE2009). Another key area that was highlighted by school nurses was further education on referrals and in particular, understanding when it is appropriate to refer people on to specialist services, when to seek help and when to refer to child protection services. Finally, training was considered necessary in issues of confidentiality, specifically, when to inform parents and break confidentiality. Most of those who had previously attended training said it had helped increase their confidence in dealing with these issues (COOKE2009). It was also suggested that involving people who self-harm in the training may help to address the issues of guilt and blame felt by healthcare professionals (DUPEROUZEL2007). Further evidence suggesting more training is necessary is apparent within research conducted by JEFFERY2002. Medical staff and psychiatrists showed limited awareness about self-harm when tested about facts and myths surrounding self-harm. The respondents who had appropriate training were clearer about self-harm. In an additional study carried out by ROBERTS-DOBIE2007 the most commonly identified need expressed by school counsellors in the US was building their knowledge and skills. In addition to more information, counsellors wanted policies and procedures to follow when working with people who self-harm. Learning mentors interviewed in a study carried out by SIMM2007 described how they had gained new understanding of self-harm from a training course on self-harm. Equally, they felt that colleagues who had little training in this area were not as aware. Particular gaps in knowledge found were in relation to subgroups of the population who are at higher risk of self-harm. Additionally, the findings suggested that training and support to help unqualified staff feel less negative and concerned about working with people who self-harm may be particularly important (WHEATLEY2009).

4.5   FROM EVIDENCE TO RECOMMENDATIONS

Service user experiences of self-harm
The evidence from the qualitative literature provided an insight into the experience of people who self-harm, as well as their carers and healthcare professionals. For many people, self-harm was an indication of an underlying problem and the reasons for self-harm vary considerably. For some, self-harm was related to traumatic life events, childhood abuse, psychiatric illness or troubled relationships. For others, self-harm was an important coping mechanism for dealing with feelings of frustration, loneliness or distress. It was also described in the literature as a cry for help, an escape or as a means of gaining support. Others mentioned that they engaged in self-harm to feel alive or cope with dissociation. Also, the meaning and motivation behind each act may differ considerably from one incident to the next. There were 14 studies in the literature reviewed that looked at reasons behind self-harm behaviour. Most of the studies were qualitative and used semi-structured interviews of mostly adult female participants; one study included participants as young as 14 years and four as young as 16 years. The mean study sample size was around 37 participants and the recruitment varied considerably from inpatient and hospital recruitments to advertisements, self-help websites and email interviews. In summary, health and social care professionals should explore the meaning of self-harm for the person and recognise that each person self-harms for individual reasons.

Self-harm may coexist with other destructive behaviours such as drug or alcohol misuse. Two particular studies highlighted these destructive behaviours; however, the participants varied from a large sample (n = 76) of female subjects who self-injured to male and female subjects (n = 20) who had stopped self-harming for at least 2 years. The literature also mentions that these coexisting behaviours may be interchangeable; however, this finding came from a small study of seven participants.

There are mixed attitudes towards ending self-harm and the process of recovery. Some people wanted to stop, whereas others valued it as a vital coping mechanism. There were three studies in the literature that looked at the views of people who currently self-injured as well as those who had stopped.

There was a paucity of evidence that looked at experience of self-harm in males. The male literature implied an expectation that men are '*stronger*' and '*able to cope*', and as a result they may resort to self-harm as an expression of their underlying emotions. There was also a suggestion from the literature that men tend to injure themselves more severely and are more likely to display public and violent self-harm, but due to the small numbers of studies available these findings need to be replicated in future research. There were only two studies that looked at the experience of self-harm in males; both of these included a small sample size of fewer than ten participants.

Access, engagement and barriers to services
Although there was considerable variation in the literature, service users' experiences of services are predominantly negative in nature. Service users reported poor access to services including delayed referral for psychosocial assessment and long waiting

lists for therapy. Service users reported feeling frustrated when organising their own aftercare because often they could not reach services through the telephone numbers provided. Health and social care professionals should ensure that people who self-harm (including children and young people, older adults, adults from black and minority ethnic groups and people with mild learning disability) have access to the full range of assessment and services.

Service users face problems with regard to communication with professionals due to inadequate sharing of information by medical staff. Individuals were not given the opportunity to be involved in decision-making about their treatment because little information was shared. This informed the recommendation that health and social care professionals should ensure that service users are fully involved in decision-making about their care, and that they foster service users' autonomy wherever possible. Service users reported a lack of rapport in their relationships with healthcare professionals and poor continuity of care. There were seven studies that highlighted these specific experiences, but care needs to be taken when interpreting these results as the sample size ranged from three participants to 84. Nevertheless, health and social care professionals should maintain continuity of therapeutic relationships wherever possible, and aim to develop a supportive and engaging relationship with people who self-harm.

Experience of treatment

The evidence suggested that the use of an empathetic, non-judgemental approach by practitioners may be associated with a more positive experience of assessment and treatment by service users. The importance of the therapeutic relationship was echoed in a total of eight studies of which the sample size ranged from only three to 76 participants, most of whom were women from a wide variety of different settings. It was also apparent from the findings that the opportunity to talk was a vital aspect of aftercare for many service users, but not all. This finding is supported by 12 studies of which the total sample size ranged from three to 89 participants, with the majority having a small-to-medium sample size recruited from a variety of settings. The population comprised a mixture of males and females, but was mostly young females between 8 and 60 years old and included those who self-injured and self-poisoned. This suggested that there was more evidence to support the importance of developing trusting and supportive relationships with people who self-harm.

Service users emphasised the need for professionals to discuss the risks and benefits associated with various medications in order for them to make a more informed decision. This finding is supported by four studies, which were conducted in a variety of non-UK settings. The number of participants ranged from three to 12 participants and included a mixture of males and females; however, they were predominantly young females. This finding might not be applicable to the UK.

Social support

Social support in the form of community support groups, support from family and friends and website support groups appeared to be important for people who self-harm as feelings of isolation, low self-esteem and alienation are very common among this group. However, these voluntary support groups and websites may be destructive if not well moderated and managed. It should be noted that this possible limitation of support groups came from the view of one individual who attended a voluntary support group a number of years ago. There were a total of eight studies that examined the importance of social support for people who self-harm with a sample size ranging from six to 89 participants, including a mixture of males and females with ages ranging from 14 to 44 years. These were conducted in a wide variety of different settings and included those who self-poisoned and self-injured. Health and social care professionals could offer advice about local and national resources regarding additional support for people who self-harm.

Overall, there is a lack of evidence examining young people's experiences of self-harm and their experiences of care. It should also be noted that most of the evidence examines the experiences of those who self-injure rather than those who self-poison, and thus the findings may not generalise to this population.

Carers' experiences were reported in a total of seven studies, but in some the sample size was very small with a range of six to 72 participants. Many parents felt excluded from their children's care planning and treatment. Carers highlighted the need for more information about suicidal behaviour in young people, skills for parenting and advice on managing further incidences. Therefore, when carers are involved in supporting the service user, health and social care professionals should provide written and verbal information on self-harm as well as information on how to support the person. Similar to service users, carers highlighted the lack of continuity of care and specifically the long duration spent waiting for CAMHS appointments. Finally, many carers found carer support networks and other forms of social support to be helpful in coping with their distress. Health and social care professionals can also support carers by providing information about carer support groups, and provide information and contacts in case of a crisis. It is important to note, however, that the majority of the carer literature focused on parents (especially mothers) of young people (in particular young women) and thus these findings may not generalise to other types of carers or service users. Moreover, these findings may not apply to parents of people who self-harm who have not come to the attention of services. Where appropriate, health and social care professionals should ask directly whether the service user wants their families or carers to be involved, subject to the service users' consent and right to confidentiality.

Healthcare professionals' attitudes, knowledge and experience
A total of 16 studies reported findings on healthcare professionals' attitudes, knowledge and experience, with sample sizes ranging from four to 290 participants and a mean sample of 83. Caution must be taken when interpreting the findings of these studies because they were mostly drawn from convenience samples and of the few that reported response rates, these ranged from only 12 to 64%. However, the healthcare professionals in the studies came from a wide variety of professional backgrounds and most included a mixture of male and female staff. The attitudes of staff in the literature reviewed were predominantly negative in nature. People who self-harm were often described by staff as 'attention seekers' and a difficult group to work with.

The literature also highlighted the emotional and psychological impact that working with this group can have on staff members. Some staff members felt that seeing the physical effects of self-harm were distressing and many reported anxiety, frustration and negativity when working with people who self-harm. This is supported by four studies, but the sample size was typically small ranging from nine to 14 healthcare professionals. Caution in interpreting these findings must be exercised because the settings varied widely, with one study being conducted with healthcare professionals in a medium secure unit for people with mild to moderate learning disabilities who self-injure.

Finally, health and social care professionals, service users, and families and carers all highlighted the lack of training and education on self-harm provided to professionals, and professionals expressed a need for continual support. This led to the GDG making a recommendation that all health and social care professionals should be trained in the process of caring for people who self-harm, which includes assessment, treatment and management. They should have routine access to supervision and support. In particular, they should consider the emotional impact of self-harm on both the professional and their capacity to practice competently and empathetically.

4.6   RECOMMENDATIONS

4.6.1   Clinical practice recommendations

Working with people who self-harm

4.6.1.1   Health and social care professionals working with people who self-harm should:
- aim to develop a trusting, supportive and engaging relationship with them
- be aware of the stigma and discrimination sometimes associated with self-harm, both in the wider society and the health service, and adopt a non-judgemental approach
- ensure that people are fully involved in decision-making about their treatment and care
- aim to foster people's autonomy and independence wherever possible
- maintain continuity of therapeutic relationships wherever possible
- ensure that information about episodes of self-harm is communicated sensitively to other team members.

4.6.1.2   Health and social care professionals who work with people who self-harm should be:
- familiar with local and national resources, as well as organisations and websites that offer information and/or support for people who self-harm, and
- able to discuss and provide advice about access to these resources.

Access to services

4.6.1.3   Children and young people who self-harm should have access to the full range of treatments and services recommended in this guideline within child and adolescent mental health services (CAMHS).

106

4.6.1.4 Ensure that children, young people and adults from black and minority ethnic groups who self-harm have the same access to services as other people who self-harm based on clinical need and that services are culturally appropriate.

4.6.1.5 When language is a barrier to accessing or engaging with services for people who self-harm, provide them with:
- information in their preferred language and in an accessible format
- psychological or other interventions, where needed, in their preferred language
- independent interpreters.

Self-harm and learning disabilities

4.6.1.6 People with a mild learning disability who self-harm should have access to the same age-appropriate services as other people covered by this guideline.

4.6.1.7 When self-harm in people with a mild learning disability is managed jointly by mental health and learning disability services, use the Care Programme Approach (CPA).

4.6.1.8 People with a moderate or severe learning disability and a history of self-harm should be referred as a priority for assessment and treatment conducted by a specialist in learning disabilities services.

Families, carers and significant others[8]

4.6.1.9 Ask the person who self-harms whether they would like their family, carers or significant others[8] to be involved in their care. Subject to the person's consent and right to confidentiality, encourage the family, carers or significant others to be involved where appropriate.

4.6.1.10 When families, carers or significant others[8] are involved in supporting a person who self-harms:
- offer written and verbal information on self-harm and its management, including how families, carers and significant others[7] can support the person
- offer contact numbers and information about what to do and whom to contact in a crisis
- offer information, including contact details, about family and carer support groups and voluntary organisations, and help families, carers or significant others[8] to access these.
- inform them of their right to a formal carer's assessment of their own physical and mental health needs, and how to access this.

4.6.1.11 CAMHS professionals who work with young people who self-harm should balance the developing autonomy and capacity of the young person with perceived risks and the responsibilities and views of parents or carers.

---

[8]'Significant other' refers not just to a partner but also to friends and any person the service user considers to be important to them.

Training and supervision for health and social care professionals

4.6.1.12   Health and social care professionals who work with people who self-harm (including children and young people) should be:
- trained in the assessment, treatment and management of self-harm and
- educated about the stigma and discrimination usually associated with self-harm and the need to avoid judgemental attitudes[9].

4.6.1.13   Health and social care professionals who provide training about self-harm should:
- involve people who self-harm in the planning and delivery of training
- ensure that training specifically aims to improve the quality and experience of care for people who self-harm
- assess the effectiveness of training using service user feedback as an outcome measure[9].

4.6.1.14   Routine access to senior colleagues for supervision, consultation and support should be provided for health and social care professionals who work with people who self-harm. Consideration should be given of the emotional impact of self-harm on the professional and their capacity to practice competently and empathically[9].

Managing endings and supporting transitions

4.6.1.15   Anticipate that the ending of treatment, services or relationships, as well as transitions from one service to another, can provoke strong feelings and increase the risk of self-harm, and:
- Plan in advance these changes with the person who self-harms and provide additional support, if needed, with clear contingency plans should crises occur.
- Record plans for transition to another service and share them with other health and social care professionals involved.
- Give copies to the service user and their family, carers or significant others if this is agreed with the service user.

4.6.1.16   CAMHS and adult health and social care professionals should work collaboratively to minimise any potential negative effect of transferring young people from CAMHS to adult services.
- Time the transfer to suit the young person, even if it takes place after they reach the age of 18 years.
- Continue treatment in CAMHS beyond 18 years if there is a realistic possibility that this may avoid the need for referral to adult mental health services.

4.6.1.17   Mental health trusts should work with CAMHS to develop local protocols to govern arrangements for the transition of young people from CAMHS to adult services, as described in this guideline.

---

[9]This recommendation also appears in Section 5.5 where the data regarding training are presented.

5   TRAINING

5.1   INTRODUCTION

Until about 30 years ago (Hawton *et al.*, 1979), there was little training in the management of self-harm offered to healthcare professionals in mental health, and still less to healthcare professionals in acute hospitals or other services. In many services, the only 'training' available was experiential 'on the job' training. Typically, responsibility for assessing people who had harmed themselves fell to the most junior trainee psychiatrists, who would receive little supervision or support. These inexperienced trainees would often face people who were in extreme distress and who posed difficult management problems. Within mainstream mental health services there was little training on offer to healthcare professionals who had to care for people with an ongoing mental health problem who continued to harm themselves.

A similar situation also developed in acute hospitals where people who required hospital treatment as a result of their self-harm received much of their care from junior doctors and nurses, often with little support from their more senior colleagues.

Over the past 15 years a wider range of clinical disciplines have become involved in working with people who self-harm. There has been a significant growth in liaison psychiatry services, which often have assumed responsibility for delivering care to this group. In some areas, the local crisis services take this role. The development of these new services has generally been associated with improved supervision, support and training of the healthcare professionals involved. The publication of the guideline for the management of self-harm in the first 48 hours (NICE, 2004a; NCCMH, 2004) highlighted the need for improved training of healthcare professionals. It also stimulated efforts to improve services, such as the project 'Improving Services to People who Self-harm' (Palmer *et al.*, 2006). Specific training for health and social care professionals who work with people who self-harm remains inconsistent. In this section, studies were reviewed when they were directly related to training of healthcare professionals who work in this area, or healthcare professionals who work in emergency departments.

5.1.1   Evidence search

A comprehensive search was developed based on the clinical question, 'Does the provision of healthcare professionals' training improve outcomes?'

An existing systematic review on healthcare professionals' attitudes (Saunders *et al.*, 2011) was identified and studies that were relevant were also reviewed. Information on the search can be found in Table 5.

Table 5: Databases searched and inclusion/exclusion criteria for clinical evidence

Electronic databases	CENTRAL, CINAHL, EMBASE, MEDLINE, PsycINFO
Date searched	Database inception to 25 January 2011
Study design	RCTs
Population	Healthcare professionals who work with people who self-harm
Outcomes	Healthcare professionals' attitudes, knowledge and psychological impact. Also service user outcomes.

5.1.2   Studies considered

A systematic review carried out by Saunders and colleagues (2011) examined attitudes, experience and training needs of healthcare professionals who come into contact with and treat people who self-harm. This review included both quantitative and qualitative studies, and the systematic search was conducted between 1971 and March 2009. Saunders and colleagues (2011) identified 11 studies relevant to training. From this, ten studies (BOTEGA2007 [Botega *et al.*, 2007], CRAWFORD1998 [Crawford *et al.*, 1998], GASK2006 [Gask *et al.*, 2006], HOLDSWORTH2001 [Holdsworth *et al.*, 2001], MAY2001 [May, 2001], MCALLISTER2009 [McAllister *et al.*, 2009], PATTERSON2007, SAMUELSSON2002 [Samuelsson & Asberg, 2002], TRELOAR2008B [Treloar & Lewis, 2008b], TURNBULL1997 [Turnbull & Chalder, 1997]) were selected for inclusion within the current guideline. One study was excluded because it was conducted in a non-UK setting. Further information about both included and excluded studies can be found in Appendix 15b.

In addition to the review, a search was conducted based on the clinical question. A total of 1,497 references were retrieved from the search. The search identified 14 primary studies which were not already included in the Saunders and colleagues' (2011) review. From this, eight studies were included (APPLEBY2000 [Appleby *et al.*, 2000], BERLIM2007 [Berlim *et al.*, 2007], CHAN2009 [Chan *et al.*, 2009], GASK2008 [Gask *et al.*, 2008], MORRISS1999 [Morriss *et al.*, 1999], MORRISS2005 [Morriss *et al.*, 2005], PFAFF2001 [Pfaff *et al.*, 2001], WALKER1996 [Walker & Osgood, 1996]) but none of them were RCTs.

Six studies were excluded based on reading the full text because they related to training in non-clinical populations or training in a non-clinical setting (that is, prisons) or the training was carried out in a non-UK setting. See Appendix 15b for the full references and study characteristics.

Within the included studies, the focus of training is identified as training focused on knowledge, attitudes and emotional impact of working with individuals who self-harm (Section 5.2) or training focused on risk and needs assessment (Section 5.3).

The GDG concluded that it was necessary to distinguish between self-harm training for general medical healthcare professionals, mental health professionals and healthcare professionals who work in emergency department because their level of existing training would vary significantly and may not be comparable across groups. Also, despite training for healthcare professionals who work in emergency departments being more related to the short-term management of self-harm, this group also deal with repeat presentations of self-harm in emergency settings and, therefore, it is important to examine the impact of training on them. The results from studies have therefore been divided, initially according the type of training (knowledge and attitudes versus risk assessment) and within that by the healthcare professionals group who were the target of the training. The initial results refer to the impact of training on knowledge and attitudes (Section 5.2) and the second set of results refer to the impact of risk and needs assessment training (Section 5.3).

Fifteen studies that looked at training utilised an uncontrolled study design that reported the self-report score change before and after training. Four studies used a control group. It is important to be cautious in the interpretation of results of studies where no control group has been used because it is difficult to be clear about the explanation of the results, given the high possibility of the presence of selection and performance bias. These studies were reviewed narratively.

5.2 IMPACT OF TRAINING ON HEALTHCARE PROFESSIONALS' KNOWLEDGE AND ATTITUDES

5.2.1 The impact of training: non-mental health professionals

Impact of training on knowledge, understanding and skills: non-mental health professionals

The impact of training on knowledge, understanding and skills in non-mental health professionals was examined by four studies (BERLIM2007, BOTEGA2007, CHAN2009, WALKER1996). BERLIM2007 conducted a 3-hour training session, comprising oral presentations and group discussions, which emphasised the acquisition of knowledge about suicidal behaviour in clinical and non-clinical hospital staff, as measured by the Suicide Behaviours and Attitudes Questionnaire (SBAQ). Following training, both sets of participants felt more capable of helping individuals who attempted suicide (clinical staff pre-training score was 5.56 [SD 3.1] and post-test score was 6.8 [SD 2.6], $p < 0.0001$; non-clinical staff pre-training score was 5.3 [SD 3.2] and post-training score was 6.95 [SD 2.5], $p = 0.001$), and reported an improved ability to perceive suicidal behaviours (clinical staff pre-training score was 5.08 [SD 2.9] and post-test score was 6.6 [SD 2.5], $p < 0.0001$; non-clinical staff pre-training score was 3.68 [SD 2.9] and post-training score was 5.49 [SD 2.9], $p = 0.001$). Healthcare professionals also felt less helpless when facing suicidal individuals (clinical staff pre-training score was 5.54 [SD 3.0] and post-test score was 4.49 [SD 2.6], $p = 0.002$; non-clinical staff pre-training score was 4.9 [SD 3.2] and post-training score was 3.38 [SD 3.1], $p = 0.005$) and were less anxious about enquiring about a service user's suicidality (clinical staff pre-training score was 4.15 [SD 3.2] and post-test score was 2.29 [SD 2.7], $p < 0.0001$; non-clinical staff pre-training score was 4.58 [SD 3.1] and post-training score was 2.54 [SD 3.1], $p = 0.001$). Another area of knowledge improvement, identified by the authors, was the understanding of the link between suicidality and mental disorders. Before training, participants in both groups estimated that less than 50% of suicidal service users were experiencing a mental disorder. Training improved this figure to approximately 75% for the clinical personnel and 67% for the non-clinical personnel. This finding was supported by similar results from BOTEGA2007 who found that participants' estimations of the presence of mental disorders within those who died by suicide increased significantly, from 40 to 60%. The impact of training on confidence was examined in a qualitative interview by CHAN2009. They found that, following training, participants had acquired an increased awareness of suicide and were more confident in caring for service users with suicide risk. The participants agreed that the programme had helped them to re-examine their existing practices and gain new perspectives on the concept of holistic care.

Additionally, after participating in the education programme the participants considered themselves more competent in assessing people with suicide risk. CHAN2009 also found an increase in knowledge about suicidal behaviour; however, this was not statistically significant at post-training or 6-month follow-up.

WALKER1996 focused on the development and effectiveness of a 3-hour suicide prevention training programme for long-term care staff working with older people. The outcomes measures assessed included knowledge of suicide and suicide prevention, and healthcare professionals' use of prevention practices. The overall mean pre-training score (12.49 [SD 3.9]) was statistically lower than the overall mean post-training score (17.44 [SD 3.17]) to a p-value of $p < 0.001$. Authors reported statistically significant gains on 15 of the 24 items on the knowledge subscale of the questionnaire; however, they provided no specific data about these items. Reported areas of improvement included identification of the group with the highest suicide rate, identifying the meaning of 'suicidal ideation' and the most common method of death by suicide among older people. Two areas of confusion for participants, even at post-training assessment, were the differences between primary and secondary interventions and the link between fear of Alzheimer's disease and suicide attempts. In terms of the influence that training had on clinical practice, the overall mean pre-training score (42.65 [SD 17.8]) was statistically lower than the overall mean post-training score (42.07 [SD 17.82]) to a p-value of $p < 0.05$. Additionally, the authors reported statistically significant improvements on two out of the 19 items. These were an increased likelihood of asking a depressed person if he or she is thinking about suicide ($p < 0.001$) and an increased likelihood of taking suicide threats by older people very seriously ($p < 0.01$); however, again, there were no raw data reported and this is only narratively explained. Even after the training, however, healthcare professionals were still unlikely to utilise assessment tools, including the Life-Satisfaction Quiz, the Depression Scale and the Michigan Alcoholism Screening Test – Geriatric version (WALKER1996).

Impact of training on attitudes: non-mental health professionals
An assessment of the impact of training on attitudes was examined by four studies
(BERLIM2007, BOTEGA2007, CHAN2009, WALKER1996).

CHAN2009 found there were statistically significant, positive changes post-training
in terms of attitudes towards suicide on the overall Suicide Opinion Questionnaire score
(pre-training mean was 155.5 [SD 10.90], 6-month post-training mean was 159.1 [SD
13.71], p = 0.006) as well as the Social Disintegration subscale (pre-training mean was
32.46 [SD 3.97], 6-month post-training mean was 33.83 [SD 4.40], p = 0.003) and
Personal Defect subscale (pre-training mean was 37.37 [SD 3.28], 6-month post-training
mean was 37.85 [SD 3.53], p = 0.035). Within the qualitative findings, participants
spoke of changing their attitude to suicide and gaining a new perspective on care, noting
that the programme had helped to clarify myths surrounding suicide and that these clar-
ifications led to changes in their attitude towards suicide. WALKER1996 found that
scores on 14 of the 21 items on the Attitude subscale demonstrated a statistically significant shift in a positive direction, with the overall attitude shift being significant to the
level of p < 0.05 (pre-training mean was 43.4 [SD 7.6]; post-training mean was 40.56
[SD 9.8]). Following training, participants were more likely to recognise the importance
of understanding the differences between male and female coping styles (p = 0.05),
more aware of the relationship between the signs of dementia and the risk of suicide
(p = 0.05), more likely to recognise that older people react to life events in a different
way (p < 0.05), more likely to appreciate the importance for older people to find new
roles to replace people they have lost (p < 0.05) and less likely to believe that hopelessness is a 'normal' emotion in older people (p < 0.001). As noted before, however, these
p-values were only reported narratively and there were no raw data available in the study.

Two studies (BERLIM2007, BOTEGA2007) used the SBAQ to measure attitude
change. BERLIM2007 found that attitude change was significantly improved for both
clinical and non-clinical staff within the Feelings Toward the Suicidal Patient subscale
(clinical staff pre-training score was 4.5 [SD 1.7] and post-test score was 2.7 [SD 1.7],
p < 0.0001; non-clinical staff pre-training score was 4.31 [SD 2.0] and post-training
score was 2.72 [SD 2.1], p < 0.0001) and Professional Capacity subscale (clinical staff
pre-training score was 4.72 [SD 2.2] and post-test score was 6.16 [SD 2.0], p < 0.0001;
non-clinical staff pre-training score was 3.84 [SD 2.15] and post-training score was 5.46
[SD 2.02], p < 0.0001), but not for the Right to Suicide subscale (clinical staff pre-training score was 6.55 [SD 1.40] and post-test score was 6.70 [SD 1.41], p > 0.01; non-
clinical staff pre-training score was 5.77 [SD 1.30] and post-training score was 6.05 [SD
1.53], p = 0.001). A similar result was also found by BOTEGA2007, and the attitude
changes remained significant at both 3- and 6-month follow-up.

5.2.2 The impact of training: mental health professionals

Impact of training on knowledge, understanding and skills: mental health
professionals
The impact of training on knowledge, understanding and skills in mental health professionals was examined by three studies (GASK2006, GASK2008, SAMUELSSON2002).

SAMUELSSON2002 conducted a 36-hour suicide prevention training session that involved lectures, discussion and case study vignettes. They found an improvement in knowledge about self-harm following training, demonstrated by a significant increase in participants' estimation of suicide risk for two service users who were featured in the training vignettes (case study 1: pre-training mean was 44.5, post-training mean was 63.3, p < 0.001; case study 2: pre-training mean was 78.3; post-training mean was 87.5, p < 0.01). Additionally, before the programme, 20% of the healthcare professionals did not think psychiatric care was needed for attempted suicide patients compared with 2% after training.

The impact of training on confidence was examined by GASK2006, who evaluated the effects of the Skills Training On Risk Management (STORM) programme. They found statistically significant improvements in healthcare professionals' confidence on all four questions both immediately after training (Item 1: pre-training mean was 54.99 [SD 21.59], post-training mean was 70.56 [SD 15.89], p = 0.00; Item 2: pre-training mean was 52.94 [SD 21.32], post-training mean was 69.27 [SD 0.89], p = 0.00; Item 3: pre-training mean was 59.57 [SD 21.88], post-training mean was 74.11 [SD 0.83], p = 0.00; Item 4: pre-training mean was 52.65 [SD 22.00], post-training mean was 69.56 [SD 0.88], p = 0.00) and at 4-month follow-up (Item 1: pre-training mean was 60.06 [SD 19.70], post-training mean was 68.99 [SD 1.54], p = 0.00; Item 2: pre-training mean was 55.92 [SD 21.25], post-training mean was 68.99 [SD 1.54], p = 0.00; Item 3: pre-training mean was 63.62 [SD 21.40], post-training mean was 74.42 [SD 16.22], p = 0.00; Item 4: pre-training mean was 55.11 [SD 21.68], post-training mean was 70.24 [SD 18.63], p = 0.00), as measured by a visual analogue scale. This was subsequently validated by qualitative results from a semi-structured interview. Participants reported specific ways in which the training had altered their clinical practice, predominantly in terms of being able to communicate more effectively with people who have attempted suicide.

Despite the above positive results in terms of confidence and clinical practice, there was no impact of training on skill level among healthcare professionals, as measured by the Suicide Intervention Response Inventory (SIRI), either immediately after training or at 4-month follow-up (GASK2006).

The impact of training on confidence was also examined in a study carried out by GASK2008, who evaluated the effects of the STORM programme on 203 healthcare professionals and service users in the UK. They found that there were significant improvements in confidence of the participants involved. Confidence scores increased significantly from baseline and immediately after training (Item 1: pre-training mean was 47.43 [SD 20.38], post-training mean was 69.62 [SD 14.84], p = 0.00; Item 2: pre-training mean was 35.35 [SD 19.93], post-training mean was 63.82 [SD 17.92], p = 0.00; Item 3: pre-training mean was 49.74 [SD 22.72], post-training mean was 69.66 [SD 17.34], p = 0.00; Item 4: pre-training mean was 41.17 [SD 21.19], post-training mean was 65.82 [SD 16.91], p = 0.00) and at 6-month follow-up (Item 1: pre-training mean was 51.69 [SD 21.60], post-training mean was 68.83 [SD 16.33], p = 0.00; Item 2: pre-training mean was 37.44 [SD 21.33], post-training mean was 58.05 [SD 20.07], p = 0.00; Item 3: pre-training mean was 49.95 [SD 23.14], post-training mean was 68.37 [SD 16.20], p = 0.00; Item 4: pre-training mean was 42.75

[SD 21.95], post-training mean was 65.98 [SD 17.16], p = 0.00), as measured by a visual analogue scale. This was subsequently validated by qualitative results from a semi-structured interview. The interviews also showed that participants felt that the training addressed attitudes and knowledge in a non-threatening way.

Impact of training on attitudes: mental health professionals
Five studies considered the effect of training on healthcare professionals' attitudes. PATTERSON2007 aimed to measure how attitudes of antipathy towards individuals who self-harm change following attendance on a 15-week academic-level course about self-harm and suicide. The participants were 69 qualified healthcare professionals (mainly mental health nurses), and antipathy was measured using the Self-harm Antipathy Scale. They found that immediately after training, healthcare professionals' level of antipathy towards service users who self-harmed was reduced. At 18-month follow-up, this reduction had continued, and the total reduction from baseline was approximately 20%. A control group was also used in this study and the intervention group demonstrated significantly lower antipathy scores at 18-month follow-up. The results from this study are particularly encouraging due to the long-term follow-up that was conducted after the completion of the course and the use of a control group. However, it should be noted that there were no details of the levels of significance for much of the data and the report of significant findings is based on the authors' description.

SAMUELSSON2002 examined the attitudes of psychiatric personnel towards service users who had attempted suicide before and after a training programme in psychiatric suicide prevention. After the training programme, there was a significant overall improvement on the Understanding of Suicide Attempt Patients Scale (pre-training mean was 19.8, post-training mean was 17.1, p < 0.01). However, there were no significant differences in understanding and willingness to care in the three case vignettes.

An evaluation of the STORM training programme (GASK2006) found a statistically significant improvement in scores on ten out of the 14 items of the Attitudes to Suicide Prevention Scale immediately after the training. Of these ten items, seven of them had maintained significant improvement at 4-month follow-up (GASK2006). As well as information about the impact of the training, the study also assessed the healthcare professionals' attitudes to the training programme itself. The key findings related to the relevance of the training to different healthcare professionals levels (that is, qualified and unqualified) and the levels of engagement in the training from different individuals. Some suggested that the training was more appropriate for qualified healthcare professionals given that, in clinical practice, unqualified healthcare professionals would not conduct formal risk assessments. There was also some disappointment expressed regarding senior healthcare professionals' unwillingness to engage in the role plays and lead by example.

The authors postulated that this feedback may have been due to the culture of the trust in which the training took place; however, this type of resistance to training may exist in other settings. Findings also related to the impact on clinical practice. With regard to positive views, risk assessment and crisis management modules were highly valued. On the contrary, there was also a viewpoint from some experienced workers that much of the training was being carried out in clinical practice already.

APPLEBY2000 conducted a STORM training programme to evaluate its impact on attitudes in three healthcare settings: mental health, primary care and A&E departments in the UK. There was an overall reduction in negative attitudes in all three professional groups; however, the results were only statistically significant for the A&E department staff, who had the most negative attitudes before training.

5.2.3 The impact of training: healthcare professionals working in emergency departments

Impact of training on knowledge, understanding and skills: healthcare
professionals in emergency departments
Four studies investigated the effect of training on knowledge, understanding and skill developments (HOLDSWORTH2001, MCALLISTER2009, TRELOAR2008B, TURNBULL1997) in healthcare professionals working in emergency departments. TURNBULL1997 conducted training with 37 emergency department and ward healthcare professionals on the nature of suicide and self-harm. Of the 37 who participated in the training, 26 participants completed post-training questionnaires. They found that the scores on a self-harm and suicide knowledge questionnaire were significantly higher following training (63% correct answers) compared with the scores prior to training (29% correct responses). Sample topic areas in the questionnaire included epidemiology and risk factors.

However, a weakness of these results is that the authors did not identify the specific areas of knowledge which were improved, thus making it difficult to identify areas of training that are useful. A study by HOLDSWORTH2001 provided a series of workshops for emergency department healthcare professionals aimed to improve healthcare professionals' risk assessment for suicide and self-harm, and their ability to provide effective short-term management of those risks. Self-reports from nurses indicated that nearly all felt that training had increased their knowledge and skill base in relation to self-harm and suicide. Improvements in knowledge included the relationship between completed suicide and non-fatal self-harm, repetition of self-harm and poor problem-solving skills, and reasons for individuals presentation at hospital and subsequent refusal of treatment. Improvements in skills included being able to elicit intent from the service users, as well as working with the carers to provide appropriate responses to the self-harm. It is important to note that these findings are based on self-report and were not assessed in any other way. Although it is encouraging that healthcare professionals felt more knowledgeable and skilful after they completed training, these findings were not validated by a knowledge or skill-based questionnaire, casting doubt on the results reported. However, further improvements, which were measured by a pre- and post-test assessment, were also identified in the areas of coping and strain felt by healthcare professionals. They revealed that, despite no alteration in the amount of stress placed on healthcare professionals by self-harm presentations, the perceived demand of these cases was reduced in almost half the participants. Similarly, there was an increase in self-confidence, and ability to cope and engage with people who self-harm, following training.

TRELOAR2008B examined the effects of training in mental health and emergency medicine practitioners who attended a clinical education programme on borderline personality disorder and attitudes towards working with people who self-harm. Training included: research findings on attitudes to borderline personality disorder, the prevalence, diagnostic criteria, aetiological factors, rates of self-harm and suicide and therapeutic responses to borderline personality disorder. They found that specific subscales, which related to skill acquisition, demonstrated the strongest impact of training. These included confidence in assessment and referral, and ability to deal effectively with service users with borderline personality disorder. In comparison, the effect of training on empathic approach and knowledge of hospital regulations was minimal.

MCALLISTER2009 also report on the positive effect of training on healthcare professionals' ability to respond appropriately to people who self-harm. The training involved 2 hours of interactive discussion, focused on understanding self-harm, followed by 1 hour of training in solution-focused nursing, which works to help healthcare professionals learn to engage with, support and encourage optimism in people who self-harm. Participants felt that the understanding gained from training had allowed them to effectively alter their response and coping styles when dealing with people who self-harm. This was demonstrated through an increased use of strategic assessment and proactive response skills, as well as improved communication ability. A key element underlying the changes in healthcare professionals' behaviour was the shift from focusing on the present situation (that is, injury containment and trying to provide an immediate cure) to focusing on the long-term (that is, the overall complexities of the behaviour, its cyclical nature and strategies to alter it). It appears that training has a positive impact on knowledge about self-harm and suicide both within the wider, clinical population and within specific groups (people with borderline personality disorder). However, none of these studies had a long follow-up; therefore, this effect may not have been maintained after training.

Impact of training on attitudes: healthcare professionals in accident and emergency departments
The effect of training on healthcare professionals' attitudes was examined in five studies (CRAWFORD1998, MAY2001, MCALLISTER2009, TRELOAR2008B, TURNBULL1997). MCALLISTER2009 found that, following training, nurses from an emergency setting reported a positive attitudinal shift towards individuals who self-harm. In particular, participants felt that the training had highlighted the complexity of self-harm and that this, in turn, reduced the likelihood of them dismissing the service user's care needs or placing blame on them. Participants also recognised how important it is to ensure that service users feel that they can ask for help and that they do not perceive themselves as a burden. This positive finding was backed up by CRAWFORD1998 who found that, following training,

there was a decrease in the number of healthcare professionals who believed that 'patients who had a past history of repeated self-harm were less likely to kill themselves than those who had only tried once'. However, the psychometric properties of the questionnaire utilised to test the knowledge and attitudes of healthcare professionals has not been tested, which casts some uncertainty on the findings reported.

TRELOAR2008B examined the effect of a borderline personality disorder education programme on healthcare professionals' attitudes about self-harm within this specific population, and found an overall improvement in attitudes, with a small to medium effect size. Authors identified some demographic information which potentially moderates the effects of training. They found that female healthcare professionals were more likely to experience a positive attitudinal shift following training compared with male healthcare professionals. The same was found for healthcare professionals who had previously engaged in undergraduate and post-graduate university training compared with those who had been trained in hospital. Individuals who worked with people who self-harm on a regular basis (that is, at least fortnightly) and had less than 15 years' experience were also more likely to benefit from training.

However, not all studies found a significant influence of training on attitudes. MAY2001 used a controlled study design to assess whether the attitudes of emergency department healthcare professionals towards suicidal behaviour could be improved through the use of poster displays and an information pack. The rationale being that these education tools are suitably flexible alternatives to formal training because they take into account the time constraints and practical difficulties of offering this to healthcare professionals who work in busy emergency departments. Results demonstrated an improvement in attitudes for the questionnaire subscale Morality and Mental Illness, which contained five out of the 16 questions in the outcome measure. However, there was no significant difference in post-intervention attitudes between the control and experimental groups in terms of the other outcome measure subscales or the questionnaire as a whole. This indicates that, overall, the educational tools had no effect on improving attitudes. Within the discussion, the author suggests that a 'hands-on' method may be a more appropriate education technique.

Results from a study carried out by TURNBULL1997 also indicate that no alteration took place between pre-training and post-training attitudes within healthcare professionals who work in emergency departments; however, authors suggest that this may be a result of a high attitudinal score at the baseline assessment, therefore leaving little room for improvement. Again, the training format may explain the ineffectiveness of the programme because it provided little opportunity for active learning, discussion or relation of the information in the lecture to personal experience (PATTERSON2007). In general, the effect of training on attitudes was positive.

Although two of the studies found that training resulted in a positive shift in attitudes, the non-significant findings from MAY2001 and TURNBULL1997 indicate that the format and method of the training may be an important consideration.

Impact of training on emotional impact: healthcare professionals in emergency departments

A frequently reported problem identified in Chapter 4 on healthcare professionals' attitudes, knowledge and experience was the emotional impact that people who self-harm had on the healthcare professionals who work with them; feelings of helplessness, anxiety and anger were repeatedly reported. Two studies looked at these negative emotions and the influence that training had on them (HOLDSWORTH2001, MCALLISTER2009). HOLDSWORTH2001 reported that training helped to decrease healthcare professionals' feelings of anxiety, helplessness and, most dramatically, irritation. However, these results should be interpreted with caution because the sample size was too small to reliably test the significance. MCALLISTER2009 found that, by shifting the treatment focus of the healthcare professionals from immediate solutions to long-term interventions, training allowed them to understand the important influence that nursing has on an individual's recovery process.

They felt that having knowledge and utilising a framework to guide care (the CARE [containment, awareness, resilience and engagement] framework model by McAllister and Walsh [2003]) allowed them to feel like they had a bigger role to play in the long-term recovery process. They also mentioned how important it is that not only individuals but all healthcare professionals both practice and adhere to a framework. This may then lead to an improvement in emergency practice.

5.3   IMPACT OF TRAINING ON CONDUCTING RISK AND NEEDS ASSESSMENT

Impact of risk assessment training: non-mental health professionals

PFAFF2001 aimed to determine the effectiveness of a training programme for GPs in recognising, assessing and managing suicide ideation in young people. Participants were assessed 6 weeks' post-workshop on their ability to improve the frequency of recognition of at-risk individuals; their frequency of enquiry about suicide ideation; their accuracy in assessing the degree of risk present; and the frequency and appropriateness of their service user management strategies. Following training, GPs' recognition rate of service users scoring above the cut-off on the Center for Epidemiological Studies Depression scale and General Health Questionnaire (- 12 item version; GHQ-12) increased significantly (by 39.5% and 48%, respectively). Moreover, post-training, GPs rated significantly higher proportions of their service users as at risk for suicide (75.5% increase). This occurred despite a lower proportion of post-workshop service users scoring above the cut-off on the Depressive Symptom Inventory Suicidality Subscale. Participants increased their level of enquiry about suicide ideation between the pre- and post-workshop audits by 32.5%, although the increase was not statistically significant. Relatively, the GPs' ability to accurately identify those service users above the cut-off on the Depressive Symptom Index Suicidality Subscale more than doubled during the post-training period. Of note is the substantial reduction of false negative cases identified by GPs between the two audit periods, with a minimal increase in false positive cases, demonstrating greater precision in detecting service users reporting suicide ideation. There was little difference between pre- and post-training samples in the proportion of participant-identified psychologically distressed service users who received follow-up clinical management. Psychologically distressed service users were significantly more likely to receive clinical management if the GP also rated them at risk for suicide. During the post-workshop phase, four fifths of the service users judged to be at risk of suicide received clinical management compared with just over half of the psychologically distressed service users deemed not at risk of suicide. The results demonstrate that enhanced recognition rates do not necessarily imply accompanying changes in service user management and this must be taken into account in future training endeavours.

Impact of risk and needs assessment training: healthcare professionals in emergency departments

CRAWFORD1998 examined the impact of a 1-hour teaching session for emergency department healthcare professionals on the quality of psychosocial assessment of service users who self-harmed, as measured by examining emergency department case notes. There was an overall improvement in the quality of the psychosocial assessment conducted by the emergency department healthcare professionals, as measured by the completeness of individuals' records. Additionally, there was a substantial increase in the numbers of healthcare professionals who felt that they had the necessary skills in the assessment and management of people who self-harm.

MORRISS1999 examined whether training via role play, modelling, video feedback and group discussion improved emergency department healthcare professionals' interview skills in suicide risk assessment, management and confidence in dealing with suicidal service users at a 1- to 2-month follow-up. Overall, the risk assessment and management skills were retained for at least 1 month after training. Neither training nor the assessment procedures themselves brought about any changes in the general interview skills of the healthcare professionals. However, there were significant improvements in risk assessment with a median score of 4 at 1-month post-training compared with a median score of 0.5 at 1-month pre-training. There were also significant improvements observed in risk management scores of the suicidal service users at 1-month post-training (median 5.8) compared with pre-training scores (median 3) but not for those who received no training. Performance was less satisfactory in relation to the management of the immediate crisis. There was an improvement in the provision of immediate support, but only one healthcare professional in each training condition removed potentially lethal weapons. There are a number of limitations that must be noted because they may alter the interpretation of the findings reported. First, the self-assessments may have overestimated the training effects of the package through a halo effect and second, the assessments made in role-played interviews may differ from those carried out in clinical practice.

Impact of risk assessment training: mixed healthcare professionals groups

McAuliffe and Perry (2007) conducted 2-day workshops of Applied Suicide Intervention Skills Training for mental health professionals, non-mental health professionals (for example, rehabilitation therapists) and healthcare professionals and students from local community mental health and social service agencies in Canada. The training programme consisted of a standardised workshop for assessing and responding to suicide risk, and aimed to provide healthcare professionals with a greater understanding of suicide and an opportunity to practice conversing with the suicidal person. The authors found there was an increase ranging from 14 to 21% in the identification of suicidal risk and a decrease in admissions, which healthcare professionals attributed to the clearer process of exploring reasons for dying, reasons for living and an increased focus on reinforcing the service user's protective factors in the community. There was also a 14.5% reduction in the average length of stay for service users admitted with suicide ideation or attempt. Furthermore, more healthcare professionals assessed their clients for suicide risk, with a 13% increase in the number of healthcare professionals who reported assessing the majority of their service users. The proportion of healthcare professionals that agreed that they had adequate ongoing training in assessment and management of service users with suicide risk increased from 30 to 80%. However only 24% 'strongly agreed' with this statement, demonstrating that suicide assessment and intervention is an area in which healthcare professionals want a great deal of ongoing educational support. Finally, informal feedback from healthcare professionals indicated that having standardised training and a common language regarding risk assessment has resulted in improved interprofessional communication.

APPLEBY2000 conducted a STORM training programme in three healthcare settings; mental health, primary care and A&E departments in the UK. The primary aims of the study were to assess the feasibility of district-wide training in the assessment and management of people at risk of suicide, and to assess the impact of training on assessment and management skills. Twenty-eight staff attending training agreed to make videotapes of interviews with suicidal 'patients' (played by actors according to predetermined vignettes). Videotapes were made pre-training and 1 to 2 months' post-training, and interview skills were rated by a psychiatrist who had been blind to whether tapes were made before or after training, according to criteria corresponding to the content of the training package. While training had a significant impact overall on skills obtained, only clinical management improved significantly post-training. The SIRI was completed on both occasions by 72 professionals; however, no differences were found between pre- and post-training scores.

A follow-up of the above study was carried out by MORRISS2005 to assess its effects on the reduction of suicide rates from 1994 to 2000. There were no significant reductions in suicide rates post-training.

5.4 FROM EVIDENCE TO RECOMMENDATIONS

The evidence surrounding training is inconclusive. Moreover, the training studies evaluated here were of poor quality and many did not have a control group. Therefore, the results are subject to many biases and the results should be interpreted with caution. In general, there may be a self-reported positive effect on healthcare professionals' knowledge, skills, attitudes and the psychological impact of suicide and self-harm. However, due to the nature of the outcome measures used there is no assessment of whether this translated into real change in healthcare professionals' behaviour and management. The small number of studies considered in this section also reduces the power of the findings.

An important aspect to consider, when interpreting the findings in the training section, is that the results from all of the training studies rely in some capacity on self-report measures and do not independently assess the effect of training on healthcare professionals. The most notable gap in this respect is the lack of service user assessment of healthcare professionals pre- and post-training, and the lack of RCTs. Therefore, although healthcare professionals generally reported a positive effect of training, it is not possible to know whether this results in actual changes in healthcare professionals' behaviour and the management they provide for their service users. Future research should consider a better quality study design (RCT), with objective outcome measures including both self-report and service users' reported outcomes.

Second, the length of follow-up used is problematic. The studies with healthcare professionals who work in emergency departments used particularly short follow-up times and, therefore, it is difficult to know the long-term impact of training programmes on knowledge, skills and attitudes, and the emotional impact of suicide and self-harm. Future research should include longer-term follow-up periods.

Third, the longer-term follow-up in the above studies demonstrates a high attrition rate that might also be differential in nature, which may lead to ascertainment bias. Also, assessments are usually performed in volunteer samples of staff who may be quite different in terms of skills, attitudes and knowledge compared with other staff who do not volunteer, which may have led to selection bias.

Finally, the format of the training varies and it is uncertain what the key element of training is. Given the differences in training models presented within the chapter, other methods for addressing the deficits in care for service users who self-harm should be considered. Investigation into the value of education and supervision would be valuable, particularly if it was guided by service user input.

On the other hand, drawing from the literature in the previous chapter, the need for some form of staff training is clearly displayed by both service users and staff, with many participants from these studies suggesting that training may lead to more positive attitudes among staff members, increased knowledge and confidence.

On the basis of the poor quality of evidence, it is not possible to make any recommendation about the particular form of training that should be provided except that using information alone, for example posters, is probably unhelpful. Given that the evidence surrounding training is inconclusive these recommendations are based on service user experience and GDG consensus.

5.4.1   Health economic evidence

No evidence on the cost effectiveness of experience of care for people who self-harm or training for healthcare professionals was identified by the systematic search of the economic literature. Details on the methods used for the systematic search of the economic literature are described in Chapter 3.

5.5   RECOMMENDATIONS

5.5.1   Clinical practice recommendations

Training and supervision for health and social care professionals

5.5.1.1   Health and social care professionals who work with people who self-harm (including children and young people) should be:
- trained in the assessment, treatment and management of self-harm and
- educated about the stigma and discrimination usually associated with self-harm and the need to avoid judgemental attitudes[10].

5.5.1.2   Health and social care professionals who provide training about self-harm should:
- involve people who self-harm in the planning and delivery of training
- ensure that training specifically aims to improve the quality and experience of care for people who self-harm
- assess the effectiveness of training using service user feedback as an outcome measure.[10]

5.5.1.3   Routine access to senior colleagues for supervision, consultation and support should be provided for health and social care professionals who work with people who self-harm. Consideration should be given of the emotional impact of self-harm on the professional and their capacity to practice competently and empathically.[10]

5.5.2   Research recommendations

5.5.2.1   The effectiveness of training compared with no formal training in assessment and management for healthcare professionals who work with people who self-harm

For healthcare professionals who work with people who self-harm, does the provision of training in assessment and management improve outcomes compared with no additional specialist training?

A well-powered RCT should examine the effectiveness of training. Researchers should consider the format and length of training. The outcomes chosen should include both healthcare professionals' and service users' evaluation of the training, and the effect on subsequent knowledge, attitude and behavioural changes. It should include longer-term follow-up of 12 months or more.

---

[10]This recommendation also appears in Section 4.6 where the data regarding the experience of care is presented.

Training

Why this is important

Current studies of training have been limited in their assessment of changes in health-care professionals' knowledge, attitudes and behaviour. Crucially, no studies have examined whether training has any impact on service users' experience and outcomes. Healthcare professionals frequently report that treating service users who self-harm is challenging and they are likely to find training helpful because it provides an opportunity to think about and understand this aspect of their work. Studies to date, however, have not looked beyond these initial outcomes of training, which are more indicative of satisfaction with training rather than addressing whether training has had an impact on practice, service user experience and outcomes. Future research should consider a wider range of outcomes – for example, attitudes, changes in assessment practice, changes in interventions and improvement in service user experience and outcomes. The longer-term impact of training should also be assessed.

6 PSYCHOSOCIAL ASSESSMENT

6.1 INTRODUCTION

The term 'psychosocial assessment' as used in this guideline refers to a comprehensive assessment including an evaluation of needs and risk. The assessment of needs is designed to identify those personal psychological and environmental (social) factors that might explain an act of self-harm. This assessment should lead to a formulation from which a management plan can be developed. This chapter aims to undertake a thorough review of risk and protective factors, and the utility of risk assessment scales. The practical aspects of conducting a psychosocial assessment are also discussed.

6.2 RISK AND PROTECTIVE FACTORS

6.2.1 Introduction

Many researchers have investigated risk factors for self-harm (Fliege *et al.*, 2009; Gratz, 2003; Owens *et al.*, 2002) and for suicide (McLean *et al.*, 2008; Nock *et al.*, 2008). However, these studies do not often distinguish risk factors for a first episode of self-harm from those risk factors for repetition of self-harm. Knowledge of these factors can provide an understanding of the characteristics of those who repeat self-harm or who go on to die by suicide. There will be an overlap between individual risk factors and risk assessment scales (see Section 6.3) which may include combinations of risk factors. Aside from traditional risk factors, those factors that may protect against repeated self-harm or suicide are also considered. Establishing causal relations between risk factors and outcome is difficult because many studies have been observational. In addition there is often a strong association between different risk factors, and measuring one may be a proxy measure for another. This section, however, is aimed at giving guidance on factors to consider in a clinical assessment and not for predicting risk.

6.2.2 Clinical review protocol

The review protocol including the review questions, information about the databases searched and the eligibility criteria used for this section of the guideline can be found in Appendix 8 (further information about the search strategy can be found in Appendix 9). Information on the review protocol can be found in Table 6.

Table 6: Clinical review protocol for the review of case identification tools

Component	Description
Review question	What are the risk and protective factors among people who self-harm that predict outcomes?
Population	People who self-harm (8 years old or above)
Critical outcomes	Non-fatal repetition; fatal repetition
Electronic databases	CINAHL, EMBASE, MEDLINE, PsycINFO
Date searched	Inception to 25 January 2011
Study design	Prospective cohort studies

6.2.3   Studies considered[11]

Forty-nine prospective cohort studies (out of 6,077 references generated by the search) providing relevant clinical evidence met the eligibility criteria for this review. The GDG decided to include only prospective cohort studies for the following three reasons. First, prospective studies are less subject to selection bias and participant recall bias than retrospective studies. Second, prospective cohort studies could identify temporal relationships between risk factors and outcome that might have implications for management. The third reason was practical: to ensure that the number of studies was manageable within the timeframe of this guideline. Of the 49 studies, all were published in peer-reviewed journals. In addition, 41 studies were excluded from the analysis. Further information about both included and excluded studies can be found in Appendix 15c.

Twenty-six out of 49 prospective studies that reported effect measures such as RRs, odds ratios (ORs) or hazard ratios (together with CIs) were selected for possible meta-analysis. These are presented as clinical evidence in Section 6.2.4 (risk factors for non-fatal repetition), Section 6.2.5 (risk factors for fatal repetition) and Section 6.2.9 (risk factors for children and young people).

The process for selection of studies for meta-analysis is described below:
- A list of risk factors examined in each of the 26 studies was drawn up.
- The studies that reported the effect measure for the same risk factor were grouped together.
- For each risk factor, a meta-analysis was conducted for studies that reported the same type of effect measure together with 95% CI (for example, two studies that reported the OR of depression were pooled). A narrative synthesis was presented for those studies that could not be pooled.

---

[11]Here and elsewhere in the guideline, each study considered for review is referred to by a study ID in capital letters (primary author and date of study publication, except where a study is in press or only submitted for publication, then a date is not used).

Other risk factors that were not reported in a way to allow outcomes to be extracted are included in the narrative synthesis presented in Sections 6.2.6, 6.2.7 and 6.2.10. These studies either did not report 95% CIs, only reported effect measures by subgroups (for example, gender or single ethnic group), only reported p-values, or comprised either a mixture of people who self-harmed for the first time or repeatedly self-harmed (in which results were not separable).

For the section concerning children and young people, studies that recruited participants up to the age of 20 years were included; for the section concerning older adults, one study was identified that included participants aged 60 years or above. These age ranges were wider than those that might be seen in clinical services, but were used in this guideline because of the age cut-offs included in the studies.

6.2.4 Clinical evidence for risk factors for repetition of self-harm in adults (non-fatal outcome)

All studies in this section included clinical populations recruited after presenting to hospital following an index episode of self-harm. Therefore, the factors examined are those associated with a higher risk of *repetition* of self-harm. As mentioned in Section 6.2.3, all risk factors reviewed below are findings from prospective studies only.

The quality of evidence is presented according to following criteria:
- Study sample – is the study representative of the population of interest with regard to key characteristics, and is it sufficient to limit potential bias to results?
- Loss to follow-up – is the loss to follow-up unrelated to key characteristics, and is it sufficient to limit potential bias?
- Putative risk factor – has this been adequately measured in study participants?
- Outcome of interest – has this been adequately measured in study participants?
- Potential confounders – have the important confounds been appropriately accounted for, limiting potential for spurious association?
- Statistical analysis – has the study used an appropriate design, which limited the potential for presentation of invalid results?

Evidence from each important outcome and the overall quality of evidence are presented. The study characteristics for studies included in the meta-analysis can be found in Appendix 15c.

History of previous self-harm as a risk factor for repetition
Pooled adjusted data
A history of previous self-harm is associated with higher risk of repetition. Three studies (COLMAN2004 [Colman *et al.*, 2004], JOHNSTON2006 [Johnston *et al.*, 2006], MCAULIFFE2008 [McAuliffe *et al.*, 2008]) with a total of approximately 5,000 participants were pooled in the meta-analysis and their combined adjusted OR was 2.7 (95% CI, 2.13 to 3.42).

The repetition rate for self-harm during follow-up (up to 2 years) was 25% (COLMAN2004), 11% (JOHNSTON2006) and 30% (MCAULIFFE2008).

Table 7: History of self-harm – adjusted factors

	COLMAN2004	JOHNSTON2006	CAULIFFE2008
Depression	Yes	No	Hopelessness
Age	Yes	No	Yes
Gender	Yes	–	Yes
Previous psychological treatment	No	Yes	No
Suicide intent	No	No	Yes
Method of self-harm	No	No	Yes
Schizophrenia	Yes	No	No
Physical health	Yes	No	No
Marital status	No	Yes	Yes
Employment	No	Yes	No
Ethnic percentage	No	Yes	No
Education	No	No	Yes

The majority of participants in COLMAN2004 (66%), JOHNSTON2006 (55%) and MCAULIFFE2008 (59%) had a history of previous self-harm. Specifically, most participants in COLMAN2004 received a psychiatric diagnosis, half of the participants in JOHNSTON2006 had received previous psychiatric treatment and a number of participants in MCAULIFFE2008 had alcohol problems. Three studies varied in the extent to which they adjusted for current symptoms related to depression. The adjusted factors can be found in Table 7.

The follow-up period ranged from 1 to 2 years. The three studies were conducted in Canada, the UK and European countries. There was no significant heterogeneity after pooling these studies.

Attenuation of the association following adjustment was examined in the two studies (COLMAN2004, MCAULIFFE2008) that reported both unadjusted and adjusted OR. The pooled unadjusted OR was 5.86 (95% CI, 3.23 to 10.65). After adjusting for depression, age and gender, the adjusted OR decreased to 3.81 (95% CI, 1.98 to 7.35).

The quality of evidence for history of self-harm as a risk factor for repetition of self-harm is summarised in Table 8.

Table 8: History of self-harm – quality of evidence

Study sample	All three studies met criteria
Loss to follow-up	None met criteria
Putative risk factor	Two of three studies met criteria
Outcome of interest	All three studies met criteria
Potential confound	One study met criteria
Statistical analysis	All three studies met criteria

Pooled unadjusted data

Five studies (BILLE-BRAHE1994 [Bille-Brahe & Jessen, 1994], COLMAN2004, JOHNSSON1996 [Johnsson *et al.*, 1996], MCAULIFFE2008, OWENS1994 [Owens *et al.*, 1994]) provided raw data and a pooled unadjusted OR of 3.09 (95% CI, 1.99 to 4.8), and an observed heterogeneity ($I^2 = 52\%$) was calculated. It is important to note that unadjusted ratios do not take confounding variables into consideration, and thus findings may result from association with another unmeasured risk factor.

Narrative synthesis

Aside from the studies reviewed above, a narrative synthesis of seven other studies (HAW2007 [Haw *et al.*, 2007], ALLGULANDER1990 [Allgulander & Fisher, 1990], KAPUR2006 [Kapur *et al.*, 2006], DIESERUD2000 [Dieserud *et al.*, 2000], SIDLEY1999 [Sidley *et al.*, 1999], VAN AAIST1992 [Van Aaist *et al.*, 1992], PETRIE1992 [Petrie & Brook, 1992]) with a total of approximately 23,000 participants reported a history of previous self-harm as a risk factor for repetition. Of these seven studies, two studies adjusted for confounding variables (HAW2007, KAPUR2006) while the remaining five did not.

Depressive symptoms as a risk factor for repetition
Pooled adjusted data

People with depressive symptoms are associated with higher risk of repetition. Three studies (CHANDRASEKARAN2008 [Chandrasekaran & Gnanaselane, 2008], COLMAN2004, DIESERUD2003 [Dieserud *et al.*, 2003]) with a total of approximately 700 participants were pooled and reported an adjusted OR of 2.63 (95% CI, 1.72 to 4.04).

The repetition rate during follow-up was 25% (COLMAN2004), 16% (DIESERUD2003) and 23% (CHANDRASEKARAN2008).

A lifetime psychiatric diagnosis was reported in the majority of participants in COLMAN2004 (66% major depression) and in a few participants in CHAN-DRASEKARAN2008 (26% depression) at baseline. The breakdown of psychiatric diagnosis was not reported in DIESERUD2003, where depressive symptoms were measured by the Beck Depression Inventory (BDI; Beck & Steer, 1987). The majority of participants in COLMAN2004 and DIESERUD2003 had a history of previous self-harm. In CHANDRASEKARAN2008, only participants who reported their index episode as their first episode of self-harm were included. The adjusted factors for each study can be found in Table 9.

The follow-up period ranged from 1 to 2 years. They were conducted in three different countries. There was no significant heterogeneity reported after pooling the three studies.

Attenuation following adjustment was examined in two of these studies (COLMAN2004, DIESERUD2003), which reported both unadjusted and adjusted OR. The pooled unadjusted OR was 2.98 (95% CI, 0.9 to 9.85). After adjusting for previous self-harm, age and gender, the adjusted OR decreased to 2.19 (95% CI, 1.25 to 3.81).

The quality of evidence for depressive symptoms as a risk factor for repetition of self-harm is summarised in Table 10.

Table 9: Depressive symptoms – adjusted factors

	COLMAN 2004	DIESERUD 2003	CHANDRASEKARAN 2008
Self-harm history	Yes	Yes	Included only participants with no history of previous self-harm
Age	Yes	Yes	No
Gender	Yes	Yes	No
Suicide intent	No	Yes	No
Schizophrenia	Yes	No	No
Physical health	Yes	No	No
Other	No	Self efficacy and esteem	Global assessment of functioning

Table 10: Depressive symptoms – quality of evidence

Study sample	Two of three studies met criteria
Loss to follow-up	One study met criteria
Putative risk factor	Two of three studies met criteria
Outcome of interest	All three studies met criteria
Potential confound	One study met criteria
Statistical analysis	All three studies met criteria

Narrative synthesis

The narrative findings from four studies (SCOLIERS2009 [Scoliers *et al.*, 2009], CHRISTIANSEN2007 [Christiansen & Jensen, 2007], KAPUR2006 and SIDLEY1999) with a total of approximately 12,000 participants also found that having depressive symptoms, scoring high on a scale measuring hopelessness, and the current use of antidepressants all increased the risk of repetition of self-harm.

KAPUR2006 and SCOLIERS2009 reported an unadjusted hazard ratio of 1.28 (95% CI, 1.14 to 1.44) and RR of 1.85 (1.23 to 2.78), respectively.

The majority of participants (over 50%) in most studies had a history of previous self-harm. The use of antidepressants (CHRISTIANSEN2007) as a risk factor was controlled for other confounds, while hopelessness and having other depressive symptoms (KAPUR2006, SCOLIERS2009, SIDLEY1999) was not controlled for other confounds. SIDLEY1999 reported hopelessness as a short-term predictor of repetition (within 6 months).

Psychiatric history as a risk factor for repetition

Pooled unadjusted data

Two studies (JOHNSSON1996 [Johnsson *et al.*, 1996], OWENS1994) with a total of approximately 1000 participants reported raw data that could be used to calculate a pooled unadjusted OR. The pooled unadjusted OR was 3.46 (95% CI, 2.26 to 5.3). This showed that people with a psychiatric history might be at a higher risk of repetition, bearing in mind this had not been adjusted for confounders. Neither study specified a diagnosis. Data were collected objectively from local psychiatric services' case registers in OWENS1994, and from psychiatric hospital records in JOHNSSON1996.

Repetition rates were reported as 40% (JOHNSSON1996) and 12% (OWENS1994) respectively. Forty-eight per cent (JOHNSSON1996) and 35% (OWENS1994) of participants had a history of previous self-harm before the index admission. JOHNSSON1996 specified the diagnosis (68% with personality disorder, 35% with major depressive disorder [MDD]), while OWENS1994 reported 33% of participants had past psychiatric contact. None of the aforementioned variables was adjusted for in the pooled ratio. There might be confounding factors that limit the strength of findings.

JOHNSSON1996 conducted the study in Sweden for 5 years and OWENS1994 followed up participants for 1 year in the UK.

The quality of evidence for psychiatric history as a risk factor for repetition of self-harm is summarised in Table 11.

Narrative synthesis

Five other studies with a total of approximately 20,000 participants reported narratively having a psychiatric history (without specifying diagnosis) as a risk factor. Three studies reported separately psychiatric treatment (JOHNSTON2006, KAPUR2006) and admission to a mental health hospital (CHRISTIANSEN2007) as a significant risk factor even after adjusting for confounding variables. Two studies (HAW2007, SIDLEY1999) reported the same but only presented unadjusted effects. In HAW2007, psychiatric diagnosis as a risk factor was only reported in participants

Table 11: Psychiatric history – quality of evidence

Study sample	All studies met criteria
Loss to follow-up	None met criteria
Putative risk factor	All studies met criteria
Outcome of interest	All studies met criteria
Potential confound	None met criteria
Statistical analysis	None met criteria

who were admitted following their first self-harm attempt (not following subsequent episodes).

Alcohol misuse as a risk factor for repetition
Two studies (KAPUR2006, WANG2006 [Wang & Mortensen, 2006) reported alcohol misuse as a risk factor for repetition. KAPUR2006 defined misuse as 'harmful use or consumed over seven units daily'. WANG2006 did not report how this factor was measured. The studies could not be meta-analysed because the reported outcomes were not comparable. Both reported adjusted estimates with suicide intent adjusted for in both studies. WANG2006 reported an adjusted effect measure of 2.57 (95% CI, 1.05 to 6.55). KAPUR2006 reported both unadjusted and adjusted hazard ratios of 1.49 (95% CI, 1.34 to 1.66) and 1.3 (95% CI, 1.16 to 1.45), respectively. Slight attenuation was observed after adjusting for previous self-harm, suicide intent, methods of self-harm, hallucinations, current psychiatric treatment and unemployment.

Narrative synthesis
In two studies (CHRISTIANSEN2007, SIDLEY1999) with a total of 2,680 participants, the outcomes were not extractable for meta-analysis. CHRISTIANSEN2007 reported alcohol or drug misuse as an independent risk factor being adjusted for other confounds, while SIDLEY1999 reported this as risk factor without adjusting for confounds.

Schizophrenia-related symptoms as a risk factor for repetition
Outcomes were extracted for two studies; however, they could not be pooled. KAPUR2006 reported hallucinations with an unadjusted hazard ratio of 1.82 (95% CI, 1.56 to 2.14) and COLMAN2004 reported a lifetime history of schizophrenia with an unadjusted OR of 4.24 (95% CI, 2.3 to 7.79). After adjusting for previous self-harm, depression, age, gender and physical health problems, the adjusted OR became 3.43 (95% CI, 1.77 to 6.66).

Narrative synthesis
Three other studies (CHRISTIANSEN2007, VAN AAIST1992, WANG2006) with a total of 2,857 participants reported that schizophrenia-related symptoms were

associated with a higher risk for repetition of self-harm. These three studies' findings were not adjusted for confounds, and should be subject to cautious interpretation. A diagnosis of schizophrenia (VAN AAIST1992), hallucinations (KAPUR2006) and the presence of any psychotic symptom (WANG2006) were reported as risk factors in these studies.

Employment status as a risk factor for repetition

Being unemployed might be a risk factor for repetition of self-harm. Outcomes were extracted from three studies (JOHNSTON2006, KAPUR2006, OWENS1994); however, they could not be pooled because they were not comparable. JOHNSTON2006 reported being unemployed as a risk factor with an adjusted OR of 1.41 (95% CI, 1.06 to 1.87), adjusted for previous self-harm, previous psychiatric treatment and marital status. KAPUR2006 reported an unadjusted hazard ratio of 1.77 (95% CI, 1.56 to 2.02); after adjusting for previous self-harm, current psychiatric treatment, alcohol misuse, suicide plans and hallucinations, the ratio lowered to 1.38 (95% CI, 1.2 to 1.59). OWENS1994 provided raw data and an unadjusted OR was calculated as 2.44 (95% CI, 1.36 to 4.38).

Similarly, JOHNSTON2006 and KAPUR2006 reported 'registered sick' as a risk factor for repetition. An adjusted OR of 1.67 (95% CI, 1.12 to 2.51) was reported and KAPUR2006 reported an unadjusted hazard ratio of 2.17 (95% CI, 1.83 to 2.57). After adjustment, the hazard ratio attenuated to 1.42 (95% CI, 1.18 to 1.71).

Narrative synthesis

Three other studies (BILLE-BRAHE1994, DIESERUD2000, PETRIE1992) with a total of 1,537 participants reported being unemployed as a risk factor for repetition of self-harm. These studies reported unemployment as a risk factor without adjustment for other confounds.

One study (BILLE-BRAHE1994) also reported early retirement as a risk factor for repetition.

Gender as a risk factor for repetition
Pooled adjusted data

Two studies (CHEN2010 [Chen, 2010], SCOLIERS2009) with a total of 1,844 participants, reported females as being at a higher risk for repetition. The studies were pooled, resulting in an adjusted RR of 1.96 (95% CI, 1.22 to 3.15). Adjusted factors can be found in Table 12.

The pooled unadjusted RR of the same two studies was 1.8 (95% CI, 1.2 to 2.71). CHEN2010 reported a repetition rate of 9.5% over 4 years, while SCOLIERS2009 reported an overall repetition rate of 30% over 5 years.

In SCOLIERS2009, 34% of participants had a history of previous self-harm. CHEN2010 did not report this information. The majority of participants were younger than 40 years old (SCOLIERS2009) and the mean age was 37 years (CHEN2010). Most of the participants were married and had less than 10 years of education (CHEN2010). Other important demographics such as employment or

Table 12: Gender – adjusted factors

	CHEN2010	SCOLIERS2009
Self-harm history	–	–
Depression	–	Yes
Age	Yes	Yes
Method of self-harm	Yes	–
Anxiety	–	Yes
Education	–	Yes
Other	–	Symptom Checklist – 90 items (SCL-90) symptoms

clinical variables were not reported in CHEN2010. SCOLIERS2009 reported that 61% of their participants had high anxiety scores and 46% had high depression scores at follow-up, but these factors were adjusted for in the statistics model.

Both studies followed-up participants for approximately 5 years. CHEN2010 was conducted in Taiwan and SCOLIERS2009 was conducted in Belgium.

The quality of evidence in the meta-analysis for gender as a risk factor for repetition of self-harm is summarised in Table 13.

Pooled unadjusted data

Four studies (CHANDRASEKARAN2008, JOHNSSON1996, KRARUP1991 [Krarup *et al.*, 1991], OWENS1994) reported raw data that could be used to calculate the unadjusted OR. However, the pooled unadjusted OR had a wide CI and thus there was no clear indication of the direction of the effect if any (OR unadjusted 1.01 [95% CI, 0.5 to 2.04]). A moderate heterogeneity was also observed ($I^2 = 53\%$), which might be explained by the uncontrolled confounding variables.

Table 13: Gender – quality of evidence in the meta-analysis

Study sample	One of two studies met criteria
Loss to follow-up	None met criteria
Putative risk factor	One of two studies met criteria
Outcome of interest	All studies met criteria
Potential confound	None met criteria
Statistical analysis	All studies met criteria

Table 14: Pooled unadjusted odds ratio – quality of evidence

Study sample	Three of four studies met criteria
Loss to follow-up	One study met criteria
Prognostic factor	Three of four studies met criteria
Outcome of interest	All studies met criteria
Potential confound	None met criteria
Statistical analysis	One of four met criteria

The quality of evidence for pooled unadjusted OR is summarised in Table 14.

Narrative synthesis

In studies where outcomes were not extractable, ZAHL2004 (Zahl & Hawton, 2004) reported young female multiple repeaters (more than two episodes) being at a higher risk compared with repeaters who had two or fewer episodes. This finding is only applicable to females.

In contrast, CHRISTIANSEN2007 reported that being male was associated with a higher risk of repeating a suicide attempt. HEATH2008 suggested that there were no gender differences in risk of repetition, based on a college sample that had a female majority. However, the finding was unadjusted for potential confounds, which should be subject to careful interpretation.

Marital status as a risk factor for repetition
Pooled unadjusted data

Some evidence suggests that not being married, or being of single status, could be a higher risk for repetition of self-harm. Four studies (BILLE-BRAHE1994, CHAN-DRASEKARAN2008, JOHNSSON1996, OWENS1994) with a total of approximately 1,700 participants reported raw data that could be used to calculate a pooled unadjusted OR. The finding was not significant, with an unadjusted OR of 1.36 (95% CI, 0.85 to 2.16), and was subject to heterogeneity ($I^2 = 63\%$). Both BILLE-BRAHE1994 and OWENS1994 reported not being married as a risk factor. Nevertheless, the reported statistics in both studies were limited because they were unadjusted.

The quality of evidence for marital status as a risk factor for repetition of self-harm is summarised in Table 15.

Narrative synthesis

Three other studies (JOHNSTON2006, KAPUR2006, DIESERUD2000) with a total of approximately 15,000 participants narratively reported not being married as a risk factor. Findings from KAPUR2006 and DIESERUD2000 were unadjusted for

Table 15: Marital status – quality of evidence

Study sample	Three of four studies met criteria
Loss to follow-up	One of four studies met criteria
Putative risk factor	Three of four studies met criteria
Outcome of interest	All studies met criteria
Potential confound	None met criteria
Statistical analysis	Two of four studies met criteria

confounds and therefore of limited conclusiveness. JOHNSTON2006 reported an adjusted OR of 1.39 (95% CI, 1.09 to 1.76), which was adjusted for previous self-harm, psychiatric treatment, employment status and ethnicity.

Suicide intent as a risk factor for repetition
Pooled unadjusted data
Two studies (OWENS1994, DIESERUD2003) were pooled to report an unadjusted OR of 0.9 (95% CI, 0.32 to 2.52), providing no conclusive evidence for suicide intent as a risk factor for repetition of self-harm; there was also substantial heterogeneity when pooling the studies ($I^2 = 78\%$). Suicide intent was defined as 'suicide threat' or 'leaving note' in OWENS1994; a cut-off score on Beck's Suicide Intent Scale (SIS) was used in DIESERUD2003.

The quality of evidence for suicide risk as a risk factor for repetition of self-harm is summarised in Table 16.

Narrative synthesis
Two studies with a total of approximately 10,000 participants reported associations with having a suicide plan (KAPUR2006) and carrying a suicide letter (WANG2006)

Table 16: Suicide risk – quality of evidence

Study sample	All studies met criteria
Loss to follow-up	None met criteria
Putative risk factor	All studies met criteria
Outcome of interest	All studies met criteria
Potential confound	None met criteria
Statistical analysis	One of two studies met criteria

as being associated with a higher risk of repetition. Both studies were adjusted for different sets of confounding factors.

However, two studies (HAW2003A, HARRISS2005B [Harriss *et al.*, 2005b]) did not find lethality nor intent scores at the index episode as being associated with repetition of self-harm. HARRISS2005B reported that the association between repetitions and suicide intent scores was different for male and female participants.

6.2.5 Clinical evidence for risk factors for completed suicide in adults

All studies in this section included clinical populations recruited after presenting to hospital after an index episode of self-harm and followed prospectively. Therefore, the factors examined are associated with higher risk for repetition of self-harm, leading to a fatal outcome.

All risk factors reviewed below are findings from prospective studies only. Quality of evidence is presented according to the following criteria:

- Study sample – is the study representative of the population of interest with regard to key characteristics, and is it sufficient to limit potential bias to results?
- Loss to follow-up – is the loss to follow-up unrelated to key characteristics, and is it sufficient to limit potential bias?
- Putative risk factor – has this been adequately measured in study participants?
- Outcome of interest – has this been adequately measured in study participants?
- Potential confounders – have the important confounds been appropriately accounted for, limiting potential for spurious association?
- Statistical analysis – has the study used an appropriate study design that limited the potential for invalid results?

Evidence from each important outcome and overall quality of evidence are presented. The study characteristics for studies included in the meta-analysis can be found in Appendix 15c.

History of previous self-harm as a risk factor for completed suicide
Pooled adjusted data
Two studies (NORDENTOFT1993 [Nordentoft *et al.*,1993], SUOKAS2001 [Suokas *et al.*, 2001]) with a total of 1,992 participants were pooled and reported an adjusted hazard ratio of 2.17 (95% CI, 1.53 to 3.09) with the general population as reference group. In comparison, COOPER2005 (Cooper *et al.*, 2005) reported an unadjusted hazard ratio of 2.97 (95% CI, 1.6 to 5.5).

In NORDENTOFT1993 and SUOKAS2001, 10.5% and 6.7% of the participants, respectively, completed suicide during the follow-up period after their index episode.

Forty-eight per cent of participants in SUOKAS2001 had a history of self-harm prior to the index episode; the exact percentage was not reported in NORDENTOFT1993. Sixty per cent of participants had previous psychiatric treatments (SUOKAS2001), 28% had a diagnosis of 'alcoholism' and 15% had a personality disorder (NORDENTOFT1993). Nevertheless, in another study 40% reported no history of mental health problems (NORDENTOFT1993). Adjusted factors can be found in Table 17.

Table 17: History of self-harm – adjusted data

	NORDENTOFT1993	SUOKAS2001
Age	Yes	–
Gender	–	Yes
Previous psychiatric treatment	–	Yes
Suicide intent	–	'Wish to die'
Living alone	Yes	–

Table 18: History of self-harm and completed suicide – quality of evidnce

Study sample	All studies met criteria
Loss to follow-up	None met criteria
Putative risk factor	All studies met criteria
Outcome of interest	All studies met criteria
Potential confound	None met criteria
Statistical analysis	All studies met criteria

Data were collected from death register and records. The follow-up period ranged from 10 to 14 years.

The quality of evidence for history of self-harm as a risk factor for completed suicide is summarised in Table 18.

Narrative synthesis

Eight other studies (HAWTON1988 [Hawton & Fagg, 1988], ALLGULAN-DER1990, CHRISTIANSEN2007, COOPER2005, HAW2007, SKOGMAN2004 [Skogman *et al.*, 2004], SUOKAS1991 [Suokas & Lonnqvist, 1991], ZAHL2004), with a total of approximately 39,000 participants, narratively reported a history of previous self-harm as a risk factor for completing suicide. Four studies (CHRISTIANSEN2007, COOPER2005, HAW2007, SKOGMAN2004) had adjusted this finding for other confounding variables. Two studies suggested that previous self-harm was gender specific. One study (SKOGMAN2004) reported that male repeaters were at a higher risk of completing suicide; by contrast, another study (HAW2007) reported that female repeaters were at a higher risk compared with females with fewer episodes of self-harm. Three other studies (ALLGULAN-DER1990, HAWTON1988, SUOKAS1991, ZAHL2004) reported this as an unadjusted factor.

Table 19: Suicide intent – adjusted factors

	SUOKAS2001 – wish to die	BJORNAAS2009 – subjective intent is suicidal	COOPER2005 – avoidance of discovery
Self-harm history	Yes	–	–
Gender	Yes	Yes	–
Previous psychiatric treatment	Yes	Seen by psychiatrist	Yes
Alcohol misuse	–	Yes	–
Physical health	Somatic disease	–	Yes
Substance misuse	–	Yes	Alcohol misuse
Socioeconomic status	–	Yes	–
Others	–	–	Not living close with relatives

Suicide intent as a risk factor for completed suicide (repetition with fatal outcome)
Pooled adjusted data
Three studies (BJORNAAS2009, COOPER2005, SUOKAS2001) with a total of approximately 10,000 participants were pooled. Suicide intent was defined differently in the three studies (see Table 19). Nevertheless, there was evidence of increased risk for those with high intent, with a pooled hazard ratio of 2.7 (95% CI, 1.91 to 3.81) being observed.

The quality of evidence for suicide intent as a risk factor for completed suicide is summarised in Table 20.

Table 20: Suicide intent as a risk factor for completed suicide – quality of evidence

Study sample	All studies met criteria
Loss to follow-up	None met criteria
Putative risk factor	Two of three studies met criteria
Outcome of interest	All studies met criteria
Potential confound	One of three studies met criteria
Statistical analysis	All studies met criteria

Narrative synthesis

Six studies, with a total of approximately 8,279 participants, narratively reported suicide ideation as a risk factor for subsequent completed suicide. Meta-analysis was not appropriate because none of the outcomes was comparable. Findings from three of these six studies (BJORNAAS2009, SKOGMAN2004, SUOKAS2001) had been adjusted for confounds. The reported 'wish to die' (SUOKAS2001) and suicidal motives (BJORNAAS2009) were reported as risk factors, and suicide ideation was found to be a risk factor for females only in SKOGMAN2004. The three other studies (HARRISS2005B, LONNQVIST1991 [Lonnqvist & Ostamo, 1991], SUOKAS1991) did not adjust for confounds. Of these, SUOKAS1991 reported that severe intention to die was predictive of subsequent suicide during follow-up. HARRISS2005B reported that suicide intent was associated with a higher risk of subsequent suicide, especially during the first year and among females.

Being male as a risk factor for completed suicide
Pooled adjusted data

Two studies (CHEN2011 [Chen *et al.*, 2011], SUOKAS2001) with a total of approximately 2,000 participants were pooled to report an adjusted hazard ratio of 2.66 (95% CI, 1.72 to 4.11) for being male as a risk factor for completed suicide.

Suicide following an index episode of self-harm was 4.4% (CHEN2011) and 6.7% (SUOKAS2001). All participants at index episode were admitted for self-poisoning in SUOKAS2001, and 43% were admitted for overdose in CHEN2011.

In SUOKAS2001, 48% had a history of previous self-harm and 60% had received previous psychiatric treatment. No such information was provided for CHEN2011.

These two studies varied in the factors they adjusted. The adjusted factors can be found in Table 21.

The follow-up period ranged from 7 to 14 years, with one study conducted in Taiwan and the other in Finland. There was no significant heterogeneity after pooling these studies.

The quality of evidence for being male as a risk factor for completed suicide is summarised in Table 22.

Table 21: Being male – adjusted factors

	CHEN2011	**SUOKAS2001**
Previous self-harm	–	Yes
Age	Yes	–
Previous psychiatric treatment	–	Yes
Suicide intent	–	Yes
Method of self-harm	Yes	–
Physical health	–	Somatic disease

Table 22: Being male – quality of evidence

Study sample	All studies met criteria
Loss to follow-up	One of two studies met criteria
Putative risk factor	All studies met criteria
Outcome of interest	All studies met criteria
Potential confound	None met criteria
Statistical analysis	All studies met criteria

Pooled unadjusted data

Two studies (CHEN2011, COOPER2005) with a total of 9,051 participants, reported unadjusted hazard ratios, and a pooled unadjusted hazard ratio of 2.72 (95% CI, 1.78 to 4.16) was calculated. It is important to note that unadjusted ratios do not take confounding variables into consideration, and thus findings may result from association with another unmeasured risk factor. Only one study (CHEN2011) reported both adjusted and unadjusted hazard ratios. After being adjusted for age and methods of self-harm, attenuation was observed from an unadjusted hazard ratio of 3.46 (95% CI, 1.92 to 6.26) to an adjusted hazard ratio of 2.47 (95% CI, 1.28 to 4.75).

Narrative synthesis

SKOGMAN2004 reported an adjusted OR of 1.92 (95% CI, 1.08 to 3.39), adjusted for previous self-harm.

Six other studies with a total of 17,306 participants reported men as being at a higher risk of completing suicide after they have been admitted following their index episode. One study (HOLLEY1998) was adjusted for confounds and four others (HAWTON1988, HAWTON2003B [Hawton *et al.*, 2003b], LONNQVIST1991, SUOKAS1991) were unadjusted for confounds. One study (RYGNESTAD1997 [Rygnestad, 1997]) separately analysed male and female samples, and found that males were at a higher risk of subsequent suicide if they were over the age of 30 years and divorced. One study (HAW2007) reported that female frequent repeaters were at an increased risk of completed suicide compared with less frequent repeaters and non-repeaters.

Physical health problems as a risk factor for completed suicide

Pooled adjusted data

Two studies (COOPER2005, HOLLEY1998) with a total of approximately 8,800 participants were pooled to report an adjusted hazard ratio of 1.59 (95% CI, 0.93 to 2.72) with the general population as a reference group. HOLLEY1998 defined physical health problems as chronic and associated with high mortality and leading to significant impairment to functioning. Physical health problems were not defined in COOPER2005.

Table 23: Physical health – adjusted factors

	HOLLEY1998	COOPER2005
Self-harm history	Yes	–
Previous psychiatric treatment	Previous psychiatric admission	Yes
Gender	Yes	–
Suicide intent	–	Avoided discovery
Alcohol misuse	'Alcohol as a factor'	Yes
Method of self-harm	Violent method used	Cutting
Psychiatric diagnosis	Yes	–
Marital status	Yes	–
Socioeconomic status	Yes	–
Others	–	Not living close to relatives

Less than 1% of participants (COOPER2005) and 6% (HOLLEY1998) completed suicide during follow-up, while 15.5% repeated self-harm (COOPER2005).

Fifty one percent of participants (COOPER2005) had a history of previous self-harm (this was not reported in HOLLEY1998). Sixty-nine per cent of participants had major depression, 24% had neuroses, and 35 to 43% reported the use of alcohol as a factor identified in the attempt (HOLLEY1998). None of the psychiatric diagnosis information was provided in COOPER2005. At least 67% participants were unemployed (HOLLEY1998). Adjusted factors can be found in Table 23.

Data were collected from the death register and records, while the risk factors assessed were collected from assessment forms. The follow-up period varied from approximately 4 years (COOPER2005) to 13 years (HOLLEY1998).

COOPER2005 reported an unadjusted hazard ratio of 2.68 (95% CI, 1.3 to 5.5); HOLLEY1998 did not report on this.

Another study (HAWTON1988), which could not be meta-analysed with the above studies, also reported poor physical health as a risk factor for increased risk of subsequent suicide.

The quality of evidence for physical health problems as a risk factor for self-harm is summarised in Table 24.

Alcohol misuse as a risk factor for completed suicide

Pooled adjusted data

Two studies (BJORNAAS2009, COOPER2005) with a total of approximately 9,000 participants were pooled to report an adjusted hazard ratio of 1.42, but the wide CI

Table 24: Physical health – quality of evidence

Study sample	One of two studies met criteria
Loss to follow-up	None met criteria
Putative risk factor	All studies met criteria
Outcome of interest	All studies met criteria
Potential confound	One of two studies met criteria
Statistical analysis	All studies met criteria

included the possibility of a small protective effect (95% CI, 0.7 to 2.8); there was also a high heterogeneity observed ($I^2 = 65\%$). COOPER2005 reported an unadjusted hazard ratio of 2.11 (95% CI, 1.23 to 3.63) and BJORNAAS2009 reported an unadjusted hazard ratio of 1.6 (95% CI, 1.2 to 2.2).

Less than 1% of participants (COOPER2005) and 7% (BJORNAAS2009) completed suicide during follow-up.

Fifty-one per cent of participants (COOPER2005) had a history of previous self-harm (this was not reported in BJORNAAS2009). BJORNAAS2009 reported that 12% were addicted to opiates and 53% had no history of alcohol misuse. No information about psychiatric diagnosis was provided in COOPER2005. Both studies adjusted for participants' psychiatric history as confounding variables. BJORNAAS2009 adjusted for gender and participants' socioeconomic status. Adjusted factors can be found in Table 25.

Data were collected from the death register and records, while data on the assessment of alcohol misuse or 'abuse' were collected from psychiatric assessments. The

Table 25: Alcohol misuse – adjusted factors

	COOPER2005	BJORNAAS2009
Self-harm history	–	–
Previous psychiatric treatment	Yes	Seen by psychiatrists before
Gender	–	Yes
Suicide intent	Avoided discovery	Yes
Method of self-harm	Cutting	–
Socioeconomic status	–	Yes
Others	Not living close to relatives	Level of consiousness

Table 26: Alcohol misuse – quality of evidence

Study sample	All studies met criteria
Loss to follow-up	None met criteria
Putative risk factor	One of two studies met criteria
Outcome of interest	All studies met criteria
Potential confound	One of two studies met criteria
Statistical analysis	All studies met criteria

follow-up period varied from approximately 4 years (COOPER2005) to 20 years (BJORNAAS2009), which might explain the heterogeneity.

Attenuation was examined by BJORNAAS2009 and COOPER2005, where both unadjusted and adjusted ORs were reported. The pooled unadjusted OR was 1.52 (95% CI, 0.79 to 2.94). After adjusting for previous psychiatric history and suicide intent, the adjusted OR was attenuated to 1.42 and the CI included no effect (95% CI, 0.7 to 2.88).

The quality of evidence for alcohol misuse as a risk factor for suicide completion is summarised in Table 26.

Narrative synthesis

One study (BECK1989 [Beck *et al.*, 1989b]) reported an association between alcohol misuse and completed suicide, reporting both adjusted and unadjusted ORs (which could not be pooled with the above hazard ratio). However, a wide confidence interval limited the conclusions that could be drawn from this study.

There is a lack of evidence to show an association between the time of alcohol consumption and the index episode of self-harm. HOLLEY1998 reported an adjusted hazard ratio of 1.1 (95% CI, 0.6 to 2.3), providing no evidence of whether there was an effect; the time period between alcohol consumption and the episode of self-harm was not specified. Sixty-nine per cent of participants had major depression, 24% had neuroses and 35 to 43% reported the use of alcohol as a factor at the time of the attempt (HOLLEY1998). Data was based upon A&E records of whether alcohol was used as a factor in the suicide attempt.

Another study (HAW2001B) compared people who had alcohol dependence and had self-harmed with those without alcohol dependence. This was a prospective study conducted in the UK over approximately 1 to 2 years. Participants were admitted to hospital for self-harm. Forty out of 150 patients with alcohol-use disorders were selected for analysis. Of these 40 participants, 80% had previously self-harmed and 90% had a comorbid psychiatric diagnosis (mostly depression). Repetition was 45% for those with alcohol dependence and 29% for those without. More participants with alcohol dependence had consumed alcohol within 6 hours of the index episode, and those with alcohol dependence were more aggressive and impulsive with poorer problem-solving skills.

Psychiatric history as a risk factor for completed suicide (repetition with fatal outcome)

Pooled adjusted data

Two studies (COOPER2005, HOLLEY1998) with a total of approximately 9,000 participants found no evidence of an association between psychiatric history and completed suicide, with an adjusted hazard ratio of 1.22 (95% CI, 0.56 to 2.64); a high heterogeneity was observed ($I^2 = 62\%$). Therefore, the meta-analysis result was inconclusive. COOPER2005 reported an unadjusted hazard ratio, which was 2.11 (95% CI, 1.22 to 3.65); HOLLEY1998 did not. Adjusted data can be seen in Table 27 and quality of evidence in Table 28.

Narrative synthesis

Seven studies with a total of approximately 12,000 participants narratively reviewed psychiatric history as a risk factor for completed suicide. Four studies (CHRISTIANSEN2007, LONNQVIST1991, SKOGMAN2004, SUOKAS2001) adjusted their findings for confounds and therefore were more robust in their results. These studies did

Table 27: Psychiatric history – adjusted data

	HOLLEY1998	**COOPER2005**
Self-harm history	Yes	–
Gender	Yes	–
Suicide intent	–	Avoided discovery
Alcohol misuse	'Alcohol as a factor'	Yes
Method of self-harm	Violent method used	Cutting
Physical health problems	Yes	Yes
Marital status	Yes	–
Socioeconomic status	Yes	–
Others	–	Not living close to relatives

Table 28: Psychiatric history – quality of evidence

Study sample	One of two studies met criteria
Loss to follow-up	None met criteria
Putative risk factor	One of two studies met criteria
Outcome of interest	All studies met criteria
Potential confound	One of two studies met criteria
Statistical analysis	All studies met criteria

not report a specific psychiatric diagnosis. Past psychiatric contact (SKOGMAN2004) and being admitted to mental health hospitals (CHRISTIANSEN2007) were regarded as similar factors. The other three studies (HAWTON1988, LONNQVIST1991, SUOKAS1991) reported psychiatric history as a risk factor without adjusting their findings. HAWTON1988 reported that a diagnosis of schizophrenia was more common than other diagnoses among people who did and did not complete suicide.

6.2.6   Narrative synthesis – risk factors for repetition of self-harm in adults

Studies included in this section concern risk factors that cannot be included in meta-analysis because the outcomes reported are not suitable. These studies either did not report 95% CIs, only reported effect measures by subgroups (for example, male or female, Asian or non-Asian, and so on), only reported p-values, or comprised a mixture of people who had either self-harmed for the first time or repeatedly self-harmed (in which results were not separable). However, these factors should not be overlooked.

Age as a risk factor for repetition
A meta-analysis was not possible due to the difference in age range reported in different studies (CHEN2010, SCOLIERS2009, WANG2006).

Narrative synthesis
Eight studies reported youth as a risk factor for repetition of self-harm; however, the definition of 'youth' had a wide age range. CHEN2010 reported the lowest age range (below 25 years) as a risk factor. SCOLIERS2009 defined youth as between 20 to 49 years (with the majority of the population's age being below 40 years), HAW2007 reported an age range below 45 years and WANG2006 reported an age range below 40 years. However, two studies (CHEN2010, HAW2007) did not provide information on psychiatric diagnosis, which might be a confounding factor. Four earlier studies (ALLUGULANDER1990, JOHNSSON1996, KRARUP1991, VAN AAIST1992) reported young age as a risk factor without defining the age range. The mean age of two studies was approximately 40 years (ALLGULANDER1990, JOHNSSON1996), and the majority of participants in KRARUP1991 were aged between 20 to 39 years. However, findings from three studies (all except ALLGULANDER1990) were unadjusted for confounds, which limited the strength of the evidence.

Method of self-harm as a risk factor for repetition
Three studies reported different self-harm methods as a predictor of repetition of self-harm. The findings from all studies were adjusted for age and one study (CHRISTIANSEN2007) adjusted for some psychiatric disorders. The two studies reported self-harm by gassing as an important predictive factor, followed by self-cutting (CHRISTIANSEN2007) or self-poisoning (CHEN2010). LILLEY2008B (Lilley *et al.*, 2008b) reported that people who cut themselves are more likely to have a history of previous self-harm and are more likely to repeat (47%) compared with people who self-poison (31%). Of those who repeated, one third switched methods.

Ethnicity as a risk factor for repetition

COOPER2006A (Cooper *et al.*, 2006a) and COOPER2008 (Cooper *et al.*, 2008) reported the rates of self-harm as being higher in South Asian females aged 16 to 24 years compared with white females in the same age group, but the results were not statistically significant.

JOHNSTON2006 reported a higher repetition of self-harm in areas of high non-white ethnic density.

COOPER2010 reported that young black women in three UK cities were more likely to self-harm; however, the risk in young South Asian people varied between the three cities in which the study was conducted. The study showed that people of both genders from ethnic minority groups were less likely to present to an emergency department after an episode of self-harm with further episodes. However, ethnic minority groups may have higher rates of other risk factors such as unemployment; therefore, unadjusted associations should be interpreted cautiously.

Living situation as a risk factor for repetition

Three studies reported living alone as a risk factor for repetition of self-harm. People who were not living with family or friends (KAPUR2006), not living at home (VAN AAIST1992) and living alone (PETRIE1992) were at higher risk of repetition. However, these factors were not adjusted for confounds. One study reported that people living alone on the day of the attempt (CHRISTIANSEN2007) were also at higher risk.

Other risk factors for repetition

The following risk factors were supported by a smaller evidence base (one or two studies). Clinical risk factors include personality disorders (HAW2007, JOHNSSON1996), anxiety disorders (CHRISTIANSEN2007, SCOLIERS2009) and substance (drug and alcohol) misuse (DIESERUD2000, CHRISTIANSEN2007). Demographic risk factors include a lower education level (CHRISTIANSEN2007, SCOLIERS2009). Personal history risk factors include having a criminal record (HAW2007, SIDLEY1999), history of abuse (KAPUR2006, YEO1993 [Yeo & Yeo, 1993]), parents' poor mental health or a family history of suicide (JOHNSSON1996, VAN AAIST1992) and an unhappy childhood (KRARUP1991). Individual psychological characteristics risk factors include poor problem-solving capacity (DIESERUD2003, MCAULIFFE2008), low self-appraisal and self-efficacy (DIESERUD2003), and poor emotion regulation (HEATH2008). Common current problems as risk factors were stress CHANDRASEKARAN2008), poor physical health (COLMAN2004), relationship problems with partner or friends (HAW2007, KAPUR2006), problems at work (KAPUR2006) and moving from a rural to an urban area (WANG2006).

6.2.7   Narrative synthesis – risk factors for completed suicide in adults

Studies under this section were not included in the meta-analysis because the outcomes reported were not suitable. These studies either did not report 95% CIs, only reported effect measures by subgroup (for example, male or female, Asian or non-Asian, and so on), only reported p-values, or comprised a mixture of people who had either self-harmed for the first time or had repeatedly self-harmed (in which results were not separable). However, these variables should not be overlooked as possible risk factors.

Depressive symptoms as a risk factor for completed suicide

Three studies reported depressive symptoms as a risk factor for suicide following an index episode of self-harm. Variables include depression (SKOGMAN2004), high hopelessness scores (COOPER2005) and use of antidepressants (CHRIS-TIANSEN2007). Only one study (COOPER2005) did not adjust for confounds.

Older age as a risk factor for completed suicide

Seven studies (with a total of 24,842 participants narratively reported age as a risk factor for completing suicide. However, all seven studies reported different age ranges. Moreover, meta-analyses were not appropriate because none of the outcomes were comparable. Three studies adjusted for confounds, of which SKOGMAN2004 defined those aged over 50 years as being at higher risk, RYGNESTAD1997 defined those aged over 30 years as being at higher risk and NORDENTOFT1993 reported an 'increasing age' without specifying the age range. The other four studies did not adjust for confounds. They reported that people aged above 35 years (COOPER2005), of 'advancing age' (HAWTON2003B, SUOKAS1991) and of 'advancing age in females' (HAWTON1988) were at higher risk of completing suicide.

Violent index attempt as a risk factor for completed suicide

Four studies with a total of approximately 52,000 participants reported that a violent attempt is indicative of subsequent suicide. RUNESON2010 (Runeson *et al.*, 2010) compared different methods of self-harm and reported that self-cutting and self-poisoning had similar risk levels. They reported that those who attempted suicide by hanging, strangulation or suffocation had the worst prognosis after adjusting for age, gender, education and coexisting psychiatric morbidities. HOLLEY1998 adjusted for the same confounds, in addition to marital status, socioeconomic status, previous self-harm and physical comorbidity. However, SKOGMAN2004 reported this association as being restricted to men. LONNQVIST1991 did not adjust for its finding and reported that the degree of lethality was a risk factor predicting subsequent suicide.

Other risk factors for completed suicide

The following risk factors were supported by a smaller evidence base (one or two studies). A non-impulsive index attempt (SUOKAS1991), the method of self-harm (jumping from heights) (CHRISTIANSEN2007, RUNESON2010) and avoidance of discovery of an attempt (COOPER2005) may be risk factors. Living alone (NORDENTOFT1993) or not living with close relatives (COOPER2005), being homeless (COOPER2005), living in a lower income area (HOLLEY1998), having no link to parents (CHRISTIANSEN2007) and having legal problems (COOPER2005) may also be risk factors for repetition of self-harm with a fatal outcome.

6.2.8   Clinical evidence summary – adults

Risk factors for non-fatal repetition of self-harm
Key factors with pooled quantitative evidence
Previous self-harm and depressive symptoms are the two risk factors with most support from quantitative and narrative evidence. The majority of participants had self-harmed prior to their index episode. The pooled adjusted or unadjusted ORs of previous self-harm as a risk factor are over 2. For depressive symptoms, there is a somewhat smaller evidence base. The pooled adjusted or unadjusted OR varied, yet there was still an association. This association should also be interpreted cautiously because a number of different measures of depressive symptoms were used in the studies.

Other factors with pooled quantitative evidence
Unspecified psychiatric history has been one of the most commonly reported risk factors. Pooled quantitative synthesis showed some support for this, but the findings were not adjusted for important confounds such as age and gender. It is noteworthy that key risk factors such as previous self-harm and depression, identified above, may overlap with this factor. Moreover, these studies did not specify or define what they meant by psychiatric history; therefore uncertainties remained. Nevertheless, there was reasonable support from the studies' reported narrative findings.

Although being female is another commonly reported risk factor for non-fatal repetition, the evidence is mixed and of relatively poor quality. Two studies reported a similar pooled adjusted and unadjusted RR. However, one important limitation is that none of the studies adjusted for participants' previous self-harm, which is itself an important risk factor. Being female is often reported as being associated with self-harm. The increase in RR of repetition in females might be a consequence of its association with a first episode of self-harm rather than a repeated episode. By contrast, one study found that being male led to a higher risk of repetition. Being female might be a generic risk factor for self-harm, but it might not necessarily be associated with a higher risk of repetition.

There is evidence to suggest that being unemployed and 'registered sick' are associated with a higher risk of repetition. Although the studies were not pooled quantitatively, each study reported a statistically significant RR. Similarly, evidence from narrative synthesis also supports this as a risk factor.

There is mixed evidence about marital status as a risk factor for repetition of self-harm. Pooled quantitative evidence did not support this as a risk factor. However, some narrative syntheses suggest an association between not being married and repetition of self-harm.

There is mixed evidence suggesting that the existence of a suicide letter or plan might mean the individual is at higher risk for non-fatal repetition. The pooled quantitative evidence did not support this; however, some narrative syntheses do support this as a risk factor. From other narrative syntheses, there is evidence suggesting that a more violent method of index attempt is predictive of further repetition. Attempts that are regarded as violent include hanging, strangulation, suffocation and jumping from heights. A summary of risk factors can be seen in Table 29.

Table 29: Summary of risk factors for self-harm population in adults

Risk factors	Outcome	Evidence base	Pooled data	Prevalence of risk factor (range)	Duration of follow-up (range)
Previous self-harm	Repetition	3 studies, N = 5264	Adjusted OR 2.70 [2.13, 3.42]	55 to 66%	6 to 24 months
		5 studies, N = 1947	Unadjusted OR 3.09[1.99, 4.80] (I^2 = 52%)	35 to 66%	1 to 5 years
	Suicide following self-harm	2 studies, N = 1992	Adjusted hazard ratio 2.17 [1.53, 3.09]	48%	10 to 14 years
Depressive symptoms	Repetition	3 studies, N = 1693	Adjusted OR 2.63 [1.72, 4.04]	26 to 66%	18 to 24 months
Psychiatric history (previous history, treatments, admissions from records)	Repetition	2 studies, N = 1034	Unadjusted OR 3.46 [2.26, 5.3]	33 to 48%	1 to 5 years
	Suicide following self-harm	2 studies, N = 8844	Adjusted hazard ratio 1.22 [0.56, 2.64] (I^2 = 62%)	7 to 24%	4 to 13 years

Risk factor	Outcome	Studies	Effect	%	Duration
Alcohol misuse	Suicide following self-harm	2 studies, N = 8914	Adjusted hazard ratio 1.42 [0.7, 2.88] (I^2 = 65%)	25 to 26%	4 to 20 years
Physical health problems	Suicide following self-harm	2 studies, N = 8844	Adjusted hazard ratio 1.59 [0.93, 2.72]	7 to 21%	4 to 13 years
Gender – female	Repetition	2 studies, N = 1331	Adjusted RR 1.96 [1.22, 3.15]	57 to 63%	5 years
		4 studies, N = 1426	Unadjusted OR 1.01 [0.50, 2.04] (I^2 = 53%)	28 to 61%	1 to 5 years
Gender – male	Suicide following self-harm	2 studies, N = 2098	Adjusted hazard ratio 2.66 [1.72, 4.11]	37 to 47%	6 to 14 years
	Suicide following self-harm	2 studies, N = 9048	Unadjusted hazard ratio 2.72 [1.78, 4.16]	37 to 43%	4 to 6 years
Marital status – single	Repetition	4 studies, N = 1719	Unadjusted OR 1.36 [0.85, 2.16] (I^2 = 63%)	16 to 85%	1 to 5 years
Suicide intent	Repetition	2 studies, N = 2023	Unadjusted OR 0.90 [0.32, 2.52] (I^2 = 78%)	35%	12 to 18 months

Factors from studies reviewed narratively
Demographics
Youth is a commonly reported risk factor. Data were not synthesised quantitatively because different studies reported different age ranges and it was unclear how some studies defined 'youth'. This factor should not be conflated with the higher prevalence of self-harm among young people. Being at risk of self-harm may not be equivalent to being at risk for repeating self-harm.

Specific psychiatric diagnosis
There is a substantial evidence base that suggests schizophrenia and related symptoms may be a risk factor for repetition. There was some quantitative support that could not be meta-analysed and remained robust after being adjusted for separately in two studies. Although the evidence base has only been narratively reviewed, schizophrenia as a factor for repetition of self-harm should be considered. Also, alcohol misuse is an additional risk factor with a strong narrative evidence base as well as unpooled quantitative support.

Risk factors for suicide following self-harm
Key factors with pooled quantitative evidence
Previous self-harm is again reported as a key risk factor for completed suicide. Although the evidence base was weaker than repetition (non-fatal outcome), the quantitative synthesis finding was robust. One limitation from the quantitative evidence was that no common confound was adjusted for in the studies. Both adjusted and unadjusted RRs were over 2. Nevertheless, a number of studies provided narrative support for this factor. More than half of those studies had individually adjusted for confounds.

Another risk factor, suicide intent, is also supported by pooled quantitative evidence, associated with higher risk of suicide following self-harm. The studies might have had different definitions, but in all the intent to die or not be discovered was expressed. All studies in the pooled analysis adjusted for participants' previous psychiatric treatment. However, unadjusted data were not provided. Nevertheless, a number of studies provided narrative support for this risk factor.

It has commonly been reported that men are at a higher risk of suicide following self-harm. This was supported by pooled quantitative data. Both adjusted and unadjusted RRs showed significance. A number of studies in the narrative synthesis also provided support for this factor.

Other factors with pooled quantitative evidence
Physical health problems might be a risk factor for completed suicide. Quantitative synthesis suggested mixed evidence for this factor, depending on whether it was adjusted for other factors. The findings did not adjust for important risk factors such as psychiatric disorder and previous self-harm. In another study, a physical health problem was reported as a risk factor but was not adjusted for other confounds.

It is unclear whether alcohol misuse was a risk factor for completed suicide. Pooled quantitative synthesis did not provide strong evidence, but other studies that could not be pooled reported higher risk for people who misuse alcohol. However, there was little support from narrative evidence and the evidence was inconclusive. In addition, the context in which alcohol was used in the self-harm episode is unclear.

Psychiatric history had a reasonable amount of support from narrative evidence, which was reasonably robust with findings being controlled for in the majority of studies. However, a pooled quantitative synthesis did not provide conclusive evidence of an association.

Factors from studies reviewed narratively
It is commonly reported that older age increases the risk of completed suicide. From the existing evidence, the age range varied widely. Some defined older age as over 30 years and others as over 50 years. Some did not define an age range. The number of studies provides reasonable evidence to suggest that older age is associated with a higher risk of suicide following self-harm.

Evidence from narrative reviews shows that violent methods of self-harm are associated with a higher risk of suicide following self-harm. Methods may include hanging, strangulation or suffocation.

6.2.9 Clinical evidence for risk factors in young people
Previous self-harm as a risk factor for repetition in young people
Pooled adjusted data
Four studies (CHITSABESAN2003 [Chitsabesan *et al.*, 2003], MIRANDA2008 [Miranda *et al.*, 2008], HULTEN2001 [Hulten *et al.*, 2001], WONG2008 [Wong *et al.*, 2008]) with a total of approximately 2,700 participants were pooled to report an adjusted OR of 3.27 (95% CI, 2.46 to 4.34). No hetereogeneity was observed. Two studies (MIRANDA2008, WONG2008) reported self-endorsed attempts and recruited a community sample. The pooled adjusted OR was 4.09 (95% CI, 1.72 to 9.74), which was higher than the pooled adjusted OR calculated from the two clinical studies (OR of 3.18 [95% CI, 2.35 to 4.29]) (CHITSABESAN2003, HULTEN2001).

Fifteen per cent (CHITSABESAN2003) and 17.2% (HULTEN2001) repeated, and 4.5% (WONG2008) and 22.5% (MIRANDA2008) self-reported repetition during follow-up.

Twenty-nine per cent (CHITSABESAN2003) and 38% (HULTEN2001) had a history of self-harm. Fifteen per cent self-reported multiple suicide attempts in MIRANDA2008. Self-reported previous self-harm was the recruitment criteria in WONG2008. Therefore, all participants self-endorsed past suicide attempts, of which 2% were attempted within the last year that the survey was conducted.

The majority of participants were diagnosed with depression and substance misuse in CHITSABESAN2003. Approximately a quarter of participants had various mood and anxiety disorders (MIRANDA2008, WONG2008). Psychiatric diagnosis was not reported in HULTEN2001. Adjusted factors can be found in Table 30 and quality of evidence in Table 31.

Two studies were long-term studies ranging in duration from 4 to 6 years (HULTEN2001, MIRANDA2008). The other two were short-term studies ranging

Table 30: Previous self-harm – adjusted factors

	MIRANDA 2008	HULTEN 2001	WONG 2008	CHITSABESAN 2003
Depression	–	–	Depressive symptoms	Yes
Age	Yes	Yes	–	–
Gender	Yes	Yes	–	–
Suicide intent	–	–	Yes	Yes
Anxiety	–	–	Yes	–
Substance misuse	–	–	Yes	–
Psychiatric diagnosis	Yes	–	–	–
Ethnicity	Yes	–	–	–
Others	–	–	Life stress	Parents' mental health; family functioning

Table 31: Previous self-harm – quality of evidence

Study sample	Three of four studies met criteria
Loss to follow-up	None met criteria
Putative risk factor	Two of four studies met criteria
Outcome of interest	Two of four studies met criteria
Potential confound	All studies met criteria
Statistical analysis	All studies met criteria

from 6 to 12 months (WONG2008, CHITSABESAN2003). Three studies reported an average age of 15 years, whilst the remaining studies' participants ranged from 15 to 19 years old.

Narrative synthesis
One study (GROHOLT2006 [Groholt *et al.*, 2006]) suggested previous self-harm history as an independent risk factor (unadjusted hazard ratio 2.8 [95% CI, 1.39 to 5.64]), which was not adjusted for.

Depressive symptoms as a risk factor for repetition in young people

Pooled adjusted data

Two studies (CHITSABESAN2003, WONG2008) with a total of approximately 1,200 participants were pooled to report a marginally significant adjusted OR of 1.05 (95% CI, 1.00 to 1.11). However, one study was conducted in a school setting, where students self-reported past suicide attempts and related outcomes in a questionnaire. Despite the difference in setting, no heterogeneity was found.

Fifteen per cent repeated (CHITSABESAN2003) and 4.5% self-reported repetition (WONG2008) during follow-up.

Twenty-nine per cent had a history of previous self-harm (CHITSABESAN2003). Self-reported previous self-harm was the recruitment criteria in WONG2008. Therefore all participants self-endorsed past suicide attempts, of which 2% were attempted within the last year the survey was conducted.

The majority of participants were diagnosed with depression and substance misuse in CHITSABESAN2003. A quarter of participants had depressive symptoms and a fifth of them had anxiety symptoms in WONG2008. Adjusted factors can be found in Table 32 and quality of evidence in Table 33.

Both studies were conducted over a relatively short period ranging from 6 months (CHITSABESAN2003) to 1 year (WONG2008). In both studies, the participants' average age was 15 in the UK and Hong Kong respectively.

Table 32: Depressive symptoms – adjusted factors

	CHITSABESAN2003	**WONG2008**
Self-harm history	Yes	Yes
Suicide intent	Yes	Yes
Anxiety	–	Yes
Substance misuse	–	Yes
Others	Parent's' mental health; family functioning	Life stress

Table 33: Depressive symptom – quality of evidence

Study sample	All studies met criteria
Loss to follow-up	None met criteria
Putative risk factor	None met criteria
Outcome of interest	One of two studies met criteria
Potential confound	All studies met criteria
Statistical analysis	All studies met criteria

One study (GROHOLT2006) suggested depressive symptoms as an independent but marginal risk factor (unadjusted hazard ratio 1.05 [95% CI, 1.02 to 1.08]), which was not adjusted for.

Narrative synthesis

Three other studies (BRENT1993 [Brent *et al.*, 1993], GROHOLT2006, NOVAKOVIC2006 [Novakovic *et al.*, 2006]) with a total of approximately 400 participants reported depression as a risk factor. BRENT1993 reported that a diagnosis of major depression at baseline, and an affective disorder that continued through follow-up predicted repetition in young people. While NOVAKOVIC2006 reported that depressive, anxious and phobic tendencies predicted repetition, GROHOLT2006 reported hopelessness as a risk factor after adjusting for confounds; a diagnosis of depression was found to be an independent risk factor in this study.

Gender as a risk factor for repetition in young people
Pooled unadjusted data

Three studies (HAWTON1992 [Hawton *et al.*, 1992], MIRANDA2008, WONG2008) with a total of approximately 3,600 participants reported raw data for the calculation of an unadjusted OR of 1.24 (95% CI, 0.7 to 2.17) for the age range of 10 to 19 years (moderate heterogeneity, $I^2 = 62\%$). The result found no evidence of an association between gender and repetitio of self-harm in young people. MIRANDA2008 reported an adjusted OR of 2.7 (95% CI, 0.4 to 16.4). The wide confidence interval meant that no conclusion could be drawn regarding the direction or size of any association.

The repetition rates were reported as 9% (HAWTON1992) and 22.5% (MIRANDA2008). Twenty per cent reported previous self-harm and 16% had a psychiatric treatment history in HAWTON1992. Approximately one quarter of participants had various mood and anxiety disorders in MIRANDA2008.

Because the result was not significant, and confounds such as previous self-harm and psychiatric diagnosis might affect the influence of gender, evidence for gender as a risk factor for repetition in young people is inconclusive.

The quality of evidence for gender as a risk factor for repetition of self-harm in young people is summarised in Table 34.

Table 34: Gender in young people – quality of evidence

Study sample	Two of three studies met criteria
Loss to follow-up	None met criteria
Putative risk factor	Two of three studies met criteria
Outcome of interest	Two of three studies met criteria
Potential confound	Two of three studies met criteria
Statistical analysis	All studies met criteria

Narrative synthesis

In a narrower age range of 12 to 14 years, HAWTON2008 [Hawton & Harriss, 2008b] reported raw data for the calculation of an unadjusted OR of 1.14 (95% CI, 0.66 to 1.98). This has not been pooled with the above studies due to the difference in age range.

Age as a risk factor for repetition in young people

Narrative synthesis

One study (HAWTON1992) provided raw data for the comparison of repetition rates between younger adolescents (10 to 14 years) and older adolescents (15 to 19 years). The unadjusted OR was 1.09 (95% CI, 0.88 to 1.35). The result was insignificant.

Repetition rate for 10- to 14-year-olds was 7.6% and for 15- to 19-year-olds was 9.1%. Because the evidence base was weak (only one study), further breakdown of age as a risk factor in a population of young people is required for future research.

Suicide intent as a risk factor for repetition in young people

Pooled adjusted data

Two studies (CHITSABESAN2003, WONG2008) with a total of approximately 1,200 participants were pooled. There was no evidence of an association between suicide intent and repetition of self-harm in young people, with an adjusted OR of 1.45 (95% CI, 0.63 to 3.37); there was considerable heterogeneity ($I^2 = 84\%$). Adjusted factors can be found in Table 35 and quality of evidence in Table 36.

Table 35: Suicide intent in young people – adjusted factors

	WONG2008	**CHITSABESAN2003**
Self-harm history	Yes	Yes
Depression	Depressive symptoms	Yes
Gender	Yes	–
Suicide intent	Yes	Yes
Alcohol misuse	–	Yes
Anxiety	Yes	–
Others	Life stress	Parents' mental health and family functioning

Table 36: Suicide intent in young people – quality of evidence

Study sample	All studies met criteria
Loss to follow-up	None met criteria
Putative risk factor	None met criteria
Outcome of interest	One of two studies met criteria
Potential confound	All studies met criteria
Statistical analysis	All studies met criteria

6.2.10 Narrative synthesis – young people

Studies under this section cannot be included in a meta-analysis because the outcomes reported are not suitable. These studies either did not report 95% CIs, reported effect measures by subgroup only (for example, male or female, Asians or non-Asians, and so on), reported p-values only, or comprised a mixture of people who self-harmed for the first time or repeatedly self-harmed (in which results were not separable). However, these factors should not be overlooked as risk factors.

Anxiety as a risk factor for repetition in young people
Three studies (MIRANDA2008, O'CONNOR2009B [O'Connor *et al.*, 2009b], NOVAKOVIC2006) narratively reported anxiety symptoms or a diagnosis of anxiety as a risk factor for repetition in young people. Meta-analysis was not appropriate because none of the outcomes was comparable. O'CONNOR2009B was the only study that adjusted its finding for potential confounds such as sexual abuse history, self-esteem, sexual orientation worries and family history of self-harm. NOVAKOVIC2006 reported that anxiety symptoms were an independent risk factor, while MIRANDA2008 reported diagnosis of anxiety disorder as an unadjusted finding but showed no evidence of association following adjustment.

Other risk factors for repetition in young people
The following risk factors were supported by a smaller evidence base (only one or two studies). Clinical variables included any psychiatric diagnosis (GROHOLT2006, MIRANDA2008), affective disorders (BRENT1993), personality disorders (GROHOLT2006), substance use (MIRANDA2008, WONG2008), 'psychoticism' and 'neuroticism' (NOVAKOVIC2006), and suicidal inpatients (BRENT1993). Those who used violent methods of self-harm (HULTEN2001), and those who were not admitted or referred to psychiatric services after an index episode (HAWTON1992), might be at higher risk of repeating. A number of risk factors relating to family were highlighted, such as parents' poor mental health

(CHITSABESAN2003, NOVAKOVIC2006), the death of a relative (BRENT1993), family financial problems (BRENT1993, NOVAKOVIC2006), not living with parents (O'CONNOR2009B) and violence in the family (NOVAKOVIC2006). Relationship problems with friends (HAWTON2008, O'CONNOR2009B) and migration (NOVAKOVIC2006) might also be risk factors. Sexual abuse history and sexual orientation worries were reported in one study (O'CONNOR2009B) as risk factors. Two studies (GROHOLT2006, O'CONNOR2009B) also reported that self-esteem might also be a risk factor.

6.2.11   Clinical evidence summary – young people

Based on the evidence review, risk factors for young people are similar to those reviewed in the section on adults.

Key factors with pooled quantitative evidence
A history of previous self-harm is the key risk factor with most support from quantitative synthesis and narrative evidence. The studies were adjusted for different confounds, yet each study still found significance in this factor. Despite the difference in follow-up length and context in which studies were conducted, the risk was similar for all studies. This finding is regarded as reasonably robust.

Other factors with pooled quantitative evidence
Depression may be a risk factor for repetition. Quantitative synthesis reported only a marginally significant result, after adjusting for important confounds. One limitation of this finding was the difference in the settings in which the studies were conducted.

There is a general lack of evidence for gender as a risk factor for repetition in young people. The quantitative synthesis result was not significant and it was not adjusted for confounds. There is no other narrative evidence to support gender as a risk factor. Thus, gender as a risk factor in young people remains unknown.

Factors from studies reviewed narratively
Psychiatric diagnosis
A diagnosis of anxiety had some evidence supporting it as a risk factor in young people. However, a major limitation was that most findings had not been adjusted for confounding variables. Substance use had some narrative evidence reporting it as a risk factor, but it was based on self-report questionnaires conducted in school settings. There is little evidence to support a general psychiatric diagnosis (such as affective disorders) as a risk factor.

Relational problems
There are some risk factors relating to family and friendships that may be unique for young people.

A summary of risk factors for young people can be found in Table 37.

Table 37: Summary of risk factors for young people who self-harm

Risk factors	Outcome	Evidence base	Pooled data	Prevalence of risk factor (range)	Duration of follow-up (range)
Previous self-harm	Repetition (combined)	4 studies, N = 2738	Adjusted OR 3.27 [2.46, 4.34]	2 to 38%	6 months to 6 years
	Repetition (clinical)	2 studies, N = 1411	Adjusted OR 3.18 [2.35, 4.29]	29 to 38%	6 months to 4 years
	Repetition (community)	2 studies, N = 1327	Adjusted OR 4.09 [1.72, 9.74]	2 to 20%	1 to 6 years
Depressive symptoms	Repetition (combined)	2 studies, N = 1246	Adjusted OR 1.05 [1.00, 1.11]	66%	6 to 12 months
	Repetition (clinical)	1 study, N = 147	Reported adjusted OR 1.85 [0.44, 7.74]	66%	6 months
	Repetition (community)	1 study, N = 1099	Reported adjusted OR 1.05 [0.99, 1.1]	Not reported	12 months

Gender – female	Repetition (combined)	3 studies, N = 3609	Unadjusted OR 1.24 [0.70, 2.17] (I^2 = 62%)	33 to 73%	1 to 14 years
	Repetition (clinical)	1 study, N = 2282	Reported unadjusted OR 1.05 [0.75, 1.47]	73%	14 years
	Repetition (community)	2 studies, N = 1327	Unadjusted OR 1.33 [0.45, 3.92] (I^2 = 71%)	33 to 63%	1 to 6 years
Suicide intent	Repetition (combined)	2 studies, N = 1246	Adjusted OR 1.45 [0.63, 3.37] (I^2 = 84%)	14%	6 to 12 months
	Repetition (clinical)	1 study, N = 147	Reported adjusted OR 1.01 [0.99, 1.02]	Not reported	6 months

6.2.12   Narrative synthesis for older adults

One study (HAWTON2006) conducted a prospective study in the UK with 20 years' follow-up, recruiting 730 older people aged 60 years or above who presented to a general hospital in Oxford following a self-harm episode. Forty-seven per cent of participants were aged between 60 and 69 years and 24% had previously self-harmed. Only 15% of the sample received psychiatric care at time of their episode. Of the 149 participants who reported suicide intent scores, nearly two thirds of the participants (65.1%) scored in the high or very high range of the Beck SIS. Repetition rate was 15.3%. It was suggested that a previous history of self-harm was the independent risk factor for suicide, with some evidence showing previous psychiatric treatment and high suicide intent being risk factors as well. This finding was confirmed by a recent, large multicentre cohort study conducted in the UK (MURPHY2011 [Murphy *et al.*, 2011]). This study had 1,177 participants aged 60 years or above, presenting to six emergency departments in Oxford, Derby and Manchester. It was reported that 12.8% of the participants repeated within 12 months of presentation and 1.5% died by suicide within 12 months. This study concluded that previous self-harm, previous psychiatric treatment and being aged between 60 and 74 years were risk factors for repetition. There were no direct comparisons of risk factors for older adults and working-age adults. However, based on this study, it appeared that the risk factors among older adults were similar to risk factors for working-age adults.

6.2.13   Clinical evidence for risk factors in subgroups

Nine studies with psychiatric diagnosis subgroups were narratively reviewed. Participants in these studies were at risk of self-harm, but may or may not have self-harmed before. Study characteristics for each study included in the meta-analysis can be found in Appendix 15c.

Depression
OQUENDO2004
OQUENDO2004 (Oquendo *et al.*, 2004) conducted a prospective study in the US over 2 years in which they recruited participants seeking treatment for depressive problems. Seventy-nine per cent had depressive disorder and 21% had bipolar disorder. Of the psychiatric population, 53% engaged in self-harm. Fourteen per cent of the sample self-harmed during follow-up (with a combination of first episodes and re-attempts). The study reported that previous self-harm, a high score on a self-reported depression scale and smoking predicted future episodes of self-harm. Pessimism and aggression or impulsivity also had an additive effect. It was also reported that repeaters of self-harm were younger, more pessimistic and impulsive, had a history of abuse and frequently had a substance-use disorder.

SOKERO2005
SOKERO2005 (Sokero *et al.*, 2005) was a prospective study conducted in Finland for 1.5 years that screened for patients with depression. All participants had a diagnosis

of depression and 32% engaged in self-harm. The majority of the sample had a psychiatric comorbidity, with anxiety disorder being the most common comorbidity (54%). Eight per cent of the sample self-harmed during follow-up (with a mixture of first episodes or re-attempts). The study reported previous self-harm, lack of a partner (that is, being single) and chronicity of depression as the most robust risk factors for repetition. These factors were adjusted for age and gender.

HOLMA2010

HOLMA2010 (Holma *et al.*, 2010) was a prospective study conducted in Finland for 5 years that recruited participants from a hospital providing secondary care psychiatric services. All participants had a *Diagnostic and Statistical Manual of Mental Disorders* of the American Psychiatric Association (4th edition; DSM-IV) diagnosis of MDD. During follow-up, 14.5% of subjects (n = 36 out of 249) attempted suicide. Of these attempts, 73% took place during a major depressive episode, 19% during partial remission and 8% during full remission. When looking at the incidence rate of suicide attempts, the study reported an incidence rate of 332 per 1000 patient-years during major depressive episodes, 62 per 1000 patient-years during partial remission and 16 per 1000 patient-years during full remission. The risk of attempting suicide was highest during the first year of observation and, furthermore, the amount of time spent in major depressive episodes was also higher in the first year of observation. There were various sociodemographic and clinical factors that were also associated with a high incidence of suicide attempts, such as age, lower perceived social support and a previous suicide attempt as well as time spent in partial remission, but the most robust predictor was time spent in major depressive episodes.

BOLTON2010

BOLTON2010 (Bolton *et al.*, 2010) was a prospective study conducted in the US over 4 years. Participants were diagnosed with MDD and were part of a nationally representative epidemiologic sample. During a 3-year follow-up, 2.7% (169 out of 6,004) of the sample had made a suicide attempt (incident or recurrent); 1.2% (63 out of 6,004) of the individuals with major depression had made an incident suicide attempt. For this group, significant predictors were age (being younger than 45 years) and anxiety disorders such as panic disorder and post-traumatic stress disorder ($p < 0.01$), as well as some personality disorders. For all suicide attempts after follow-up, respondents with factors such as age (less than 45 years) and never being married were more likely to attempt suicide. The study also reported that specific features of MDD such as lifetime suicide ideation and lifetime suicide attempt are associated with suicide attempts, as well as anhedonia, feelings of worthlessness and guilt, and the amount of depressive symptoms endorsed.

Mood disorders
NORDSTROM1995

NORDSTROM1995 (Nordstrom *et al.*, 1995) was a prospective study conducted in Sweden for approximately 6 years. Participants were recruited from hospitalised patients with mood disorders. Twenty-seven per cent engaged in self-harm. The study reported that mood disorder patients with self-harm episodes were at a higher risk than those without a mood disorder for completing suicide. Neither age nor gender were found to be risk factors predicting subsequent suicide; however, it should be noted that findings from this study had not been adjusted for confounds.

Alcohol dependence
PREUSS2003
A prospective study, PREUSS2003 (Preuss *et al.*, 2003), conducted in the US for 5 years recruited participants seeking treatment for alcohol dependence. A large majority of the sample had a substance-induced psychiatric disorder (mostly depression). Fifteen per cent had a history of self-harm and the repetition rate was 29%. The study reported that previous self-harm predicted repetition. Being young, or being diagnosed with alcoholism or substance misuse-induced depression, were found to lead to a higher risk of self-harm. These factors were adjusted for confounds. Being female and unemployed at baseline were not predictive of repetition; however, they were associated with previous self-harm. It should be noted that those who were not followed up were less likely to be Caucasian, had a later onset of alcohol dependence and a higher intake of drinks per day. These could be potential confounds.

Borderline personality disorder
SOLOFF2008
A prospective study, SOLOFF2008 (Soloff & Fabio, 2008) conducted in the US for 2 to 5 years. Participants were recruited from both in and outpatient services for people with borderline personality disorder. Eighty-two per cent of the population engaged in self-harm. Nineteen per cent attempted suicide within a year of study, of which 92% were prior attempters. The study reported that predictors changed over time. In the short term (12 months), comorbid depression and poor social adjustment increased risk. In the intermediate term (12 to 18 months), psychiatric hospitalisation prior to any attempts, together with poor social adjustment, increased risk. In the long term (2 to 5 years), psychiatric hospitalisation remained a significant risk factor, whereas outpatient medication visits decreased risk. Because poor social adjustment carried through the short and intermediate periods as a risk factor, it was suggested that interventions for this population should focus on social adjustment to prevent self-harm.

Schizophrenia
CARLBORG2010
A prospective study conducted in Sweden, CARLBORG2010 (Carlborg *et al.*, 2010) followed participants with schizophrenia spectrum psychosis for 25 years to assess suicide attempts and suicide risks. Participants were recruited from hospital psychiatric wards and 32% had a history of attempted suicide. During follow-up, 8% (18 out of 224) participants died by suicide. There was a strong association ($p < 0.001$) between those who had made a previous suicide attempt and completed suicide during follow-up. This study also reported gender-specific specificity, sensitivity, positive predictive values and negative predictive values of attempted suicide and for

suicide. The probability for dying by suicide with a previous suicide attempt was 28% in males and 14% in females (18% in the total sample). The NPV indicated that there was a low probability that a person with no history of suicide attempt will complete suicide.

6.2.14 Clinical evidence summary – subgroups

The evidence base for risk factors among psychiatric subgroups is limited. The study participants were recruited on the basis of treatment of psychiatric problem – they might or might not have self-harmed before. Therefore, the risk factors associated with psychiatric problems might not be indicative of a further repetition of self-harm (but could be a generic risk factor for self-harm). One common risk factor shared across all diagnostic subgroups was previous self-harm. People with psychiatric problems who had a previous history of self-harm might be more likely to self-harm in the future. In addition, depression might be associated with a higher risk of self-harm.

6.2.15 Prevalence of psychiatric disorders in patients who self-harm

A systematic review conducted by Hawton and colleagues (2011) was adopted in this section for narrative review. This review aimed to explore the extent to which self-harm is associated with psychiatric disorders. The authors included 46 studies, of which seven were UK-based. All participants were recruited after presenting at the hospital following an episode of self-harm. Diagnosis was made according to DSM-IV for all ages. Studies were excluded where assessment was made only for a single disorder or a retrospective diagnosis. Populations with a learning disability and those residing in psychiatric hospitals were excluded.

An overall prevalence rate of 84% (95% CI, 75 to 92%) was observed among adults or mixed samples with a very high heterogeneity ($I^2 = 99\%$) in 30 studies. In the young people population (up to the age of 25 years), an overall prevalence of 81% was observed with very high heterogeneity ($I^2 = 97\%$) from nine studies. Prevalences for specific disorders were reported: 61% (95% CI, 41 to 79%) mood disorders were observed, mostly in females, of which the most frequent diagnosis was depression (52%; 95% CI, 43 to 64%); anxiety had a prevalence of 37% (95% CI, 24 to 52%); substance misuse had a prevalence of 36% (95% CI, 22 to 52%) and alcohol misuse was more common than drug misuse. Prevalence was higher in males for substance misuse, personality disorders had a prevalence rate of 28% (95% CI, 18 to 39%) in all adult populations and adjustment disorders had a prevalence rate of 22% (95% CI, 6 to 45%). Lastly, psychotic disorders and eating disorders had prevalence rates of less than 10%. It was observed that the prevalence rate of multiple diagnosis (94.1%, 95% CI, 88 to 98%) was greater than single diagnosis (75%, CI, 63 to 86%). There were no major gender differences in overall prevalence rates of psychiatric disorders.

The limitations to this review lay in the heterogeneity observed in pooled prevalence rates. This could be due to the variation in diagnostic measures (research or clinical diagnosis) and different definitions of self-harm. Studies were cross-sectional, which might make them susceptible to unstable diagnosis. Nevertheless, there was a high prevalence rate (around 80 to 90%) of psychiatric disorders (most commonly depression, anxiety and alcohol misuse) among people who presented to hospital for self-harm. This underlies the importance of careful psychosocial assessment for people who self-harm, in order to treat the underlying disorders and manage their self-harm.

6.2.16   Clinical evidence for protective factors

In this section, studies that looked at protective factors that might protect against repeated self-harm or suicide were reviewed.

A meta-analysis was not conducted because the outcomes were not comparable across studies. Studies were therefore narratively reviewed.

Problem-solving skills as a protective factor
MCAULIFFE2006
MCAULIFFE2006 (McAuliffe *et al.*, 2006) conducted a prospective study with data collected from 12 European regions for 12 months among the clinical population. The repetition rate was 29.6%.

The authors reported that the strongest of five problem-solving dimensions associated with repetition was passive avoidance. Passive-avoidance tendency is characterised by a preoccupation with problems, feeling an inability to change the situation, worries about the past and a greater likelihood of giving in so as to avoid difficult situations. This finding was adjusted for gender and age; however, it was diminished when self-esteem was considered in the model. The next best dimension was active handling of problems, which had also been adjusted for age and gender. It should be noted that 32% of participants had alcohol-use problems and the attrition rate was high (48%). Participants who were not followed up were more likely to be men, have a lower level of education and to have drinking problems. This study suggested that improving passive-avoidance (together with self-esteem) and active handling may be protective against further self-harm.

MCAULIFFE2008
A prospective study conducted by MCAULIFFE2008 in Ireland for 12 months among patients admitted for self-harm. The repetition rate was 20.4%. It was found that among those who had self-harmed for the first time, optional thinking ability (that is, difficulty generating alternative solutions) was associated with repetition within 12 months. This was not the case for repeaters (that is, had a history of previous self-harm at baseline). The authors also reported previous self-harm as a risk factor for repetition. Based on the reported risk and protective factors, the authors suggested that interventions involving optional thinking skills should be delivered to people immediately after their first self-harm episode to prevent further repetition. The male participants in this study were significantly older than the female participants, and more of the females participants were married and more highly educated than males.

The statistical model had adjusted for these factors; therefore, this finding is reasonably robust.

SANTOS2009

SANTOS2009 (*Santos et al.*, 2009) conducted this prospective study in Portugal for 9 months among people admitted to hospital for self-harm compared with a group with identical characteristics (age, gender and residence) who did not self-harm. The repetition rate was 24%.

Compared with the matched control group, participants with better problem-solving skills and self-concept were protected against repetition. However, the findings had not been adjusted for confounding variables. The majority of participants were female (82%) and 60% of those who self-harmed were students. Seventy-seven per cent of those who self-harmed mentioned their affective problems and 23.5% of them were on psychotropic drugs; 17.6% of participants had a history of psychiatric hospitalisation. The reported outcomes relied on self-report questionnaires completed at home. For these reasons, this study's conclusion should be noted with caution.

O'CONNOR2011A

This was both a cross-sectional study with data collected at baseline and a prospective study with data collected at follow-up in Edinburgh, by O'CONNOR2011a (O'Connor *et al.*, 2011a). Five hundred and fifty patients who self-harmed were recruited in the community. Three hundred and twenty participants completed the study at a mean follow-up period of approximately 6 months. Repetition rate was 46%, of which 31% repeated more than once between baseline and Time 2. Results from prospective analysis showed poor problem-solving skills were associated with repetition of self-reported self-harm at 6 months. This association remained after adjustment for previous self-harm and baseline suicide ideation. It was also found that being of a younger age and being single were risk factors for repetition. However, all outcomes were collected from self-report questionnaires.

Other protective factors
SPIRITO2003

This was a prospective study conducted by SPIRITO2003 (Spirito *et al.*, 2003) in the US for 3 months among youths admitted to children's hospital for self-harm. The repetition rate was 12%. This study reported that good family environment characteristics (such as general functioning and communication) served as a protective factor against repetition. However, the effect was lost when depression was factored into the model. Unlike other common findings, previous self-harm, suicide intent or a psychiatric diagnosis did not predict repetition in this sample. This may be explained by the heterogeneous population because it involved both inpatients and outpatients. Moreover, this was a short-term study that differed from the majority of longer-term studies. Repetition rates relied on self-endorsed re-attempts. This study suggested that good family functioning and communication may be independently protective against repetition. However, many confounding variables might have attenuated the effect.

GROHOLT2006

GROHOLT2006 has been included in the narrative synthesis of risk factors among a population of children (Section 6.2.11); however, one of its findings relates to protective factors. Parental bonding (particularly with the father) was found to be an important factor adjusted for other variables (such as hopelessness and number of diagnoses).

PETRIE1992

PETRIE1992's prospective study was conducted in New Zealand for 6 months among a clinical population. Repetition rate was 11%, and 2% of this included a fatal outcome. This study reported that a good sense of coherence was more closely related to future attempts than depression, hopelessness or self-esteem. However, this had not been adjusted for confounding variables. The study also found that previous self-harm, unemployment and living alone were risk factors for repetition. In fact, over half of the participants (54%) had a history of self-harm. These risk factors might have reduced the effect of sense of coherence when they were considered together in the statistical model. This study suggested that a sense of coherence might be independently protective against repetition. However, it is subject to the influence of other potential confounds.

A number of factors might have a protective effect and these were mentioned in Section 6.2.6. Individual psychological characteristics such as problem-solving capacity (DIESERUD2003, MCAULIFFE2008), self-appraisal and self-efficacy (DIESERUD 2003), and emotion regulation (HEATH2008) may have protective effects.

6.2.17   Clinical evidence summary – protective factors

The evidence base for protective factors is not strong. Some narrative evidence shows that problem-solving skills are protective for further repetition. It is unclear whether the effect may diminish after adjusting for other confounding variables. In younger populations, there is some evidence regarding a healthy family environment and parental bonding as protective factors for further repetition.

6.2.18   Narrative synthesis – social care and adversity as risk factors

It is important to note the absence of some commonly reported social risk factors in the reviews above, such as childhood experience of physical abuse, sexual abuse, being a 'looked-after child' and other stressful childhood experiences. These studies are often conducted retrospectively, depending on participants' recollection of their childhood experiences. As a result, these did not meet the inclusion criteria set by the GDG and were not included in the above review. However, these factors cannot be overlooked.

The technical team identified a few relevant systematic or literature reviews that were deemed to cover these risk factors. In addition, some key studies were also provided by some GDG members.

It is important to take note of the limitations to these studies. Retrospective studies are subject to participants' recall bias, when recollecting childhood experiences in particular. Also, the findings from the review and studies did not specify whether these factors were associated with repetition of self-harm or incidence of self-harm behaviour.

Childhood experience of physical abuse
FLIEGE2009 conducted a systematic review targeted at non-suicidal self-harm and found 12 cross-sectional studies reporting an association between childhood experiences of physical abuse and self-harm. STEELE2007 (Steel & Doey, 2007) systematically searched for literature in the children and young people population and reported a similar association. Similarly, EVANS2005 (Evans *et al.*, 2005) systematically searched the literature regarding young people (mostly aged 12 to 20 years) and found four studies reporting an association between physical abuse and self-harm. Of these, two studies conducted multivariate analysis that controlled for confounding variables such as age and gender, and an independent association with suicide attempts remained significant.

Nevertheless, the mechanism between physical abuse and self-harm is not completely understood. GRATZ2003 concluded that the relationship between physical abuse and self-harm was inconclusive. The evidence was mixed for both clinical and non-clinical populations. People with a history of abuse are often associated with various psychiatric problems that are found to be a risk factor for self-harm. Therefore, an independent and direct relationship between physical abuse and self-harm behaviour remains unclear.

Childhood experience of sexual abuse
One prospective study (YEO1993) was identified. One hundred and seventy-eight patients who presented at a hospital for self-harm were divided into 'abused' (8%) or 'non-abused' (92%) groups. They were then followed up prospectively for 6 months. Sixty-eight per cent of the participants had a history of self-harm and 54% of them had a psychiatric history. The overall repetition of self-harm rate was 15%. The repetition rate of self-harm among the sexually abused group was 50% and among the non-abused group was 12%. The study concluded that patients with a history of childhood sexual abuse were at a higher risk of repeating self-harm, with a cluster effect of four major risk factors (unemployment, previous self-injury or self-poisoning and psychiatric illness).

Systematic reviews
FLIEGE2009 found 21 cross-sectional studies reporting associations between childhood experiences of sexual abuse and self-harm. STEELE2007 reported similar findings and suggested that sexual abuse might be a stronger predictor of suicide attempts for male than female young people. EVANS2005 reported associations between sexual abuse and self-harm in five studies. In addition, the strength of association might depend on the severity of the abuse. In a multivariate analysis, when the psychiatric outcomes (depression and conduct disorders) were controlled for, the independent

association was found only among people who had experienced 'serious' abuse (involving sexual intercourse). The association with 'less serious' abuse was no longer found to be statistically significant when other confounds were controlled for. A recent review, CHEN2010, conducted a systematic review (of case-control and cohort studies) to assess the association between sexual abuse and a lifetime diagnosis of psychiatric disorders. The review found a significant association between sexual abuse and many psychiatric disorders, including suicide attempts (OR 4.14, 95% CI, 2.98 to 5.76). When factors such as age and sex were controlled, the association remained the same. Thirty-seven studies were reviewed and 27 of these looked at abuse that occurred in childhood, two studies looked at adult and childhood abuse and one study looked at adult abuse only. The majority of the population reviewed was female.

It should be noted that KLONSKY2008 (Klonsky & Moyer, 2008) conducted a meta-analysis that cast doubt on the degree of association between childhood sexual abuse and self-harm. Forty-three studies were included in the analysis, which reported a relatively small association (with significant heterogeneity) between sexual abuse and non-suicidal self-harm. The moderator analysis suggested that the heterogeneity was not related to age or gender. The type of participant (clinical and non-clinical) moderated the effect, where a stronger relationship was found between sexual abuse and self-harm among the clinical sample. Studies that controlled for psychiatric variables were reported not to have found an association between childhood sexual abuse and self-harm. The authors indicated the possibility of publication bias, which inflates the association between sexual abuse and self-harm.

Also, two literature reviews (GRATZ2003, ROGERS2003 [Rogers, 2003]) doubted the direct association between childhood sexual abuse and self-harm. The definition of childhood sexual abuse was inconsistent in the literature. Information was often collected retrospectively from self-reports or gathered from semi-structured interviews, which are both subject to recall bias. Moreover, the selection of samples was often biased towards clinical samples. From the analysis perspective, different studies controlled for different confounding variables, which makes the establishment of a unique association impossible.

There is evidence to support the link between childhood sexual abuse and self-harm; however, the association is complex because evidence suggests it also interacts with other confounding variables. This may imply that childhood sexual abuse can be conceptualised as a proxy risk factor.

Other stressful experiences in childhood

The role of physical and emotional neglect and family history of self-harm might be risk factors for self-harm, but they are relatively less well researched. GRATZ2003 reported that the association between neglect and self-harm was inconsistent. However, there was some evidence suggesting that emotional neglect has a stronger relationship with self-harm compared with physical neglect. STEELE2007 reported that an impaired relationship between parents and children increases the risk of suicide attempts; however, this association was no longer significant when children's psychopathology was controlled for. Furthermore, some studies examined childhood separation and the affective quality of childhood attachment as risk factors. However, conclusions cannot be drawn from the very limited amount of low quality studies.

STEELE2007 echoed the narrative findings from the earlier section where parental psychopathology was associated with adolescent suicidal behaviour in retrospective studies. It was reported that a family history of suicide is a key risk factor, and some evidence suggests that the immediate family members of people dying by suicide were at highest risk.

Klomek and colleagues (2010) reviewed the association of suicidal behaviours and bullying in 31 cross-sectional and longitudinal studies of children and young people. Studies were identified by electronic literature search of PsycNET and MEDLINE (no date specified in search) and by selecting relevant studies from reference lists of articles. This review reported findings that those involved in bullying, as well as victims of bullying, had a high prevalence of suicide ideation and suicide attempts. It is unclear whether there is an association between the gender of bullies and the risk of suicide ideation because this review reported inconsistent findings. There might be an association in particular between the frequency of bullying and suicide ideation or suicide attempts in males and females (Klomek *et al.*, 2007). For example, in females, if bullying is infrequent, there is still a risk of suicide ideation or suicide attempts compared with males, where only frequent bullying is associated with suicide ideation (not attempt). Klomek and colleagues (2010) also reported findings of studies that looked at cyber bullying (via the internet or email); however, there was limited research in this area. The main methodological problem of the studies looked at in this review is that the cross-sectional studies only provide evidence for a correlation between bullying and suicidality and cannot establish causality, unlike longitudinal studies. This review reports that there is limited (and inconclusive) evidence in longitudinal studies that look at the long-term consequences of bullying and suicidality.

Kim and colleagues (2005) conducted a longitudinal study and found that school bullying is a significant risk factor for suicide ideation or behaviour after 10 months; however, these findings were based on Korean young people so may not be generalisable to all populations.

A prospective study by Klomek and colleagues (2009) showed that the association between being bullied (as young as 8 years) and suicidal behaviour later in life is affected by gender. For example, females who were victims of frequent bullying were associated with making suicide attempts and having suicide ideation later in life, but this was not found in males, when controlling for childhood conduct and depression symptoms. The main limitation to examining studies in this review was that there was inconsistent terminology used for bullying, peer victimisation, and suicidal thoughts and behaviours.

Looked-after children
Stanley and colleagues (2005) aimed to look at the mental health needs of 80 looked-after children who were considered to have high levels of need and were aged between 5 and 16 years in two local authorities in England. Data from social services case files were analysed to look at health and education, experiences of the looked-after

system before entering and while being in the system, mental health needs and how these needs were met by services. A set of indicators of need was constructed that included emotional, social, behavioural/developmental and high-risk indicators. Children who scored highly on all indicators were considered to have high need. The majority of the study group were being looked after in foster or residential care settings and had entered the looked-after system because of abuse (mainly physical abuse) or neglect. When looking at the frequency and severity of mental health needs, it was evident that there were high levels of low self-esteem, angry or hostile emotions and aggressive behaviour in as much as 50% of the sample. Less frequent behaviours included drug misuse, bullying and absconding. There were high rates of self-harm in the sample, which included seven cases of overdosing, 12 of cutting and 17 of other forms of self-harm. A limitation to this study was that the sample consisted of children who were considered to have high needs and were challenging to the services. The data were limited to records of social services files and there was a limited number of reports from mental health professionals kept on file. This study highlights the need to explore the occurrence and management of self-harm in looked-after children and the need for support and training for families and carers of children and young people who self-harm.

Richardson and Lelliott (2003) reviewed the problems faced by looked-after children with regard to their mental and physical health, and education. Young people who leave care were found to be at particularly high risk of social disadvantages such as ill health and risk-taking behaviours. Saunders and Broad (1997) conducted a small study looking at 48 young care leavers and found that 35% of them had engaged in self-harm since the age of 15 years. Nearly double this number of subjects had reported suicide ideation and four out of ten subjects had made a suicide attempt.

Summary

One prospective study that was identified reported a history of childhood sexual abuse as a risk factor for repetition of self-harm. This finding was supported by systematic reviews of retrospective studies. Therefore, this risk factor should be considered in assessments bearing in mind the less robust quality of the largely retrospective research evidence. In addition, there is an association between poor mental health and people with history of childhood sexual abuse. Poor mental health may act as a mediator between history of childhood sexual abuse and self-harm.

6.3 RISK ASSESSMENT TOOLS AND SCALES

6.3.1 Introduction

There is increasing emphasis on the assessment of risk in clinical services. Risk assessment in mental health is a broad concept that covers a judgement not only of the likelihood of an adverse outcome, such as suicide or self-harm, but also of violence, risk to children, risk of exploitation and environmental risks such as safety in the home. This guideline focuses on risk of self-harm and suicide. Risk assessment in the UK is carried out by undertaking a clinical interview and this often includes a checklist of risk factors derived from an assessment scale. In the UK, there is no consistency in the risk assessment tools used by different mental health services. Despite the widespread use of these instruments, there is no clear evidence that their use makes any difference to patient outcome. The usefulness of any particular risk assessment scale for repeated self-harm depends on the ability to distinguish those who go on to self-harm from those who do not. Whilst the risk of repeated self-harm is important, healthcare professionals will be most concerned about the risk of suicide. This is more difficult to predict given the relative rarity of suicide even in a population at high risk such as those who have self-harmed.

Risk assessment is not the same as risk management and simply assessing risk without developing a management plan contingent on the level and nature of the risk is unlikely to improve patient outcomes. Previous guidelines (NICE, 2004a) have emphasised that risk scales should not replace a full psychosocial assessment and there is evidence that the latter is associated with better outcomes (Bergen *et al.*, 2010b; Hickey *et al.*, 2001; Kapur *et al.*, 2002).

A further issue to consider is the context in which the risk assessment takes place, in the emergency department after an episode of self-harm, in the community or at the point of admission to or discharge from an inpatient unit.

6.3.2 Clinical review protocol

The review protocol, including the review questions, information about the databases searched and the eligibility criteria used for this section of the guideline, can be found in Appendix 8. Further information about the search strategy can be found in Appendix 9. Also, see Table 38 for the clinical review protocol.

6.3.3 Studies considered[12]

A total of 7,642 studies were identified by the electronic search. Of these, 7,573 were excluded at the screening stage on the basis of reading the title and/or abstract. The remaining 69 references were assessed for eligibility on the basis of the full text. Sixteen prospective cohort and case-control studies providing clinical evidence for risk assessment measures met the eligibility criteria for this section of the guideline. These are: BECK1985 (Beck *et al.*, 1985), BECK1999 (Beck *et al.*, 1999), BISCONER2007 (Bisconer & Gross, 2007), CARTER2002 (Carter *et al.*, 2002), COOPER2006B (Cooper *et al.*, 2006b), COOPER2007 (Cooper *et al.*, 2007), CORCORAN1997 (Corcoran *et al.*, 1997), GALFAVY2008 (Galfavy *et al.*, 2008), HARRISS2005A (Harriss & Hawton, 2005a), KAPUR2005 (Kapur *et al.*, 2005), NIMEUS1997

---

[12]Here and elsewhere in the guideline, each study considered for review is referred to by a study ID in capital letters (primary author and date of study publication, except where a study is in press or only submitted for publication, then a date is not used).

Table 38: Clinical review protocol

Review question	For people who self-harm, do formal risk assessment, needs assessment and psychosocial assessment improve outcomes?
Electronic databases	CINAHL, EMBASE, MEDLINE, PsycINFO
Date searched	Inception to 25 January 2011
Study design	Prospective cohort or case-control studies
Patient population	People who experience self-harm (or suicide ideation, where the study clearly reports a history of self-harm). This includes all types of self-harm, irrespective of motive.
Intervention(s)	N/A
Comparison	N/A
Critical outcomes	Prediction of repeated self-harm or suicide measured by sensitivity and specificity values.
Note. Impact of setting/organisational context and content of assessment to be taken into account if data available).	

(Niméus *et al.*, 1997), NIMEUS2000 (Niméus *et al.*, 2000), NIMEUS2002 (Niméus *et al.*, 2002), OSMAN1999 (Osman *et al.*, 1999), OSMAN2001 (Osman *et al.*, 2001) and WAERN2010 (Waern *et al.*, 2010). Seven studies were identified for psychosocial assessment (BERGEN2010B, HAW2003b, HICKEY2001, KAPUR2003 [Kapur *et al.*, 2003], KAPUR2008 [Kapur *et al.*, 2008], OUGRIN2011 [Ougrin *et al.*, 2011], WITTOUCK2010 [Wittouck *et al.*, 2010]) and two studies were identified for needs assessment (CEDEREKE2007 [Cedereke & Öjehagen, 2007], KEENE2005 [Keene, 2005]).

For risk assessment, the inclusion criteria are prospective cohort or case-control studies that report sensitivity and specificity data. The populations used in the studies include people who self-harm, or have suicide ideation if the study clearly reports a history of self-harm. The studies used tools or scales (these terms are used interchangeably) to predict a repetition of self-harm or suicide.

Based on reading the full text of studies for risk assessment scales, 56 references were excluded because they were either not a self-harm population, did not look at prediction of self-harm or suicide, did not report sensitivity or specificity or did not use a risk tool or scale to predict suicide or self-harm. Studies were also excluded if it was unclear how many people in the population had self-harmed in the past. Studies that used another scale as a reference standard to measure the outcome of the study were also excluded. Studies that used a case-control design were excluded if the population of the control group was a general and not self-harm population, for example OSMAN1998. The study characteristics for studies that were included in the meta-analysis can be found in Appendix 15d, which also includes details of excluded studies.

For a full list of the scales reviewed in this chapter and the studies that have reported the predictive validity of these scales, see Table 39.

Table 39: Risk assessment scales and corresponding study ID

Scale	Study ID
Beck Hopelessness Scale (BHS)	BECK1985 BECK1999 GALFAVY2008 NIMEUS1997
Beck Depression Inventory (BDI)	GALFAVY2008
Scale for Suicide Ideation (SSI)	BECK1999 GALFAVY2008
Suicide Probability Scale (SPS)	BISCONER2007
Reasons for Living Inventory (RFL)	GALFAVY2008 OSMAN1999
Adult Suicide Ideation Questionnaire (ASIQ)	BISCONER2007 OSMAN1999
Edinburgh Risk of Repetition Scale (ERRS)	CARTER2002 HAWTON1995
Hamilton Depression Rating Scale (HDRS)	GALFAVY2008
Manchester Self-harm Rule (MSHR)	COOPER2006B COOPER2007
Global Clinical Assessment (GCA)	COOPER2007 KAPUR2005
Suicide Assessment Scale (SUAS)	NIMEUS2000 WAERN2010
Suicide Behaviours Questionnaire – Revised (SBQ-R)	OSMAN2001
Suicide Intent Scale (SIS)	HARRISS2005A NIMEUS2002
Statistical model	CORCORAN1997

6.3.4 Methods

The psychometric properties of the scales examined included sensitivity, specificity, positive predictive value (PPV) and negative predictive value (NPV), using pre-defined cut-off scores. Sensitivity and specificity can be calculated using true positive (TP), true negative (TN), false positive (FP) and false negative (FN) values.

In this guideline, sensitivity is defined as the proportion of those who go on to repeat self-harm who have been identified as at high risk of repetition of self-harm on the basis of their scores on the risk scale or measure (sensitivity = TP / [TP + FN]). Specificity is defined as the proportion of those who do not go on to repeat self-harm and who have been identified as at low risk of self-harm repetition on the basis of their scores on the risk scale or measure (specificity = TN / [FP + TN]). Predictive values may be more useful than sensitivity and specificity in clinical practice. PPV measures the probability that a person with a positive test result really has self-harmed (TP / [TP + FP]). Finally, the negative predictive validity measures the probability that a person with a negative test result really is free of self-harm (TN / [FN + TN]).

The GDG agreed that the desired psychometric properties of scales would vary according to the outcome being predicted and the context in which the scale would be used. For example, a scale predicting repetition in routine practice should help health-care professionals identify a person who is at high risk of repeating an episode of self-harm, without including too many who do not repeat (that is, has a low false positive rate). However, for a scale predicting suicide the consequences of missing individuals who would go on to die by suicide are so serious that the false negative rate should be very low.

Each study has been narratively reviewed and details of the impact of setting or organisational context have been included, if available, as well as the content of assessment scales.

6.3.5 Scales that predict suicide

There were six cohort studies that used scales to predict suicide (BECK1985, BECK1999, HARRISS2005A, NIMEUS1997, NIMEUS2000, NIMEUS2002).

The Beck Hopelessness Scale (BHS; Beck *et al.*, 1974a) is a self-report instrument that consists of 20 true–false statements constructed to measure the extent of positive and negative beliefs about the future during the past week in psychiatric patients. Typical items are 'My future seems dark to me' and 'I might as well give up because there is nothing I can do about making things better for myself'. Each of the 20 statements is scored 0 or 1. Responses are summed to give a score of 0 to 20. The severity of hopelessness is rated as 0 to 3 minimal, 4 to 8 mild, 9 to 14 moderate and 15 to 20 severe.

BECK1985 used the BHS in a cohort study of 207 psychiatric inpatients hospitalised for suicide ideation. Thirty-two per cent had previously attempted suicide. Participants were followed up for 5 to 10 years. The aim was to see if the BHS could predict the eventual number of suicides. Eleven out of 165 participants used in the analysis died by suicide within the study period. The results showed that, with a cut-off score of 10 or more, the BHS had a sensitivity of 90.9% and a specificity of 50.6% in identifying repetition (reported in Beck *et al.*, 1989a). The review team for this guideline calculated a PPV of 11.6% and an NPV of 98.7%. A limitation to drawing conclusions from this study of those with suicide ideation and little history of self-harm is that it cannot necessarily be extrapolated to guiding the longer-term management of those presenting following an episode of self-harm. Another limitation in the interpretation of the results is that this study uses a lengthy follow-up period of up to 10 years, which is not useful in a clinical assessment where the concern is the risk of suicide in the shorter term.

The Scale for Suicide Ideation (SSI) was designed by Beck and colleagues (1979) to assess the severity of suicide ideation in psychiatric patients. It consists of 19 items and each item consists of three alternative statements graded in intensity using a three-point scale ranging from 0 to 2. The items assess a person's wish to die, their desire to make an active or passive attempt, the duration and frequency of suicide ideation, sense of control over making an attempt and how much preparation they have contemplated. The scores for each response are added up to give a possible total score of 0 to 38. Higher scores are associated with a greater suicide risk. The SSI – Current (SSI-C) measures a person's current intensity of specific attitudes, behaviours and plans to commit suicide (Beck *et al.*, 1979) and the SSI at Worst Point (SSI-W) is rated when the suicide ideation is at the worst point in their lives. The SSI-C and SSI-W have high internal and good concurrent validity (Beck *et al.*, 1997).

Beck and colleagues (1999) used the SSI-C, SSI-W and BHS in a cohort study of 3,701 outpatients evaluated at the Centre for Cognitive Therapy in Pennsylvania in the US. Of the participants, 13.3% made a prior suicide attempt. Participants were followed up for 15 years. The aim was to see if the scales could predict the eventual number of suicides. Thirty out of 3,701 participants died by suicide. The results showed that, with a cut-off score of 2 or more, the SSI-C reported a sensitivity of 53%, a specificity of 83% and a PPV of 2.4%. An NPV of 99.5% was calculated from these results. The SSI-W (cut-off score of 16 or more) had a sensitivity of 80%, a specificity of 78% and a PPV of 2.8%. An NPV of 99.7% was calculated from these results. The BHS (cut-off score of 8 or more) had a sensitivity of 90%, a specificity of 42% and a PPV of 1.3%. An NPV of 99.7% was calculated from these results. There are a number of limitations that must be addressed before coming to any firm conclusions about using these scales to predict suicide. First, the study used a sample of outpatients and only a small percentage of them had a history of self-harm. Second, this study, along with the previous studies by Beck and colleagues (such as BECK1985), also had a lengthy follow-up period, which is not useful for a clinical assessment.

The SIS (Beck *et al.*, 1974b) is administered by interview and designed to measure the level of a person's intent to complete suicide once they have already made an attempt. It takes into consideration behaviour and attitudes before, during and after an episode. The scale comprises 15 items that are rated on a two-point Likert scale. The total score ranges from 0 to 30 and is calculated by adding up the scores of each individual item. The completion time is approximately 10 minutes and it is administered by a trained clinician. The scale can be divided into two parts. Part 1 is comprised of the first eight items, which measure the objective circumstances of self-harm. Part 2 is comprised of the remaining seven items, which measures the thoughts and feelings of a person at the time of self-harm.

HARRISS2005A examined the SIS in a cohort study on 1,049 males and 1,440 females who presented to a general hospital following self-harm. Participants were assessed by members of the psychiatric service or data were obtained by records completed in the emergency department. Participants were followed up for 3 to 7 years (5.2 mean year follow-up). The aim was to see if the SIS could predict the eventual number of suicides. Thirty male and 24 female participants used in the analysis died by suicide within the study period. The results showed that, with a cut-off score of 10, the SIS reported a sensitivity of 76.7%, a specificity of 48.8% and a PPV of 4.2% in male participants. In females, using a cut-off score of 14, the sensitivity rate was 66.7%, the specificity was 75.3% and the PPV was 4%. The NPV score calculated by the review team for this guideline was 98.6% (males) and 99.2% (females). The study also provided scores for Part 1 of the SIS in females. The sensitivity was 75% with a cut-off score of 6 and the specificity was 72.6%. The PPV remained at 4% and had an NPV of 99.4%, as calculated by the review team for this guideline. If the cut-off score was increased to 7, this yielded a higher specificity of 80.9% but a lower sensitivity of 66.7%. This study does not provide results that combine male and female subjects, which makes it difficult to generalise to a mixed male and female population of people who self-harm.

NIMEUS2002 used the SIS in a cohort study of 555 participants who were evaluated by a psychiatrist within 12 hours to 5 days following a suicide attempt, and most often as an inpatient of the medical intensive care unit. The participants were followed up from 10 months to 8 years and 10 months (with a mean time of 4 years and 6 months). Twenty-two participants died by suicide during the follow-up period. With a cut-off score of 19, the reported sensitivity for the SIS was 59%, the specificity was 77% and the PPV was 9.7%. The review team for this guideline calculated an NPV of 97.8%. This study also looked at the predictive value of the SIS with participants who were aged 55 years and above. Ten out of 88 participants in this age group died by suicide during follow-up. The reported sensitivity, specificity and PPV were 90%, 60% and 23%, respectively. The review team for this guideline calculated an NPV of 97.9%.

NIMEUS1997 used the BHS in a cohort study on 212 suicide attempters evaluated in the Medical Intensive Care Unit and during psychiatric hospitalisation. Participants were asked to participate in a suicide research programme and were followed up for a mean period of 4 years and 4 months. Thirteen out of 212 participants used in the analysis died by suicide. The results showed that with a cut-off score of 9, the BHS reported a sensitivity of 77%, a specificity of 42% and a PPV of 8%. The review team for this guideline calculated an NPV of 96.5%. When a cut-off score of 13 was used, the sensitivity was still 77% but with a specificity of 61.3% and a PPV of 13% (calculated NPV was 97.6%).

The Suicide Assessment Scale (SUAS) was developed by Stanley and colleagues (1986) and is a clinician-rated scale designed to measure changes in levels of suicidality over time. It consists of 20 items and each item is rated on a four-point Likert scale. Typical items are: 'sadness and despondency', 'hostility' and 'anergia'. Ratings are interview based and the completion time is approximately 20 to 30 minutes.

NIMEUS2000 used the SUAS in a cohort study of 191 suicide attempters evaluated in a medical intensive care unit and asked to participate in a suicide research programme. They were followed up for 12 months and eight out of 191 died by suicide during this time. The results showed that with a SUAS cut-off score of 39 the sensitivity of the scale was 75%, the specificity was 86% and the PPV was reported as 19.4%. One important note about this study is that, due to the low prevalence of suicide, the study used a case control design to calculate the predictive validity by comparing the suicide cases with a matched control of 40 participants who did not die by suicide. Using data from the study the review team for this guideline calculated an NPV of 98.7%. A major limitation to drawing a firm conclusion about the usefulness of this scale to predict suicide, based on this study, is that a case control method was used for the analysis of predictive values and therefore any interpretations cannot be generalised to make a clinical assessment.

6.3.6   Clinical evidence summary of scales that predict suicide

There are six studies (all cohort design) that looked at predicting a fatal outcome such as suicide in people who have self-harmed. A scale that has a sensitivity of 100% means that there will be zero false negatives identified by the scale and therefore it will be unlikely to miss any people who will then go on to die by suicide. The scale that reported the highest sensitivity of 91% and the lowest false negative rate of 1 is the BHS used by BECK1985. However, there are major limitations to the interpretations of these results, such as the use of a small sample of mainly suicide ideators and a lengthy follow-up period of 5 years. Furthermore the BHS would identify 76 false positives for every true positive, severely compromising its clinical utility.

Another drawback for these scales is that they all have low PPV scores (between 1% and 13%), therefore identifying many false positives, which makes them of limited use. The low PPV scores are a result of the low prevalence of suicide. A final point to note is that the follow-up period is extremely long in some studies (between 4 and 15 years), in order to increase prevalence. The greatest concern to healthcare professionals is to be able to predict suicide in the next few weeks and months. In the shorter term, the PPV of these scales will be even lower. For these reasons, the use of scales to predict the risk of suicide cannot be recommended in clinical practice. For more information on the predictive scales, see Table 40.

6.3.7   Scales that predict a repetition of self-harm

Six cohort design studies looked at non-fatal outcomes (CARTER2002, COOPER2006B, COOPER2007, CORCORAN1997, GALFAVY2008, KAPUR2005, WAERN2010).

Table 40: Scales that predict suicide

Study ID	Scale (cut-off score)	Sensitivity (%)	Specificity (%)	PPV (%)	NPV (%)	Prevalence
BECK 1985	BHS (≥10)	91	50.6	11.6	98.7	11/165 (6%)
BECK 1999	BHS (≥8)	90	42	1.3	99.7	30/3701 (0.8%)
	SSI-W (>16)	80	78	2.8	99.7	30/3701 (0.8%)
	SSI-C (≥2)	53	83	2.4	99.5	30/3701 (0.8%)
HARRISS 2005A	SIS (10 for males)	76.7	48.8	4.2	98.6	30/1049 (2%)
	SIS (14 for females)	66.7	75.3	4	99.2	24/1440 (1%)
NIMEUS 1997	BHS (9)	77	42	8	96.5	13/212 (6%)
NIMEUS 2000	SUAS (39)	75	86	19	98.7	8/191 (4%)
NIMEUS 2002	SIS (19)	59	77	9.7	97.8	22/555 (3%)

The Manchester Self-harm Rule (MSHR; COOPER2006B) is a clinician-rated screening tool designed for the initial assessment of self-harm in emergency departments. It contains four questions assessing history of self, past or present psychiatric treatment, and whether the service user has had a benzodiazepine overdose. The assessment of risk is divided into two categories: perceived low risk and perceived moderate or high risk.

COOPER2006B used the MSHR in a cohort study of consecutive service users who presented themselves to five hospital emergency departments following self-harm. The participants were followed up for 6 months and 373 out of 2,095 service users made a repeat attempt to self-harm, 14 of whom died by suicide. The reported sensitivity was 97% (95% CI, 95 to 98%), specificity was 26% (95% CI, 24 to 29%), PPV was 22% (95% CI, 20 to 24%) and NPV was 97% (95% CI, 96 to 99%).

COOPER2007 conducted an analysis of people who self-harmed and presented to an emergency department, 8,825 of whom completed the MSHR and 8,722 of whom had a Global Clinical Assessment (GCA) completed by emergency department clinicians or mental health specialists. The participants were followed up for 6 months, with 1,506 of those completing the MSHR and 1,481 of those completing the GCA making a repeat attempt to self-harm in that period, 59 of whom died by suicide. For the MSHR, the reported sensitivity was 94% (95% CI, 92 to 95%), specificity was 26% (95% CI, 24 to 27%), PPV was 21% (95% CI, 19 to 21%) and NPV was 96% (95% CI,

94 to 96%). For the GCA, the reported sensitivity was 85% (95% CI, 83 to 87%), specificity was 38% (95% CI, 37 to 39%), PPV was 22% (95% CI, 21 to 23%) and NPV was 92% (95% CI, 91 to 93%).

KAPUR2005 conducted a cohort study using the GCA to examine the risk of repetition in 3,828 people who presented to a hospital emergency department following self-harm. The assessment was conducted by emergency department clinicians and mental health staff. For the purpose of this guideline, only the findings of the assessment undertaken by mental health staff are presented here. Participants were followed up for 12 months and 549 patients repeated self-harm, 18 of whom died by suicide. The reported sensitivity was 17% (95% CI, 14.1 to 20.5%), specificity was 92% (95% CI, 90.7 to 92.6%), PPV was 26% (95% CI, 21.3 to 30.2%) and the review team calculated an NPV of 87%.

Kreitman and Foster (1991) developed a clinical and research scale to predict the repetition of self-harm within 12 months. The Edinburgh Risk of Repetition Scale (ERRS) has 11 variables including history of psychiatric treatment, marital status and age between 25 and 54 years old. A positive answer for each item is scored as 1 and scores are added up to give a possible total score of 0 to 11. The ERRS for research use has specific weightings for each item when it is scored.

Hawton and Fagg (1995) conducted two 1-year cohort studies in 1,180 people assessed in routine clinical practice at a UK general hospital following a suicide attempt. The study aimed to compare the performance of a clinical version of the ERRS (with non-weighted items), a research version (with weighted items) and a shorter version (comprising six items) of a scale developed in Edinburgh in 1974 (Buglass & Horton, 1974). Performance was examined in two ways: first, based on the method used by Kreitman and Foster (1991), that is, based on suicide attempts where a repeat attempt within that year indicated repetition (analysis Type A); second, based on individual persons (rather than episodes of attempts) where a repeat attempt within a 1-year period indicated repetition, measured by hospital re-admission (analysis Type B). The results showed that there was little difference in the performance of the clinical and research versions of the ERRS scales when compared with each other, using analysis Type A. These results were compared with analysis Type B, where both versions performed more poorly than in analysis Type A. The performance for the Buglass and Horton (1974) scale was similar to the clinical version of the ERRS, using analysis Type B. It is important to note that this study does not report sensitivity and specificity data, and has been reviewed to illustrate the background and development of the ERRS.

CARTER2002 used the ERRS scale by rating the items based on clinical interview, service user self-report and case notes. This cohort study used 1,317 people who self-poisoned and presented for hospital treatment. The participants were followed up for 12 months and 180 participants made a repeated presentation for self-poisoning. A cut-off score of 8 or more for male subjects and 6 or more for female subjects was used. The ERRS reported a sensitivity of 26%, a specificity of 84% and a PPV of 21%. The review team for this guideline calculated an NPV of 86.7%.

The following scales, as well the BHS and the SSI scales, which have been described above, was used in a study by GALFAVY2008.

The Hamilton Depression Rating Scale (HDRS; Hamilton, 1960) is a clinician-rated scale and consists of 17-items designed to measure the severity of depressive symptoms in people diagnosed with affective disorder of depressive type. Scores on each item are measured on a five-point Likert scale ranging from 0 to 4 (0 = absent, 1 = mild or trivial, 2 = moderate, 3 = severe, 4 = incapacitating), or they can be measured on a three-point scale (0 = absent, 1 = slight or doubtful, 2 = clearly present). The total score is the sum of the item scores and can range from 0 to 53. A score of 0 to 7 is considered clinical remission and at least 20 is low severity. It is advised to have two raters independently score a patient at the same interview and the administration time is approximately 20 to 30 minutes.

The BDI (Beck & Steer, 1987) is a self-report instrument that consists of 21 items constructed to measure the current severity of depression in psychiatric patients. Each of the items is rated on a four-point scale with scores ranging from 0 to 3). Scores for responses are added up to give a possible total score of 0 to 63. The severity of depression is rated as 0 to 9 minimal, 10 to 16 mild, 17 to 29 moderate and 30 to 63 severe.

The Reasons for Living Inventory (RFL; Linehan *et al.*, 1983) is a 48-item self-report measure designed to assess beliefs and expectations for wanting to live as an alternative to suicide in adults and young people. As such, the scale is one of the few instruments that assesses protective factors or beliefs defending against suicidal behaviour rather than focusing on risk factors. Typical items are 'I believe I can find a purpose in life, a reason to live' and 'I believe I can find other solutions to my problems.' Each item of the inventory is rated at six levels of importance ranging from 1 ('not at all important') to 6 ('extremely important'). Based on factor analyses with adults, the RFL consists of six domains of reasons for living: (1) survival and coping beliefs, (2) responsibility to family, (3) child related concerns, (4) fear of suicide, (5) fear of social disapproval and (6) moral objections. The RFL yields a total score as well as six subscale scores corresponding to each of the above domains.

GALFAVY2008 conducted a cohort study with 304 depressed psychiatric research centre participants, 54% of whom had a history of previous self-harm. Participants were administered the BHS, SSI, RFL, HDRS and BDI, and were followed up for 2 years. Fifty-two participants made a suicide attempt during follow-up, four of whom died by suicide. The BHS (cut-off score 5) had a sensitivity of 0% and a specificity of 100%. For this guideline, the NPV was calculated as 82.8%. The SSI (cut-off score 10) reported a sensitivity of 54% and a specificity of 75%. The PPV was calculated as 30.8% and the NPV as 88.7%. The RFL (0.25 probability cut off) scale reported a sensitivity of 35% and a specificity of 79%. The review team for this guideline calculated a PPV of 25.5% and an NPV of 85.4%. The HDRS (cut-off score 2) had a sensitivity of 4% and a specificity of 94%. The review team for this guideline calculated a PPV of 12% and an NPV of 82.5%. The BDI (cut-off score 16) had a sensitivity of 31% and a specificity of 83%. The review team for this guideline calculated a PPV of 27.3% and an NPV of 85.3%. When interpreting these results, it is important to note that this is not a study of a pure self-harm population but a study of depressed people, some of whom have a history of self-harm.

The SUAS has been described in Section 6.3.5. WAERN2010 used a modified version of the SUAS (Nimeus *et al.*, 2006) in a cohort study of 162 people admitted to an emergency ward and interviewed following a suicide attempt. Participants were followed up for 6 months and 61 participants repeated a suicide attempt, including five suicides. The results showed that, with a cut-off score of 24, SUAS reported a sensitivity of 61% and a specificity of 40%. The review team for this guideline calculated a PPV of 38% and an NPV of 62.9%.

CORCORAN1997 used a statistical model created by entering 11 predictor variables into a logistic regression analysis to identify people who were at high risk of repeated self-harm. The variables included items such as any previous act of self-harm, main method of self-harm used, alcohol taken at the time of the act, and so on (for more details on the method used for identification of these variables, see CORCORAN1997). One hundred and twenty-two participants were admitted to a general or psychiatric hospital following an episode of self-harm and had their data entered into a computer. Participants were followed up for 6 months, of which 26 repeated self-harm. Results were reported for a range of cut-point probabilities, ranging from 0.2 to 0.5. With a cut-off point probability of 0.2 (which has the highest sensitivity score), the analysis gave a sensitivity of 96% and a specificity of 81%. The review team for this guideline calculated a PPV of 60% and an NPV of 99%. It is important to note that data for 100 participants (from the original sample total of 212 participants) could not be entered into the analysis because there was incomplete information for at least one of the 11 variables. The study did report, however, that there was no difference between the excluded and included participants with regards to the predictor variables.

The search identified three case control design studies (BISCONER2007, OSMAN1999, OSMAN2001) that met the inclusion criteria for this guideline. The studies looked at non-fatal outcomes and reported the sensitivity and specificity of the following scales.

The Suicide Probability Scale (SPS) by Cull and Gill (1988) is a 36-item, self-report measure designed to measure the probability of suicidal behaviour in adults and young people aged 14 years and older. Individuals rate the frequency of their subjective experience and past behaviours using a four-point Likert scale, ranging from 'none or a little of the time' to 'most or all of the time'. It has a total weighted score and four subscales based on factor analysis: hopelessness, suicide ideation, negative self-evaluation and hostility. Typical items include: 'I feel so lonely I cannot stand it'; 'In order to punish others I think of suicide', 'Things seem to go well for me'; and 'I feel I tend to be impulsive.' The suicide probability score can be interpreted in relation to an assessed risk level: a score of 0 to 24 represents a subclinical risk level, 25 to 49 represents a mild risk level, 50 to 74 represents a moderate risk level and 75 to 100 represents a severe risk level.

The Adult Suicide Ideation Questionnaire (ASIQ; Reynolds, 1991) is a 25-item self-report measure designed to measure the frequency of suicidal thoughts in clinical and non-clinical adult populations. There are 25 descriptions of negative thoughts and behaviours that a person might experience over 1 month. Individuals rate the frequency of their experience and behaviours using a seven-point Likert scale ranging from 0 ('I never had this thought') to 6 ('almost every day'), and this yields a total score with a corresponding *T* score and percentile score.

BISCONER2007 conducted a sensitivity and specificity analysis for the SPS and the ASIQ in a case control study on inpatients from an acute psychiatric hospital. Participants were divided into either Group 1 (n = 25), who were admitted for suicide ideation or gesture (suicide risk group), or Group 2 (n = 42), who were admitted for other reasons (comparison group) but also had a history of suicide gestures. The aim was to determine the extent to which the SPS and the ASIQ could correctly classify subjects into their groups. The results showed that with a cut-off score of 50, the SPS reported a sensitivity of 52% and a specificity of 78%. The review team for this guideline calculated a PPV of 70.8% and an NPV of 60.9%. The ASIQ, with a cut-off score of 31, reported a sensitivity of 51% and a specificity of 78%. The review team for this guideline calculated a PPV of 72% and an NPV of 59.5%.

The Suicide Behaviours Questionnaire (SBQ) was designed by Linehan (1981) to measure past suicidal thoughts and behaviour. It is a self-report measure comprising 34 items. To date, many different versions of the SBQ have been used and, furthermore, OSMAN2001 validated a revised version – the SBQ-R. This is a self-report measure comprising of four items, each touching on a different domain of suicide behaviour. These include past suicide attempt (Item 1), frequency of suicide ideation (Item 2), threat of suicidal behaviour (Item 3) and the likelihood of a future attempt (Item 4). Each item is scored using a weighted summary score and the total score ranges from 3 to 18. For Item 1, response is scored on a four-point Likert scale ranging from 1 ('never') to 4 ('I have attempted suicide'), the total score, therefore, ranges from 1 to 4.

OSMAN2001 used the SBQ-R in a case control study on psychiatric inpatients. They grouped adult participants into a suicidal risk subgroup (n = 51) based on hospital admission for recent suicide attempts or serious threats, or a non-suicidal risk subgroup (n = 69) for patients who were admitted for other reasons. The young people were also divided into a suicidal risk and a non-suicidal risk subgroup based on this criteria. The analysis used a SBQ-R total score and Item 1 only from the SBQ-R, to distinguish suicidal versus non-suicidal individuals. The results showed that with a cut-off score of 8, in adults, the SBQ-R reported a sensitivity of 80%, a specificity of 91%, a PPV of 87% and an NPV of 86%. In young people, the reported sensitivity was 87%, specificity was 93%, PPV was 90% and NPV was 99%. For Item 1 of the SBQ for adults, the sensitivity was 80%, specificity was 97%, PPV was 95% and NPV was 87%. For young people, the reported scores were a sensitivity of 100%, specificity of 96%, PPV of 95% and an NPV of 100%.

OSMAN1999 used the ASIQ and the RFL scale in a case control study on psychiatric inpatients. They grouped the participants into a 'suicide attempter group' (n = 75) and a psychiatric control group (n = 130). The suicide attempter group had made prior or current suicide attempts with an established intent to die. This was measured from assessments by intake staff using various other scale measures (Minnesota Multiphasic Personality Inventory-2, SIS, BHS and the Positive and Negative Affect Scale) as well as the ASIQ and RFL. Group assignment was further endorsed by a review of medical records. The control group did not have a history of suicide attempt. The results showed that the sensitivity (the proportion of suicide attempters that were correctly identified as suicide attempters) using a cut-off score of 14 in the ASIQ identified the maximised sensitivity of 96% and maximised specificity (the proportion of psychiatric controls who were correctly identified as non-suicide attempters) of 79%. The reported PPV was 72% and the NPV was 97%. The RFL showed that a cut-off score of 3.8 yielded greatest accuracy in giving a sensitivity of 61% and a specificity of 81.5%. The reported PPV was 65.7% and the NPV was 75.5%.

6.3.8   Clinical evidence summary of scales that predict repetition of self-harm

There were ten studies (three case control and seven cohort designed) that looked at predicting repetition of self-harm (see Table 41 and Table 42). Sensitivity,

Table 41: Scales that predict repetition of self-harm (prospective cohort studies)

Study ID	Scale (cut-off score)	Sensitivity (%)	Specificity (%)	PPV (%)	NPV (%)	Prevalence
KAPUR 2005	GCA	17	92	26	86.8	549/3828 (14%)
CARTER 2002	ERRS (>8 for male, >6 for female)	26	84	21	87.6	180/1317 (13%)
COOPER 2006B	MSHR	97	26	22	97	373/2095 (17%)
COOPER 2007	MSHR	94	26	21	96	1506/8825 (17%)
	GCA	85	38	22	92	1481/8722 (16%)
CORCORAN 1997	Statistical Model (0.2)	96	81	60	99	26/112 (23%)
GALFAVY 2008	HDRS (2)	4	94	12	82.5	52/304 (17%)
	BDI (16)	31	83	27.3	85.3	52/304 (17%)
	BHS (5)	0	1	N/A	82.8	52/304 (17%)
	SSI (10)	54	75	30.8	88.7	52/304 (17%)
	RFL (0.25)	35	79	25.5	85.4	52/304 (17%)
WAERN2010	SUAS (24)	61	40	38	62.9	61/162 (37%)

Table 42: Scales that predict repetition of self-harm (case-control studies)

Study ID	Scale (cut-off score)	Sensitivity (%)	Specificity (%)	PPV (%)	NPV (%)
BISCONER2007	BDI (50)	52	78	70.8	60.9
	ASIQ (31)	51	78	72	59.5
OSMAN1999	ASIQ (14)	96	79	72	97
	RFL (3.8)	61	81.5	65.7	75.5
OSMAN2001	SBQ-R (8) Adults	80	91	87	86
	SBQ-R (8) Young people	87	93	90	99

specificity, PPV and NPV scores from case control studies may be less generalisable to a real world clinical context than those obtained from cohort studies. The GDG came to the consensus that the evidence needed to potentially formulate recommendations would be derived from studies that used the stronger prospective cohort design.

The prospective studies were examined in more detail to describe the sample and the sample size so that the utility and generalisability of the findings and precision of the estimates could be assessed. All studies with the exception of one included participants who presented to an emergency department following self-harm. The length of follow-up used by these studies varied between 6 months to 3 years. The tool that reported the highest sensitivity of 97% was the MSHR used by COOPER2006B. The limitation of this tool in terms of its clinical utility was its low specificity of only 26%. All the scales had relatively low PPVs ranging from 12 to 60%. This meant that many individuals were wrongly identified as people who would repeat self-harm, thus limiting the clinical utility of these scales and possibly resulting in unnecessary intervention in some individuals.

6.4 NEEDS ASSESSMENT

6.4.1 Introduction

While psychosocial assessment includes several components, the most important are the assessment of needs and the assessment of risks. The assessment of needs is designed to identify those personal (psychological) and environmental (social) factors that might explain an act of self-harm. This assessment should lead to a formulation, based upon which a management plan can be developed. The main components of an assessment of need after self-harm therefore include:

● social situation and environmental issues (including current living arrangements, work and debt, access to means of self-harm)
● family and personal relationships (including recent breakdown of a significant relationship)
● recent life events and current difficulties
● psychiatric history and mental state examination, including any history of previous self-harm and alcohol or drug use
● an assessment of physical health issues
● psychological characteristics that are known to be associated with self-harm (for example, hopelessness, problem solving ability, impulsivity)
● possible protective factors
● current episodes of self-harm including motivation for the act
● attitudes to help/care
● establishment of problem list with service user
● exposure to suicide or self-harm by others (family, environment, media, internet).

Information about the psychiatric, social and psychological factors and contexts of the act can then be brought together into a formulation that describes the antecedents of the episode of self-harm. The formulation should therefore include:

● Long-term vulnerability factors including early loss or separation from parents, difficult relationships with parents signified by rejecting or overprotective parenting styles, or abuse in early life. Although sexual abuse has been associated with self-harm, emotional or physical abuse are also important.
● Enduring psychological characteristics and psychiatric problems.
● Short-term vulnerability including current difficulties in relationships and lack of social support, work or health-related problems, drug and alcohol misuse, or exacerbation of psychological symptoms.
● Precipitating factors are likely to be stressors experienced in the few days immediately prior to self-harm. Again, relationship problems, financial worry, anniversaries, deaths or other losses can act as precipitators to the act of self-harm.

6.4.2   Narrative synthesis

The following section summarises two identified studies, which examined the assessment of need in people who self-harm.

CEDEREKE2007 aimed to look at the specific needs of people who have self-harmed by using a comprehensive needs assessment tool – the Camberwell Assessment of Need. Semi-structured interviews were conducted for participants (N = 140) 1 month and 12 months following emergency treatment for a suicide attempt. The Camberwell Assessment of Need looks at whether a need exists (as rated by a service user) and the severity of the need in 22 areas of 'every-day living'. The most common areas of need were 'safety to self (self-harm), psychological distress and physical health'. The aim of the study was to investigate the help that service users received from services (formal help), support from friends and family (informal help), whether help from services was considered adequate and, lastly, whether the amount of help received and its level of adequacy differed between service users who repeated suicide attempts during follow-up. There were 23 service users who repeated self-harm between 1 and 12 months, and 117 who did not. The results showed that after 1 month, a high rate of formal and informal help was received in the most common areas of need, mentioned above. But in areas of need such as intimate relationships, and needs in daytime activities, company and sexual expression, there was little (formal or informal) help received. After 12 months the need for 'safety to self' fell, but the highest rate of help received was still both in this area and psychological distress. There was no difference between repeaters and non-repeaters in that they rated the same main areas and the same severity of need. Furthermore, the help received did not differ at 1 month after the index episode of self-harm. After 12 months, however, repeaters had significantly more needs, such as 'safety to self, psychological distress and intimate relationships' to name a few. With regard to the help received, repeaters received more help for psychological distress, intimate relationships and company. Both groups found help from services to be adequate, with the exception of needing more information.

KEENE2005 conducted a descriptive cross-sectional study to look at the assessed needs and service use of a self-harm population. This population comprised people who had self-harmed by self-poisoning, asphyxiation, cutting, burning and other self-inflicted injuries. The first part of this study aimed to look at the assessment of need, including mental health and substance misuse needs. The second part assessed the inter-agency service use of this population, such as health and social care services, and compared it with utilisation patterns of a wider emergency department population. Results showed that 53% (n = 427) had an assessed mental health problem, 18% with drug or alcohol problems and 15% with a dual diagnosis. Only 10% had no assessed need. Results also looked at the proportion of each assessed need group and their referral to the relevant external agencies. Seventy per cent of those who had self-harmed and had mental health problems were referred to mental health services, 64% with drug problems were referred to a drug agency and 35% with alcohol problems were referred an alcohol agency or for detoxification from alcohol. Overall, 37% of those with at least one assessed need were referred to mental health services, 3% to a drug agency, 6% to an alcohol agency, 15% to social services, 16% to a GP, 15% to follow-up or outpatient services and 9% were discharged with no further service. When comparing those who self-harmed with the rest of the emergency department population over 3 years, it could be seen that the former were three times more likely to contact social services and ten times more likely to attend drug or alcohol agencies. This study described the service use of a small population of those who had self-harmed in the hope that inter-agency integrated care services could provide a better service for this population and help inform the development of integrated care initiatives.

6.5   INTEGRATED PSYCHOSOCIAL ASSESSMENT

Models and definitions of psychosocial assessment vary, but in this guideline the GDG uses the term to denote a comprehensive assessment of personal circumstances, social context, mental state, risk and needs (Kapur *et al.*, 2008). Many of the main areas of inquiry are listed in Section 6.4 (on needs assessment). A psychosocial assessment following an act of self-harm should be regarded as an opportunity to engage a service user in a collaborative investigation of the complex interplay of factors that led to their act of self-harm.

6.5.1   Narrative synthesis

The following section summarises identified studies, which examine the psychosocial assessment of people who have self-harmed. Some studies that are relevant to answering the clinical question, investigated whether receiving an assessment had an effect on repetition of self-harm or adherence to treatment (BERGEN2010b, HICKEY2001, KAPUR2008, OUGRIN2011, WITTOUCK2010). These studies compared groups of participants who received an assessment with those who did not or those who were given treatment as usual. A further two studies (HAW2003b, KAPUR2003) looked at these outcomes but did not make a comparison between groups of participants in their study design.

HICKEY2001 conducted a study where they looked at people who presented to hospital over 2 years following self-harm, comparing those who received a psychosocial assessment with those who were discharged from hospital without an assessment, and whether these participants differed in characteristics and subsequent self-harm. A psychiatric team conducted the assessments in a general hospital in the UK. When comparing their characteristics, the non-assessed participants (n = 145) were more likely to have a history of self-harm ($p < 0.02$), were recorded as showing difficult behaviour ($p < 0.02$), were uncooperative during physical examination ($p < 0.05$), took early discharge from the emergency department ($p < 0.0001$) and were less likely to have further healthcare arrangements made ($p < 0.0001$), compared with the assessed participants (n = 101). The non-assessed group also had more incidence of self-poisoning (74%) as opposed self-injury, compared with the assessed group (79%).

In a follow-up study, after 12 months of the index presentation, non-assessed participants were matched on characteristics (age, sex and type of self-harm) with assessed participants (control) and there were 88 matched pairs in this comparison. The participants' GPs were contacted for information on psychosocial variables of the participants within 1 year of the index presentation. There was no significant difference between the groups in terms of psychosocial problems, although these were more common in the non-assessed group. According to the monitoring system data, more non-assessed participants repeated self-harm within 28 days of the index episode compared with assessed participants, although this was not statistically significant. After 12 months, three times as many non-assessed participants repeated self-harm compared with assessed participants. When these data were combined with GP data, the results showed that 37.5% of the non-assessed participants repeated self-harm within 12 months compared with 18.2% of the assessed participants. One limitation to this study is that it excluded participants who were in inpatient psychiatric care at the time of the index presentation; therefore, few participants had a history of psychiatric care or self-harm and so the results might not be generalisable to all people who self-harm.

KAPUR2008 carried out a large multicentre research project in the UK for people who presented to hospitals following self-harm. The study aimed to establish factors associated with receiving or not receiving a specialist psychological assessment and whether this was associated with repetition of self-harm. Taking into account various social and clinical characteristics of the 7,344 participants, and also the type of substance or method they used to self-harm, key characteristics were associated with an increased likelihood of having an assessment in hospital. These were being aged over 55 years, having current psychiatric treatment, being admitted into a medical ward and taking antidepressants. A person less likely to receive an assessment was: unemployed, used self-cutting, chose to self-discharge from hospital and attended a hospital outside working hours. Overall, a repeated subsequent attempt could not be predicted based on whether one has or has not received an assessment. However, in some hospitals having an assessment appeared to reduce the risk of repeated self-harm and these hospitals tended to have a higher proportion of assessed episodes, whereas in others having an assessment appeared to increase the risk and these hospitals had a lower proportion of assessed episodes. Only 60% of self-harm episodes resulted in an assessment, overall. The findings of this and other similar studies need to be interpreted in the context of their observational design, which means that the observed associations may not be causal and could well have been influenced by unmeasured confounders.

BERGEN2010b carried out a survival analysis to examine, first, the association between psychosocial assessment by a specialist mental health practitioner following self-harm and a subsequent repeated episode, and, second, the association between having a psychosocial assessment after an episode of self-harm and the survival time until the repeated episode. The study was conducted in three UK centres where 13,966 participants had made a hospital presentation for a first episode of self-harm in the study period (2003 to 2005) and 55.6% had received a specialist psychosocial assessment. There were 18,483 repeated episodes of self-harm within the following 2 years, which included up to the first six episodes only for each person. Participants received a specialist psychosocial assessment for 54.7% of these episodes. The following results look at 'short term repetition' or the time to the first repeated episode. For participants who did not have a history of psychiatric treatment, the risk of repeating an episode of self-harm was 51% (95% CI, 42 to 58%) less if they received an assessment compared with not receiving an assessment. Likewise, for participants who did have a history of psychiatric treatment, having an assessment reduced the likelihood of a repeat episode by 26% (95% CI, 8 to 34%) compared with not having an assessment, with other variants controlled. For recurrent repetition, for all six episodes, results showed that participants who did not have a history of psychiatric treatment, the risk of repetition was 57% (95% CI, 51 to 63%) less if they received an assessment at the last episode compared with not receiving an assessment, controlling for covariates. Likewise, for those who had a psychiatric treatment history, having an assessment reduced the likelihood of a repeated episode by 26% (95% CI, 11 to 41%) compared with not having an assessment.

OUGRIN2011 conducted an RCT with young people who self-harmed to examine whether therapeutic assessment compared with assessment as usual improves attendance and engagement during a 3-month follow-up period. This study was set in CAMHS settings in London. Assessment as usual involved standard psychosocial evaluation and standard disposition planning. The therapeutic assessment was carried out by trained healthcare professionals and involved the same components as assessment as usual in addition to a brief therapeutic intervention. When looking at the attendance rate of the first follow-up session, results showed that subjects in the therapeutic assessment group had better attendance rates (OR 5.19, 95% CI, 2.22 to 12.10). Subjects were also given the Strengths and Difficulties Questionnaire (SDQ) and the results showed that although there was an improvement in scores for all subjects, there was no significant differences in changes of scores between the groups (mean difference -0.37, 95% CI, -3.25 to 2.53) and this was also seen in the Children Global Assessment Scale scores (mean difference 4.49, 95% CI, -0.98 to 9.96). There was insufficient evidence to make any conclusions regarding the difference between therapeutic assessment and assessment as usual. Limitations of this study include a short follow-up period and that the effectiveness of standard clinical practice interventions for young people who self-harm is questionable.

WITTOUCK2010 conducted a longitudinal study to examine people who attempted suicide and their compliance with aftercare following standardised psychosocial assessment. The study group was assigned to assessment using the Instrument for Psychosocial Evaluation and Care of Suicide Attempters (IPEO) (n = 93) compared with people who attempted suicide and received a non-IPEO based psychosocial assessment (n = 38). Semi-structured interviews were conducted at 1 and 6 months' follow-up (FU1 and FU2, respectively) after an index episode (within the study period). Outcomes measured included contact with emergency department staff (during hospital admission), GP and mental health services. The results showed that participants who had no inpatient history (OR 2.73, 95% CI, 1.18 to 6.29) or those who had only had one inpatient admission for treatment (OR = 7.15, 95% CI, 1.43 to 35.7) were more likely to receive an IPEO-based assessment compared with participants with two or more previous inpatient admissions for treatment. There was no difference between the study groups in terms of the treatment advice received and compliance with fixed referrals; however, participants in the IPEO group were more likely to have treatment options discussed with them than the non-IPEO group (OR 3.2, 95% CI, 1.23 to 8.45). During FU1, 62% of the participants who visited their GPs did so within 1 week of their index attempt. There was no difference between the study groups in the number of participants who visited their GP. However, during the period of discharge from hospital to visiting the GP, the non-IPEO group visited their GP 3.6 times less within 1 week after the index attempt (95% CI, 1.1 to 11.9). During FU2 there was no difference in the groups regarding the regularity of visits to a GP. At FU1, there was no difference between the groups in receiving mental healthcare, outpatient mental healthcare or pharmacological treatment. However, the non-IPEO group was more likely to receive inpatient mental healthcare than the IPEO group (OR 3.1, 95% CI, 1.4 to 6.8). At FU2, no differences in treatment received remained between the two groups. There was a high dropout rate of 37% between FU1 and FU2.

HAW2003B conducted a prospective study on 135 participants who presented to a general hospital in the UK following self-harm and were given an assessment by the hospital self-harm service, a specialist service that aimed to provide a rapid psychosocial assessment and aftercare for people who have self-harmed. After the index hospital presentation, participants were followed up for between 12 and 20 months to assess repetition of self-harm, treatment adherence and satisfaction. One hundred and six patients (79%) reported how satisfied they felt with their psychiatric assessment at follow-up and a majority felt that the assessor showed understanding and that their problems were taken seriously.

Only 33 (24%) of the participants who were assessed were offered an outpatient appointment by the self-harm service because there was a criteria for this offer, such as being at high risk for further self-harm. Twenty (61%) of these participants attended their first follow-up appointment, but there was no statistical difference between the characteristics of these people and those who refused an appointment or did not turn up. Nineteen (60%) participants had a follow-up interview and the majority of these were satisfied with the care that they had received from the self-harm service. Four out of those 19 (21%) participants who reported satisfaction levels of the treatment received had also reported a further episode of self-harm, whereas 30 out of 87 (35%) participants who were not offered treatment reported a repeat episode of self-harm. Although the repetition rate of participants who received aftercare was low, there was no statistical difference between these groups.

The self-harm service provided 53 (39%) participants who were thought to be at high risk of further self-harm with an emergency telephone number if needed in a crisis. Forty one of those 53 (77%) participants were seen at follow-up and six (15%) reported a repeat episode of self-harm during this period.

When interpreting the findings of this study, it is important to note that the authors defined self-harm as including self-poisoning and self-injury but excluded self-cutting that was considered part of a repetitive pattern of self-mutilation. Another limitation to interpreting the findings of this study is that the sample size of participants offered outpatient appointments and interviewed regarding satisfaction of the psychosocial assessment that they received is small. Furthermore, experiences of the psychiatric assessment were measured after the 12- to 20-month follow-up period, where 15 participants could not then remember or report on the assessors' attitude towards their problems. This study had an original sample of 150 participants presenting to hospital for self-harm. Ninety per cent of these received an assessment; however, this study did not compare outcomes between groups of participants who received and did not receive a psychosocial assessment.

KAPUR2003 conducted a prospective study to look at the differences in six UK hospitals with regards to their management (including rate of psychosocial assessments received by participants) and direct costs associated with participants presenting for self-poisoning. Three of these hospitals had a multidisciplinary self-harm team consisting of medical or nursing staff as well as social workers who carried out the assessments. Over a 5-month study period there were 1,778 episodes of self-poisoning involving 1,306 people aged over 16 years. When looking at differences between hospitals, rates of admission following an episode of self-harm varied from 16.5 to 81.3%, rates of psychosocial assessment varied from 28.5 to 57.7%, rates of admission to a psychiatric bed varied from 1.8 to 6.2% and the rate of specific follow-up being arranged by the hospital varied from 16.3 to 58.6%. Hospital costs (including capital charges and general services) ranged from £228 to £422. The rate of repetition varied from 10.3 to 16.1%, but the difference between hospitals was not statistically significant. Furthermore, the rate was similar in the hospitals with a self-harm team (14%) and with no such team (15.2%). Six hundred and four participants who had presented in the first 8 weeks of the study were followed up to measure repetition of self-poisoning within 12 weeks of their index presentation of which 88 (14.6%) participants repeated self-poisoning. This study found that the repetition rate of participants receiving an assessment was 9.8% compared with 17.9% in those who did not receive an assessment, and this association reached statistical significance (p < 0.005) even when adjusted for differences in participants' characteristics such as age, sex, substance dependence, previous self-harm and current contact with psychiatric services (adjusted OR 0.42, 95% CI, 0.25 to 0.71, p <0.005). One limitation of this study is that it did not measure rates of repetition in a larger sample. If this had been done, there may have been more significant differences noticed between teaching and district hospitals, hospitals with or without specialist teams and in terms of aspects of management.

6.5.2   Summary

Due to the studies being very different from each other and therefore not meta-analysable, there was insufficient evidence to draw any conclusions regarding the association between psychosocial assessment and improvement in outcomes. Nevertheless, psychosocial assessment is an important part of developing care and management plans for self-harm. Reviews conducted in Section 6.2 and Section 6.3 may inform areas to explore during psychosocial assessment.

6.6   FROM EVIDENCE TO RECOMMENDATIONS

Risk assessment

Based on the evidence review conducted in Section 6.2, the following risk factors in particular should be considered when assessing risk of repeated self-harm or suicide: previous self-harm and depressive symptoms. These two factors were supported by pooled quantitative analysis. Previous self-harm before an index episode is the most robust risk factor predicting both repetition and suicide following self-harm. The size of the evidence base and the adjustment of confounding variables provide stronger support for this risk factor. Another factor, depressive symptoms, is also important but less robust.

Other risk factors, such as psychiatric illness and current and past suicidal intent, should also be taken into account. The personal and social context associated with the behaviour and any other specific antecedent factors should be noted. Individual risk and protective factors that may increase or decrease risks associated with repetition of self-harm are important as well. Interpersonal relationships with family or significant others may also lead to possible changes (positive or negative) in the level of risk. It is important to note that risk factors often overlap with each other, and measuring one may be a proxy measure for another. The association between factors does not imply any causal relations. Therefore, the evidence review in Section 6.2 is only intended to give guidance on factors to consider in psychosocial assessment, and should not be used for predicting risk.

Risk assessment tools and scales

No risk scale can be recommended for use in isolation to distinguish people at risk of repeated self-harm from those who are not. Based on the evidence reviewed in Section 6.3, there are major limitations to making a recommendation for the use of a scale alone to predict whether a person who has a history of self-harm will go on to die by suicide. The results of the risk assessment scales show that is it also almost always likely to miss people who will go on to die by suicide. The main limitation is that suicide in nature is a rare outcome, therefore, the prevalence will always be low which makes it difficult for scales, when tested, to correctly identify the probability that a person with a positive test result really has self-harmed.

There are also limitations for making a recommendation for the use of a scale alone to predict a repeated non-fatal episode of self-harm. Although some scales perform well in correctly identifying the number of people who self-harm and were classified as high risk, they perform poorly in correctly identifying those who were categorised at low risk. Furthermore, the scales will identify many individuals as high risk, who do not go on to self-harm, reducing their clinical utility. As a result, risk tools and scales should not be used to predict future repetition or suicide following self-harm; neither should risk tools or scales be used to determine treatment offers or discharge decisions. However, risk tools may be considered to prompt, add detail and help structure psychosocial assessments.

In addition, it is also good practice to identify and agree with service users the specific risks for them. Healthcare professionals should differentiate between long-term and more immediate risks, and monitor any changes in risks and associated factors.

Psychosocial assessment

Based on current literature reviewed in Sections 6.4 and 6.5, it is difficult to draw conclusions regarding the association between psychosocial assessment and improvement in outcomes. Nevertheless, an integrated psychosocial assessment should be regarded as part of the therapeutic process to engage the service user.

A comprehensive psychosocial assessment including an assessment of needs and risk should be carried out on all those who have self-harmed. This includes people from black and minority ethnic groups, children and young people, as well as people older than 65 years of age. Assessment should follow the same principles as for adults who self-harm in each subgroup.

In Chapter 4, the qualitative literature highlights the importance of exploring the meaning and functions of self-harm for each individual. Health and social care professionals should treat each episode in its own right and acknowledge each person who self-harms does so for individual reasons.

6.7   RECOMMENDATIONS

6.7.1   Recommendations

General principles of care
Primary care

6.7.1.1   If a person presents in primary care with a history of self-harm and a risk of repetition, consider referring them to community mental health services for assessment. If they are under 18 years, consider referring them to CAMHS for assessment. Make referral a priority when:
- levels of distress are rising, high or sustained
- the risk of self-harm is increasing or unresponsive to attempts to help
- the person requests further help from specialist services
- levels of distress in parents or carers of children and young people are rising, high or sustained despite attempts to help.

6.7.1.2   If a person who self-harms is receiving treatment or care in primary care as well as secondary care, primary and secondary health and social care professionals should ensure they work cooperatively, routinely sharing up-to-date care and risk management plans. In these circumstances, primary health and social care professionals should attend CPA meetings.

6.7.1.3   Primary care professionals should monitor the physical health of people who self-harm. Pay attention to the physical consequences of self-harm as well as other physical healthcare needs.

Psychosocial assessment in community mental health services and other specialist mental health settings: integrated and comprehensive assessment of needs and risks

6.7.1.4   Offer an integrated and comprehensive psychosocial assessment of needs (see recommendations 6.7.1.5 to 6.7.1.8) and risks (see recommendations 6.7.1.9 to 6.7.1.11) to understand and engage people who self-harm and to initiate a therapeutic relationship.

Assessment of needs

6.7.1.5   Assessment of needs should include:
- skills, strengths and assets
- coping strategies

- mental health problems or disorders
- physical health problems or disorders
- social circumstances and problems
- psychosocial and occupational functioning, and vulnerabilities
- recent and current life difficulties, including personal and financial problems
- the need for psychological intervention, social care and support, occupational rehabilitation, and also drug treatment for any associated conditions
- the needs of any dependent children.

6.7.1.6   All people over 65 years who self-harm should be assessed by mental health professionals experienced in the assessment of older people who self-harm. Assessment should follow the same principles as for working-age adults who self-harm (see recommendations 6.7.1.4 and 6.7.1.5). In addition:
- pay particular attention to the potential presence of depression, cognitive impairment and physical ill health
- include a full assessment of the person's social and home situation, including any role they have as a carer, and
- take into account the higher risks of suicide following self-harm in older people.

6.7.1.7   Follow the same principles as for adults when assessing children and young people who self-harm (see recommendations 6.7.1.4 and 6.7.1.5), but also include a full assessment of the person's family, social situation, and child protection issues.

6.7.1.8   During assessment, explore the meaning of self-harm for the person and take into account that:
- each person who self-harms does so for individual reasons, and
- each episode of self-harm should be treated in its own right and a person's reasons for self-harm may vary from episode to episode.

Risk assessment

A risk assessment is a detailed clinical assessment that includes the evaluation of a wide range of biological, social and psychological factors that are relevant to the individual and, in the judgement of the healthcare professional conducting the assessment, relevant to future risks, including suicide and self-harm.

6.7.1.9   When assessing the risk of repetition of self-harm or risk of suicide, identify and agree with the person who self-harms the specific risks for them, taking into account:
- methods and frequency of current and past self-harm
- current and past suicidal intent
- depressive symptoms and their relationship to self-harm
- any psychiatric illness and its relationship to self-harm
- the personal and social context and any other specific factors preceding self-harm, such as specific unpleasant affective states or emotions and changes in relationships

- specific risk factors and protective factors (social, psychological, pharmacological and motivational) that may increase or decrease the risks associated with self-harm
- coping strategies that the person has used to either successfully limit or avert self-harm or to contain the impact of personal, social or other factors preceding episodes of self-harm
- significant relationships that may either be supportive or represent a threat (such abuse or neglect) and may lead to changes in the level of risk
- immediate and longer-term risks.

6.7.1.10 Consider the possible presence of other coexisting risk-taking or destructive behaviours, such as engaging in unprotected sexual activity, exposure to unnecessary physical risks, drug misuse or engaging in harmful or hazardous drinking.

6.7.1.11 When assessing risk, consider asking the person who self-harms about whether they have access to family members', carers' or significant others'[13] medications.

6.7.1.12 In the initial management of self-harm in children and young people, advise parents and carers of the need to remove all medications or, where possible, other means of self-harm available to the child or young person

6.7.1.13 Be aware that all acts of self-harm in older people should be taken as evidence of suicidal intent until proven otherwise.

Risk assessment tools and scales

Risk assessment tools and scales are usually checklists that can be completed and scored by a clinician or sometimes the service user depending on the nature of the tool or scale. They are designed to give a crude indication of the level of risk (for example, high or low) of a particular outcome, most often suicide.

6.7.1.14 Do not use risk assessment tools and scales to predict future suicide or repetition of self-harm.

6.7.1.15 Do not use risk assessment tools and scales to determine who should and should not be offered treatment or who should be discharged.

6.7.1.16 Risk assessment tools may be considered to help structure risk assessments as long as they include the areas identified in recommendation 6.7.1.9.

Developing an integrated care and risk management plan

6.7.1.17 Summarise the key areas of needs and risks identified in the assessment (see recommendations 6.7.1.5 to 6.7.1.11) and use these to develop a care plan (see recommendations 6.7.1.20 to 6.7.1.21) and a risk management plan (see recommendations 6.7.1.22 and 6.7.1.23) in conjunction with the person who self-harms and their family, carers or significant others[13] if this

---

[13]'Significant other' refers not just to a partner but also to friends and any person the service user considers to be important to them.

is agreed with the person. Provide printed copies for the service user and share them with the GP.

6.7.1.18 If there is disagreement between health and social care professionals and the person who self-harms about their needs or risks, consider offering the person the opportunity to write this in their notes.

Longer-term treatment and management of self-harm

Provision of care

6.7.1.19 Mental health services (including community mental health teams and liaison psychiatry teams) should generally be responsible for the routine assessment (see recommendations 6.7.1.4 to 6.7.1.5), and the longer-term treatment and management of self-harm. In children and young people this should be the responsibility of tier 2 and 3 CAMHS[14].

Care plans

6.7.1.20 Discuss, agree and document the aims of longer-term treatment in the care plan with the person who self-harms. These aims may be to:
- prevent escalation of self-harm
- reduce harm arising from self-harm or reduce or stop self-harm
- reduce or stop other risk-related behaviour
- improve social or occupational functioning
- improve quality of life
- improve any associated mental health conditions.

Review the person's care plan with them, including the aims of treatment, and revise it at agreed intervals of not more than 1 year.

6.7.1.21 Care plans should be multidisciplinary and developed collaboratively with the person who self-harms and, provided the person agrees, with their family, carers or significant others[15]. Care plans should:
- identify realistic and optimistic long-term goals, including education, employment and occupation
- identify short-term treatment goals (linked to the long-term goals) and steps to achieve them
- identify the roles and responsibilities of any team members and the person who self-harms
- include a jointly prepared risk management plan (see recommendations 6.7.1.22 to 6.7.1.25)
- be shared with the person's GP.

Risk management plans

6.7.1.22 A risk management plan should be a clearly identifiable part of the care plan and should:

---

[14]Tier 2 CAMHS: primary care; Tier 3 CAMHS: community mental health teams.

[15]'Significant other' refers not just to a partner but also to friends and any person the service user considers to be important to them

- address each of the long-term and more immediate risks identified in the risk assessment
- address the specific factors (psychological, pharmacological, social and relational) identified in the assessment as associated with increased risk, with the agreed aim of reducing the risk of repetition of self-harm and/or the risk of suicide
- include a crisis plan outlining self-management strategies and how to access services during a crisis when self-management strategies fail
- ensure that the risk management plan is consistent with the long-term treatment strategy.

Inform the person who self-harms of the limits of confidentiality and that information in the plan may be shared with other professionals.

6.7.1.23 Update risk management plans regularly for people who continue to be at risk of further self-harm. Monitor changes in risk and specific associated factors for the service user, and evaluate the impact of treatment strategies over time.

Provision of information about the treatment and management of self-harm

6.7.1.24 Offer the person who self-harms relevant written and verbal information about, and give time to discuss with them, the following:
- the dangers and long-term outcomes associated with self-harm
- the available interventions and possible strategies available to help reduce self-harm and/or its consequences (see 4.6.1.1 and 7.7.1.1)
- treatment of any associated mental health conditions (see Sections 7.3 and 8.5).

6.7.1.25 Ensure that people who self-harm, and their families, carers and significant others[16] where this is agreed with the person, have access to the 'Understanding NICE guidance' booklet for this guideline and for the short-term management of self-harm (NICE Clinical Guideline 16).

6.8   RESEARCH RECOMMENDATION

6.8.1   Research recommendation

6.8.1.1 The effectiveness of psychosocial assessment with a valid risk scale, compared with psychosocial assessment, for the management of people who self-harm (including young people)

For people who self-harm (including young people), does the provision of psychosocial assessment with a validated risk scale, compared with psychosocial assessment alone, improve outcomes?

---

[16]'Significant other' refers not just to a partner but also to friends and any person the service user considers to be important to them.

Psychosocial assessment

This question should be answered using a well-conducted RCT. The assessment should be conducted by mental health professionals in CMHTs. The main outcomes should include both hospital-reported and self-reported repetitions of self-harm. Outcomes such as service users' experience of assessment and the impact on therapeutic engagement should also be included. The duration of the study should be at least 6 months.

Why this is important
There are many different scales aimed at predicting the risk of self-harm and these are widely used in clinical practice. The sensitivity and specificity of these scales are, at best, modest. While individual scales may provide useful prompts for making a psychosocial assessment, it is possible that they may disrupt engagement and encourage clinicians to treat risk as dichotomous rather than continuous. It is therefore important to establish how they are used, how their use is experienced and whether scales do or do not improve tangible service-user outcomes.

7 PSYCHOLOGICAL AND PSYCHOSOCIAL INTERVENTIONS

This chapter provides an evaluation of the evidence for psychological and psychosocial interventions for the management and treatment of people who self-harm.

As discussed in the short-term guideline (NICE, 2004a), self-harm is not a medical diagnosis but a heterogeneous set of behaviours that can have different meanings in different contexts. Therefore, psychological and psychosocial interventions need to take account of this complexity (Hjelmeland *et al.*, 2002; O'Connor *et al.*, 2011b) and recognise that there is no 'one size fits all' intervention for self-harm. A key aim of any intervention is to reduce self-harm through understanding the specific contributing factors in each individual.

7.1 INTRODUCTION

Management of self-harm takes place in a wide range of health and social care settings involving services for children, young people and adults. Provision of self-harm services in the UK appears to be variable (Bennewith *et al.*, 2004; Kapur *et al.*, 1998) and many individuals do not receive specialist follow-up or interventions (Kapur *et al.*, 1999). Self-harm is also a key factor in the treatment of a wide range of psychiatric disorders and difficulties, including borderline personality disorder (Bateman & Fonagy 2009; Clarkin *et al.*, 2007) and substance misuse (Gunnell *et al.*, 2008; Sinclair *et al.*, 2010b).

The treatment of self-harm can be through distinct stand-alone psychological therapies (O'Connor *et al.*, 2011b) or adjunctive treatments that operate alongside standard care, such as contact by letter, postcard, telephone or provision of crisis cards (Kapur *et al.*, 2010a). The setting in which treatment is provided is also important, for example at home or in community mental health settings. Who provides the treatment also needs to be considered. Generic mental health services and the voluntary sector have important roles in contemporary service provision, and specialist multidisciplinary self-harm teams in secondary care are becoming increasingly common.

Interventions for self-harm might focus on the behaviour itself or take a more holistic approach by dealing with relationships, cognitions and social factors. Interventions may be delivered individually or in groups. Therapeutic engagement is very important in this group of service users who some professionals might find hard to treat (Ougrin *et al.*, 2011). There may be some benefit in differentiating between individuals who have a transient relationship with self-harm and those whose self-harm occurs over long periods of time. Despite the range of treatments and service provision, the evidence to date in terms of the effectiveness of psychological or psychosocial interventions remains unclear.

Aim of review

This review aims to explore the effect of psychological and psychosocial interventions on the repetition of self-harm. This was selected as the main outcome because of its clinical importance, the relationship between repeated self-harm and suicide and its inclusion as an outcome in the majority of studies to date. However, it is accepted that this is not always the only outcome of interest in clinical settings. The effect of interventions on a range of psychological factors and engagement with services was therefore also reviewed.

7.2 PSYCHOLOGICAL AND PSYCHOSOCIAL SERVICE-LEVEL INTERVENTIONS

7.2.1 Studies considered[17]

An existing systematic review was identified (Hawton *et al.*, 2011) for which the authors made their data available to the NCCMH team. The review included 49 studies, of which five reviewed pharmacological interventions (see Chapter 8). This chapter included 34 studies relating to psychosocial interventions (ALLARD1992 [Allard *et al.*, 1992], BENNEWITH2002, BROWN2005 [Brown *et al.*, 2005], CARTER2005 [Carter *et al.*, 2005], CEDEREKE2002 [Cedereke *et al.*, 2002], CLARKE2002 [Clarke *et al.*, 2002], COTGROVE1995 [Cotgrove *et al.*, 1995], DONALDSON2005 [Donaldson *et al.*, 2005], DUBOIS1999 [Dubois *et al.*, 1999], EVANS1999A [Evans *et al.*, 1999a], FLEISCHMANN2008 [Fleischmann *et al.*, 2008], GIBBONS1978 [Gibbons *et al.*, 1978], GUTHRIE2001 [Guthrie *et al.*, 2001], HARRINGTON1998 [Harrington *et al.*, 1998], HAWTON1981 [Hawton *et al.*, 1981], HAWTON1987 [Hawton *et al.*, 1987], HAZELL2009 [Hazell *et al.*, 2009], LIBERMAN1981 [Liberman & Eckman, 1981], MCLEAVEY1994 [McLeavey *et al.*, 1994], MORGAN1993 [Morgan *et al.*, 1993], PATSIOKAS1985 [Patsiokas & Clum, 1985], SALKOVSKIS1990 [Salkovskis *et al.*, 1990], SLEE2008, SPIRITO2002 [Spirito *et al.*, 2002], STEWART2009 [Stewart *et al.*, 2009], TORHORST1987 [Torhorst *et al.*, 1987], TORHORST1988 [Torhorst *et al.*, 1988], TYRER2003 [Tyrer *et al.*, 2003], VAIVA2006 [Vaiva *et al.*, 2006], VANDERSANDE1997 [van der Sande *et al.*, 1997], VANHEERINGEN1995 [van Heeringen *et al.*, 1995], WATERHOUSE1990 [Waterhouse & Platt, 1990], WELU1977 [Welu, 1977], WOOD2001 [Wood *et al.*, 2001]). Seven studies looked specifically at interventions treating populations with borderline personality disorder (BATEMAN2009, GRATZ2006 [Gratz & Gunderson, 2006], LINEHAN1991 [Linehan *et al.*, 1991], LINEHAN2006 [Linehan *et al.*, 2006], MCMAIN2009 [McMain *et al.*, 2009], TURNER2000 [Turner, 2000], WEINBERG2006 [Weinberg

---

[17]Here and elsewhere in the guideline, each study considered for review is referred to by a study ID in capital letters (primary author and date of study publication, except where a study is in press or only submitted for publication, then a date is not used).

et al., 2006]), and one (EVANS1999B [Evans *et al.*, 1999b]) looked at treatment for personality disorder. These studies were excluded from the current analysis because they were reviewed in the *Borderline Personality Disorder* guideline (NCCMH, 2009), but a brief summary of the overall findings of these studies has been included in Section 7.2.6. Treatment for associated borderline personality disorder should follow the NICE *Borderline Personality Disorder* guideline (NICE, 2009e).

Additional systematic searches were undertaken to update the review in January 2011. A further additional two studies were identified (CARTER2007 [Carter *et al.*, 2007], BEAUTRAIS2010 [Beautrais, 2010]). Further to this, an additional unpublished study was identified by contacting researchers known to be working in the area of self-harm (GREEN2011 [Green *et al.*, 2011]).

The categories into which studies in the review (Hawton *et al.*, 2011) had been grouped was maintained (with one exception: intensive interventions in Section 7.2.2).

Psychological interventions included in the meta-analysis (see Section 7.2.2) were:
● problem-solving therapy
● CBT
● psychodynamic therapy
● interpersonal problem-solving skills training.

Psychosocial service-level interventions included in the meta-analysis (see Section 7.2.2) were:
● intensive interventions
● emergency card interventions
● telephone supportive contact
● postcard interventions.

Psychosocial service-level interventions included in the narrative synthesis (see Section 7.2.4) were:
● long- or short-term therapy
● continuity of therapist
● home or outpatient interventions
● general hospital admission or discharge to GP
● compliance enhancement
● case management
● GP letters.

The primary outcome is repetition of self-harm. Other dichotomous outcomes included death by suicide and treatment attendance. Continuous outcomes such as depression, hopelessness and suicide ideation scores were also extracted where reported.

The clinical evidence for psychological and psychosocial interventions that were meta-analysed are presented in Section 7.2.2, followed by narrative synthesis of single trials in Section 7.2.4. The review of trials for children and young people can be found in Section 7.2.7.

For a summary of study characteristics of trials comparing psychological interventions with treatment as usual, see Table 43. The study characteristics for studies included in the meta-analysis can be found in Appendix 15e, which also includes details of excluded studies.

Table 43: Summary of study characteristics of trials comparing psychological interventions versus treatment as usual

	Psychological interventions versus treatment as usual
Total number of trials (N)	10 RCTs (1458)
Study ID	1) GIBBONS1978 2) PATSIOKAS1985 3) HAWTON1987 4) SALKOVSKIS1990 5) DUBOIS1999 6) GUTHRIE2001 7) TYRER2003 8) BROWN2005 9) SLEE2008* 10) STEWART2009*
Diagnosis	1) 44% had diagnosis of depressive neurosis, 2% phobic neurosis, 2% affective psychosis and 1% schizophrenia. No baseline difference between groups. 2) Not reported. No baseline difference in demographics, psychiatric diagnosis, previous attempts or suicide intent. 3) Not reported. No baseline difference in demographics, previous psychiatric problems, previous self-harm or psychiatric symptoms. 4) Not reported 5) Unclear 6) 55% had psychiatric history 7) 42% diagnosed with personality disorder (ICD-10). No difference in baseline characteristics. 8) 68% had a diagnosis of substance abuse and 77% MDD (SCID-DSM-IV). No baseline difference in demographics and psychiatric diagnosis. 9) Not reported. No baseline difference in demographics. 10) Not reported
Recruitment setting	1) Patients who presented to A&E after deliberate self-poisoning 2) Patients admitted to psychiatric ward for suicide attempt 3) Patients admitted to general hospital for self-poisoning 4) Patients who were referred by a psychiatrist following antidepressant self-poisoning and assessed in A&E 5) Patients attending emergency department after a suicide attempt. Not hospitalised for more than 24 hours.

Continued

Table 43: (*Continued*)

	Psychological interventions versus treatment as usual
	6) Patients presenting to hospital after self-poisoning 7) Patients presenting to hospital after self-harm 8) Patients presenting to hospital after suicide attempt. Received medical/psychiatric evaluation within 48 hours. 9) Patients presenting to hospital/mental health centre following self-harm 10) Patients presenting to a hospital after a suicide attempt
Number of sessions and treatment length	1) Unclear: number of sessions up to 3 months 2) Ten sessions (60 minutes each) for 3 weeks 3) Average of three sessions (range one to eight sessions lasting 54 minutes). 4) Five sessions lasting 60 minutes each for 1 month 5) Five sessions for 1 month 6) Four weekly 50-minute sessions 7) Up to five sessions (plus two booster sessions) 8) Ten weekly or biweekly sessions for 10 to 20 weeks 9) 12 sessions (plus three follow-up sessions) for 5.5 months 10) Four and seven sessions of 60 minutes each
Country	1) UK 2) US 3) UK 4) UK 5) France 6) UK 7) UK 8) US 9) Netherlands 10) Australia
Intervention	1) Home-based problem-solving intervention 2) Non-home-based cognitive structuring and problem-solving intervention 3) Non-home-based problem-solving intervention 4) Home-based problem-solving intervention 5) Brief psychotherapy 6) Home-based psychodynamic intervention focused on interpersonal problem-solving 7) Non-home-based, manual-assisted cognitive behavioural therapy (MACT) 8) Non-home-based cognitive therapy

Continued

Table 43: *(Continued)*

	Psychological interventions versus treatment as usual
	9) Non-home-based cognitive behavioural intervention 10) Non-home-based cognitive behavioural and problem-solving interventions
Control	1) Usual care: 54% were referred to their GP, 33% received a psychiatric referral and 13% received unspecified referral 2) Non-directive therapy: open discussion about suicidal behaviour, problems and daily life 3) GP care (individual support, marital therapy) 4) Usual care 5) Treatment as usual: attended an assessment by a clinical psychiatrist and were followed-up by a psychiatrist or psychologist 6) Usual care: in most cases assessment by doctor in emergency department and referral to psychiatry outpatient, addiction services or GP 7) Normally psychiatric assessment, outpatient care, occasional day-patient care or referral back to GP 8) Usual care from clinicians in the community. Case managers track patients on regular basis and refer to CMHT or social services when necessary. 9) Treatment as usual: for example, psychotropic medication, psychotherapy and hospitalisation 10) Treatment as usual: community follow-up by telephone visits, appointments with the psychiatrist, liaison with the client's GP or networking with social supports (no specialised therapy)
Source for primary outcome (repetition) and follow-up period	1) Hospital records (plus GP notes) (at 6 to 12 months) 2) Did not report this outcome 3) Mixture (interviews, GP interviews, hospital). Did not report outcomes for each separately (at 6 to 12 months). 4) Hospital records (at 0 to 6 months and over 12 months) 5) Unclear (at 6 to 12 months) 6) Mixture (majority self-report repetitions with no hospital treatment; some self-reported re-admission to hospitals and a few identified from computer records) (at 0 to 6 months) 7) Interviews checked with hospital record (at 6 to 12 months) 8) Unclear (over 12 months) 9) Interviews checked with hospital record (at 6 to 12 months) 10) Hospital records (at 0 to 6 months)
* New studies since short-term guideline (NCCMH, 2004)	

7.2.2   Clinical evidence for psychological and psychosocial interventions

Psychological interventions versus treatment as usual

Ten studies were combined to investigate the effects of psychological interventions compared with treatment as usual on the treatment of self-harm. Given the variation in modality and duration of psychological interventions, components of standard care and prevalence of psychiatric disorders in these studies, the results should be interpreted with caution.

Psychological interventions included problem-solving therapy, CBT and psychodynamic interpersonal therapy. They were conducted either at home (home-based therapies) or in outpatient settings. Evidence from each important outcome and overall quality of evidence are presented after each review. The full evidence profiles and associated forest plots for studies that were included in the meta-analysis can be found in Appendix 17a and Appendix 16a, respectively.

Effects on repetition (up to 6 months)

Three studies (GUTHRIE2001, SALKOVSKIS1990, STEWART2009) measured repetition up to 6 months since trial entry. Fewer people from the treatment group had a repetition of self-harm compared with the treatment as usual group. A statistically significant RR of 0.33 (95% CI, 0.15 to 0.72) (K = 3, N = 171) was observed. There was no heterogeneity; however, the outcome was of low quality.

Effects on repetition (6 to 12 months)

Five studies (DUBOIS1999, GIBBONS1978, HAWTON1987, SLEE2008, TYRER2003) measured repetition from 6 to 12 months since trial entry. Fewer people from the treatment group had a repetition of self-harm compared with the treatment as usual group. An RR of 0.89 (95% CI, 0.76 to 1.02) (K = 5, N = 1067) was observed, but it was not statistically significant. The outcome was of moderate quality and there was no heterogeneity.

Effects on repetition (more than 12 months)

Two studies (BROWN2005, SALKOVSKIS1990) measured repetition over 12 months since trial entry. Fewer people from the treatment group had a repetition of self-harm compared with the treatment as usual group. A statistically significant RR of 0.5 (95% CI, 0.31 to 0.82) (K = 2, N = 105) was observed with no heterogeneity. The outcome was of low quality.

Effects on repetition (at last follow-up)

As in the review conducted by Hawton and colleagues (2011), the GDG also considered repetition at its last follow-up as an outcome. This approach allowed consideration of the combined findings of all nine studies. There was a statistically significant 24% reduction in chance of repetition in the treatment group compared with treatment as usual (RR 0.76, 95% CI, 0.61 to 0.96) (K = 9, N = 1323) with an acceptable degree of heterogeneity of 30%. The outcome was of low quality.

The results of the above analysis should be interpreted with caution. The source of repetition data varied across the studies and included a mixture of hospital records, GP interviews, and self-reports. Repetition data from hospital records included only hospital-treated episodes, which might underestimate the true number of repetitions of self-harm that did not require medical attention. Similarly, self-reported data might over estimate the effect detected.

Effects on depression scores (at 6 months)
Four studies measured depression using the Hospital Anxiety and Depression Scale (TYRER2003) and the BDI (BROWN2005, GUTHRIE2001, SLEE2008). There was no evidence of effect in depression scores (SMD −0.33, 95% CI, −0.71 to 0.05) (K = 4, N = 660) compared with treatment as usual. However, a high degree of heterogeneity was observed ($I^2 = 78\%$) and the outcome was of low quality.

Effects on depression scores (at 12 months)
Five studies measured depression using the Hospital Anxiety and Depression Scale (TYRER2003) and the BDI (BROWN2005, HAWTON1987, SALKOVSKIS1990, SLEE2008). There was a statistically significant moderate improvement in depression scores, favouring treatment (SMD −0.54, 95% CI, −1.01 to −0.07) (K = 5, N = 656) compared with treatment as usual. However, a high degree of heterogeneity was observed ($I^2 = 83\%$) and the outcome was of low quality.

Effects on depression scores (over 12 months)
Two studies measured depression using the BDI (BROWN2005, GIBBONS1978). There was no statistically significant effect between groups on this outcome (SMD −0.22, 95% CI, −0.48 to 0.05) (K = 2, N = 225) compared with treatment as usual. No heterogeneity was observed; however, the outcome was of low quality.

Effects on depression scores (at last follow-up)
All seven studies (BROWN2005, GIBBONS1978, GUTHRIE2001, HAWTON1987, SALKOVSKIS1990, SLEE2008, TYRER2003) reported in the previous paragraphs were combined for reporting depression scores at its last follow-up. There was a small statistically significant improvement in depression scores (SMD −0.43, 95% CI, −0.76 to −0.12) (K = 7, N = 878) favouring treatment over treatment as usual. However, a high degree of heterogeneity was observed ($I^2 = 75\%$) and the outcome was of low quality, limiting confidence in drawing any firm conclusions for this outcome.

Effects on hopelessness scores (up to 6 months)
Three studies measured hopelessness using the BHS (BROWN2005, STEWART2009, PATSIOKAS1985). There was a statistically significant moderate improvement (SMD −0.52, 95% CI, −0.86 to −0.18) (K = 3, N = 149) favouring treatment over treatment as usual. No heterogeneity was observed and the outcome was of moderate quality.

Effects on hopelessness scores (at 12 months)
Two studies measured hopelessness using the BHS (BROWN2005, SALKOVSKIS1990). There was no statistically significant difference between groups (SMD −0.7, 95% CI, −1.76 to 0.35) (K = 2, N = 121). Moreover, a high degree of heterogeneity was observed (I^2 = 74%) and the outcome was of very low quality.

Number of participants with improved problems (at 4 months)
Two trials of problem-solving measured participants' perceived social problems experienced in various life areas (GIBBONS1978, HAWTON1987). There was a statistically significant improvement favouring treatment over treatment as usual (RR 1.28, 95% CI, 1.09 to 1.49) (K = 2, N = 231). No heterogeneity was observed; however, the outcome was of low quality.

Number of participants with improved problems (at last follow-up)
The last assessment point for GIBBONS1978 is 12 months and 9 months for HAWTON1987. The effect was no longer statistically significant at last follow-up (RR 1.32, 95% CI, 0.89 to 1.96) (K = 2, N = 211). A high degree of heterogeneity was observed (I^2 = 81%) and the outcome was of very low quality. Compared with the effect observed at 4 months, this might imply that the beneficial effect was not sustained in the longer term.

Effects on suicide ideation scores (up to 6 months)
Three studies measured suicide ideation using the Beck SSI (GUTHRIE2001, STEWART2009) and the SSI (PATSIOKAS1985). There was a statistically significant moderate improvement (SMD −0.54, 95% CI, −0.92 to −0.16) (K = 3, N = 142). No heterogeneity was observed; however, the outcome was of low quality.

Completed suicides at last follow-up
Four out of the eight psychological interventions reported the number of completed suicides (K = 8, N = 770) and no suicides occurred in the remaining four studies. Because suicide was a rare event, meta-analysis was not possible. Overall, there were more suicides among participants in the treatment as usual group (seven out of 382) than the treatment group (two out of 388). For both HAWTON1987 and TYRER2003 there was one suicide in each of the treatment arms; in BROWN2005 and SLEE2008 one suicide occurred in each of the control groups; and five suicides occurred in the control group in TYRER2003. No conclusions could be drawn from these data.

Attendance at treatment
Low attendance rates or missing data might lead to an overestimation of study effects. This issue was addressed somewhat by employing ITT analysis for all dichotomous outcomes. Nevertheless, no firm conclusions could be drawn from the evidence below.

All participants in the treatment group completed all therapy sessions, in contrast to a dropout rate of 21% (nine out of 42) from the comparison group in SLEE2008. Overall, 34% in the CBT group and 38% in the problem-solving group completed the sessions as opposed to 26% in the control group in STEW-ART2009.

Most studies reported adherence data for the intervention group only. In BROWN2005, 50% received ten or more treatment sessions. Eighty-six per cent (50 out of 58) completed more than half the treatment sessions and 60% (35 out of 58) completed all treatment sessions in GUTHRIE2001. Forty per cent of participants did not attend treatment sessions in TYRER2003. Finally, 49% completed one to eight sessions and 22% attended no sessions (HAWTON1987).

Summary of treatment components
The treatments in the pooled studies were delivered by a range of professionals and varied in terms of settings, length of treatment and modality of treatment. Three studies were home-based interventions (GIBBONS1978, GUTHRIE2001, SALKOVSKIS1990). Social workers or nurses conducted home-visits ranging from four to five sessions within 1 to 3 months. Both home-based treatments started within 1 week of the index episode (GUTHRIE2001, SALKOVSKIS1990). The non-home-based interventions were conducted in outpatient or clinic settings. They ranged from three to 12 sessions delivered by a range of therapists including psychiatrists, psychologists, counsellors, community psychiatric nurses and social workers. The treatment sessions (where reported) ranged from 50 to 60 minutes each. Common treatment modalities included cognitive therapy, CBT, problem-solving therapy, and psychodynamic interpersonal therapy. Most studies did not report details of staff training; however, the majority of the studies employed therapists who had significant experience with people who self-harm. Adherence to protocols was ensured by video or audio taping treatment sessions in four studies (BROWN2005, GUTHRIE2001, PATSIOKAS1985, SLEE2008). HAWTON1987 provided details of training including standard assessment and treatment procedures. Training consisted of specific reading, closely supervised assessment and treatment experience, and attending daily supervision meetings with a senior psychiatrist. SLEE2008 also provided 2 days of training in standardised protocols. Therapists met biweekly (BROWN2005) or monthly (SLEE2008) for feedback.

Other psychological and psychosocial interventions versus treatment as usual
Other psychological and psychosocial interventions versus treatment as usual are summarised in Table 44.

Intensive multi-modal intervention versus treatment as usual
In *Self-harm: the Short-term Physical and Psychological Management and Secondary Prevention of Self-harm in Primary and Secondary Care* (NCCMH, 2004), six studies were grouped under comparison of 'intensive intervention plus outreach versus standard aftercare' (ALLARD1992, CEDEREKE2002, HAWTON1981, VANDERSANDE1997, VANHEERINGEN1995, WELU1977). For

Table 44: Other psychological and psychosocial interventions versus treatment as usual

	Intensive multi-modal intervention versus treatment as usual	Emergency card versus treatment as usual	Telephone contact versus treatment as usual
Total number of trials (N)	2 RCTs (270)	2 RCTs (1039)	2 RCTs (821)
Study ID	1) ALLARD1992 2) WELU1977	1) MORGAN1993 2) EVANS1999A	1) CEDEREKE2002 2) VAIVA2006
Diagnosis	1) 87% (n = 131) had diagnosis of depression, 53% (n = 80) substance abuse 45% (n = 68) personality disorder. All according to according to DSM-III. 2) Not reported	1) Most common diagnosis was depressive disorder (22%) (diagnostic tool not reported) 2) 85% (n = 707) had diagnosis of any psychiatric disorder (diagnostic tool not reported)	1) 91% (n = 197) had diagnosis of mood disorder by DSM-III-R 2) Not reported
Recruitment setting	1) Patients presenting to hospital for a suicide attempt 2) Patients admitted to an accident and emergency department for self-harm	1) Patients admitted to hospital following first episode of self-harm 2) Patients admitted to general hospital following self-harm episode	1) Patients treated in hospital after suicide attempt 2) Patients presenting to hospital after drug overdose
Number of sessions and treatment length	1) Unclear number of sessions for 12 months 2) Weekly or bi-weekly contacts for 4 months	1) 12 months 2) 6 months	1) 8 months (telephone calls ranged from 20 to 45 minutes) 2) One telephone call (duration not specified)
Country	1) Canada 2) US	1) UK 2) UK	1) Sweden 2) France

Continued

Table 44: *(Continued)*

	Intensive multi-modal intervention versus treatment as usual	Emergency card versus treatment as usual	Telephone contact versus treatment as usual
Intervention	1) Various interventions (for example psychoanalytic psychotherapy, psychosocial, drug or behavioural therapy) or therapy provided where needed 2) Special outreach programme: a CMHT contacted participants immediately after discharge and at home visit arranged as soon as possible. Various modalities involved	1) Standard care plus emergency green card (emergency card indicating that a doctor was available by telephone and how to contact them) 2) Emergency card plus treatment as usual: participants were provided with an emergency card offering 24-hour service for crisis telephone consultation with an on-call psychiatrist	1) Telephone contact 2) Telephone contact
Control	1) Treatment as usual (no details on usual care other than this group was 'treated by regular personnel of hospital') 2) Treatment as usual (routine treatment programme: psychiatric consultation at request of treating physician. Participants were given a next-day appointment for evaluation at the CMHT centre. Any further contact after discharge was up to the patient to decide)	1) Treatment as usual (for example referral back to the primary healthcare team, psychiatric inpatient admission) 2) Treatment as usual	1) Treatment as usual 2) Treatment as usual (mostly referred back to GP)

Continued

Table 44: *(Continued)*

	Intensive multi-modal intervention versus treatment as usual	**Emergency card versus treatment as usual**	**Telephone contact versus treatment as usual**
Source for primary outcome (repetition) and follow-up period	1) Hospital records, coroner's office plus interview with participants and other informants 2) Self-report, hospital records and interview with family/friends	1) Hospital, psychiatric and GP records 2) Hospital records	1) Interviews checked against patient and admission charts 2) Self-report and hospital records

this guideline, however, four of these studies were included in either single modality or less intensive treatment comparisons (CEDEREKE2002, HAWTON1981, VANDERSANDE1997, VANHEERINGEN1995). The remaining two studies (ALLARD1992, WELU1977) were combined to investigate the effects of intensive multi-modal interventions compared with treatment as usual and included service users presenting to hospital after a suicide attempt. ALLARD1992 and WELU1977 involved the implementation of a range of psychological and pharmacological interventions, which could be combined according to the needs of the service user, including psychoanalytic psychotherapy, behavioural therapy, family counselling and a range of drug treatments among others. Wherever possible, the staff involved established contact immediately after the suicide attempt and scheduled visits with the individual.

Effects on repetition (at last follow-up)
There was insufficient evidence to determine the clinical effectiveness between an intensive intervention and treatment as usual. These studies measured repetition of self-harm, one at 24 months' (ALLARD1992) and the other at 4 months' (WELU1977) follow-up. Overall, fewer people from the treatment group compared with treatment as usual repeated self-harming behaviour. An RR of 0.67 (95% CI, 0.18 to 2.49) (K = 2, N = 245) was observed but it was not statistically significant, with significant heterogeneity ($I^2 = 74\%$). Also, the results must be interpreted with caution as the study was of low quality. Some possible reasons for this heterogeneity were the difference in the length of follow-up or treatment (8 months longer in WELU1977), or the time difference between studies (almost 20 years). The variabilities in the above studies limited the ability to draw conclusions concerning the clinical effectiveness of intensive interventions on repetition of self-harm in the longer term.

Attendance

Data were reported separately for each study. In ALLARD1992, the experimental group attended more sessions by 12 months' follow-up (mean 12.35 versus 1.54 sessions; p <0.001). After the first year, participants in the intervention group were referred to standard psychiatric services. At 24 months' follow-up participants in the intervention group continued to attend more sessions (mean 2.11 versus 0.64 sessions; p = 0.071).

Suicides

ALLARD1992 reported suicides during the follow-up period of 2 years. Three suicides were reported in the intensive intervention group versus one in the treatment as usual group. The number of suicides in WELU1977 was unclear. No conclusions could be drawn from these data given the rarity of this outcome.

Emergency card plus treatment as usual versus treatment as usual

Two studies (EVANS1999A, MORGAN1993) were combined to investigate the effects of emergency card use compared with treatment as usual on the treatment of self-harm. These interventions emphasised the importance of having easy access to on-call professionals in the event of difficulties. In both studies the majority of participants consisted of those who had self-harmed by drug overdose (98% in both studies). However, in MORGAN1993 the participants had no history of previous self-harm, whereas in EVANS1999A 48% of the participants had a history of previous self-harm. The emergency card treatment consisted of access to either telephone consultation with a trainee psychiatrist (EVANS1999A) or the choice between telephone or face-to-face consultation with a doctor or trainee psychiatrist with the offer of admission to a psychiatric ward if necessary (MORGAN1993).

Effects on repetition (at 12 months)

There was insufficient evidence to determine the clinical effectiveness between emergency card intervention and treatment as usual. A longer-term follow-up study (EVANS2005) and MORGAN1993 measured repetition of self-harm at 12 months. Overall, fewer people from the treatment group compared with treatment as usual repeated. An RR of 0.83 (95% CI, 0.35 to 1.97) (K = 2, N = 1039) was observed, but it was not statistically significant, with a high degree heterogeneity ($I^2 = 67\%$) and low quality. Some possible reasons for this high heterogeneity are the differences noted above in the history of previous self-harm and the longer treatment period in MORGAN1993 (6 versus 12 months). This limited the ability to draw any conclusions from this finding.

Suicides

Only one study (EVANS1999A) reported suicides during the follow-up period of 1 year. Two suicides were reported in the emergency card group versus one in the treatment as usual group. No suicides occurred in MORGAN1993. No conclusions can be drawn from these data due to the small evidence base.

Telephone contact plus treatment as usual versus treatment as usual
Two studies (CEDEREKE2002, VAIVA2006) were combined to investigate the effects of telephone contact compared with treatment as usual on the treatment of self-harm. The active approach of establishing contact with participants aimed to increase motivation and engagement with treatment. Both studies consisted of participants who were treated after a suicide attempt and the majority were repeat attempters. Telephone contact consisted mainly of contact with an experienced therapist over the phone at two different time periods (4 and 8 months in CEDEREKE2002, and 1 and 3 months in VAIVA2006).

Effects on repetition (at last follow-up)
There was insufficient evidence to determine the clinical effectiveness between telephone contact plus routine care and treatment as usual. VAIVA2006 reported repetition of self-harm both at 1 and 3 months' follow-up, and CEDEREKE2002 reported one outcome (repetitions between 1 and 12 months). There was no statistical difference between telephone contact and treatment as usual after a period of 1 month (RR 0.89, 95% CI, 0.62 to 1.28) (K = 2, N = 674) or 3 months (RR 0.79, 95% CI 0.54 to 1.16). No heterogeneity was observed and both of these studies are of moderate quality. No conclusions could be drawn due to the small evidence base.

Treatment attendance (at 12 months' follow-up)
CEDEREKE2002 found no difference in the number of participants attending treatment (60 out of 83) at least once during the 12 months' follow-up compared with the control group (58 out of 89).

Suicides
Studies reported suicides at follow-up periods of 12 months (CEDEREKE2002) and 13 months (VAIVA2006). Because suicide was a rare event, the results were not meta-analysed. One suicide was reported in both the treatment group and treatment as usual group in CEDEREKE2002, and two suicides were reported in the treatment as usual group in VAIVA2006. No conclusions could be drawn from these data.

Postcard interventions plus treatment as usual versus treatment as usual
Two studies (CARTER2005, BEAUTRAIS2010) looked at the effectiveness of postcard interventions in addition to treatment as usual compared with treatment as usual alone (see Table 45). The intervention consisted of sending a series of postcards following participants' index presentation of self-harm.

Effects on repetition (at 12 months)
There was insufficient evidence to determine whether there was a clinically significant difference between intervention and treatment as usual during the 12 months since trial entry (RR 0.92, 95% CI, 0.73 to 1.18) (K = 2, N = 1099). No heterogeneity was observed and the study was of moderate quality. A follow-up study measured repetition at 24 months and found no statistical significant differences between groups (RR 0.93, 95% CI, 0.71 to 1.21) (K = 2, N = 772).

Table 45: Summary study characteristics of trials comparing postcard interventions versus treatment as usual

	Postcard interventions versus treatment as usual	Postcard interventions versus treatment as usual
Total number of trials (N)	1 RCT (772)	1 RCT (327)
Study ID	1a) CARTER2005 1b) CARTER2007 (24 months' follow- up study of CARTER2005)	BEAUTRAIS2010
Diagnosis	43% had diagnosis of any affective disorder, 13% alcohol misuse and/or dependence, 40% other substance related disorders, 22% personality disorder	Unclear
Recruitment setting	1a & 1b) Patients presenting to hospital toxicology service after deliberate self-poisoning	Patients presented to psychiatric emergency services after self-harm/attempted suicide
Treatment length	12 months	12 months
Country	Australia	New Zealand
Intervention	Eight postcards sent at 1, 2, 3, 4, 6, 8, 10 and 12 months after discharge plus usual care	Six postcards sent at 2 and 6 weeks, and 3, 6, 9 and 12 months after discharge plus usual care
Control	Treatment as usual	Treatment as usual – crisis assessment and referral to inpatient community-based mental health services
Source for primary outcome (repetition) and follow-up period	Hospital database	Psychiatric emergency services and hospital medical records

Effects on number of episodes per patient

Although the proportion of participants who repeated self-harming behaviour was not statistically significant between groups, participants in the experimental group had a much lower mean number of self-harm episodes during the first 12 months (CARTER2005, CARTER2007). However, this result had to be interpreted with caution as it was derived from 18 participants with multiple repeated episodes. An unadjusted incidence RR (IRR) showed a significant reduction in the number of repetitions in the treatment group (IRR 0.55, 95% CI, 0.35 to 0.87) compared with the control group. This difference persisted at 2 years' follow-up (IRR 0.49, 95% CI, 0.33 to 0.73). BEAUTRAIS2010 reported similar findings with an unadjusted IRR 0.73 (95% CI, 0.56 to 0.95). However, when adjusted for previous self-harm, the effect is no longer significant (adjusted IRR 1.07, 95% CI, 0.8 to 1.43). This attenuation in effect after adjustment for previous self-harm might indicate the observed results were derived from a small subgroup who repeatedly self-harm.

Suicide

In the first year following trial entry, there were two suicides in the intervention group and four in the control group (CARTER2005). At 24 months after trial entry there were no further suicides in the intervention group, but a total of five in the control group (CARTER2007). Both suicides in the intervention group occurred in males and four in the control group were males. The number of suicides was not reported in BEAUTRAIS2010.

Results should be interpreted with caution as these two postcard studies varied in a number of ways. In CARTER2005 and CARTER2007 more postcards were sent compared with BEAUTRAIS2010. In addition, CARTER2005 and CARTER2007 recruited only people who had self-poisoned, whereas BEAUTRAIS2010 recruited a mixture of people who self-poisoned and self-cut. The postcard intervention might have reduced the number of repeated episodes per participant. This was, however, confounded by the history and chronicity of previous self-harm. An important limitation to note in CARTER2005 and CARTER2007 was the small proportion (less than 20%) of participants who repeated self-harm more than once. This highly skewed subgroup might result in an overestimation of the effect of the intervention for most service users. In BEAUTRAIS2010, there were baseline differences between treatment and comparison groups on the history of previous self-harm. After adjustment, the clinical benefit of treatment was no longer valid.

7.2.3   Clinical evidence summary

Psychological and psychosocial interventions (regardless of treatment modality) might be effective in improving outcomes compared with treatment as usual. The uncertainty lies in the variability found in the population and treatment modalities, as well as comparison arms. The variability was reflected by considerable heterogeneity in a number of outcomes.

There was some evidence drawn from summarising the effect of psychological interventions on reducing per protocol repetition (the primary outcome), suicide ideation scores, and mixed evidence on depression and hopelessness scores. However, the quality of these outcomes was poor for several reasons. First, there were variability and uncertainties in terms of the comparability of the population. Six of nine studies (in meta-analyses) did not report psychiatric diagnosis of their included population and, in addition, six studies did not report the percentage of the population who had a previous history of self-harm. For those that did report these data, it ranged from 30 to 100% of participants who had at least one previous attempt prior to study entry. Previous history of self-harm might modify the effect of treatment (for example, treatments might be effective for those presenting with their first self-harm episode but not for those with a past history). Second, the treatment sessions and length varied from 3 to 12 sessions (average 6 sessions) delivered from 3 weeks to 5.5 months. Third, the treatment modalities and settings differed across trials. Fourth, it was uncertain whether psychological interventions had any adverse events because these studies did not report data on this.

A number of other psychosocial interventions were reviewed, namely intensive intervention, provision of emergency cards, establishing contact by telephone support and sending postcards to individuals. However, compared with usual care, there was insufficient evidence to determine clinical effects between interventions and routine care in the reduction of the proportion of participants who repeated self-harm. Thus, no conclusions could be made regarding psychosocial interventions for reducing repetitions of self-harm.

7.2.4 Narrative synthesis of single trials

Psychological and psychosocial interventions versus other comparator
Interpersonal problem-solving skills training (IPSST) versus brief problem-oriented therapy
MCLEAVEY1994 conducted a small study to compare IPSST with brief problem-oriented therapy. Thirty-four subjects completed treatment and 31 subjects were available after a 1-year follow-up.

Effects on repetition (at 12 months)
There was insufficient evidence to determine clinical difference between IPSST and brief problem-oriented therapy (RR 0.84, 95% CI, 0.27 to 2.67). Repetition was assessed as being a 'self-poisoning act' within 1 year of treatment.

Effects on other outcomes
There were no suicides in either treatment group. Results showed that the mean scores of hopelessness measured during the first 6 months in the experimental group did not differ from the control group (SMD 0.07, 95% CI −0.62 to 0.75).

Results reported by the investigators suggest an equal benefit of both treatments in reducing the number of presenting problems and in reducing hopelessness. However, it was reported that IPSST was significantly more effective in interpersonal cognitive problem-solving, self-rated personal problem-solving ability, perceived ability to cope with ongoing problems and self-perception.

Attendance
Three (15%) subjects in the control group and two (11%) in the treatment group did not complete treatment.

Inpatient behaviour therapy versus insight-oriented therapy
One study made the comparison between inpatient behaviour therapy versus insight-oriented therapy (LIBERMAN1981). Here behaviour therapy covered social skills training, anxiety management, family work, and insight-oriented therapy involving individual therapy, group therapy, psychodrama and family therapy. Both groups received approximately 32 hours of therapy over 10 days.

Effects on repetition
There was insufficient evidence to determine if there was a clinically significant difference between inpatient behaviour therapy and insight-oriented therapy on reducing the likelihood of repetition of self-harm (RR 0.67, 95% CI, 0.13 to 3.3).

Effects on depression scores
After 24 weeks, patients who received behaviour therapy had a large reduction in depression scores (SMD -0.98, 95% CI, -1.84 to -0.12) but this effect was not seen at 36 weeks. Behaviour therapy was also of benefit to participants in terms of reported suicide ideation at 6 months and 36 weeks after trial entry.

c) Long-term therapy versus short-term therapy
Only one study made the comparison between long-term and short-term therapy (TORHORST1988). It compared outcomes following 12 monthly therapy sessions with 12 weekly sessions. The type of therapy offered was not specified. Outcomes were measured at the end of treatment for each group.

Effects on repetition
There was insufficient evidence to determine if there was a clinically significant difference between long-term therapy and short-term therapy on reducing the likelihood of repetition of self-harm (RR 1, 95% CI, 0.44 to 2.26).

Attendance
The attendance of the long-term group 'dropped drastically' by the second session to under 40%, but this was not seen in the 3-month group. The overall attendance rate was very low in both groups (mean sessions for the long-term group was 2.6 out of a possible 12 sessions and 3.9 of a possible 12 sessions in the short-term group; thus,

approximately 23% attendance compared with approximately 33% attendance at sessions). Nevertheless, information was available on 97% of the sample at the end of the study.

Effect of treatment on depression
'Self-evaluated depressivity improved considerably more' for participants in the 12-week programme as compared with the 12-month group. Data were not given numerically but on a graph; the difference was reported to be 'significant'.

For a summary of single trials comparing psychosocial interventions versus another comparator, see Table 46.

Table 46: Summary study characteristics of single trials comparing psychosocial interventions versus other comparator

	IPSST versus brief problem-orientated therapy	Inpatient behaviour therapy versus insight-oriented therapy	Long-term versus short-term therapy
Total number of trials (N)	1 RCT (39)	1 RCT (24)	1 RCT (80)
Study ID	MCLEAVEY1994	LIBERMAN1981	TORHORST1988
Diagnosis	23% had diagnosis of dysthymia, 15% dependent personality disorder and 13% alcohol abuse	All had diagnosis of depressive neurosis. Most met criteria for personality disorder.	Unclear
Recruitment setting	Patients admitted to an A&E department following self-poisoning	Patients were referred by the psychiatric emergency service or the A&E department following self-harm	Patients who had deliberately self-poisoned referred to liaison service of toxicological ward

Table 46: (*Continued*)

	IPSST versus brief problem-orientated therapy	Inpatient behaviour therapy versus insight-oriented therapy	Long-term versus short-term therapy
Treatment length	5 weeks, follow-up over 12 months	10 days, follow-up over 24 months	Long-term therapy: once a month for 12 months; short-term therapy: once a week for 3 months
Country	Ireland	US	Germany
Intervention	Five sessions lasting 60 minutes. Manualised training consisting of instruction, active discussion, reflective listening, modelling, coping strategy, role playing, sentence completion and prompting.	Inpatient treatment with behaviour therapy for self-poisoning plus aftercare at community mental health centre/ private therapy	Following hospitalisation for self-poisoning (duration: approximately 3 days) long-term therapy: one therapy session per month over 12 months
Control	Brief problem-solving therapy: therapy focused on patient's current problems and prevention by helping patient gain insight into problems; no specific skills training	Inpatient treatment with insight orientated therapy plus aftercare at community mental health centre/private therapy	Following hospitalisation for self-poisoning (duration: approximately 3 days) short-term therapy: 12 weekly therapy sessions over a period of 3 months

Same therapist versus different therapist in different settings
One study made this comparison (TORHORST1987). All participants received a motivational interview, letter and assessment of motivation towards therapy. This was designed to increase engagement with treatment. Participants in the experimental group then received therapeutic contact with the original hospital therapist in an outpatient setting, whereas participants in the control group received therapy in a specialised suicide prevention centre with a different therapist. This made it hard to assess the effect of treatment. In addition, and despite randomisation, at baseline participants in the same therapist group had more risk factors for repetition of self-harm than those in the different therapist group, including being more likely to be older, male and divorced, and having more episodes of self-harm in the year before the index episode. These differences could wholly account for the differences in repetition.

Effects on repetition
There was limited evidence suggesting that there was a clinically significant difference favouring different therapist over same therapist on reducing the likelihood of repetition of self-harm (RR 0.31, 95% CI, 0.09 to 1.11).

Attendance
There were significantly more patients in 'same therapist' group; 49 out of 68 attended treatment at least once compared with the different therapist group (36 out of 73).

Suicide
There was insufficient evidence to determine if there was a clinically significant difference between receiving a different therapist and receiving the same therapist on reducing the likelihood of death by suicide 9 months after treatment (two suicides in the treatment and three suicides in the control group).

Effects on depression scores
There was no significant difference in depression scores between the groups at 12 months after trial entry (SMD −0.17, 95% CI, −0.52 to 0.18).

Home versus outpatient problem-solving therapy
HAWTON1981 compared the delivery of brief problem-oriented counselling in two different ways, namely flexibly-timed home-based therapy (including access via telephone services to the general hospital psychiatric service) versus treatment in weekly outpatient clinics.

Effects on repetition
During the year following treatment entry, the repetition of self-harm was measured. There was no significant difference in repetition, which occurred in five out of 48 participants in the home treatment group compared with seven out of 48 in the outpatient group (RR 0.71, 95% CI, 0.24 to 2.09).

Attendance

A greater number of participants in the home treatment group attended one treatment session or more (45 out of 48) when compared with the outpatient group (35 out of 48).

Effects on depression scores

There was no statistically significant difference in mean depression scores post-treatment (adjusted for pre-treatment differences) in the home treatment group 2.91 (N = 44) and the outpatient group 2.71 (N = 44) (F = 0.09). After 6 months, the home treatment group mean score was 2.49 (N = 42) versus an outpatient group mean score of 2.61 (N = 40) (F = 0.03), which was not statistically significant. The study did not report SDs.

General hospital admission versus discharge

One study assessed the effect of general hospital admission versus non-admission in a group of self-harm 'parasuicide' patients attending an emergency room who had 'no immediate medical or psychiatric treatment needs' (WATERHOUSE1990). In this study no additional treatment was offered to either group, although all patients were advised to contact their GP on discharge. Average length of admission was 17 hours. Only those who did not require hospital admission because of medical or psychiatric needs were included in the study and the majority of patients were not randomised because they were considered to pose too great a risk to be assigned to the non-admission group. Therefore, the patients included in the study constitute an extremely biased sample.

Effects on repetition

There was insufficient evidence to determine if there was a clinically significant difference between general hospital admission and discharge on reducing the likelihood of repetition (RR 0.77, 95% CI, 0.18 to 3.21).

Effects on hopelessness scores

There was also no significant difference in hopelessness scores as measured after 1 week (mean 10.29, SD 5.68 versus mean 10.21, SD 4.97); however, the numbers of patients in each group were not reported for this outcome.

Effects on suicide ideation scores

At 4 months, there was also no evidence of a difference in suicide ideation scores between the two groups (SMD 0.28, 95% CI, -0.26 to 0.83).

For a comparative summary of these three types of intervention, see Table 47.

Compliance enhancement versus treatment as usual

Some service users do not attend outpatient appointments arranged after discharge from hospital following self-harm. In a study by VANHEERINGEN1995, compliance enhancement via a nurse visit at home resulted in significantly more service users attending the outpatient clinic at least once compared with a group of service users who did not receive this extra intervention (129 out of 252 versus 102 out of 256).

Table 47: Summary study characteristics of single trials comparing psychosocial interventions versus other comparator

	Same versus different therapist	Home versus outpatient problem-solving therapy	General hospital admission versus discharge
Total number of trials (N)	1 RCT (141)	1 RCT (96)	1 RCT (77)
Study ID	TORHORST1987	HAWTON1981	WATERHOUSE 1990
Diagnosis	Uncertain	Not reported	Not mentioned. None had a psychiatric diagnosis of a depressive illness.
Recruitment setting	Patients hospitalised after suicide attempt	Patients admitted to a general hospital following deliberate self-poisoning	Patients admitted to A&E for self-harm. No immediate medical or psychiatric treatment needs.
Treatment length	3 months	Not stated; up to 60 minutes per session	Not applicable
Country	Germany	UK	UK
Intervention	Short crisis intervention during hospital stay, fixed outpatient appointment with same therapist as was seen in hospital. Motivational interview, letter and assessment of motivation towards therapy.	Domiciliary (home-based) therapy. Open telephone access to the general hospital service/ flexible sessions. Treatment was brief, and terminated when patient's current crisis was resolved. During first 2	General hospital admission. No additional treatment or counselling.

Continued

Table 47: *(Continued)*

	Same versus different therapist	Home versus outpatient problem-solving therapy	General hospital admission versus discharge
		months of treatment, sessions could be as frequent but during third month, maximum of two sessions was allowed.	
Control	Short crisis intervention during hospital stay, fixed outpatient appointment with a different therapist than was seen in hospital. Motivational interview, letter and assessment of motivation towards therapy.	Outpatient therapy of one session per week	Discharge from hospital

Effects on repetition
There was also a substantial but non-significant reduction in the repetition of self-harm during the 12 months after trial entry (RR 0.61, CI, 0.37 to 1.02).

Suicides
There was, however, no evidence of a difference between treatment groups in the occurrence of suicides during this period (six out of 196 versus seven out of 195).

Case management versus treatment as usual
One study made the comparison between case management and treatment as usual (CLARKE2002). The intervention involved case management combined with routine management, including medical and psychiatric assessment. Usual care consisted of triage, medical and psychosocial assessment and treatment as required.

Effects on readmission
There was insufficient evidence to determine if there was a clinically significant difference between nurse-led case management and standard aftercare on reducing

the likelihood of people who self-harm being readmitted to hospital (RR 0.85, 95% CI, 0.48 to 1.51). However, investigators reported that multiple re-admission was much more common in the experimental group than the control (nine out of 220 versus two out of 247). At 36 months' follow-up, one suicide had occurred in each treatment group.

Supportive contact versus treatment as usual
One study conducted as a multicentre investigation in 'suicide attempters' in five low- and middle-income countries (Brazil, India, Sri Lanka, Iran and China) assessed the effect of brief contact over 18 months by home visits or telephone contacts by a clinician after an information session at the time of discharge from hospital with treatment as usual (FLEISCHMANN2008). Participants were recruited in the emergency departments after their suicide attempts. The intervention included an individual 1-hour session, in addition to regular follow-up contacts after discharge. The therapist provided information that aided the understanding of suicidal behaviour and provided contacts or referral options. A person with clinical experience (range of doctors, nurses, psychologists or students in psychology or social work who received 1 day of special training) conducted contacts at 1, 2, 4, 7, and 11 weeks, and 4, 6, 12 and 18 months after discharge. Treatment as usual was limited to acute management of index suicide attempts. It did not include psychosocial assessment or any treatment. In some sites, participants were discharged to outpatient mental health services.

Effects on repetition
There was no difference in repeat suicide attempts at 18 months (RR 0.98, 95% CI, 0.7 to 1.37). There were significantly fewer suicides in the experimental group at 18 months (two out of 872 versus 18 out of 827) (FLEISCHMANN2008). However these data should be interpreted cautiously as they were based on informant report rather than official data sources and data were not available for those lost to follow-up.

Effects on contact with services
It was reported that the utilisation of psychological services following self-harm was low in both experimental (5.7%) and treatment as usual (5%) groups, and it was not statistically significant.

GP letter versus standard aftercare
One study made the comparison between a GP letter versus standard aftercare (BENNEWITH2002). In this study, which was cluster randomised by GP practice, participants were sent a letter by GPs from practices allocated to the experimental group inviting them to make an appointment for a consultation.

Effects on repetition
There was insufficient evidence to determine whether there was a clinically significant difference between using a GP letter and standard aftercare on reducing the likelihood of repetition of self-harm (RR 1.12, 95% CI, 0.94 to 1.34).

Effects on contact with services

During the first 6 weeks after trial entry, there was no difference between treatment conditions in the number of contacts made with services (351 out of 599 versus 387 out of 681).

Intensive inpatient and community treatment versus treatment as usual

One study (VANDERSANDE1997) compared the impact of brief psychiatric inpatient admission followed by outpatient appointments and 24-hour access to the unit with treatment as usual.

Effects on repetition

There was insufficient evidence to determine whether there was a clinically significant difference on reducing the likelihood of repetition of self-harm at 12 months (RR 1.15, 95% CI, 0.67 to 1.98). VANDERSANDE1997 reported one suicide in the treatment group and two suicides in the treatment as usual group.

Attendance

In VANDERSANDE1997, more participants attended one or more treatment sessions in the intensive intervention condition (119 out of 140) compared with the comparison group (64 out of 143) at 12 months' follow-up. However, there was no difference in the mean number of treatment sessions participants attended (SMD 0.11, 95% CI, −0.13 to 0.35).

Effects on depression scores

VANDERSANDE1997 had lower depression scores after 12 months; however, the difference was not significant (SMD −0.31, 95% CI, −0.66 to 0.03).

Effects on hopelessness scores

VANDERSANDE1997 had lower hopelessness scores after 12 months; however, the difference was not significant (SMD −0.26, 95% CI, −0.61 to 0.08).

For a comparative summary of these five types of intervention, see Table 48.

7.2.5   Clinical evidence summary for narrative synthesis

Section 7.2.4 presented narrative syntheses of single trial psychological or psychosocial interventions that could not be meta-analysed. In terms of reducing repetition, there was insufficient evidence of a treatment difference between the following interventions: interpersonal problem-solving skills training versus brief problem-oriented therapy; inpatient behaviour therapy versus insight-oriented therapy; long-term (12 months') versus short-term (3 months') therapy; and general hospital admission versus discharge.

There was limited evidence suggesting that the same versus a different therapist is associated with a reduction in self-harm repetition. However, this conclusion was subject to many uncertainties and biases. Thus, based on only a single trial, no conclusions could be drawn.

Table 48: Summary study characteristics of single trials comparing psychosocial interventions versus treatment as usual

	Compliance enhancement versus treatment as usual	Case management versus treatment as usual	Supportive contact versus treatment as usual	GP letter to patient/enhanced care versus treatment as usual	Intensive inpatient and community treatment versus treatment as usual
Total number of trials (N)	1 RCT (516)	1 RCT (467)	1 RCT (1867)	1 RCT (1932)	1 RCT (240)
Study ID	VANHEERINGEN1995	CLARKE2002	FLEISCHMANN2008*	BENNEWITH 2002	VANDERSANDE1997
Diagnosis	15% had a diagnosis of mood disorder, 3% of anxiety disorder	17% had psychiatric history, 13% alcohol problems, 3% schizoaffective disorder	Not reported	Not reported	32% had diagnosis of mood disorder and adjustment disorder
Recruitment setting	Patients treated in A&E after a suicide attempt	Patients presenting to hospital for deliberate self-harm	Patients attending an emergency care setting with a diagnosis of self-harm or self-poisoning	Participants found in hospital case register for self-harm	Patients admitted to hospital following a suicide attempt

Treatment length	Unclear	Up to 6 months	18 months	Unclear	Flexible appointments usually on weekly basis
Country	Belgium	UK	Brazil	UK	Netherlands
Intervention	Compliance enhancement plus usual care – home visits were made to participants who did not keep outpatient appointments, the reasons for not attending appointments were discussed and the patient was encouraged to attend.	Case management consisting of psychosocial assessment, a negotiated care plan and 'open access' to a case manager who helped the patient identify and access suitable services plus usual care.	Treatment as usual plus brief intervention ('information about suicidal behaviour as a sign of psychological and/or social distress, risk and protective factors, basic epidemiology, repetition, alternatives to suicidal behaviours, and referral options') plus follow-up contact (via phone or visits; referral support) at 1, 2, 4, 7 and 11 weeks, and 4, 6, 12 and 18 months).	Letter from GP for consultation in surgery	Brief psychiatric unit admission, encouraging participants to contact unit on discharge. CPN assigned to establish therapeutic relationship with the patient. Treament by CPN based on problem-solving approach. Outpatient therapy plus 24-hour emergency access to unit.

Continued

Table 48: (*Continued*)

	Compliance enhancement versus treatment as usual	Case management versus treatment as usual	Supportive contact versus treatment as usual	GP letter to patient/enhanced care versus treatment as usual	Intensive inpatient and community treatment versus treatment as usual
Control	Outpatients appointments only; non-compliant participants were not visited.	Usual care consisting of triage, medical and psychosocial assessment and treatment as required. For patients who were admitted from A&E for further treatment, usual treatment generally involved a request for a psychiatric assessment.	Treatment as usual 'according to the norms prevailing in the respective emergency departments' (typically, treatment for somatic problems).	Usual GP care. No structured feedback about patient management. GPs in control group had initiated contact with only 15% (97 out of 642) of patients, compared with 58% (352 out of 612) in the intervention group.	Usual care. Patients were assigned by the routine clinical service and could consist of all currently available alternative treatments. 75% were discharged from hospital; of these patients, almost 90% were referred to an outpatient clinic. 25% were referred for hospitalisation in a psychiatric clinic.

Note. *New studies since short-term guideline (NICE, 2004a).

For the same outcome (repetition) compared with routine care, there was insufficient evidence to establish clinical effectiveness for psychosocial interventions such as case management, supportive contact in low to middle income countries, GP letters, and intensive inpatient and community care.

There was a trend showing that enhancing compliance by visiting participants who did not attend an outpatient appointment may reduce repetition 12 months after trial entry. This was based on a single trial of poorer quality, and therefore no conclusions could be drawn.

7.2.6   Narrative synthesis of interventions for specific subgroups

This section includes brief summaries of studies that looked at interventions for specific subgroups and reported repetition of self-harm as an outcome. For the management of each specific condition, please refer to the relevant NICE guideline.

Borderline personality disorder
A total of nine studies examined the effectiveness of DBT for the reduction of self-harm, all in people with borderline personality disorder with a history of self-harm. Eight of these studies (Carter *et al.*, 2010; Koons *et al.*, 2001; Linehan *et al.*, 1991; Linehan *et al.*, 1999; Linehan *et al.*, 2002; Linehan *et al.*, 2006; Turner, 2000; van den Bosch *et al.*, 2002) were reviewed in the NICE guideline *Borderline Personality Disorder* (NCCMH, 2009), which can be consulted for further details on the study characteristics and findings. There was also an additional study (McMain *et al.*, 2009), which was published after the guideline was produced.

In summary, the evidence for DBT showed some benefit in reducing rates of self-harm. Two studies (Koons *et al.*, 2001; van den Bosch *et al.*, 2002) displayed significant differences between DBT and treatment as usual in the reduction of self-harm. Two further studies reported significant differences between DBT and community treatment by experts (Linehan *et al.*, 2006) and client-centred therapy (Turner, 2000) in reducing self-harm, suicide attempts and suicide ideation. Most of the evidence is of moderate quality. The sample size in these nine studies ranged from 23 to 180 participants with a total of 578 participants. The average duration of DBT treatment was 1 year with the treatment length ranging from 6 months to 1 year. Trials all followed the manualised treatment designed by Linehan (1993), although several modified it. DBT, in outpatient settings, comprised four treatment components: weekly individual cognitive-behavioural psychotherapy sessions with the primary therapist; weekly skills training groups lasting 2 to 2.5 hours per session; weekly supervision; and consultation meetings for the therapists and phone consultation. Participants were encouraged to obtain coaching in the application of new skills by telephoning their primary therapists either during or outside office hours. These results should be interpreted with caution as the populations examined varied considerably with some populations having coexisting substance misuse (Linehan *et al.*, 1999; Linehan *et al.*, 2002; van den Bosch *et al.*, 2002) and some involved female veterans (Koons *et al.*, 2001). The treatment setting also varied greatly, including outpatients, primary care and referrals to a community mental health outpatient clinic following emergency department treatment for a suicide attempt. Five out of nine studies compared DBT with treatment as usual; however, there were four studies in which the comparator varied, including comprehensive validation therapy (Linehan *et al.*, 2002), community treatment by experts (Linehan *et al.*, 2006), a combination of psychodynamically informed therapy and symptom-targeted medication management (McMain *et al.*, 2009) and client-centred control (Turner, 2000). Finally, participants were mostly women, thus limiting the applicability of the findings.

There were two studies that examined MACT, a brief cognitive-oriented and problem-focused therapy, against treatment as usual (Evans *et al.*, 1999b; Weinberg *et al.*, 2006). One was in a population of people with personality disturbance within the flamboyant personality cluster (N = 34) who had a history of self-harm aged 16 to 50 years (Evans *et al.*, 1999b) and the other was in a population with borderline personality disorder (N = 30) aged 18 to 40 years (Weinberg *et al.*, 2006). The first trial was reviewed in *Self-harm: the Short-term Physical and Psychological Management and Secondary Prevention of Self-harm in Primary and Secondary Care* (NCCMH, 2004) and the second in *Borderline Personality Disorder* (NCCMH, 2009), which can be consulted for further details of study characteristics and findings. In summary, both treatments lasted for 6 months with a range of two to six sessions and incorporated DBT, CBT and bibliotherapy. Evans and colleagues (1999b) found that the rate of self-harm episodes was lower in the MACT group compared with the treatment as usual group but not significantly so. On the other hand, Weinberg and colleagues (2006) found that MACT was associated with significantly less frequent self-harm post-treatment and at 6 months' follow-up when compared with the treatment as usual group. These results should be interpreted with caution given the following limitations. The participants were mostly women thus limiting the applicability of the findings reported. Both had small sample sizes and the populations differed in their diagnosis with one being diagnosed with borderline personality disorder and the other population being a mixture of personality disorders within the flamboyant personality cluster.

There was an additional RCT (Doering *et al.*, 2010) that examined the efficacy of transference-focused psychotherapy compared with treatment by community psychotherapists in reducing self-harm in 104 female outpatients with borderline personality disorder. Transference-focused psychotherapy is a modified psychodynamic psychotherapy consisting of two 50-minute sessions per week over a period of 1 year and focused on the experiences of dysfunctional early relationships. Significantly fewer participants dropped out of the transference-focused psychotherapy group compared with the community psychotherapists group (38.5 versus 67.3%), significantly fewer attempted suicide and there was a reduction in need for psychiatric inpatient treatment in the transference-focused psychotherapy group. However, there were no significant differences in the reduction of self-harm in either group. These findings should be interpreted with caution as this was in a group of women thus limiting the generalisability of the findings. There was also a high dropout rate and low participation in the follow-up assessment with only 47% completing the 1-year treatment, which might introduce bias favouring the results.

A comprehensive review of treatment options for people with a diagnosis of borderline personality disorder can be found in the *Borderline Personality Disorder* NICE guideline (NCCMH, 2009).

Alcohol misuse
An RCT conducted by Crawford and colleagues (2010) looked at the effect of referral for brief interventions for people who had self-harmed and were misusing alcohol. The study was carried out after an earlier trial showed a statistically significant reduction in re-attendance at the emergency department for an unselected group of individuals screened for alcohol misuse and given brief treatment (Crawford *et al.*, 2004). Alcohol misuse was defined as consuming more than eight units (for men) or six units (for women) per drinking session on a weekly basis, or if participants reported their self-harm was related to the use of alcohol. Participants were recruited from an emergency department following a self-harm episode, and if they met the criteria for alcohol misuse. The brief intervention consisted of an appointment card for a 30-minute session with an alcohol specialist nurse, together with a health information leaflet. The alcohol specialist nurse conducted an assessment of current and past drinking behaviour using a person-centred and non-confrontational approach. The control group received a blank card together with the same health information leaflet. There was no statistical significant difference between treatment and control on re-admission for repetition (RR 0.62, 95% CI, 0.26 to 1.48) at 6 months' follow-up. There were a number of limitations for this study including the low attendance of appointments in the treatment group (47%) and the high prevalence of what was probably personality disorder among the participants.

7.2.7 Clinical evidence for interventions for children and young people

For a summary of the study characteristics comparing group psychotherapy versus treatment as usual, see Table 49. For a summary of the study characteristics of trials of other psychological or psychosocial interventions, see Table 50. The study characteristics for studies included in the meta-analysis can be found in Appendix 15e, which also includes details of excluded studies. The full evidence profiles and associated forest plots can be found in Appendix 17a and Appendix 16a, respectively.

Developmental group psychotherapy plus treatment as usual versus treatment as usual
Three studies (WOOD2001, HAZELL2009, GREEN2011) explored the effectiveness of developmental group psychotherapy for young people with repeated self-harm. This therapy was designed to tackle difficulties experienced by young people by using positive corrective therapeutic relationships. It involved a number of treatment principles including problem-solving, cognitive-behavioural interventions, DBT and psychodynamic therapy. It comprised of six 'acute' group sessions plus routine care, followed by weekly group therapy in the longer term that could be terminated when participants felt ready to leave. HAZELL2009 was a replica of the original study conducted in Australia. GREEN2011 was a larger-scale multicentre study conducted by the original developer of the intervention.

Table 49: Summary of the study characteristics of trials comparing group psychotherapy versus treatment as usual

	Group psychotherapy versus treatment as usual
Total number of trials (N)	K = 3 (501)
Study ID	1) WOOD2001 2) HAZELL2009* 3) GREEN2011
Diagnosis	1) Major depressive disorder in 83 to 84% of groups. 75% (experimental) and 62% (control) had conduct or oppositional disorder diagnosis (assessed by K-SADS and DSM-IV). 2) 4% had alcohol problems; 0% had substance misuse problems; 57% had depression; 7% had a diagnosis of conduct/oppositional defiant disorder (all assessed using Schedule for Affective Disorders and Schizophrenia for School-age Children [K-SADS]) 3) ~60% depressive disorder; ~30% behavioural disorder
Recruitment setting	1) Referred to CAMHS following self-harm 2) Referred to CAMHS with reported self-harm 3) Young people with two or more episodes of self-harm during previous 12 months in CAMHS, north-west UK
Treatment length	All six sessions
Country	1) UK 2) Australia 3) UK
Intervention	Developmental group psychotherapy involved a variety of techniques, including interventions involving problem-solving, CBT, DBT and group psychodynamic psychotherapy
Control	Routine care
Note. *New studies since short-term guideline (NCCMH, 2004).	

Table 50: **Summary of the study characteristics of trials of other psychological or psychosocial interventions**

	CBT versus treatment as usual	Home-based family intervention versus treatment as usual	Standard disposition planning with and without added compliance enhancement	Emergency card versus treatment as usual
Total number of trials (N)	1 RCT (39)	1 RCT (162)	1 RCT (76)	1 RCT (105)
Study ID	DONALDSON2005*	HARRINGTON1998	SPIRITO2002	COTGROVE1995
Diagnosis	29% (9 out of 31) had diagnosis of MDD. 19% (6 out of 31) had diagnosis of alcohol-use disorder	64.5% had diagnosis of major depression; 10.5% had diagnosis of conduct disorder	37% had a diagnosis of either dysthymia, major depression, oppositional defiant disorder, conduct disorder, alcohol abuse or drug abuse/dependence	6% had major psychiatric disturbance (not specified)
Recruitment setting	Patients presenting to a general paediatric emergency department or inpatient unit of an affiliated child psychiatric hospital after a suicide attempt	Participants had no self-injury by cutting or hanging but had all self-poisoned. Patients referred to mental health teams in four hospitals.	Patients presenting to hospital after a suicide attempt	Patients admitted to hospital following self-harm

Continued

Table 50: (*Continued*)

	CBT versus treatment as usual	Home-based family intervention versus treatment as usual	Standard disposition planning with and without added compliance enhancement	Emergency card versus treatment as usual
Treatment length	6 individual sessions plus 1 family session; 3 maintenance sessions	5 sessions	8 weeks	12 months
Country	US	UK	US	UK
Intervention	Skills-based treatment focused on problem-solving and affect management skills; taught problem-solving and cognitive and behavioural strategies and given homework assignments to strengthen skills. Treatment comprised two parts: (a) active treatment (first 3 months) included six individual sessions and one adjunct family session with two additional family sessions and two crisis sessions available at therapist's	Home-based family therapy plus routine care	Compliance enhancement intervention plus standard disposition planning: single, 1-hour session that reviewed expectations for outpatient treatment and factors likely to impede attendance. Addressed treatment misconceptions and encouraged the young person and parent to make a verbal contract to attend treatment. Participants were also	Standard care plus emergency green card: green card acted as a passport to re-admission into a paediatric ward in the local hospital.

discretion; (b) maintenance treatment (last 3 months) included three sessions.

contacted by telephone at 1, 2, 4 and 8 weeks after discharge regarding their compliance with treatment.

Standard follow-up and treatment from a clinic or child psychiatry department.

Control — Supportive relationship therapy focused on young people's mood and behaviour; unstructured sessions which addressed reported symptoms and problems; specific skills not taught, designed to be close to usual care for this population in this community.

Routine psychiatric aftercare. Visits to the clinic by the of young person and family. A diverse range of interventions, including sessions with psychiatrists and with psychiatric nurses.

Standard disposition planning: treatment based on judgement psychiatric clinician who conducted the evaluation. Some attempters in both groups had a brief inpatient psychiatric stay prior to receiving outpatient care. Remainder received outpatient care at a local mental health centre.

Note.*New studies since short-term guideline (NCCMH, 2004).

Effects on repetition

There was no evidence to determine whether group psychotherapy plus routine care had an effect compared with routine care alone. At 7 (WOOD2001) and 12 months' follow-up (HAZELL2009, GREEN2011), an RR of 0.95 (95% CI, 0.63 to 1.45) with a 79% heterogeneity is observed. The heterogeneity might be explained by the large difference in effect size for WOOD2001 being effective, but not for the other two studies.

Effects on suicide ideation and depression scores

There was no evidence of an effect when group psychotherapy plus routine care was compared with routine care alone at the last follow-up (SMD −0.03, 95% CI, −0.21 to 0.15) (K = 3, N = 471) for suicide ideation scores. Similarly, there was no evidence of effect on depression scores (SMD −0.17, 95% CI, −0.52 to 0.18) (K = 2, N = 129).

Suicides

There were no suicides in the treatment nor the treatment as usual groups (WOOD2001, GREEN2011).

CBT versus treatment as usual for children and young people

One small study assessed CBT versus nondirective supportive therapy, which was designed to be as close to usual care for young people who self-harm (DONALD-SON2005). The treatment condition focused on problem-solving and affect-management skills. Young people were taught problem-solving and cognitive behavioural strategies for affect management. The comparator was supportive in nature and sessions were unstructured. It involved exploratory questioning, encouraging affect; however, specific skills were not taught.

Effects on repetition

There was little difference between psychological therapy and treatment as usual in the number of participants in each group who repeated self-harm at 6 months after trial entry (RR 1.71, 95% CI, 0.35 to 8.29). No participants died by suicide.

Attendance

All participants attended at least one treatment session. There was no statistical evidence of a difference in the mean number of treatment sessions attended in each group (mean 9.70 versus mean 9.50). A greater proportion of control group participants completed treatment (13 out of 21 versus 13 out of 18), but the difference was, again, not significant.

Effects on other outcomes

Depression scores at 6 months after trial entry were somewhat lower in the treatment group, but the small sample size might explain its statistical insignificance (SMD −0.38, 95% CI, −1.09 to 0.33). A similar, but not statistically significant finding was reported for suicide ideation scores at 6 months (SMD 0.14, 95% CI, −0.86 to 0.58).

*Home-based family intervention versus treatment as usual for children
and young people*

One study (HARRINGTON1998) compared home-based family therapy under-taken by two social work masters-level students with 'standard aftercare' involving no home visits. The experimental intervention involved a single home-based assessment and four treatment sessions at home. All participants were under 16 years old and none of them was seriously suicidal; nearly 90% were female and over 60% were reported as having major depression. All were routine referrals to mental health services.

Effects on repetition

There was insufficient evidence to determine if there was a clinically significant difference between home-based family therapy and standard aftercare on reducing the likelihood of repetition of self-harm (RR 1.01, 95% CI, 0.47 to 2.19). One participant in the experimental treatment group died by suicide and no suicides occurred in the control group.

Attendance

More participants in the home-based group completed treatment (39 out of 84 versus 28 out of 77).

Effects on other efficacy outcomes

There was insufficient evidence to suggest a clinically significant difference between home-based family therapy and standard aftercare on reducing hopelessness scores in children and young people (SMD 0.06, 95% CI, –0.26 to 0.38), problem-solving scores (SMD −0.04, 95% CI, −0.36 to 0.28), or reducing suicide ideation scores (SMD −0.13, 95% CI, –0.45 to 0.19).

*Standard disposition planning with and without added compliance enhancement for
children and young people*

One study assessed the effect of standard disposition planning with and without an added compliance enhancement intervention in young people after a self-harm episode (SPIRITO2002).

Effects on repetition

Fewer participants in the intervention group had repeat self-harm episodes at 3 months after trial entry, but the difference was not significant (RR 0.70, 95% CI, 0.18 to 2.69). The compliance enhancement group had fewer repeat self-harm episodes compared with participants in the control group (mean 0.10 versus mean 0.15). No participants died by suicide.

Attendance

No significant difference was found between the groups in relation to the number of participants attending at least one treatment session (27 out of 29 versus 31 out of 34). While participants in the experimental group (that with compliance enhancement) attended more treatment sessions (mean 7.70 versus mean 6.40) and more completed treatment (17 out of 29 versus 16 out of 34), neither of these differences was significant.

7.2.8 Clinical evidence summary for interventions for children and young people

In the NICE guideline *Self-harm: the Short-term Physical and Psychological Management and Secondary Prevention of Self-harm in Primary and Secondary Care* (NICE, 2004a), group psychotherapy was recommended for children and young people based on evidence from a study by WOOD2001. However, results from more recent studies did not replicate the clinical effect observed in WOOD2001. Group psychotherapy plus routine care did not appear to be effective in reducing the repetition of self-harm when compared with routine care alone, among young people with a history of self-harm. The difference in effect might be explained by differences in the participants. For example, a replication study in Australia (HAZELL2009) and a more recent multicentre RCT (GREEN2011) used wider referral samples, which tended to consist of more severe, complex and chronic participants. This contrasted with the single district participant pool used by WOOD2001. Another explanation could be a higher level of service provision and use in routine care in more recent years, which might diminish the relative treatment effect.

For all other studies included in the narrative review, there were no statistically significant findings in reducing the repetition of self-harm. There were no differences between treatments such as CBT and home-based family interventions when compared with routine care. Furthermore, there was no evidence showing enhanced compliance had an effect in standard disposition planning among children and young people who self-harm.

7.2.9 Health economic evidence

Evidence review

The systematic literature search identified three economic studies that assessed the cost effectiveness of specific psychological or psychosocial interventions compared with treatment as usual or routine care. All three studies were conducted in the UK (BYFORD1999 [Byford *et al.*, 1999], BYFORD2003 [Byford *et al.*, 2003], GREEN2011).

GREEN2011 was identified during an update search. The authors used a cost-effectiveness analysis, comparing group psychotherapy plus routine care with routine care alone for young people aged between 12 and 17 years who had at least two past episodes of self-harm within the previous 12 months. The analysis was conducted alongside an RCT in the northwest of England with a sample population of 181 for group therapy and 183 for routine care. The group psychotherapy comprised six weekly sessions initially followed by a booster of weekly sessions for as long as was needed, while routine care was made up of local children and young people's mental health services provided by CAMHS teams. The perspective of the analysis was societal with broad service use from the NHS, social services, education services, voluntary services and criminal justice services. The indirect cost due to productivity lost was tested in the sensitivity analysis. The primary outcome was proportion of participants who had not harmed themselves over the preceding 6 months at 12-month follow-up.

The reported total mean cost per young person (in 2005/06 prices) over the 12-month period was £21,761 (SD £38,794) for group therapy and £15,354 (SD £24,981) for routine care. No statistically significant difference in the two mean costs was detected. For the primary outcome result, the proportion of those young people who received group therapy and did not have any episode of self-harm over the follow-up period was 38.9% while that of the routine care arm was 41.9%. The reported incremental cost-effectiveness ratio (ICER) was £2,020 per 1% increase in the proportion of young people not self-harming, with the probability of group therapy being an optimal strategy ranging from 12 to 28% as willingness to pay for outcome improvement increased.

The application of the economic evidence of this study in the guideline is limited given that the perspective considered is societal and the final outcome was not measured in terms of quality of life values. Also, according to the authors, and from the estimated likelihood of the cost effectiveness of group therapy at increasing willingness-to-pay thresholds, the addition of group therapy to routine care is probably not more cost effective than routine care alone.

The second study by BYFORD2003 evaluated the cost effectiveness of MACT compared with treatment as usual for adult patients (16 to 65 years) with a history of self-harm recruited after presenting with an episode of self-harm. Their analysis was based on the clinical trial by Tyrer and colleagues (2003). Those requiring inpatient psychiatric treatment, or with psychotic or bipolar disorder or alcohol or drug dependence were excluded. The MACT group was given a treatment manual each and offered up to seven sessions of cognitive therapy while those in the treatment as usual group were offered standard treatment, which varied between the three studies and included problem-solving, psychotherapy, GP or voluntary group referral, and short-term counselling. A societal perspective was adopted for the analysis. Resource-use items included hospital and community health services, social services, voluntary sector services, community accommodation, criminal justice system, and participants' living expenses and productivity losses. The primary outcome measure used in the analysis was the proportion of participants who experienced a repeat episode of self-harm during 12-month follow-up. Quality of life years (QALYs) were also measured, by calculating European Quality of Life−5 Dimensions (EQ-5D) utility scores, taken at baseline, 6 and 12 months.

The total mean cost over 12 months was £13,454 in the MACT group and £14,288 in the treatment as usual group (1999/2000 prices). The reported percentage of participants experiencing a repeat episode of self-harm over the 12-month period of follow-up was 7% lower in the MACT group whilst QALYs were 0.0118 lower in the MACT group. Taking treatment as usual as the base case, the reported ICERs when compared with MACT were -£120 per 1% reduction in percentage of participants with a repeat episode of self-harm (thus MACT was the dominant strategy) and £66,000 per QALY gained. Cost-effectiveness acceptability curves (CEACs) showed that MACT had more than a 90% probability of being cost-effective when using the percentage of repeat episodes of self-harm as an outcome. With QALYs as an outcome, MACT has higher probability of being cost effective at a threshold less than or equal to £66,000 per QALY. However, at different threshold values, the probability of MACT being more cost effective ranges between 44 and 88%. Extrapolating approximately from the CEACs, the probability of MACT being cost effective at a willingness-to-pay threshold of £20,000 and £30,000 were 65 and 60%, respectively.

The results of this study are highly applicable to this guideline in terms of the population, healthcare system, interventions and outcomes considered. However, the broader perspective, other than NHS and personal social services (PSS), taken by the study may be relevant to the population resource use but not recommended by NICE (2009d). Other limitations with the study findings were that uncertainty around the effectiveness measures were not presented. Given the small differences between the two treatment groups in terms of QALYs and percentage of repeat self-harm episodes, it is possible that these differences were not statistically significant and may explain why differences in percentage of repeat episodes but not QALYs favoured the MACT group. In addition, as noted by the authors, the chance that any coping mechanism could possibly improve quality of life may be plausible. In other words, with self-harm as a coping mechanism, such interventions that result in least reduction in repeat episodes of self-harm may be associated with more gain in quality of life than other interventions with significant reduction in repeat episodes of self-harm. Consequently, this calls for more caution in the interpretation of the direction of QALYs gained or lost with respect to self-harm interventions.

The third study, by BYFORD1999, evaluated the cost effectiveness of a home-based social work intervention plus routine care compared with routine care for children and young people (age range 10 to 16 years) who had self-poisoned. The home-based social work intervention delivered by two psychiatric social workers consisted of an assessment session and four intensive sessions targeted towards intra-familial communication, behavioural techniques and problem-solving. Routine care involved the visitation of psychiatric and psychiatric nurses in the clinic on an outpatient basis. The analysis was based on an RCT of 6 months' follow-up with outcome measures and costs reported for 162 children (77 for routine care and 85 for the intervention group).The perspective of the analysis included the NHS, PSS as well as the educational and voluntary sector. Resource use included assessment sessions, hospital services (inpatient, day-patient, intensive care unit, outpatient care and A&E services), GP visits, school nurses and doctors, community psychiatric nurses, counsellors, educational welfare officers, educational psychologists, social workers and foster and residential care.

The primary outcome measures used in the study were the Suicidal Ideation Questionnaire and BHS both of which were completed by the individual, and the Family Assessment Device (a measure of family functioning) completed separately by both the young person and their parents. No statistically significant differences were detected in any of the primary outcomes at 6 months between the two treatment groups. Similarly, no statistically significant differences in costs between the intervention and routine care (£1,455 versus £1,751; p = 0.6) were detected.

Regarding the applicability of this study to the guideline, it has a number of methodological limitations although the participant population, interventions and healthcare system considered in the study are all relevant. Firstly, there was no synthesis of incremental costs and outcomes or use of the QALY as a final outcome measure. Secondly, the short time horizon may not have allowed for full evaluation of all the important costs and effects associated with the intervention. Finally, the uncertainties of the result estimates were not tested.

Details on the methods used for the systematic search of the economic literature are described in Section 3.6.1. Information on the methods used and the results reported in the economic studies included in the systematic literature review are presented in the form of evidence tables in Appendix 14.

Economic modelling
Introduction – objective of economic modelling
The systematic review of clinical evidence and meta-analysis demonstrated that psychological interventions in addition to treatment as usual for people who self-harm are clinically effective in reducing the repetition of self-harm episodes when compared with treatment as usual alone. The subsequent repetition of self-harm could affect the service user's HRQoL (Sinclair *et al.*, 2010b) and further use of NHS or PSS resources (Sinclair *et al.*, 2010a). It is thus necessary to identify the cost effectiveness of delivering a psychological intervention in addition to treatment as usual to people who self-harm. The existing economic evidence from the reviewed literature (BYFORD1999, BYFORD2003, GREEN2011) was found to have some limitations to reliably inform the guideline recommendations given the short time horizon in estimation of the health benefits and costs, uncertainties in the use of QALYs and broader perspective of the analyses. Hence the need for an economic model aiming to assess the cost effectiveness of psychological interventions added to treatment as usual relative to treatment as usual alone for people who self-harm, from the perspective of the NHS and PSS, is important.

Though the recommended outcome is the QALY (NICE, 2009d), the final outcome used in this analysis was the number of people prevented from repetition of self-harm because the two quality-of-life studies (BYFORD2003, Sinclair *et al.*, 2010b) identified from the systematic literature search (see Appendix 12) were not sufficiently reliable. The HRQoL data reported in the study by Sinclair and colleagues (2010b) were collected using both the EQ-5D and Short-Form Health Survey, Version 11 (SF36-11) questionnaires. However, the results were neither presented in the form of utility scores nor in any value sets that could be converted into utility scores by using existing health states value sets for the general UK population. Also, the study by BYFORD2003 was limited in its application because the utility scores were reported in a way to determine the incremental

QALYs between the two treatment arms in the trial study and were not specific for utilities of different possible self-harm health states used in this model. In addition, the methodology used in the valuation of the health utilities was not given and there was an associated significant level of uncertainty with the reported health utilities in the later study. Therefore, the GDG was not convinced regarding the reliability of these utility data in developing the economic model for this guideline.

Economic modelling methods
Intervention considered in the analysis
The economic analysis considered interventions that were shown to be effective in reducing the number of repeated self-harm episodes according to the systematic review and meta-analysis of the clinical evidence. For the purposes of the economic model, the GDG identified a more realistic psychological intervention for reducing repetition of self-harm episodes to consist of six sessions delivered by a skilled and competent mental health worker with each session lasting for 60 minutes while the treatment as usual was described as consisting of a basic treatment provided by the CMHT to service users who self-harm after the initial hospital management of any associated acute physical and/or mental health problem. For the group receiving psychological interventions, treatment as usual is considered as a baseline intervention with the psychological intervention serving as an additional intervention. The psychological intervention is delivered either at the service user's home or in a clinic.

Model structure
The model structure construct aims to elaborate the natural history of the self-harm population as much as possible. Identified literature on the risk of repetition of self-harm showed a varied self-harm repeat risk ranging from 15 to 33% (Lilley *et al.*, 2008b; Owens *et al.*, 2002; Zahl & Hawton, 2004). Given the insufficient data on self-harm mortality and quality-of-life outcomes, a simple decision tree incorporating Markov nodes (represented by 'M' in Figure 3, and Markov health states (self-harm and no self-harm) with an annual cycle length was constructed using Excel workbook 2007 to partly capture the treatment effects and costs of psychological interventions over a period of time in the future. According to the model structure, 1000 hypothetical cohorts of people aged 8 years and above who self-harm were provided with a psychological intervention plus treatment as usual or treatment as usual alone. People in each cohort either self-harmed after treatment, or were prevented from self-harming with 'no self-harm' taken as the absorbing state (see Figure 3). In the base-case analysis, the time horizon was taken to be 12 months based on the meta-analysis of the treatment effect of the psychological intervention lasting up to 12 months. A longer time horizon of up to 24 months was tested in the sensitivity analysis assuming the treatment effect was sustained till the end of the second year. A schematic diagram of the decision tree is provided in Figure 3.

Figure 3: Model decision tree

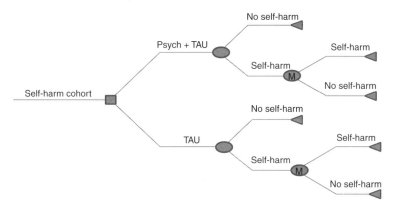

Costs and outcomes considered in the analysis

The economic analysis adopted the perspective of the NHS and PSS, as recommended by NICE (2009d) and reported in 2010 prices. Costs consisted of intervention costs (psychological intervention) and annual costs of care of a person who self-harms. The cost of treatment as usual was not considered in the analysis, as this was common to both arms of the model. The measure of outcome was the number of people prevented from a repeat episode of self-harm.

Clinical input parameters

Clinical input parameters consisted of the RR of repetition of self-harm associated with provision of a psychological intervention plus treatment as usual compared with treatment as usual alone, and annual baseline risk of repetition of self-harm following treatment as usual. Data were derived from the guideline systematic review and meta-analysis of clinical evidence. The baseline risk of repetition of self-harm estimated by Lilley and colleagues (2008b) to be 33% was found to be comparable with the pooled self-harm repetition risk from nine studies included in the meta-analysis. Given the possibility that the baseline risk of self-harm repetition used in the base-case analaysis can be an overestimation of risk of repetition of self-harm, as some people may not be presenting to services, a lower risk of repetition of self-harm is tested in the sensitivity analysis. In the base-case analysis, the economic model used the outcome measure assessed at last follow-up period (12 months on average) as agreed by the GDG.

Cost data

Cost of psychosocial intervention: The cost of intervention was estimated based on the descriptions of resource use identified from the psychological intervention studies included in the systematic review, confirmed by the GDG to be consistent with clinical practice in the UK. The intervention is a brief psychological therapy consisting of six sessions, which is provided by a nurse (mental health) specialist with each session lasting for 60 minutes. To estimate the intervention cost, the unit cost of a nurse specialist per hour of client contact reported in Curtis (2010) as £91 per hour was used. Calculation of this unit cost was based on the median full-time equivalent basic salary for Agenda for Change Band 6 of the January to March 2010 NHS staff earnings for qualified nurses. The estimation also included the salary oncosts, qualification costs, overheads and capital overheads (Curtis, 2010). Adjustment was made for those interventions provided at the person's home by adding the cost of travel time to hourly cost of client contact. The total mean cost of the psychological intervention was then estimated as the average cost of both home-based and non-home-based psychological interventions by multiplying the quantity of resource use by the respective unit costs (see Table 51).

Cost of self-harm: The estimation of costs incurred by a service user following an episode of self-harm was based on a retrospective cost analysis by Sinclair and colleagues (2010a), conducted in the UK. This study estimated costs following an episode of self-harm from the perspective of the NHS and PSS with a mean follow-up period of 10.9 years, which was divided into 6-month cost intervals. Among the 150 participants recruited into the cost study, 78 service users with available resource use in each time period were analysed. Resources measured in the study included primary care services, emergency department services, hospital services such as medical and surgical inpatient bed days, outpatient consultations, laboratory investigations, and inpatient psychiatric care. Other resources included were outpatient psychiatric care, psychotropic prescriptions, social service visits and social service residential placements. The cost estimate was reported as cost per episode of self-harm per 6-month interval and was £2,994 in 2004/05 prices. This estimate was inflated to 2010 price year using Hospital and Community Health Services pay and price inflator (Curtis, 2010) and also doubled to approximately estimate the annual cost of care for a person who self-harms to reach £6,998. According to GDG opinion, the cost incurred by people prevented from future episodes of self-harm after receiving a psychological intervention or treatment as usual was assumed to be negligible. Table 52 provides the details of the clinical and cost input parameters described above with their probability distributions. For costs beyond 12 months, cost adjustment using a discount rate of 3.5% was applied as recommended by NICE (NICE, 2009d).

Data analysis and presentation of the results
In the base-case analysis, the cost effectiveness of a psychological intervention plus treatment as usual versus treatment as usual alone at the 12-month time horizon was evaluated. Subsequently, evaluation at a longer time horizon of up to 24 months was made in the sensitivity analysis assuming the treatment effect was sustained till the end of the second year. Sensitivity analaysis was also conducted for other key parameters of the model. Two methods were employed to analyse the input parameter data and present the results of the economic analysis.

First, a *deterministic* analysis was undertaken, where data were analysed as point estimates; results are presented as mean total costs and outcomes associated with each

Table 51: Summary of the average costs of psychosocial intervention

Intervention	Resource use	Sessions (A)	Measure of resource use	Unit cost (B)	Number of hour(s) per session (C)	Valuation (A*B *C)	Reference
Home-based psychological intervention	Nurse specialists' time	6	Per hour of client contact	£91	1	£546	Curtis, 2010; GDG expert opinion
	Nurse specialists' travel time	6	Per visit	£1.5	–	£9	Curtis, 2010
					Total for home-based	£555	
Non-home-based psychosocial intervention	Nurse specialists' time	6	Per hour of client contact	£91	1	£546	Curtis, 2010
					Average cost (home-based and non-home based)	£550.5	

Table 52: Summary of the base-case input parameters of the economic model

Parameter	Distribution	Point estimate	Probability distribution	Reference and comment
Baseline risk of repetition of self-harm	Beta	0.33	Alpha = 211 Beta = 437	Self-harm repetition risk pooling following treatment as usual alone (from nine meta-analysed studies)
RR	Log normal	0.76	95% CIs: 0.61 to 0.96	Meta-analysis
Self-harm intervention cost	Gamma	£550.50	Alpha = 6.25 Beta = 88.08	Curtis, 2010; price year 2010
Annual cost of care of person who self-harms	Gamma	£6,998	Alpha = 2.78 Beta = 2519.45	Sinclair *et al.*, 2010a; price year 2010

intervention. Subsequently, an ICER was calculated, expressing the additional cost per additional unit of benefit associated with one intervention relative to its comparator. Estimation of such a ratio allows consideration of whether the additional benefit is worth the additional cost when choosing one treatment option over another. Alternatively, if one intervention is less costly and more effective than its comparator, then this is obviously the most cost-effective option (dominant) and no ICER needs to be calculated.

To test the robustness of the results under different scenarios, one-way and two-way sensitivity analyses were conducted. The following scenarios were explored:

- A resource-intensive scenario comprising 12 psychological intervention session delivered by a Band 7 clinical psychologist was considered to reflect the possible variations in resource inputs and the associated ICER.
- A scenario of 50% variability in the cost of self-harm from Sinclair and colleagues (2010a) was tested to examine the effect on the ICER level since the reported cost of the self-harm estimate has a wide standard deviation around the mean cost.
- It was assumed that people prevented from self-harming following a psychological intervention incurred a negligible future cost. The possibility that these people may incur some cost such as four subsequent GP visits (per clinic consultation

lasting 17.2 minutes is £53 inclusive of direct care cost [Curtis, 2010]) was tested to examine the implication of such extra cost on the ICER level.

● A lower baseline risk of repetition of self-harm of 24% following an index episode was tested given that the baseline risk used in the base case was based on those presenting to services with the possibility of overestimating the risk as some individuals will not present to service. From the literature, the annual risk of repetition of self-harm varies from 15 to 33% (Lilley *et al.*, 2008b; Owens *et al.*, 2002; Zahl & Hawton, 2004) with 24% as an approximate estimate of the average annual risk of repetition of self-harm.

● Variations in the effectiveness of the psychological intervention using the upper and lower values of the 95% confidence interval of the relative risk and baseline risk of repetition of self-harm episodes was also tested.

In addition to deterministic analysis, a probabilistic analysis was also conducted. In this case, all model input parameters were assigned probability distributions (rather than being expressed as point estimates), to reflect the uncertainty characterising the available clinical and cost data. Subsequently, 10,000 iterations were performed, each drawing random values out of the distributions fitted onto the model input parameters. This exercise provided more accurate estimates of mean costs and benefits for each intervention assessed (average results from the 10,000 iterations), by capturing the non-linearity characterising the economic model structure (Briggs *et al.*, 2006). The distributions assigned to each of the input parameters are shown in Table 52.

Results of probabilistic analysis are presented as mean costs and effects derived from 10,000 iterations, as well as in the form of CEACs, which demonstrate the probability of each intervention being cost effective at different levels of willingness-to-pay per unit of effectiveness (that is, at different cost-effectiveness thresholds the decision-maker may set).

Results of economic modelling

For clarity, the results the analyses were presented as follows:

● For the base-case analysis, the probabilistic and deterministic estimates showing the mean cost and mean effect of both psychological and treatment as usual strategies with the resultant ICER evaluated at the end of the last follow-up period (that is, 12 months) (see Table 53).

● The sensitivity analysis showing the value of ICERs for a given parameter(s) of interest evaluated both at the end of the last follow-up period and 24-month time horizon.

Table 53 shows the mean costs and number of people prevented from self-harm repetition for each of the interventions assessed in the analysis. The ICER evaluated as £ per additional person prevented from repetition of self-harm episode was £164 (probabilistic analysis). The ICER estimate by deterministic analysis was £46. The ICER estimate from the probabilistic analysis is relatively higher than the deterministic estimate and is regarded as more reliable given the variations around the parameter inputs.

Table 53: Base-case analysis at 12-month time horizon

Analytical method	Strategy	Cost (£)	Effect (people prevented from self-harm)	Incremental value		ICER (£/person prevented from self-harm repeat)
				Cost	Effect	
Probabilistic	Treatment as usual alone	2,281,636	674.43	–	–	
	Psychological + treatment as usual	2,294,166	750.85	12,530	76.42	164
Deterministic	Treatment as usual alone	2,278,819	674	–	–	
	Psychological + treatment as usual	2,282,403	753	3,583	78.15	46

Sensitivity analysis

Deterministic sensitive analysis: The result of the deterministic sensitivity analysis as shown in Table 54 demonstrated that ICER value is sensitive to most of the range values of the parameters tested. However, the ICER estimate is highly robust when the subsequent costs incurred by people prevented from future episodes of self-harm is tested.

In the longer term of up to 24 months, psychological intervention becomes a dominant strategy and also tends towards a more cost-effective option for all other parameters tested separately. In two-way sensitivity analysis, different combinations of the intervention cost and RR of self-harm repetition give rather varied ICER estimates when compared with the base-case ICER value. The combination of low risk of self-harm repetition and a resource-intensive intervention option results in psychological intervention being a dominant strategy in both the short- and the long-term. Conversely, lower treatment effect and higher cost of self-harm care when combined results in an extra high cost for each additional person prevented from self-harming showing the extent of uncertainty around the treatment effect estimate.

Probabilistic sensitive analysis: The result of the probabilistic sensitivity analysis presented as a CEAC in Figure 4 shows the likelihood that a chosen intervention will be cost effective relative to the alternative option at various levels of willingness-to-pay threshold. For example, at a willingness-to-pay threshold of £1000 and above, the probability that a psychological intervention plus treatment as usual will be cost

Table 54: Deterministic sensitivity analysis

One way sensitivity analysis			
		ICER	
Variables	**Value**	**At last follow-up (12 months)**	**At 24 months**
All model parameters (base case)	–	£164	Psychological intervention dominates
Resource-intensive intervention option (12 sessions by a clinical psychologist) (base case = £550)	£1,149	£7,704	£6,682
Further cost of care of treated people (assuming they have four extra GP visits) (base case = £0)	£212	£258	Psychological intervention dominates
50% increase in cost of self-harm care (base case = £6,998)	£10,498	Psychological intervention dominates	Psychological intervention dominates
50% decrease in cost of self-harm care (base case = £6,998)	£3,499	£3,545	£2,805
Low baseline risk of self-harm repetition (base case = 0.33)	0.24	£2,559	Psychological intervention dominates
Two-way sensitivity analysis			
Higher effect size (lower CI of RR) and resource-intensive intervention option	0.61 and £1,149	£2,049	Psychological intervention dominates
Low baseline risk of self-harm repetition and 50% increase in the cost of self-harm	0.24 and £10,498	Psychological intervention dominates	Psychological intervention dominates
Low effect size (upper CI of RR) and 50% of increase in the cost of self-harm	0.96 and 10,498	£31,768	£39,634

Figure 4: Cost-effectiveness acceptability curve

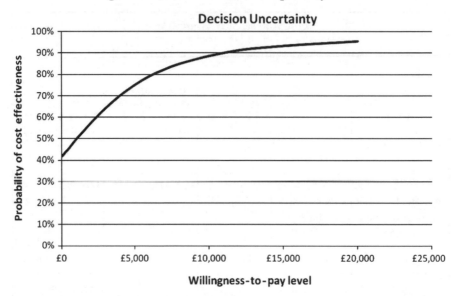

effective if implemented ranges from 50% and above. For various willingness-to-pay threshold levels tested, the likelihood that a psychological intervention will be an optimal strategy ranges from 42 to 97%.

Discussion

The economic analysis undertaken examined the cost effectiveness of a psychological intervention as an additional intervention to treatment as usual compared with treatment as usual alone. The result of the economic modelling showed that to prevent an additional person from repeating an episode of self-harm by choosing six sessions of a psychological intervention delivered by a nurse specialist instead of treatment as usual alone, the NHS will be incurring an additional cost of approximately £200. Also demonstrated by this analysis was that the psychological intervention plus treatment as usual has a greater likelihood of being cost effective compared with treatment as usual alone at various willingness–to-pay levels of £1000 and above. Hence, choosing the psychological intervention will depend more on the service provider's level of willingness-to-pay for an additional person prevented from self-harm repetition.

An important point in this analysis is the resources used to deliver the psychological intervention. The model analysed a realistic option as suggested by the GDG comprising six sessions delivered by a skilled and competent nurse. Nevertheless, some of the reviewed studies described up to 12 sessions delivered by a clinical psychologist. Though the benefit of extra sessions and service delivery by a clinical psychologist could not be ascertained from the reviewed studies, it may be worth examining further to identify the advantages and/or possible disadvantages of such an intensive option. However, from the sensitivity analysis in Table 54, such an intensive option may be incurring a much higher cost compared with the realistic option should the benefit of the two options be similar. Also, when the long-term resource impact of implementing a psychological intervention is considered, the model shows that psychological intervention has the potential to be a more cost-effective option notwithstanding significant uncertainty around some parameters.

Limitations of the analysis
The major issue that may limit the usefulness of this analysis is the non-availability of QALYs estimates. Nevertheless, from the reported potential gain of more QALYs following treatment as usual compared with fewer QALYs gained following MACT in the study by BYFORD2003, it is uncertain whether QALY gain or loss is a useful measure of outcome in long-term self-harm management. In the same study, the authors were of the opinion that self-harm as a coping mechanism may be associated with improvement in quality of life than other measures used to prevent it.

Another limitation is variation in the modalities of psychological interventions among the studies included in the meta-analysis. Though the probabilistic method used in this analysis substantially accounts for the associated uncertainties, it is important to interpret the result of this analysis with caution especially in relation to the cost of intervention and the RR.

7.2.10   From evidence to recommendations

Based on the clinical review, there is some evidence showing clinical benefit of a psychological interventions in reducing repetition of self-harm episodes, compared with routine care. However, there is considerable uncertainty and heterogeneity with respect to the population, treatment length and treatment modality and settings, which lowers the quality of the evidence. Interventions in the analysis included cognitive-behavioural, psychodynamic, or problem-solving elements. The number of sessions in studies varied with an average of six sessions and the GDG opted to recommend a range of three to twelve sessions. Therapists in these studies were experienced in working with people who self-harm. They worked collaboratively with service users to identify problems causing distress, or factors maintaining their self-harm.

From the health economic evidence, there is some evidence to suggest that a psychological intervention is potentially cost effective in reducing repetition of self-harm episodes. In the long term, its health and economic benefit is also significant. However, given the extent of uncertainty around the treatment effect estimate, there is a need to be cautious in the implementation of a psychological intervention. Further research is necessary to determine the extent of the benefit of intensive psychological intervention, the usefulness of the QALY as an outcome in self-harm interventions, and the effect of the settings in which the intervention is delivered.

In light of the clinical and health economic evidence, health and social care professionals may consider providing psychological interventions specifically structured for people who self-harm.

7.2.11 Clinical practice recommendations

Interventions for self-harm

7.2.11.1 Consider offering 3 to 12 sessions of a psychological intervention that is specifically structured for people who self-harm, with the aim of reducing self-harm. In addition:

- The intervention should be tailored to individual need, and could include cognitive-behavioural, psychodynamic or problem-solving elements.
- Therapists should be trained and supervised in the therapy they are offering to people who self-harm.
- Therapists should also be able to work collaboratively with the person to identify the problems causing distress or leading to self-harm.

7.2.11.2 Provide psychological, pharmacological and psychosocial interventions for any associated conditions, for example those described in the following published NICE guidance:

- *Alcohol-use Disorders: Diagnosis, Assessment and Management of Harmful Drinking and Alcohol Dependence* (NICE, 2011b)
- *Depression* (NICE, 2009a)
- *Schizophrenia* (NICE, 2009b)
- *Borderline Personality Disorder* (NICE, 2009e)
- *Drug Misuse: Psychosocial Interventions* or *Drug Misuse: Opioid Detoxification* (NICE, 2007a and 2007b)
- *Bipolar Disorder* (NICE, 2006)[18].

7.2.12 Research recommendations

7.2.12.1 Clinical and cost effectiveness of psychological therapy with problem-solving elements for people who self-harm

For people who have self-harmed, does the provision of a psychological therapy with problem-solving elements, compared with treatment as usual, improve outcomes? What is the differential effect for people with a past history of self-harm, compared with people who self-harm for the first time?

This question should be answered using a well-conducted RCT. Consider six sessions of psychological therapy with problem-solving elements, delivered immediately after discharge for the index episode of self-harm. The therapist should be trained and experienced in working with people who self-harm. Participants' history of previous self-harm, methods used and psychiatric history should be noted. Primary outcomes should include both hospital-reported and self-reported repetitions of self-harm. Other important outcomes, such as quality of life, depressive symptoms, service users' experience and adverse events (for example, distress or exacerbation of symptoms associated with therapy), should be included. The study design should take

---

[18]This recommendation also appears in Section 8.5 where the pharmacological data is presented.

into account the complex motives that underpin self-harm. Studies needs to be large enough to determine the intervention's costs and cost effectiveness.

Why this is important
Although review of the research evidence suggests that psychological therapy with problem-solving elements offers promise, it is not clear which components are the active ingredients of any such intervention, or whether such an intervention is effective for people with a past history of self-harm compared with those who have self-harmed for the first time. Further, only a few studies have looked at a broad range of outcomes for different populations who self-harm.

7.2.12.2   Clinical effectiveness of low-intensity/ brief psychosocial interventions for people who self-harm
For people who self-harm, does the provision of potentially cheap low-intensity/brief psychosocial interventions, compared with treatment as usual, improve outcomes?

This question should be answered using a well-conducted RCT. Consider using a variety of approaches, including postcards, emergency cards, phone calls, or the use of electronic media in community mental health settings. The outcomes should include service users' engagement and experience, and hospital-reported and self-reported repetitions of self-harm. Other important outcomes, such as quality of life, depressive symptoms and adverse events (for example, distress or exacerbation of symptoms associated with contact with services) should be included.

Why this is important
Many people do not engage with available treatments following self-harm. If acceptable, alternative approaches, such as the low-intensity contact interventions indicated above, can be relatively easily and widely implemented, with the potential to improve outcomes, at relatively low cost, in individuals who may be otherwise difficult to engage.

7.3   HARM REDUCTION

7.3.1   Introduction

The most desirable outcome for the treatment and care of people who self-harm would be to permanently stop self-harming, recover from any underlying psychiatric disorder and to have a good quality of life. However, for some people not self-harming may not be immediately attainable nor possible in the medium to long term, and there are individuals for whom self-harm functions to prevent suicide. For many people who self-harm, there will be a period in which the aim of treatment will be to reduce harm to the individual, either by reducing the frequency of self-harm, or reducing the harm associated with acts of self-harm.

This approach to harm reduction has been tried with significant success in helping people with substance misuse (including drugs and alcohol) and smoking, and in relation to sexual activity ('safe sex') to prevent transmission of HIV and other sexually transmitted diseases. Indeed, harm reduction has been an acceptable, secondary aim of treatment in a broad range of chronic medical conditions where cure is either not possible or not immediately attainable. The application of this approach to self-harm has been controversial. The GDG nevertheless took the view that harm reduction should be considered in line with the above. In addition, the GDG decided to review the evidence available on the specific approach to harm reduction termed 'harm minimisation'.

7.3.2 Definition of harm minimisation

The term 'harm minimisation' has been used in a number of ways. For example, Pembroke states, 'Harm minimisation is about accepting the need to self-harm as a valid method of survival until survival is possible by other means. This does not condone or encourage self-injury but is about facing the reality of maximising safety in the event of self-harm' (Pembroke, 2007). For some people, self-harm is a way of taking control (see Chapter 4); and treatment regimes that focus on removing control by enforcing abstinence may be counterproductive or even dangerous. For some people, harm minimisation rather than abstinence may be a more realistic goal.

Harm minimisation is sometimes described as 'harming oneself safely' (for example using a sterile, sharp blade to cut and being aware of the location of veins and arteries; see for example National Self Harm Network, 2000), but many health and social care professionals may find this concept troubling. One concern is that by highlighting the dangers of certain activities, staff may actually be alerting service users to them. Understandably, staff can be worried that this may been seen as condoning or endorsing harmful behaviours. It is widely agreed, however, that poisoning with any substance cannot be done 'safely': there is no safe way of self-poisoning (NICE, 2004a).

7.3.3 Clinical review protocol

The review protocol, including the review questions, information about the databases searched, and the eligibility criteria used for this section of the guideline, can be found in Appendix 8. Further information about the search strategy can be found in Appendix 9. Information on the review protocol can be found in Table 55.

7.3.4 Studies considered

The search strategy generated 4,747 references, for which titles and abstracts were sifted by the technical team. Full studies were retrieved where team members regarded them as having potential relevance. However, no RCTs or cohort studies met the inclusion criteria.

The GDG therefore selected three publications that would help illustrate some different approaches to harm reduction in the context of self-harm. One study looked at the different attitudes among healthcare professionals in a locality and within

Table 55: Clinical review protocol for the review of harm reduction strategies

Review question	For people who self-harm, does the provision of self-management and/or harm reduction strategies, compared with no treatment or treatment as usual, improve outcomes?
Electronic databases	CINAHL, EMBASE, MEDLINE, PsycINFO
Date searched	All literature to 25 January 2011
Study design	N/A
Patient population	Self-harm population
Intervention(s)	Harm reduction strategies (such as replacement therapy, positive emotion technique and so on)
Comparison	N/A
Critical outcomes	Repetition (reduction in frequency or severity)

national professional organisations to a harm minimisation handbook. The second approach involved teaching young people techniques on how to cope better when the urge to self-harm occurred so as to prevent self-harm, backed up by a process of ward exclusion in the event of self-harm. The final study describes using a 'positive risk taking' approach in a female forensic service. It was acknowledged that these studies did not constitute evidence in the terms set out for this guideline.

7.3.5   Narrative synthesis

Pengelly and colleagues (2008) developed a handbook for people who repeatedly self-harm, to encourage collaboration between service users and front-line healthcare professionals. The *Alternatives to Self-harm Handbook* (Pengelly & Ford, 2005) was designed for use within the Selby and York Primary Care Trust. It gives factual information about self-harm, helps identify support networks, and covers areas such as understanding why people self-harm, types of therapy of possible benefit and techniques for problem-solving. The booklet also provides advice on harm reduction, including alternative behaviour to help distraction from the urge to self-harm, and some advice on damage limitation.

Alternative behaviours suggested to help distract a person from the urge to self-harm included pinching, squeezing an ice cube for a short time, snapping rubber bands on one's wrist, exercising, yoga, and kicking and punching something soft such as a pillow.

Advice on damage limitation techniques included using a clean and sharp blade, avoiding cutting areas near major veins and arteries, not sharing instruments used to self-harm so as to avoid infections and to ensure each person had tetanus protection.

The approach also included having access to first aid and a basic knowledge of medical care; avoiding alcohol/drug use in association with self-harm as this may lead to more severe wounding; and, finally, to focus on reducing the severity and frequency of episodes.

This study reported feedback received about the handbook, from service users, mental health professionals from the York and Selby Primary Care Trust and a solicitor. The Royal College of Psychiatrists and the Nursing and Midwifery Council were also approached for their comments and views.

Service users were pleased with the handbook's advice on harm reduction as they felt it was encouraging a shift in attitude of professionals who expect service users to stop self-harm completely; reducing the frequency and severity of self-harm was considered a more realistic goal.

Local healthcare professionals expressed a range of views. For example, a psychiatrist had the opinion that service users should decide on which alternatives should be considered. A psychodynamic therapist thought the handbook misunderstood the nature of self-harm as an act aimed at harming/hurting oneself and that harm reduction was missing this point. Moreover, advising on alternative forms could raise legal issues as it may be seen as encouraging self-harm. These behaviours could be misinterpreted or used to excess and are still harmful as they could cause bruising or bleeding. It is more important to understand the meaning of self-harm and the motivation behind it for that individual.

Perhaps unsurprisingly, the legal view of the handbook from the trust solicitor drew attention to possible legal challenges if it was implemented, but did acknowledge that telling a person not to self-harm, or threatening detention, is often unrealistic. The Nursing and Midwifery Council underlined the need for practitioners to consult with a wider clinical team before decisions are made and follow the Code of Professional Conduct. The Royal College of Psychiatrists stressed the importance of a full psychosocial assessment along with offering a comprehensive care package to service users. It is important to note that this handbook was not intended to be a self-help book but to be used as part of a comprehensive care plan.

Livesey (2009) conducted a pre-post design study set in an acute psychiatric inpatient and day patient unit for young people who self-harm by cutting or over-dosing. The interventions used in this study were two-fold. Firstly, they introduced introduction of a 'no self-harm' policy, also described as a therapeutic contract. The failure to comply with the no self-harm policy resulted in immediate suspension from the unit. Subjects were then called back for an interview with their care giver, to reconsider negotiating their therapeutic contract. Failure to comply a second time would result in discharge from the unit. Secondly, staff encouraged the use of alternative techniques such as ice, rubber bands and marker pens instead of sharp objects. They also encouraged the use of diaries, relaxation, distraction and other therapeutic interventions to address underlying distress and problems that a young person may have. The results reported that 2 weeks following the introduction of the new therapeutic regime, the mean number of self-harm episodes recorded per week fell from a 6 month baseline level of 1.2 (SD 1.3) to 0.2 (SD 0.59). There was no control group, the study was in a single unit and the numbers were small.

Birch and colleagues (2011) carried out an audit of self-harm and non-fatal overdose seen in 45 women from a women's forensic service, who had long-standing and complex mental health problems. The setting comprised three units in which the women resided: a medium secure unit, a community ward and supported community flats. The study analysed the pattern and frequency of self-harm using a positive risk-taking approach. Positive risk-taking uses both harm reduction and 'relational security', which is described as developing a relationship with a service user, where the healthcare professional and service user reach a psychological understanding of the meaning of self-harm to that individual and agree on a risk management plan. If the intention of self-harm was communicated, it was met by a response which was supportive but emphasised the importance of acting on feelings in other ways than self-harm. Communication by talking was encouraged in group or individual therapy sessions. The units reflected home-like environments with household objects that could be used to self-harm. Continuous observation was used but not one-to-one observation. The idea behind this approach was that self-harm is an individual's choice and it should not be stopped until other forms of expression are found. Positive risk-taking aims to work with the self-harm rather than against it. During the study length of 6 years, data were collected from incidence forms that were completed in the unit (from 2004 to 2009). The results showed an overall decrease in the frequency of self-harm during admission and over time, across all three units. The study had no control group, had a small number of participants and was undertaken within a single service. The design was essentially an audit.

7.3.6   From evidence to recommendations

The GDG found no evidence to support or to contradict a harm reduction approach for people who self-harm. However, the GDG took the view that the resistance to employing harm reduction approaches in this context had no evidential support whilst there was significant evidence supporting harm reduction strategies in other areas of healthcare, most notably in the field of drug misuse. The GDG could not make broad generalised recommendations for harm reduction approaches for all people who self-harm, but instead opted to, on the basis of consensus, recommend tentative approaches to harm reduction for some people who self-harm. The GDG also considered the role of the inpatient unit in harm reduction, and whilst the GDG recognised that for some individuals admission may reduce self-harm, for others, this may exacerbate it. The GDG therefore decided to make no recommendation about the use or the role of inpatient units in harm reduction.

7.3.7   Clinical practice recommendation

7.3.7.1   If stopping self-harm is unrealistic in the short term:
- consider strategies aimed at harm reduction; reinforce existing coping strategies and develop new strategies as an alternative to self-harm where possible

- consider discussing less destructive or harmful methods of self-harm with the service user, their family, carers or significant others[19] where this has been agreed with the service user, and the wider multidisciplinary team
- advise the service user that there is no safe way to self-poison.

7.3.8   Research recommendation

7.3.8.1   An observational study exploring different harm-reduction approaches following self-harm

What are the different approaches to harm reduction following self-harm in NHS settings?

A study should be carried out to investigate the different approaches to harm reduction following self-harm currently in use in NHS settings. This could use survey methodology with all, or a selected sample of, mental health service providers. Audit data should be used to provide a preliminary evaluation of potential utility. Promising interventions might be tested in small-scale pilot RCTs, which use frequency and severity of self-harm, and standard measures of distress and psychological symptoms, as outcome measures. Other outcomes such as quality of life, service users' experience and adverse events should be included.

Why this is important

Although cessation of the behaviour remains the treatment goal for many professionals providing care to people who self-harm, this may not be realistic or possible in the short term for some individuals. An alternative strategy for services is to reduce the severity and frequency of self-harm. Anecdotally, a variety of approaches to harm reduction are used in health service settings - for example minimising the physical harm associated with episodes or suggesting alternatives to self-harming behaviours. However, the extent to which such management strategies are used across services is uncertain, as is their effectiveness.

---

[19]'Significant other' refers not just to a partner but also to friends and any person the service user considers to be important to them.

8   PHARMACOLOGICAL INTERVENTIONS

8.1   INTRODUCTION

Many people who self-harm take psychotropic medication (Murphy *et al.*, 2007), often as treatment for associated conditions such as depression. However evidence for the efficacy of pharmacological interventions to reduce self-harm is lacking. Some research suggests that lithium and clozapine may have specific anti-suicidal properties (Cipriani *et al.*, 2005; Meltzer *et al.*, 2003). Other studies have reported that prescription of certain classes of antidepressants (for example, selective serotonin reuptake inhibitors [SSRIs]) may be associated with an increase in suicidal behaviour particularly in young people (Barbui *et al.*, 2009; Fergusson *et al.*, 2005). Those who self-harm are at increased risk of future episodes, including overdoses of medication. There are large differences in the toxicity of medication prescribed to people who self-harm (Hawton *et al.*, 2010).

Other NICE guidelines discuss the pharmacological treatment of conditions that may be associated with self-harm (for example, NICE, 2009a, 2009b and 2009e). The aim in the current chapter is to review the RCT evidence specifically for pharmacological treatment of self-harm. Because of variation in the toxicity of medication, a discussion of studies that could help to inform safer prescribing practices is also included.

8.2   PHARMACOLOGICAL INTERVENTIONS

8.2.1   Studies considered[20]

An existing systematic review was identified (Hawton *et al.*, 2011) and the authors made their data available to the NCCMH team. The review for this guideline includes five studies (BATTAGLIA1999 [Battaglia *et al.*, 1999]; HALLAHAN2007 [Hallahan *et al.*, 2007], HIRSCH1982 [Hirsch *et al.*, 1982]; MONTGOMERY1979 [Montgomery *et al.*, 1979]; LAUTERBACH2008 [Lauterbach *et al.*, 2008]). The GDG decided to exclude two studies (MONTGOMERY1983 [Montgomery *et al.*, 1983], VERKES1998 [Verkes *et al.*, 1998]) from the meta-analysis because they looked at people who had a diagnosis of personality disorder. Pharmacological treatment options in the treatment of personality disorder are partly covered in the NICE *Borderline Personality Disorder* guideline (NICE, 2009e).

---

[20]Here and elsewhere in the guideline, each study considered for review is referred to by a study ID in capital letters (primary author and date of study publication, except where a study is in press or only submitted for publication, then a date is not used).

Additional systematic searches were undertaken to update the review. The last search was dated in January 2011. No additional studies that met inclusion criteria were found.

Further information about both included and excluded studies can be found in Appendix 15f.

8.2.2 Clinical evidence for antidepressants versus placebo

One study compared antidepressants with placebo (HIRSCH1982). This was reviewed in the NICE guideline *Self-harm: the Short-term Physical and Psychological Management and Secondary Prevention of Self-harm in Primary and Secondary Care* (NICE, 2004a) and there were no new studies identified for this comparison.

Evidence from each important outcome and overall quality of evidence are presented in Table 56. The full evidence profiles and associated forest plots can be found in Appendix 17b and Appendix 16b, respectively.

There was insufficient evidence to differentiate clinical effectiveness between treatment and placebo on the reduction of repetition during the first 6 weeks of treatment (N = 114; RR 1.6, 95% CI, 0.63 to 4.04). There was insufficient evidence to determine the effect on death by suicide, or the acceptability of treatment.

Table 56: Summary study characteristics of trials comparing antidepressants versus placebo

	Antidepressants versus placebo
Total number of trials (N)	1 RCT (N = 114)
Study ID	HIRSCH1982
Diagnosis	Not reported
Recruitment setting	Patients were admitted to hospital after deliberate self-poisoning
Treatment length	6 weeks
Country	UK
Previous self-harm	Not reported
Intervention	30 to 60 mg mianserin or 75 to 150 mg nomifensine
Control	Placebo

Borderline personality disorder

Two studies (MONTGOMERY1983, VERKES1998) compared antidepressants versus placebo among people with personality disorders. All participants in MONT-GOMERY1983 and 92% of participants in VERKES1998 had a diagnosis of personality disorder. Thus, the GDG decided not to include these two studies in the meta-analysis. In MONTGOMERY1983 participants took 30 mg of mianserin for 6 months. Participants in VERKES1998 took 40 mg paroxetine for 12 months and both groups received psychotherapy. However, there was insufficient evidence to determine differences between groups.

8.2.3   Clinical evidence for antipsychotic medication versus placebo or low-dose antipsychotic medication

Two studies included antipsychotics as one of their treatment arms (BATTAGLIA1999, MONTGOMERY1979). A narrative synthesis for each study was included in the NICE guideline on the short-term management of self-harm (NICE, 2004a) and no new studies had been identified since then. In MONTGOMERY1979, flupenthixol depot (20 mg) or placebo was administered every 4 weeks for 6 months. In BATTAGLIA1999, 12.5 mg of fluphenazine or 1.5 mg fluphenazine was administered once a month for 6 months. Study characteristics can be found in Table 57.

There was limited evidence (MONTGOMERY1979) suggesting that there was a statistically significant clinical difference between flupenthixol and placebo on reducing repetition of self-harm (N = 37; RR 0.29, 95% CI, 0.1 to 0.81). Despite the observed effect, a wide variability in the CI was observed due to the small sample size. No statisticaly significant difference was found between groups regarding treatment complaince (N = 37; RR 0.92, 95% CI, 0.67 to 1.26). There were a total of seven dropouts, two of which were due to Parkinsonian side effects and the remaining five were not specified. As a result, it was not possible to make a recommendation based on this single trial.

There was insufficient evidence (BATTAGLIA1999) to differenitate clinical effectiveness between 12.5 mg and ultra low-dose 1.5 mg fluphenazine on reducing repetitions during 6 months after trial entry (N = 53; RR 1.28, 95% CI, 0.65 to 2.52). There were no suicide deaths reported in either trial arm. It was also unclear how the different dosage reduced the likelihood of leaving treatment early (N = 58; RR 1.12, 95% CI, 0.71 to 1.76).

8.2.4   Clinical evidence for other pharmacological interventions versus placebo

Two studies (HALLAHAN2007, LAUTERBACH2008) included medication other than antidepressants or antipsychotics. In LAUTERBACH2008, lithium was administered using a fixed schedule of dose augmentation increased by 200 mg per week for 3 to 4 weeks. At 1 year, the doses were reduced by half and discontinued at the 13th

Table 57: Summary study characteristics of trials comparing antipsychotics versus other comparators

	Antipsychotic medication versus placebo or low-dose antipsychotic medication	
Total number of trials (N)	1 RCT (N = 37)	1 RCT (N = 58)
Study ID	MONTGOMERY1979	BATTAGLIA1999
Diagnosis	Not reported	79% diagnosis of substance abuse, 35% mood disorder, 29% anxiety disorder
Recruitment setting	Patients admitted to a general hospital following a suicidal act	Patients presenting to a psychiatric hospital for suicide attempt
Treatment length	6 months	6 months
Country	UK	US
Previous self-harm	All were repeaters	Suicide attempt within 30 days before study entry and at least two prior attempts
Intervention	20 mg intramuscular flupenthixol decanoate/4 per week	Low dose (12 mg) fluphenazine decanoate
Comparison	Placebo	Ultra low-dose (1.5 mg) fluphenazine decanoate

month. The majority of the participants had a diagnosis of depression. In HALLA-HAN2007, participants were randomised to receive omega-3 fatty acid supplement (n = 22) of 1.2 g eicosapentaenoic acid and 0.9 g decosahexaenoic acid, or placebo for 12 weeks. Four identical capsules were given each morning to each group containing either an active ingredient or placebo. The active capsules contained a total dose equal to 2,128 mg per day of eicosapentaenoic acid plus decosahexaenoic acid. Patients continued to receive psychiatric care. The majority of participants had a diagnosis of personality disorder. Study characteristics can be found in Table 58.

There were no statistically significant clinical differences between lithum and placebo on any reported outcomes (LAUTERBACH2008) and no differences in reducing repetition of self-harm at 12 months from trial entry (N = 167; RR 0.99, 95% CI,

Table 58: Summary study characteristics of trials comparing other medications versus placebo

	Other medications versus placebo	
Total number of trials (N)	1 RCT (N = 167)	1 RCT (N = 49)
Study ID	LAUTERBACH2008	HALLAHAN2007
Diagnosis	DSM-IV 76% had diagnosis of MDD, 19% adjustment disorder, 5% other. Comorbidity: 8% substance-use disorder, 7% anxiety disorder, 34% personality disorder	41% had diagnosis of alcohol misuse and 82% personality disorder
Recruitment setting	Patients presenting to the emergency department following a suicide attempt at one of five study centres	Patients presenting to hospital after deliberate self-harm
Treatment length	3 to 4 weeks	12 weeks
Country	Germany	Ireland
Previous self-harm	44% were repeaters	All are recurrent repeaters
Intervention	Lithium 200 mg per week	Omega-3 fatty acid supplement (EPAX 5500 capsules) plus usual psychiatric care
Comparison	Placebo	Placebo plus usual psychiatric care

0.36 to 2.69). There were also no differences in terms of depression scores (measured by Hamilton Depression Rating Scale) at 3 months (SMD -0.05, 95% CI, -0.42 to 0.33), 6 months (SMD 0.07, 95% CI, -0.36 to 0.50) and 12 months (SMD -0.05, 95% CI, -0.54 to 0.44), and no differences in BHS score at 3 months (SMD -0.1, 95% CI, -0.49 to 0.3), 6 months (SMD -0.12, 95% CI, -0.67 to 0.42) and 12 months (SMD -0.03, 95% CI, -0.58 to 0.52). Three suicides occurred in the placebo arm and none in the treatment arm, but it should be noted that these suicides occurred within the context of a depressive spectrum disorder. Several limitations should be noted: there were more people who had personality disorders (p $<$ 0.05) and multiple suicide attempts (p $<$ 0.001) in the lithium group, and participants in the placebo group had higher baseline suicide ideation scores (p < 0.05). Furthermore, the high proportion of participants lost to follow-up (approximately 60%) might indicate the results were overestimated.

There was no statistically significant difference between omega-3 fatty acid supplement and placebo group during 12 weeks' treatment when looking at repetition as an outcome (N = 49; RR 1.23, 95% CI, 0.51 to 2.97) (HALLAHAN2007).

There was limited evidence to show a small reduction in depression scores (N = 49; SMD = -0.3, 95% CI, -0.87 to 0.26). Fewer participants in the treatment group reported suicide ideation at 12 weeks after trial entry compared with placebo (N = 49; RR 0.47, 95% CI, 0.24 to 0.9); there were slightly more participants (but not statistically significant) completing treatment (N = 49; RR 1.17, 95% CI, 0.88 to 1.54). A few limitations should be noted: at baseline, there were more married partic ipants in the treatment group, and the depression scores in the treatment group were higher than the placebo group. These limitations might inflate the effects.

8.2.5   Clinical evidence summary

The evidence base for the pharmacological treatment of self-harm remains very limited since the publication of the NICE guideline *Self-Harm: the Short-term Physical and Psychological Management and Secondary Prevention of Self-harm in Primary and Secondary Care* (NICE, 2004a). With regard to the effects of antidepressants and antipsychotics on the reduction of self-harm behaviour, no new trials were identified. The clinical efficacy of these medications remains uncertain. The variations in the treatment lengths, follow-up period, and participants' psychiatric diagnosis in these trials made it more difficult to make any conclusions about the clinical effects of these medications.

There were two new trials looking at effects of lithium and omega-3 fatty acid supplement versus placebo. There was no evidence of reduction in repetitions in either trial. There might be a small improvement in a few symptom measures; however, these trials were too small to detect a statistically significant effect. There were baseline differences between groups in the two studies that might overestimate the clinical effects for some measures. Moreover, the population of these two studies had a high prevalence of psychiatric disorders (depressive disorder, alcohol misuse and personality disorder), which might limit generalisability of the findings.

8.2.6   Health economic evidence

No evidence on the cost effectiveness of pharmacological interventions for the management of self-harm was identified by the systematic search of the economic literature. Details on the methods used for the systematic search of the economic literature are described in Section 3.6.1.

According to the guideline systematic review of clinical evidence, the clinical efficacy of pharmacological interventions for the treatment of self-harm is uncertain; therefore, no economic modelling was undertaken in this area.

8.3   SAFER PRESCRIBING

The issue of safer prescribing is not limited to treatment with psychotropic medications and is relevant to all prescribing to those with a known history of self-harm or who are at risk of self-harm. Prescribed medications may also be used to effect self-harm either as an end in itself, or as a consequence of use for other aims, for example the manipulation of, or neglect of insulin regimes to influence weight. The risks associated with the prescription of other potentially dangerous drugs such as warfarin should be assessed with reference to the health consequences of not prescribing it and considering alternatives.

There have been wider public health measures to limit the volumes of potentially hazardous drugs in the population. Consideration of some of these measures are beyond the remit of this guideline, but the recent limitation on prescription of co-proxamol has already been shown to result in fewer deaths from poisoning with no increase in those due to other analgesics (Hawton *et al.*, 2009).

Generally, prescription of potentially toxic psychotropic medications such as lithium is undertaken in secondary care with close attention to the risks of overdose. The majority of antidepressants are prescribed in primary care. Commonly, SSRIs are regarded as being of low toxicity and knowledge of the variation within this group as well as differences between SSRIs, selective noradrenaline reuptake inhibitors and other antidepressants may not be widely appreciated.

8.3.1   Studies considered

A comprehensive search was conducted that resulted in 6,183 references being generated. Sifting was conducted by three members of the technical team based on the titles and abstracts of the references. Full texts of the studies of potential relevance were retrieved. Studies were excluded on the basis of the outcomes reported. Studies in which the fatal toxicity index or case fatality index were reported were included. A total of 18 studies met these criteria, of which the GDG decided to include only the most recent. Due to the changes in regulatory policy and development of newer drugs over years, only studies published in the last 5 years were reviewed. AFSHARI2005 (Afshari *et al.*, 2005), HAUKKA2009 (Haukka *et al.*, 2009) and HAWTON2010 (Hawton *et al.*, 2010) were included. Due to the small number of studies, these have been narratively synthesised.

Toxicity is the primary outcome examined in the review. Toxicity can be measured by the fatal toxicity index or case fatality index. Fatal toxicity index is calculated by the number of deaths divided by the number of prescriptions of a particular drug.

However, the interpretation of toxicity using the fatal toxicity index can be confounded by differential prescribing of drugs to particular groups of people (for example, people at highest risk of self-harm being preferentially prescribed particular medications). This is referred to as confounding by indication. Case fatality index is calculated by dividing the number of suicides by the number of fatal and non-fatal poisonings of a particular drug. Case fatality index might be a more reliable indicator of toxicity because it partly accounts for this 'confounding by indication'.

Further information about both included and excluded studies can be found in Appendix 15f.

8.3.2   Narrative synthesis

AFSHARI2005
This study was conducted in Scotland and aimed to look at the relative toxicity of co-proxamol in overdose compared with co-codamol and co-dydramol. Prescription data, number of overdoses and deaths relating to these popular paracetamol–opioid compound analgesics were collected. Co-proxamol was ten times more toxic than co-codamol or co-dydramol in terms of its fatal toxicity index, even after the differences in prescription data were accounted for.

HAUKKA2009
This study, conducted in Finland, aimed to look at a national cohort of antidepressant users and how antidepressants related to the risk of suicide from 1999 to 2003. Data included in the study were the participants' years of usage and the number of suicides relating to that drug. Data were reported both by drug class and by individual drug. It was possible to calculate the fatal toxicity index for drug classes or individual drugs based on the data reported in the study. This showed that tricyclic antidepressants (TCAs) were more toxic than SSRIs. When individual drugs were considered, mirtazapine was the most toxic followed by venlafaxine and then moclobemide. It was unclear whether confounding by indication was accounted for. People at higher risk of self-harm might be prescribed a certain drug, which might not be accounted for in the calculation of the fatal toxicity index.

HAWTON2010
This was an observational study of prescriptions and suicide by self-poisoning in the UK that aimed to provide updated toxicity data of antidepressants, to aid clinicians' decision-making about prescriptions. Data included the death rate by suicide, prescriptions rate and self-poisoning rate for each individual antidepressant for people aged over 10 years from 2000 to 2006. The fatal toxicity index and case fatality index were then calculated. Data can be found in Appendix 16c. The study reported a very high correlation between the rankings of the results from the fatal toxicity and case fatality index (which may be a more reliable indicator of potential toxicity because case fatality index accounted for confounding by indication). The findings showed that TCAs as a drug class were more toxic than SSRIs. Dosulepin

and doxepin were the most toxic antidepressants in terms of the fatal toxicity index and case fatality index.

In addition, the study reported venlafaxine was less toxic in overdose than other TCAs. It was, however, still more toxic than SSRIs. Although SSRIs generally had lower toxicity, not all drugs within the class were the same. There was a greater than three-fold variation in case fatality rates between individual SSRIs.

8.3.3   Clinical evidence summary

Three recent studies reviewed the toxicity of different drugs that were commonly used for self-poisoning (analgesics and antidepressants). These studies included different individual drugs in their comparison, hence it was not possible to synthesise the toxicity data across these studies. Nevertheless, a common finding could be concluded for antidepressants. TCAs as a drug class were more toxic than SSRIs.

8.4   FROM EVIDENCE TO RECOMMENDATIONS

There was insufficient evidence to determine whether the provision of pharmacological treatment would reduce the likelihood of repetition of self-harm. No new trials looking at antidepressants or antipsychotics had been identified. Hence, no recommendations could be made.

It is recommended that healthcare professionals provide pharmacological interventions for any associated conditions as described in the relevant NICE guidelines. When prescribing drugs, toxicity of prescribed drugs in overdose should be taken into consideration. There was recent evidence suggesting TCAs as a drug class were more toxic than SSRIs. When clinicians are considering antidepressants, SSRIs might be preferred in those at risk of suicidal behaviour. In particular, the more toxic TCAs such as dosulepin should be avoided.

8.5   RECOMMENDATIONS

8.5.1   Clinical practice recommendations

8.5.1.1   Do not offer drug treatment as a specific intervention to reduce self-harm.

8.5.1.2   Provide psychological, pharmacological and psychosocial interventions for any associated conditions, for example those described in the following published NICE guidance:
- *Alcohol-use Disorders: Diagnosis, Assessment and Management of Harmful Drinking and Alcohol Dependence* (NICE, 2011b)
- *Depression* (NICE, 2009a)
- *Schizophrenia* (NICE, 2009b)
- *Borderline Personality Disorder* (NICE, 2009e)

- *Drug Misuse: Psychosocial Interventions or Drug Misuse: Opioid Detoxification)* (NICE, 2007a and 2007b)
- *Bipolar Disorder* (NICE, 2006)[21].

8.5.1.3   When prescribing drugs for associated mental health conditions to people who self-harm, take into account the toxicity of the prescribed drugs in overdose. For example, when considering antidepressants, selective serotonin reuptake inhibitors (SSRIs) may be preferred because they are less toxic than other classes of antidepressants. In particular, do not use tricyclic antidepressants, such as dosulepin, because they are more toxic.

---

[21]This recommendation also appears in Section 7.3 where the psychosocial data is presented.

9 CONSENT, CAPACITY AND CONFIDENTIALITY

9.1 INTRODUCTION

The ongoing management of self-harm can be complex and the issues that arise when individuals refuse the treatment that healthcare professionals feel they need are especially difficult (David *et al.*, 2010). Often healthcare professionals are unsure whether they should provide treatment to a person under these circumstances. Another important principle of care is confidentiality. There is a need to balance the protection of sensitive data with the appropriate sharing of information in order to ensure optimal care.

The focus of this chapter is on issues of consent and confidentiality. There are important overlaps between this chapter and Chapter 6 of *Self-harm: the Short-term Physical and Psychological Management and Secondary Prevention of Self-harm in Primary and Secondary Care* (NCCMH, 2004). However, there have been significant legislative changes in the interim, particularly with respect to the introduction of the Mental Capacity Act 2005 (HMSO, 2005).

9.2 MENTAL CAPACITY

Mental capacity refers to the ability of an individual to make a decision (or take a particular course of action) at a time when it is needed (HMSO, 2007b). Capacity can change over time, for example if an individual's level of consciousness changes or they are under the influence of alcohol or drugs. It is also important to note that capacity may vary according to the decision that needs to be made. An individual may have capacity to make simple everyday decisions but may lack capacity to make more complex decisions about treatment. Assessment of capacity should therefore be made on a case by case basis.

9.2.1 Mental Capacity Act 2005

The Mental Capacity Act 2005 (HMSO, 2005) provides a legal basis to enable decisions to be made on behalf of those who lack the mental capacity to make decisions for themselves. The Act is based on principles previously established by individual legal cases (that is, 'common law'). All people aged 16 years and over are presumed to have capacity. Any decision made on behalf of someone who lacks capacity must be made in their best interests. The Act aims to balance an individual's right to make decisions for themselves with their right to be protected from harm.

Text Box 2 summarises the five statutory principles of the Act (HMSO, 2007b).

271

Text Box 2: The Mental Capacity Act establishes five principles (HMSO, 2007)

A person must be assumed to have capacity unless it is established that he lacks capacity.

A person is not to be treated as unable to make a decision unless all practicable steps to help him to do so have been taken without success.

A person is not to be treated as unable to make a decision merely because he makes an unwise decision.

An act done, or decision made, under this Act for or on behalf of a person who lacks capacity must be done, or made, in his best interests.

Before the act is done, or the decision is made, regard must be had to whether the purpose for which it is needed can be as effectively achieved in a way that is less restrictive of the person's rights and freedom of action.

Assessing capacity

To enable a person to make a decision about receiving medical treatment, that person must receive sufficient information about the specific treatment that is being offered and in a form that can be understood by him/her. Information must be provided about the seriousness and nature of the problems associated with the condition under question, the objectives of the treatment, the consequences of being treated and also the consequences of not being treated. Throughout, treatment attempts must be made to provide information when necessary and to obtain the person's consent.

Any individual assessing capacity should do so as part of a two-stage process, as outlined in Text Box 3 (HMSO, 2007b).

A person will be deemed to be unable to make a particular decision if they cannot perform the tasks set out in Text Box 4.

Text Box 3: Two stages for assessing capacity from Mental Capacity Act Code of Practice

Stage 1: Does the person have an impairment of, or a disturbance in the functioning of, their mind or brain?

Stage 1 requires proof that the person has an impairment of the mind or brain, or some sort of or disturbance that affects the way their mind or brain works. If a person does not have such an impairment or disturbance of the mind or brain, they will not lack capacity under the Act.

Stage 2: Does the impairment or disturbance mean that the person is unable to make a specific decision when they need to?

For a person to lack capacity to make a decision, the Act says their impairment or disturbance must affect their ability to make the specific decision when they need to. But first people must be given all practical and appropriate support to help them make the decision for themselves. Stage 2 can only apply if all practical and appropriate support to help the person make the decision has failed.

Text Box 4: Assessing ability to make informed decisions

A person is unable to make a decision if they cannot:

1. understand information about the decision to be made (the Act calls this 'relevant information')
2. retain that information in their mind
3. use or weigh that information as part of the decision-making process, or
4. communicate their decision (by talking, using sign language or any other means).

Who can make assessments of capacity?

In practice, in most healthcare settings it will be the professional providing care for the individual at the time the decision needs to be made who makes the assessment of capacity. Multidisciplinary teams may be involved in the process but the final decision must be made by the person proposing the treatment. There is no prerequisite that the assessor must have mental health experience. More complex or difficult decisions may require assessments of capacity by professionals whose role is to advise the decision maker (for example psychiatrists, psychologists, social workers and occupational therapists). Examples of complex decisions include: those with potentially serious consequences; those where there is disagreement between family members and carers; those where the person being assessed has expressed different views to different people or has repeatedly made decisions that has put them at risk or caused harm (HMSO, 2007b). Legal advice should be available to assessors through their NHS organisations.

Factors that affect capacity

Factors that can impair capacity include long-term mental illness or disability, or more temporary factors such as impairment due to medication, drugs, alcohol, acute illness, or emotional distress. In such circumstances, staff should decide whether the treatment of a person should be withheld (if it is considered safe to do so) until the person regains capacity.

9.2.2 Advance decisions and statements

In England and Wales the Mental Capacity Act 2005 (HMSO, 2005) allows individuals aged 18 years and over who are capable of making an informed choice to refuse specified medical treatment at a time in the future, even if this might result in death. These refusals are referred to as 'advance decisions' in the Mental Capacity Act and are legally binding (HMSO, 2007b). Although people can make advance decisions to refuse treatment, there is no legal right to demand specific treatment (either at the time or in the future). However, people can state their preferences for treatment in the form of 'advance statements', which healthcare professionals can take into account, but they do not carry the same imperative as advance decisions.

Advance decisions should specify which treatment is to be refused and include as much detail as possible regarding the circumstances under which the advance decision will apply. They will only come into force once an individual has lost the capacity to make a particular treatment decision for themselves. Healthcare professionals need to be satisfied that an advance decision is valid and applicable and they should consult as widely as possible in order to establish this. Decisions may not be valid or applicable if the person concerned has done anything that clearly goes against their decision, has withdrawn their decision, has conferred the power to make a decision on an attorney, or would have changed their decision if they had known more about the current circumstances. Decisions to refuse life saving treatment must satisfy the requirement of the Mental Capacity Act (see Text Box 5).

Text Box 5: Advance decisions (HMSO, 2007)

If the advance decision refuses life-sustaining treatment, it must:

- be in writing;
- be signed and witnessed; and
- state clearly that the decision applies even if life is at risk.

9.2.3   Young people

The Mental Capacity Act does not in general apply to children under 16 years, the care and treatment of whom will be determined by common law principles. Most provisions of the Mental Capacity Act apply to young people aged 16 to 17 years old, with the exception of making advance decisions (individuals need to be 18 years old and over to make advance decisions). If a young person aged 16 to 17 years has capacity and refuses treatment there may be difficulties if those with parental responsibility wish to consent on their behalf. The Family Division of the High Court can rule on such cases (HMSO, 2007b).

For those aged 16 to 17 years who lack capacity, parents can consent on their behalf if the decision to be made is considered to be within the zone of parental control. However, it should be noted that healthcare professionals are able to provide treatment regardless of whether parental consent has been given as long as the principles of the Act are followed and the course of action is judged to be in the young person's best interests.

Healthcare professionals who have contact with young people should be aware of the Mental Health Act (1983; amended 1995 and 2007; HMSO, 2007), the Mental Health Act code of practice (HMSO, 2008) and the Children Acts (HMSO, 1989; amended 2004) and how these relate to capacity and consent in young people.

9.2.4   Capacity and advance decisions in the context of self-harm

The ethical and practical issues raised by treatment refusals and advance decisions are complex, but are even more difficult in the context of suicidal behaviour. In clinical practice there is often sufficient doubt about an individual's capacity after self-harm to justify treatment. For example, if a person seems relatively calm in making their decision to refuse treatment and expresses a wish to die by suicide, this could be rebutted by providing evidence that the person: does not understand the consequence of their decision; that their decision is influenced by another person; that their judgement is impaired by emotional distress, or that they are ambivalent about their decision. However, if the person in question is judged to be mentally capable of making a decision about whether or not to receive treatment, then this decision must be respected, even if it may cause a permanent risk to that person's health or premature death.

With respect to advance decisions, one of the most important questions is whether someone who has completed an advance decision refusing treatment should be allowed to die from the consequences of a suicidal act. The Mental Capacity Act states that health workers will be protected from liability for not providing treatment if they reasonably believe that a valid advance decision exists. However, it has also been argued that advance decisions to refuse treatment following episodes of suicidal behaviour raise a number of specific issues (Kapur *et al.*, 2010b). It has been suggested that clinicians should proceed especially cautiously, in view of the acute distress, ambivalence and changeability that often characterise suicidal thoughts and behaviour (Kapur *et al.*, 2010b).

If an individual is detained under the Mental Health Act 2007 (HMSO, 2007a), physical healthcare can be administered as long as it is part of the treatment for the mental disorder and its consequences (HMSO, 2007b). Therefore treating the physical consequences of the patient's suicidal behaviour is authorised under the Mental Health Act if that behaviour has been caused by the patient's mental disorder. Apart from advance decision to refuse electroconvulsive therapy, an advance decision to refuse treatment is not valid if the treatment is being provided under Part 4 of the Mental Health Act. If treating under the Mental Capacity Act, staff must act in the person's best interest and within good medical practice. The use of minimal force or restraint should only be considered when immediately necessary and as a last resort.

9.3   PRINCIPLES INTO PRACTICE

Treatments for underlying psychological symptoms or psychiatric disorders will generally involve informed consent, or less commonly, administration under the Mental Health Act. General principles that healthcare professionals should take into account include:

● Offering comprehensive information about the intervention and any consequences if it is not carried out. In many cases, spending time with the individual, listening to their concerns, explaining the issues in a comprehensible fashion and reducing the overall emotional tone of the situation can lead to the individual making a decision to consent to treatment.

- Not gaining consent through being coercive (for example, threats to use the Mental Health Act if the person refuses).
- Involving family members and friends in decision-making, within the bounds of confidentiality. Healthcare professionals might also be advised to consult with colleagues (if appropriate) and come to a consensus as to the proper course of action. Making a decision in isolation should be avoided.
- Considering the content of any crisis card or advance decisions and statements.
- Recording all actions and the reasons behind them.

9.4   CONFIDENTIALITY

Protecting the personal information of service users is a key principle in the provision of health services. Healthcare professionals have a legal and professional obligation to protect confidentiality, but there are circumstances in which personal information can be disclosed (General Medical Council, 2009) as outlined in Text Box 6.

Text Box 6: Confidentiality

- If it is required by law (for example, by regulatory bodies or judges).
- If the patient consents implicitly for the sake of their own care (for example, disclosure to other members of the care team or for local clinical audit) or if the patient consents specifically for other purposes (for example, disclosure to employers, insurers or benefit agencies).
- If it is justified in the public interest (for example, to protect society or individuals from harm, or to enable medical research or other uses of data that will benefit society over time).

For disclosures to be made in the public interest, the risks posed by non-disclosure need to outweigh the risks posed by disclosure. One situation that may be particularly relevant to the management of self-harm is disclosure to protect the individual themselves. The General Medical Council (2009) guidance suggests that professionals should usually abide by a competent adult's refusal to consent to disclosure even if this decision leaves them (but no one else) at risk of serious harm. Individuals should be encouraged to consent to disclosure under these circumstances, be warned of the possible consequences of non-disclosure and be given information about possible sources of help. However, disclosures without consent are permitted if non-disclosure exposes other people to a risk of death or serious harm (for example, in situations where a serious crime might be prevented or detected). Disclosures are also permitted in situations where individuals lack capacity, as long as this is in their best interests.

Sharing information with families is often a difficult issue, particularly so in the management of individuals who self-harm. It is important to establish with service users who they would like their information shared with and the circumstances under which this should occur. If a family member wishes to share their concerns about an individual, healthcare professionals should not refuse to discuss these on the basis of confidentiality. This information may be helpful in informing management. It should be made clear to the family members that the details of the conversation may be relayed to the individual themselves. However, before talking to family members in this way, guidance suggests that professionals should consider whether the service users would regard such conversations as a breach of trust (General Medical Council, 2009).

Confidentiality issues for children and young people

Issues of confidentiality are particularly challenging with children and young people[22] who self-harm and have capacity yet refuse the involvement of their parents or carers in their treatment or refuse consent to disclose issues relating to their safety to their parents or carers. In these circumstances healthcare professionals need to carefully weigh the rights of the young person to confidentiality and the risk to the therapeutic relationship of a breach of confidentiality against providing the family and carers with sufficient information to enable them to appropriately protect and care for the young person. The younger the service user and the more risky or severe the self-harm, the less justifiable the decision to maintain confidentiality may be considered to be. Healthcare professionals making these judgements are encouraged to discuss with a senior colleague and/or consult with the named doctor or nurse for safeguarding. If the healthcare professional decides on balance that a breach of confidentiality is warranted, involving the young person as much as possible in how and when this is done can mitigate some of the damage to the therapeutic relationship.

9.5   SAFEGUARDING

Although it is essential to work collaboratively with people who self-harm, it is also important to recognise that those dependent upon them may also need help, and sometimes protection, according to the Common Assessment Framework[23]. The care co-ordinator or key worker may need to ensure that children's services are alerted to the need for assessment and possible help for the child. Similarly, when dependent or vulnerable adults are involved, the vulnerable adult may need to be assessed at home, the risks assessed and any necessary safeguarding procedures initiated.

Young people who self-harm may present safeguarding concerns either because of the nature of the social circumstances in which they live, for example, a young person caring for a parent with a chronic illness who self-harms daily by cutting to manage difficult emotions about their circumstances, or because of the frequent and potential

---

[22]Where it refers to children and young people, this applies to all people who are between 8 and 17 years inclusive.

[23]www.cwdcouncil.org.uk/caf.

lethality of their behaviour, for example, a young person who frequently ties ligatures around their neck and often stands on a high bridge contemplating jumping off. Healthcare professionals should consider, both during initial assessment and treatment, whether safeguarding concerns warrant involvement of other agencies. Often the named safeguarding doctor or nurse, as well as social services departments, can provide advice. In circumstances where social circumstances are germane to the causation of the self-harm or where repeated self-harm is potentially lethal, multi-agency treatment plans may need to be developed. Such plans need to be based on a comprehensive assessment of the young person's health, educational and social needs. In endeavouring to serve the needs of young people with complex needs, occasionally the involvement of one agency may decrease the involvement of another or even, in some circumstances, precipitate their withdrawal. This is never helpful nor is it consistent with prioritising the needs of the young person. Healthcare professionals may need to provide training to staff in other agencies to help them understand their role in supporting/helping a young person who self-harms because self-harm is often medicalised solely as a mental health issue and wider contextual factors are either ignored or misunderstood.

Treatment is particularly challenging in the context where a young person is at high risk and where there is a need to balance their immediate safety with improving longer-term outcomes, which may require a degree of positive risk taking. In these situations, multi-agency involvement to agree the balance of risks and benefits of different treatment options may prove helpful in forming an intervention plan. These discussions must involve the young person and his or her family in decision making.

9.6   RECOMMENDATIONS

9.6.1   Clinical practice recommendations

General principles of care
Consent and confidentiality

9.6.1.1   Health and social care professionals who work with people who self-harm should be trained to:
- understand and apply the principles of the Mental Capacity Act (2005) and Mental Health Act (1983; amended 1995 and 2007)
- assess mental capacity, and
- make decisions about when treatment and care can be given without consent.

9.6.1.2   Be familiar with the principles of confidentiality with regard to information about a person's treatment and care, and be aware of the circumstances in which disclosure of confidential information may be appropriate and necessary.

9.6.1.3   Offer full written and verbal information about the treatment options for self-harm, and make all efforts necessary to ensure that the person is able, and has the opportunity, to give meaningful and informed consent.

9.6.1.4   Take into account that a person's capacity to make informed decisions may change over time, and that sometimes this can happen rapidly in the context of self-harm and suicidal behaviour.

9.6.1.5   Understand when and how the Mental Health Act (1983; amended 1995 and 2007) can be used to treat the physical consequences of self-harm.

9.6.1.6   Health and social care professionals who work with people who self-harm should have easy access to legal advice about issues relating to capacity and consent.

9.6.1.7   Health and social care professionals who have contact with children and young people who self-harm should be trained to:
- understand the different roles and uses of the Mental Capacity Act (2005), the Mental Health Act (1983; amended 1995 and 2007) and the Children Act (1989; amended 2004) in the context of children and young people who self-harm
- understand how issues of capacity and consent apply to different age groups
- assess mental capacity in children and young people of different ages.

They should also have access at all times to specialist advice about capacity and consent.

Safeguarding

9.6.1.8   CAMHS professionals who work with children and young people who self-harm should consider whether the child's or young person's needs should be assessed according to local safeguarding procedures[24].

9.6.1.9   If children or young people who self-harm are referred to CAMHS under local safeguarding procedures:
- use a multi-agency approach, including social care and education, to ensure that different perspectives on the child's life are considered
- consider using the Common Assessment Framework[25]; advice on this can be sought from the local named lead for safeguarding children.

If serious concerns are identified, develop a child protection plan.

9.6.1.10   When working with people who self-harm, consider the risk of domestic or other violence or exploitation and consider local safeguarding procedures for vulnerable adults and children in their care. Advice on this can be obtained from the local named lead on safeguarding adults.

---

[24]www.safeguardingchildren.org.uk
[25]www.cwdcouncil.org.uk/caf (note that the Common Assessment Framework is not applicable in Wales).

10 SUMMARY OF RECOMMENDATIONS

10.1 GENERAL PRINCIPLES OF CARE

Working with people who self-harm

10.1.1 Health and social care professionals working with people who self-harm should:
- aim to develop a trusting, supportive and engaging relationship with them
- be aware of the stigma and discrimination sometimes associated with self-harm, both in the wider society and the health service, and adopt a non-judgemental approach
- ensure that people are fully involved in decision-making about their treatment and care
- aim to foster people's autonomy and independence wherever possible
- maintain continuity of therapeutic relationships wherever possible
- ensure that information about episodes of self-harm is communicated sensitively to other team members.

10.1.2 Health and social care professionals who work with people who self-harm should be:
- familiar with local and national resources, as well as organisations and websites that offer information and/or support for people who self-harm, and
- able to discuss and provide advice about access to these resources.

Access to services

10.1.3 Children and young people who self-harm should have access to the full range of treatments and services recommended in this guideline within child and adolescent mental health services (CAMHS).

10.1.4 Ensure that children, young people and adults from black and minority ethnic groups who self-harm have the same access to services as other people who self-harm based on clinical need and that services are culturally appropriate.

10.1.5 When language is a barrier to accessing or engaging with services for people who self-harm, provide them with:
- information in their preferred language and in an accessible format
- psychological or other interventions, where needed, in their preferred language
- independent interpreters.

280

Self-harm and learning disabilities

10.1.6   People with a mild learning disability who self-harm should have access to the same age-appropriate services as other people covered by this guideline.

10.1.7   When self-harm in people with a mild learning disability is managed jointly by mental health and learning disability services, use the Care Programme Approach (CPA).

10.1.8   People with a moderate or severe learning disability and a history of self-harm should be referred as a priority for assessment and treatment conducted by a specialist in learning disabilities services.

Training and supervision for health and social care professionals

10.1.9   Health and social care professionals who work with people who self-harm (including children and young people) should be:
- trained in the assessment, treatment and management of self-harm, and
- educated about the stigma and discrimination usually associated with self-harm and the need to avoid judgemental attitudes.

10.1.10   Health and social care professionals who provide training about self-harm should:
- involve people who self-harm in the planning and delivery of training
- ensure that training specifically aims to improve the quality and experience of care for people who self-harm
- assess the effectiveness of training using service-user feedback as an outcome measure.

10.1.11   Routine access to senior colleagues for supervision, consultation and support should be provided for health and social care professionals who work with people who self-harm. Consideration should be given of the emotional impact of self-harm on the professional and their capacity to practice competently and empathically.

Consent and confidentiality

10.1.12   Health and social care professionals who work with people who self-harm should be trained to:
- understand and apply the principles of the Mental Capacity Act (2005) and Mental Health Act (1983; amended 1995 and 2007)
- assess mental capacity, and
- make decisions about when treatment and care can be given without consent.

10.1.13   Be familiar with the principles of confidentiality with regard to information about a person's treatment and care, and be aware of the circumstances in which disclosure of confidential information may be appropriate and necessary.

10.1.14   Offer full written and verbal information about the treatment options for self-harm, and make all efforts necessary to ensure that the person is able, and has the opportunity, to give meaningful and informed consent.

10.1.15   Take into account that a person's capacity to make informed decisions may change over time, and that sometimes this can happen rapidly in the context of self-harm and suicidal behaviour.

10.1.16   Understand when and how the Mental Health Act (1983; amended 1995 and 2007) can be used to treat the physical consequences of self-harm.

10.1.17   Health and social care professionals who work with people who self-harm should have easy access to legal advice about issues relating to capacity and consent.

10.1.18   Health and social care professionals who have contact with children and young people who self-harm should be trained to:
- understand the different roles and uses of the Mental Capacity Act (2005), the Mental Health Act (1983; amended 1995 and 2007) and the Children Act (1989; amended 2004) in the context of children and young people who self-harm
- understand how issues of capacity and consent apply to different age groups
- assess mental capacity in children and young people of different ages.

They should also have access at all times to specialist advice about capacity and consent.

Safeguarding

10.1.19   CAMHS professionals who work with children and young people who self-harm should consider whether the child's or young person's needs should be assessed according to local safeguarding procedures[26].

10.1.20   If children or young people who self-harm are referred to CAMHS under local safeguarding procedures:
- use a multi-agency approach, including social care and education, to ensure that different perspectives on the child's life are considered
- consider using the Common Assessment Framework[27]; advice on this can be sought from the local named lead for safeguarding children.

If serious concerns are identified, develop a child protection plan.

10.1.21   When working with people who self-harm, consider the risk of domestic or other violence or exploitation and consider local safeguarding procedures for vulnerable adults and children in their care. Advice on this can be obtained from the local named lead on safeguarding adults.

---

[26]www.safeguardingchildren.org.uk.
[27]www.cwdcouncil.org.uk/caf. It should be noted that the Common Assessment Framework is not applicable in Wales.

Families, carers and significant others[28]

10.1.22   Ask the person who self-harms whether they would like their family, carers or significant others to be involved in their care. Subject to the person's consent and right to confidentiality, encourage the family, carers or significant others to be involved where appropriate.

10.1.23   When families, carers or significant others are involved in supporting a person who self-harms:
● offer written and verbal information on self-harm and its management, including how families, carers and significant others can support the person
● offer contact numbers and information about what to do and whom to contact in a crisis
● offer information, including contact details, about family and carer support groups and voluntary organisations, and help families, carers or significant others to access these
● inform them of their right to a formal carer's assessment of their own physical and mental health needs, and how to access this.

10.1.24   CAMHS professionals who work with young people who self-harm should balance the developing autonomy and capacity of the young person with perceived risks and the responsibilities and views of parents or carers.

Managing endings and supporting transitions

10.1.25   Anticipate that the ending of treatment, services or relationships, as well as transitions from one service to another, can provoke strong feelings and increase the risk of self-harm, and:
● Plan in advance these changes with the person who self-harms and provide additional support, if needed, with clear contingency plans should crises occur.
● Record plans for transition to another service and share them with other health and social care professionals involved.
● Give copies to the service user and their family, carers or significant others if this is agreed with the service user.

10.1.26   CAMHS and adult health and social care professionals should work collaboratively to minimise any potential negative effect of transferring young people from CAMHS to adult services.
● Time the transfer to suit the young person, even if it takes place after they reach the age of 18 years.

---

[28]'Significant other' refers not just to a partner but also to friends and any person the service user considers to be important to them.

- Continue treatment in CAMHS beyond 18 years if there is a realistic possibility that this may avoid the need for referral to adult mental health services.

10.1.27 Mental health trusts should work with CAMHS to develop local protocols to govern arrangements for the transition of young people from CAMHS to adult services, as described in this guideline.

10.2 PRIMARY CARE

10.2.1 If a person presents in primary care with a history of self-harm and a risk of repetition, consider referring them to community mental health services for assessment. If they are under 18 years, consider referring them to CAMHS for assessment. Make referral a priority when:
- levels of distress are rising, high or sustained
- the risk of self-harm is increasing or unresponsive to attempts to help
- the person requests further help from specialist services
- levels of distress in parents or carers of children and young people are rising, high or sustained despite attempts to help.

10.2.2 If a person who self-harms is receiving treatment or care in primary care as well as secondary care, primary and secondary health and social care professionals should ensure they work cooperatively, routinely sharing up-to-date care and risk management plans. In these circumstances, primary health and social care professionals should attend CPA meetings.

10.2.3 Primary care professionals should monitor the physical health of people who self-harm. Pay attention to the physical consequences of self-harm as well as other physical healthcare needs.

10.3 PSYCHOSOCIAL ASSESSMENT IN COMMUNITY MENTAL HEALTH SERVICES AND OTHER SPECIALIST MENTAL HEALTH SETTINGS: INTEGRATED AND COMPREHENSIVE ASSESSMENT OF NEEDS AND RISKS

10.3.1 Offer an integrated and comprehensive psychosocial assessment of needs (see recommendations 10.3.2–10.3.5) and risks (see recommendations 10.3.6–10.3.8) to understand and engage people who self-harm and to initiate a therapeutic relationship.

Assessment of needs
10.3.2 Assessment of needs should include:
- skills, strengths and assets
- coping strategies

- mental health problems or disorders
- physical health problems or disorders
- social circumstances and problems
- psychosocial and occupational functioning, and vulnerabilities
- recent and current life difficulties, including personal and financial problems
- the need for psychological intervention, social care and support, occupational rehabilitation, and also drug treatment for any associated conditions
- the needs of any dependent children.

10.3.3　All people over 65 years who self-harm should be assessed by mental health professionals experienced in the assessment of older people who self-harm. Assessment should follow the same principles as for working-age adults (see recommendations 10.3.1 and 10.3.2). In addition:

- pay particular attention to the potential presence of depression, cognitive impairment and physical ill health
- include a full assessment of the person's social and home situation, including any role they have as a carer, and
- take into account the higher risks of suicide following self-harm in older people.

10.3.4　Follow the same principles as for adults when assessing children and young people who self-harm (see recommendations 10.3.1 and 10.3.2), but also include a full assessment of the person's family, social situation, and child protection issues.

10.3.5　During assessment, explore the meaning of self-harm for the person and take into account that:

- each person who self-harms does so for individual reasons, and
- each episode of self-harm should be treated in its own right and a person's reasons for self-harm may vary from episode to episode.

Risk assessment

A risk assessment is a detailed clinical assessment that includes the evaluation of a wide range of biological, social and psychological factors that are relevant to the individual and, in the judgement of the healthcare professional conducting the assessment, relevant to future risks, including suicide and self-harm.

10.3.6　When assessing the risk of repetition of self-harm or risk of suicide, identify and agree with the person who self-harms the specific risks for them, taking into account:

- methods and frequency of current and past self-harm
- current and past suicidal intent
- depressive symptoms and their relationship to self-harm
- any psychiatric illness and its relationship to self-harm

- the personal and social context and any other specific factors preceding self-harm, such as specific unpleasant affective states or emotions and changes in relationships
- specific risk factors and protective factors (social, psychological, pharmacological and motivational) that may increase or decrease the risks associated with self-harm
- coping strategies that the person has used to either successfully limit or avert self-harm or to contain the impact of personal, social or other factors preceding episodes of self-harm
- significant relationships that may either be supportive or represent a threat (such as abuse or neglect) and may lead to changes in the level of risk
- immediate and longer-term risks.

10.3.7   Consider the possible presence of other coexisting risk-taking or destructive behaviours, such as engaging in unprotected sexual activity, exposure to unnecessary physical risks, drug misuse or engaging in harmful or hazardous drinking.

10.3.8   When assessing risk, consider asking the person who self-harms about whether they have access to family members', carers' or significant others' medications.

10.3.9   In the initial management of self-harm in children and young people, advise parents and carers of the need to remove all medications or, where possible, other means of self-harm available to the child or young person.

10.3.10   Be aware that all acts of self-harm in older people should be taken as evidence of suicidal intent until proven otherwise.

Risk assessment tools and scales

Risk assessment tools and scales are usually checklists that can be completed and scored by a clinician or sometimes the service user depending on the nature of the tool or scale. They are designed to give a crude indication of the level of risk (for example, high or low) of a particular outcome, most often suicide.

10.3.11   Do not use risk assessment tools and scales to predict future suicide or repetition of self-harm.

10.3.12   Do not use risk assessment tools and scales to determine who should and should not be offered treatment or who should be discharged.

10.3.13   Risk assessment tools may be considered to help structure risk assessments as long as they include the areas identified in recommendation 10.3.6.

Developing an integrated care and risk management plan

10.3.14   Summarise the key areas of needs and risks identified in the assessment (see recommendations 10.3.1–10.3.8) and use these to develop a care plan (see recommendations 10.4.2–10.4.3) and a risk management plan (see recommendations 10.4.4–10.4.5) in conjunction with the person who self-harms and their family, carers or significant others if this is agreed with the person. Provide printed copies for the service user and share them with the GP.

10.3.15　If there is disagreement between health and social care professionals and the person who self-harms about their needs or risks, consider offering the person the opportunity to write this in their notes.

10.4　LONGER-TERM TREATMENT AND MANAGEMENT OF SELF-HARM

Provision of care

10.4.1　Mental health services (including community mental health teams and liaison psychiatry teams) should generally be responsible for the routine assessment (see Section 10.3) and the longer-term treatment and management of self-harm. In children and young people this should be the responsibility of Tier 2 and 3 CAMHS[29].

Care plans

10.4.2　Discuss, agree and document the aims of longer-term treatment in the care plan with the person who self-harms. These aims may be to:
- prevent escalation of self-harm
- reduce harm arising from self-harm or reduce or stop self-harm
- reduce or stop other risk-related behaviour
- improve social or occupational functioning
- improve quality of life
- improve any associated mental health conditions.

Review the person's care plan with them, including the aims of treatment, and revise it at agreed intervals of not more than 1 year.

10.4.3　Care plans should be multidisciplinary and developed collaboratively with the person who self-harms and, provided the person agrees, with their family, carers or significant others. Care plans should:
- identify realistic and optimistic long-term goals, including education, employment and occupation

---

[29]Tier 2 CAMHS: primary care; Tier 3 CAMHS: community child and adolescent mental health teams.

- identify short-term treatment goals (linked to the long-term goals) and steps to achieve them
- identify the roles and responsibilities of any team members and the person who self-harms
- include a jointly prepared risk management plan (see below)
- be shared with the person's GP.

Risk management plans

10.4.4   A risk management plan should be a clearly identifiable part of the care plan and should:
- address each of the long-term and more immediate risks identified in the risk assessment
- address the specific factors (psychological, pharmacological, social and relational) identified in the assessment as associated with increased risk, with the agreed aim of reducing the risk of repetition of self-harm and/or the risk of suicide
- include a crisis plan outlining self-management strategies and how to access services during a crisis when self-management strategies fail
- ensure that the risk management plan is consistent with the long-term treatment strategy.

Inform the person who self-harms of the limits of confidentiality and that information in the plan may be shared with other professionals.

10.4.5   Update risk management plans regularly for people who continue to be at risk of further self-harm. Monitor changes in risk and specific associated factors for the service user, and evaluate the impact of treatment strategies over time.

Provision of information about the treatment and management of self-harm

10.4.6   Offer the person who self-harms relevant written and verbal information about, and give time to discuss with them, the following:
- the dangers and long-term outcomes associated with self-harm
- the available interventions and possible strategies available to help reduce self-harm and/or its consequences (see recommendations 10.1.1 and 10.4.10)
- treatment of any associated mental health conditions (see Section 10.5).

10.4.7   Ensure that people who self-harm, and their families, carers and significant others where this is agreed with the person, have access to the 'Understanding NICE guidance' booklet for this guideline and for the short-term management of self-harm (NICE, 2004a).

Interventions for self-harm

10.4.8   Consider offering 3 to 12 sessions of a psychological intervention that is specifically structured for people who self-harm, with the aim of reducing self-harm. In addition:
   ● the intervention should be tailored to individual need, and could include cognitive-behavioural, psychodynamic or problem-solving elements.
   ● therapists should be trained and supervised in the therapy they are offering to people who self-harm.
   ● therapists should also be able to work collaboratively with the person to identify the problems causing distress or leading to self-harm.

10.4.9   Do not offer drug treatment as a specific intervention to reduce self-harm.

Harm reduction

10.4.10   If stopping self-harm is unrealistic in the short term:
   ● consider strategies aimed at harm reduction; reinforce existing coping strategies and develop new strategies as an alternative to self-harm where possible
   ● consider discussing less destructive or harmful methods of self-harm with the service user, their family, carers or significant others where this has been agreed with the service user, and the wider multidisciplinary team
   ● advise the service user that there is no safe way to self-poison.

10.5   TREATING ASSOCIATED MENTAL HEALTH CONDITIONS

10.5.1   Provide psychological, pharmacological and psychosocial interventions for any associated conditions, for example those described in the following published NICE guidance:
   ● *Alcohol-use Disorders: Diagnosis, Assessment and Management of Harmful Drinking and Alcohol Dependence* (NICE, 2011b)
   ● *Depression* (NICE, 2009a)
   ● *Schizophrenia* (NICE, 2009b)
   ● *Borderline Personality Disorder* (NICE, 2009e)
   ● *Drug Misuse: Psychosocial Interventions* or *Drug Misuse: Opioid Detoxification* (NICE, 2007a and 2007b)
   ● *Bipolar Disorder* (NICE, 2006).

10.5.2　　When prescribing drugs for associated mental health conditions to people who self-harm, take into account the toxicity of the prescribed drugs in overdose. For example, when considering antidepressants, selective serotonin reuptake inhibitors (SSRIs) may be preferred because they are less toxic than other classes of antidepressants. In particular, do not use tricyclic antidepressants, such as dosulepin, because they are more toxic.

11   APPENDICES

APPENDIX 1:
SCOPE FOR THE DEVELOPMENT OF THE
CLINICAL GUIDELINE

1   GUIDELINE TITLE

Self-harm: the longer-term management of self-harm[30]

1.1   SHORT TITLE

Self-harm (longer-term management)

2   THE REMIT

The Department of Health has asked NICE: 'To prepare a clinical guideline on the management of self-harm (intentional self-poisoning or self-injury, irrespective of the apparent purpose of the act) to include the role of mental health professionals in ensuring service users who have self-harmed receive appropriate treatment for underlying problems that may have led to the act of self-harm.' It will cover the longer-term management of self-harm in a variety of settings.

This guideline follows on from 'Self-harm: the short-term physical and psychological management and secondary prevention of self-harm in primary and secondary care' (NICE clinical guideline 16 [NICE, 2004a]).

3   CLINICAL NEED FOR THE GUIDELINE

3.1   EPIDEMIOLOGY

The prevalence of self-harm is difficult to estimate. A national interview survey in 1999 suggested between 4.6% and 6.6% of people in the UK have self-harmed. A more recent international survey of young people aged 15 to 16 years found the prevalence of self-harm (in the past year) in the UK was 3.2% in boys and 11.1% in girls. The lifetime prevalence for self-harm in the UK was 4.8% in boys and 16.7% in girls.
a. A survey of general hospitals in Oxford, Manchester and Leeds found 7,344 people presented with a total of 10,498 episodes of self-harm. Most episodes

---

[30]In the course of guideline development the title changed to 'Self-harm: Longer-term Management'.

(80%) were due to self-poisoning and the rest to self-injury (mainly self-cutting). Although most research to date has been hospital-based, it is likely that many self-harm episodes do not come to the attention of health services.

b. A recent systematic review in the UK found that there was a higher prevalence of self-harm in South Asian women than in either South Asian men or white women.

3.2   CURRENT PRACTICE

a. Self-harm is usually managed in secondary care. This includes hospital medical care and mental health services. About half of the people who present to an accident and emergency (A&E) department after self-harming are assessed by a mental health professional. Treatments include psychosocial interventions, pharmacological interventions and harm minimisation.

b. People who self-harm often also have contact with primary care. About half of the people who attend an emergency department after self-harming will have visited their GP in the previous month. A similar proportion will visit their GP within 2 months of attending an A&E department after self-harming.

4   THE GUIDELINE

The guideline development process is described in detail on the NICE website (see Section 6, 'Further information').

This scope defines what the guideline will (and will not) examine, and what the guideline developers will consider. The scope is based on the referral from the Department of Health.

The areas that will be addressed by the guideline are described in the following sections.

4.1   POPULATION

4.1.1   Groups that will be covered

a. All people aged 8 years or older who self-harm.

4.1.2   Groups that will not be covered

a. Children younger than 8 years.
b. People with a neurodevelopmental disorder with repetitive stereotypical self-injurious behaviour (SIB), for example, head-banging in people with a significant learning disability.

4.2 HEALTHCARE SETTING

a. Care received in primary, secondary, tertiary and community healthcare settings from healthcare professionals who have direct contact with people who self-harm, and who make decisions about risk assessment, needs assessment, treatment and management of care for people who self-harm.
b. The guideline will not provide specific recommendations for A&E departments, paramedic services, prison medical services, the police and those who work in the criminal justice, social care and education sectors, but the guideline will be relevant to their work.

4.3 CLINICAL MANAGEMENT

4.3.1 Key clinical issues that will be covered

a. Medium and longer-term care management of people who self-harm.
b. Ongoing psychosocial assessment for the longer-term management of people who have self-harmed. This will include an assessment of needs and risk and how these are integrated.
c. Psychosocial interventions for the specific treatment of self-harm compared with control groups and other active interventions. For example, but not exclusively, self-help, problem-solving therapy, mentalisation-based treatment, cognitive behavioural therapy, dialectical behaviour therapy, cognitive analytic therapy, psychodynamic psychotherapy and family therapy.
d. Pharmacological interventions for the specific treatment of self-harm compared with control groups and psychological interventions. For example, antidepressants, anxiolytics and antipsychotics when used as a specific treatment for self-harm.
e. Safe prescribing for people with a history of self-harm.
f. Treatment of groups who may have specific care needs. For example, those from black and minority ethnic groups, people who self-injure, young people and older adults.
g. Harm minimisation and other strategies aimed at reducing the risks and/or harm associated with self-harm. For example, advice on safer cutting, distraction techniques and exploring alternatives to self-harm.
h. Possible adverse effects associated with treating self-harm.
i. Training for healthcare professionals treating people who self-harm.
j. When to refer to other NICE guidelines for the treatment and management of any accompanying or underlying mental health problems.

4.3.2 Clinical issues that will not be covered

a. Acute physical, psychiatric and psychological care of people who have just self-harmed. For the immediate care of people who have self-harmed, please see

'Self-harm: the short-term physical and psychological management and second-ary prevention of self-harm in primary and secondary care' (NICE clinical guideline 16 [NICE, 2004a]).
b. The treatment and management of any mental health problem or substance use disorder that may accompany, underlie or be associated with self-harm. However, the guideline will refer to other relevant NICE guidance (see section 5.1.2).
c. Longer-term management of the physical consequences of self-harm, such as reconstructive surgery, pain management and infection arising from injuries.

4.4   MAIN OUTCOMES

a. Self-harm and self-harm repetition (for example, self-poisoning or self-cutting).
b. Suicide.
c. Quality of life.
d. Service user determined outcomes.
e. Secondary outcomes such as social and psychological functioning, other causes of mortality, and resource use.

4.5   ECONOMIC ASPECTS

Developers will take into account both clinical and cost effectiveness when making recommendations involving a choice between alternative interventions. A review of the economic evidence will be conducted and analyses will be carried out as appropriate. The preferred unit of effectiveness is the quality-adjusted life year (QALY), and the costs considered will usually be only from an NHS and personal social services (PSS) perspective. further detail on the methods can be found in 'The guidelines manual' (see Section 6 'Further information').

4.6   STATUS

4.6.1   Scope

This is the final scope.

4.6.2   Timing

The development of the guideline recommendations will begin in November 2009.

5   RELATED NICE GUIDANCE

5.1   PUBLISHED GUIDANCE

5.1.1   NICE guidance to be updated

When reviewing the evidence for this guideline a need maybe identified to update the section on 'Psychological, pharmacological and psychosocial interventions for the management of self-harm' in *Self-harm: the Short-term Physical and Psychological Management and Secondary Prevention of Self-harm in Primary and Secondary Care*, NICE clinical guideline 16 (2004). Available from www.nice.org.uk/CG16.

5.1.2   Other related NICE guidance

- Schizophrenia. NICE clinical guideline 82 (2009 [NICE, 2009b]). Available from www.nice.org.uk/CG82
- Borderline personality disorder. NICE clinical guideline 78 (2009 [NICE, 2009e]). Available from www.nice.org.uk/CG78
- Antisocial personality disorder. NICE clinical guideline 77 (2009 [NICE, 2009f]). Available from www.nice.org.uk/CG77
- Bipolar disorder. NICE clinical guideline 38 (2006 [NICE, 2006]). Available from www.nice.org.uk/CG38
- Obsessive-compulsive disorder. NICE clinical guideline 31 (2005 [NICE, 2005b]). Available from www.nice.org. uk/CG31
- Depression in children and young people. NICE clinical guideline 28 (2005 [NICE, 2005a]). Available from www.nice.org.uk/CG28
- Post-traumatic stress disorder. NICE clinical guideline 26 (2005 [NICE, 2005c]). www.nice.org.uk/CG26
- Violence. NICE clinical guideline 25 (2005 [NICE, 2005d]). Available from www.nice.org.uk/CG25
- Depression. NICE clinical guideline 23 (2004, amended 2007 [NICE, 2004b]). Available from www.nice.org.uk/CG23
- Anxiety. NICE clinical guideline 22 (2004, amended 2007 [NICE, 2004c]). Available from www.nice.org.uk/CG22
- Eating disorders. NICE clinical guideline 9 (2004 [NICE, 2004d]). Available from www.nice.org.uk/CG9

5.2   GUIDANCE UNDER DEVELOPMENT

NICE is currently developing the following related guidance (details available from the NICE website).

- Depression in adults (update). NICE clinical guideline. Publication expected October 2009.[31]
- Depression in adults with a chronic physical health problem. NICE clinical guideline. Publication expected October 2009.[32]

6   FURTHER INFORMATION

Information on the guideline development process is provided in:
- 'How NICE clinical guidelines are developed: an overview for stakeholders' the public and the NHS'
- 'The guidelines manual'.

These are available from the NICE website (www.nice.org.uk/guidelinesmanual). Information on the progress of the guideline will also be available from the NICE website (www.nice.org.uk).

---

[31]This guideline has subsequently been published (NICE, 2009a).
[32]This guideline has subsequently been published (NICE, 2009c).

APPENDIX 2:

DECLARATIONS OF INTERESTS BY GUIDELINE DEVELOPMENT GROUP MEMBERS

With a range of practical experience relevant to the treatment and management of self-harm in the GDG, members were appointed because of their understanding and expertise in healthcare for people who self-harm and support for their families/carers, including: scientific issues; health research; the delivery and receipt of healthcare, along with the work of the healthcare industry; and the role of professional organisations and organisations for people who self-harm and their families/carers.

To minimise and manage any potential conflicts of interest, and to avoid any public concern that commercial or other financial interests have affected the work of the GDG and influenced guidance, members of the GDG must declare as a matter of public record any interests held by themselves or their families which fall under specified categories (see below). These categories include any relationships they have with the healthcare industries, professional organisations and organisations for people who self-harm and their families/carers.

Individuals invited to join the GDG were asked to declare their interests before being appointed. To allow the management of any potential conflicts of interest that might arise during the development of the guideline, GDG members were also asked to declare their interests at each GDG meeting throughout the guideline development process. The interests of all the members of the GDG are listed below, including interests declared prior to appointment and during the guideline development process.

Categories of interest
Paid employment

Personal pecuniary interest: financial payments or other benefits from either the manufacturer or the owner of the product or service under consideration in this guideline, or the industry or sector from which the product or service comes. This includes holding a directorship, or other paid position; carrying out consultancy or fee paid work; having shareholdings or other beneficial interests; receiving expenses and hospitality over and above what would be reasonably expected to attend meetings and conferences.

Personal family interest: financial payments or other benefits from the healthcare industry that were received by a family member.

Non-personal pecuniary interest: financial payments or other benefits received by the GDG member's organisation or department, but where the GDG member has not personally received payment, including fellowships and other support provided by the healthcare industry. This includes a grant or fellowship or other payment to sponsor a post, or contribute to the running costs of the department; commissioning of research or other work; contracts with, or grants from, NICE.

Personal non-pecuniary interest: these include, but are not limited to, clear opinions or public statements made about individuals who self-harm, holding office in a professional organisation or advocacy group with a direct interest in self-harm, other reputational risks relevant to self-harm.

Guideline Development Group – declarations of interest	
Professor Navneet Kapur – Chair, Guideline Development Group	
Employment	Professor of Psychiatry and Population Health (University of Manchester) Honorary Consultant Psychiatrist (Manchester Mental Health and Social Care Trust)
Personal pecuniary interest	None
Personal family interest	None
Non-personal pecuniary interest	I am an academic and researcher in the field of suicidal behaviour. I am currently an investigator on several large research grants provided by the Department of Health, the National Patient Safety Agency, and the National Institute of Health Research. As part of my work, I apply for research funding from government and charitable organisations.
Personal non-pecuniary interest	I am an academic and researcher in the field of suicidal behaviour. I have published and presented widely in this area, expressing views on a number of diverse issues related to self-harm service provision.
Professor Tim Kendall – Facilitator	
Employment	Director, NCCMH Medical Director, Sheffield Health and Social Care Trust Consultant Adult Psychiatrist Visiting Professor, Research Department of Clinical, Educational and Health Psychology, University College London

Personal pecuniary interest	None
Personal family interest	None
Non-personal pecuniary interest	Grant holder for £1.44 million per year (approximately) from NICE for guidelines work. Work with NICE International. Undertake some research into mental health, and the mental health workforce for the Department of Health, Royal College of Psychiatrists and the Academy Of Medical Royal Colleges.
Personal non-pecuniary interest	None
Mr Gareth Allen	
Employment	Service user/carer representative
Personal pecuniary interest	None
Personal family interest	None
Non-personal pecuniary interest	None
Personal non-pecuniary interest	None
Mr Simon Baston	
Employment	Lead Nurse Liaison Psychiatry, Sheffield Health and Social Care NHS Foundation Trust
Personal pecuniary interest	None
Personal family interest	None
Non-personal pecuniary interest	None
Personal non-pecuniary interest	None
Mr Andrew Briggs	
Employment	Consultant Child and Adolescent Psychotherapist, Kent & Medway NHS and Social Care Partnership Trust
Personal pecuniary interest	None
Personal family interest	None
Non-personal pecuniary interest	None
Personal non-pecuniary interest	None

Professor Stephen Briggs	
Employment	Consultant Social Worker, Tavistock And Portman NHS Foundation Trust Professor Of Social Work, University Of East London
Personal pecuniary interest	None
Personal family interest	None
Non-personal pecuniary interest	Co-editor of a book, *Relating to Self-harm and Suicide: Psychoanalytic Perspectives on Practice, Theory and Prevention* (London: Routledge, 2008)
Personal non-pecuniary interest	Clinician in a mental health service for young people and deliver a 10-week training on working with suicidal and self-harming young people. Have undertaken research and written on suicidal and self-harming young people, evaluated a respite centre (Maytree) and currently lead on a research project on self-harm in an emergency department.
Ms Julia Britton	
Employment	Child and Adolescent Psychotherapist and Head of Services, Open Door Young People's Consultation Service
Personal pecuniary interest	None
Personal family interest	None
Non-personal pecuniary interest	None
Personal non-pecuniary interest	None
Mr Anthony Cox	
Employment	Service user/carer representative PAPYRUS – Prevention of Young Suicide
Personal pecuniary interest	None
Personal family interest	None
Non-personal pecuniary interest	None
Personal non-pecuniary interest	Coordinator for PAPYRUS – Prevention of Young Suicide, a national charity

	which operates a telephone helpline and works to improve services for young people who may self-harm or attempt suicide. We give support and practical advice to young people worried about themselves or to anyone concerned about a young person who they know.
Dr Jonathan Evans	
Employment	Consultant Senior Lecturer, University of Bristol
Personal pecuniary interest	None
Personal family interest	None
Non-personal pecuniary interest	None
Personal non-pecuniary interest	None
Dr Paul Gill	
Employment	Consultant in Liaison Psychiatry, Sheffield Health and Social Care Chair, Faculty of Liaison Psychiatry, Royal College of Psychiatrists
Personal pecuniary interest	None
Personal family interest	None
Non-personal pecuniary interest	None
Personal non-pecuniary interest	None
Ms Kate Hunt	
Employment	Lead Professional Consultant Clinical Psychologist, Acute & Crisis Services, Sussex Partnership NHS Foundation Trust
Personal pecuniary interest	None
Personal family interest	None
Non-personal pecuniary interest	None
Personal non-pecuniary interest	Led an audit of levels of self-harm within the Women's Secure & Forensic Services, which led me to believe that the positive risk-taking approach we

	used pointed to it being an effective intervention in reducing the frequency and severity of self-harming behaviours. We are planning to publish the results of this audit. However, this approach is recommended in the *Mainstreaming Gender and Women's Mental Health: Implementation Guidance* (Department of Health, 2003).
Dr Suzanne Kearney	
Employment	GP
Personal pecuniary interest	None
Personal family interest	None
Non-personal pecuniary interest	None
Personal non-pecuniary interest	None
Professor Rory O'Connor	
Employment	Professor of Psychology, University of Stirling
Personal pecuniary interest	None
Personal family interest	None
Non-personal pecuniary interest	None
Personal non-pecuniary interest	None
Mr Richard Pacitti	
Employment	Chief Executive, Mind in Croydon Service user/carer representative
Personal pecuniary interest	None
Personal family interest	None
Non-personal pecuniary interest	None
Personal non-pecuniary interest	None
Dr Michaela Swales	
Employment	Consultant Clinical Psychologist, North Wales Adolescent Service & Senior Lecturer, School of Psychology, Bangor University

Personal pecuniary interest	Under contract to write a book about problem-solving in the context of DBT.
Personal family interest	My husband is the managing director of, and a major shareholder in, Integral Business Support Ltd, a company that is the sole UK provider of training in DBT, a treatment considered by the self-harm guideline.
Non-personal pecuniary interest	Director of the British Isles Training Team that provides training in DBT to mental health professionals and health-care organisations throughout the UK and Eire. I fulfil this role as part of my University appointment within the School of Psychology, University of Wales, Bangor. The School of Psychology receives the income from my training in dialectical behaviour therapy. This income funds my secretary at the university, training for clinicians in my local NHS Trust (North Wales NHS Trust) and at times part funds a psychology assistant post in the clinical service in which I am employed (also North Wales NHS Trust).
	The School of Psychology was also in receipt of a grant from the Economic and Social Research Council, under the Knowledge Transfer Programme, to further develop training in DBT and increase dissemination of the treatment. The grant was awarded to the School of Psychology working jointly with Integral Business Support Ltd (see section above on Personal Family Interests). The grant from the Economic and Social Research Council was worth £104,707 over 3 years (ended September 2010). The company partner will contribute £50,760 to the project over the 3-year period.
	I have written a book on DBT from which I will receive royalties.

Personal non-pecuniary interest	Director of the British Isles DBT Training Team which is responsible for delivering all training in DBT in the UK and is in possession of a licence to deliver the training from the American Training Company, BTech LLC. I regularly present at conferences and deliver training in DBT.
Dr Alison Wood	
Employment	Consultant in Adolescent Psychiatry, Cheshire and Mersey Regional Tier 4 Adolescent Service
Personal pecuniary interest	None
Personal family interest	None
Non-personal pecuniary interest	None
Personal non-pecuniary interest	None
NCCMH team	
Mr Benedict Anigbogu	
Employment	Health Economist, NCCMH (from October 2010)
Personal pecuniary interest	None
Personal family interest	None
Non-personal pecuniary interest	None
Personal non-pecuniary interest	None
Ms Henna Bhatti	
Employment	Research Assistant, NCCMH
Personal pecuniary interest	None
Personal family interest	None
Non-personal pecuniary interest	None
Personal non-pecuniary interest	None
Ms Melissa Chan	
Employment	Systematic Reviewer, NCCMH
Personal pecuniary interest	None

Personal family interest	None
Non-personal pecuniary interest	None
Personal non-pecuniary interest	None
Mr Matthew Dyer	
Employment	Health Economist, NCCMH (until September 2010)
Personal pecuniary interest	None
Personal family interest	None
Non-personal pecuniary interest	None
Personal non-pecuniary interest	None
Ms Naomi Glover	
Employment	Research Assistant, NCCMH
Personal pecuniary interest	None
Personal family interest	None
Non-personal pecuniary interest	None
Personal non-pecuniary interest	None
Ms Marie Halton	
Employment	Research Assistant, NCCMH
Personal pecuniary interest	None
Personal family interest	None
Non-personal pecuniary interest	None
Personal non-pecuniary interest	None
Ms Katherine Leggett	
Employment	Project Manager, NCCMH
Personal pecuniary interest	None
Personal family interest	None
Non-personal pecuniary interest	None
Personal non-pecuniary interest	None
Mr Nick Meader	
Employment	Systematic Reviewer, NCCMH
Personal pecuniary interest	None

Personal family interest	None
Non-personal pecuniary interest	None
Personal non-pecuniary interest	None
Ms Sarah Stockton	
Employment	Senior Information Scientist, NCCMH
Personal pecuniary interest	None
Personal family interest	None
Non-personal pecuniary interest	None
Personal non-pecuniary interest	None
Dr Clare Taylor	
Employment	Senior Editor, NCCMH
Personal pecuniary interest	None
Personal family interest	None
Non-personal pecuniary interest	None
Personal non-pecuniary interest	None

APPENDIX 3:
SPECIAL ADVISORS TO THE GUIDELINE DEVELOPMENT GROUP

Professor Keith Hawton, Professor of Psychiatry, Oxford University/Consultant Psychiatrist, Oxfordshire and Buckinghamshire Mental Health NHS Foundation Trust
Professor Richard Jones, Consultant, Morgan Cole LLP

APPENDIX 4:
STAKEHOLDERS WHO RESPONDED TO EARLY
REQUESTS FOR EVIDENCE

None.

APPENDIX 5:

STAKEHOLDERS AND EXPERTS WHO SUBMITTED COMMENTS IN RESPONSE TO THE CONSULTATION DRAFT OF THE GUIDELINE

Stakeholders

Association of Child Psychotherapists
British Association for Counselling and Psychotherapy
British Psychological Society
Calderstones Partnership NHS Foundation Trust
Department of Health
Derbyshire Healthcare NHS Foundation Trust
Healthcare Inspectorate Wales
National Self Harm Network
NIHR (National Institute for Health Research) Evaluation, Trials and Studies Coordinating Centre
NHS Direct
Nottinghamshire NHS Trust
PAPYRUS
Royal College of General Practitioners
Royal College of Nursing
Royal College of Paediatrics and Child Health
Royal College of Psychiatrists in Scotland
Royal College of Psychiatrists in Wales
Royal Society of Medicine
SANE
Stonewall
University of Manchester
Wish

Experts

Dr Jim Bolton, Consultant Liaison Psychiatrist, St Helier Hospital

Professor David Gunnell, Professor of Epidemiology, School of Social and Community Medicine, University of Bristol

Professor Keith Hawton, Professor of Psychiatry, Oxford University;
Consultant Psychiatrist, Oxfordshire and Buckinghamshire Mental Health NHS Foundation Trust

Professor Richard Jones, Consultant, Morgan Cole LLP

Professor Richard Morriss, Professor of Psychiatry and Community Mental Health, Faculty of Medicine and Health Science, University of Nottingham

APPENDIX 6:
RESEARCHERS CONTACTED TO REQUEST INFORMATION ABOUT UNPUBLISHED OR SOON-TO-BE PUBLISHED STUDIES

Dr Mari A. Bjornaas, Department of Acute Medicine, Oslo University Hospital, Norway

Dr Prathiba Chitsabesan, Lead Consultant, Child Psychiatrist for Stockport CAMHS

Professor Ian Colman, Assistant Professor, School of Public Health, University of Alberta, Canada

Ms Kerry Gutridge, Research Associate, Bristol University

Professor Keith Hawton, Professor of Psychiatry Oxford University; Consultant Psychiatrist, Oxfordshire and Buckinghamshire Mental Health NHS Foundation Trust

Dr Agnes Hultén, National Swedish and Stockholm County Centre for Suicide Research and Prevention of Mental Ill-health, Stockholm, Sweden

Ms Cheryl Hunter, Post-graduate, University of Manchester

Professor Sunita Stewart, Department of Psychiatry, University of Texas Southwestern Medical Center, Dallas, Texas, US

Ms Sue Waterhouse, National Deputy Equality Lead, National Mental Health Development Unit

Dr Alison Wood, Consultant in Adolescent Psychiatry, Cheshire and Mersey Regional Tier 4 Adolescent Service

APPENDIX 7:

ANALYTIC FRAMEWORK AND CLINICAL

QUESTIONS

For the following clinical questions, separate analyses will be conducted (where data are available) for groups identified in the scope that have specific care needs:
- young people and older adults
- black and minority ethnic groups.

1. **Assessments**
   1.1. For people who self-harm, does formal risk assessment, needs assessment and psychosocial assessment improve outcomes?
   (*Note:* Impact of setting/organisational context and content of assessment to be taken into account if data are available)
   1.2. What are the risk and protective factors (internal and external) amongst people who self-harm that predict outcomes (for example, suicide, non-fatal repetition, other psychological outcomes)?

2. **Psychological and psychosocial interventions**
   2.1. For people who self-harm, do psychological and psychosocial interventions (compared with no treatment or other interventions) improve outcomes? What are the associated adverse effects?
   - Interventions: problem-solving, interpersonal therapy, CBT, peer support groups, self-help, computer-based interventions, DBT, counselling, psychodynamic interventions, family interventions, group therapy, postcards, assertive outreach, multi-systemic therapy, respite care, crisis management (refer to *Borderline Personality Disorder* guideline)
   2.2. For people who self-harm, do psychological and psychosocial interventions in combination with pharmacological interventions (compared with psychosocial or pharmacological interventions alone) improve outcomes? What are the associated adverse effects?

3. **Pharmacological interventions**
   3.1. For people who self-harm, do drug treatments improve outcomes? What are the associated adverse effects?
   - Interventions: Antidepressants, antipsychotics, lithium, anticonvulsants (for example, valproate, carbamazepine, lamotrigine), benzodiazepines, analgesics.
   3.2. For people who self-harm, what are the key principles underlying safer prescribing?

Consider:
- prescribing frequency (weekly, monthly)
- toxicity of drug.

4. **Self-management and harm minimisation**

4.1. For people who self-harm, does the provision of self-management and/or harm minimisation strategies, compared with no treatment or treatment as usual, improve outcomes?

Interventions include: replacement therapy, positive emotion technique.

5. **Training**

5.1. Does the provision of staff training (knowledge, skills based) improve outcomes (for example, staff attitudes, user satisfaction, user engagement with services)?

(*Note*: Impact of setting and content of training to be taken into account if data are available.)

APPENDIX 8:
REVIEW PROTOCOLS

Risk and needs assessment

Topic	Risk and needs assessment
Review question(s)	For people who self-harm, do formal risk assessment, needs assessment and psychosocial assessment improve outcomes? (*Note*: impact of setting/organisational context and content of assessment to be taken into account if data available)
Sub-question(s)	Are self-harm or suicide prediction scales clinically useful in predicting a repetition of self-harm?
Chapter	6 Psychosocial assessment
Sub-section	Section 6.3 Risk assessment scales Section 6.4 Needs assessment Section 6.5 Psychosocial assessment
Topic group	Jonathan Evans (Editor) Rory O'Connor, Kate Hunt, Simon Baston, Suzanne Kearney, Michaela Swales
Sub-section lead	Jonathan Evans and Rory O'Connor
Objectives	See sub-question
Criteria for considering studies for the review	
● Intervention	N/A
● Comparator	N/A
● Types of participants	People who experience self-harm (or suicide ideation, where the study clearly reports a history of self-harm). This includes all types of self-harm, irrespective of motive.
● Critical outcomes	Prediction of repeated self-harm or suicide measured by sensitivity and specificity values.

● Important, but not critical outcomes	N/A
● Other outcomes	N/A
● Study design	Prospective cohort or case control studies
● Include unpublished data?	No
● Restriction by date?	No
● Dosage	N/A
● Minimum sample size	N/A
● Study setting	Inpatient and outpatient (as long as participants had history of previous self-harm).
Search strategy	**Databases:** EMBASE, MEDLINE, PsycINFO **New search:** CINAHL
Searching other resources	GDG members identified if any key studies were missed.
Existing reviews	
● Updated	N/A
● Not updated	N/A
General search filter used	See search strategy in Appendix 9
Question specific search filter	See search strategy in Appendix 9
Amendments to filter/ search strategy	See search strategy in Appendix 9
The review strategy	The studies could not be meta-analysed. Each study was narratively summarised. The studies that look at risk assessment scales were divided into sub-sections of those that predict a fatal and those that predict a non-fatal outcome.
Additional assessments	1. Exclude retrospective studies design 2. Exclude general population (without history of previous self-harm) 3. Exclude studies that use another scale as a reference standard to measure repetition of self-harm.

Risk and protective factors

Topic	Risk and protective factors
Review question(s)	What are the risk and protective factors (internal and external) amongst people who self-harm that predict outcomes (for example, suicide, non-fatal repetition, other psychological outcomes)?
Sub-question(s)	N/A
Chapter	6 Psychosocial assessment
Sub-section	Section 6.2 Risk and protective factors
Topic group	Jonathan Evans (Editor) Kate Hunt, Simon Baston, Suzanne Kearney, Michaela Swales
Sub-section lead	Kate Hunt
Objectives	To explore the risk and protective factors associated with a repetition of self-harming behaviour
Criteria for considering studies for the review	
● Intervention	N/A
● Comparator	N/A
● Types of participants	Participants (aged 8 years old or above) admitted to hospital for treatment of index episode of self-harm). Self-endorsed self-harming behaviour is also included.
● Critical outcomes	Repetition (fatal and non-fatal outcome)
● Important, but not critical outcomes	N/A
● Other outcomes	N/A
● Study design	Prospective cohort studies
● Include unpublished data?	No
● Restriction by date?	No
● Dosage	N/A

● Minimum sample size	N/A
● Study setting	Inpatient and outpatient (as long as participants had history of previous self-harm).
Search strategy	**Databases:** CINAHL, EMBASE, HMIC, MEDLINE, PsycBOOKS, PsycEXTRA, PsycINFO **New search:**
Searching other resources	Experts in the field were contacted to identify if any key studies were missed.
Existing reviews	
● Updated	N/A
● Not updated	N/A
General search filter used	See search strategy in Appendix 9
Question specific search filter	See search strategy in Appendix 9
Amendments to filter/ search strategy	See search strategy in Appendix 9
The review strategy	Two independent reviewers will review the studies for their eligibility according to the inclusion criteria. Studies that meet eligibility will be examined to see if they could be meta-analysed. The criteria for inclusion in meta-analysis are the report of effects measure and its confidence interval. Studies that do not report the effects measure and confidence interval will be reviewed in a narrative manner.
Additional assessments	1. Exclude retrospective studies design 2. Exclude general population (without history of previous self-harm).

Psychological interventions

Topic	Psychological and psychosocial interventions
Review question(s)	For people who self-harm, do psychological and psychosocial interventions (compared with no treatment or other interventions) improve outcomes? What are the associated adverse effects?
Sub-question(s)	2.2 For people who self-harm, do psychological and psychosocial interventions in combination with pharmacological interventions (compared with either interventions alone) improve outcomes? What are the associated adverse effects?
Chapter	7 Psychological and psychosocial interventions
Sub-section	
Topic group	7 – Rory O'Connor, Paul Gill, Stephen Briggs, Andrew Briggs, Alison Wood
Sub-section lead	N/A
Objectives	To review the effectiveness of interventions for the management of repetition of self-harm behaviour.
Criteria for considering studies for the review	
● Intervention	Chapter 7 – problem-solving, interpersonal therapy, CBT, peer support groups, self-help, computer-based interventions, DBT, counselling, psychodynamic interventions, family interventions, group therapy, postcards, assertive outreach, multi-systemic therapy, respite care, crisis management (refer to *Borderline Personality Disorder* guideline)
● Comparator	Treatment as usual
● Types of participants	Participants (aged 8 years old or above) admitted to hospital for treatment of index episode of self-harm). Self-endorsed self-harming behaviour is also included.
● Critical outcomes	Repetition (fatal outcome: completed suicide; non-fatal repetition)

● Important, but not critical outcomes	Depression, hopelessness, suicide ideation scores
● Other outcomes	N/A
● Study design	RCTs
● Include unpublished data?	No
● Restriction by date?	No
● Dosage	N/A
● Minimum sample size	Ten in each treatment arm
● Study setting	Inpatient and outpatient (as long as participants had history of previous self-harm)
Search strategy	**Databases:** CINAHL, EMBASE, MEDLINE, HMIC, PsycBOOKS, PsycEXTRA, PsycINFO **New search:**
Searching other resources	Experts in the field were contacted to identify if any key studies were missed.
Existing reviews	
● Updated	Hawton and colleagues' (2011) updated Cochrane review for self-harm interventions.
● Not updated	N/A
General search filter used	See search strategy in Appendix 9
Question specific search filter	See search strategy in Appendix 9
Amendments to filter/ search strategy	See search strategy in Appendix 9
The review strategy	Data from the Cochrane review update will be used for meta-analysis. Studies will be checked for the inclusion criteria.
Additional assessments	1. Exclude non-randomised studies 2. Exclude studies that were designed for people with borderline personality disorder (refer to the NICE guideline).

Pharmacological interventions

Topic	Pharmacological interventions
Review question(s)	For people who self-harm, do pharmacological interventions (compared with no treatment or other interventions) improve outcomes? What are the associated adverse effects?
Sub-question(s)	3.2 For people who self-harm, what are the key principles underlying safer prescribing?
Chapter	8 – Pharmacological interventions
Sub-section	
Topic group	8 – Suzanne Kearney, Alison Wood, Paul Gill
Sub-section lead	N/A
Objectives	To review the effectiveness of interventions for the management of repetition of self-harm behaviour
Criteria for considering studies for the review	
● Intervention	Chapter 8 – Antidepressants, antipsychotics, lithium, anticonvulsants (for example, valproate, carbamazepine, lamotrigine), benzodiazepines, analgesics
● Comparator	Treatment as usual or placebo
● Types of participants	Participants (aged 8 years old or above) admitted to hospital for treatment of index episode of self-harm). Self-endorsed self-harming behaviour are also included.
● Critical outcomes	Repetition (fatal outcome: completed suicide; non-fatal repetition)
● Important, but not critical outcomes	Depression, hopelessness, suicide ideation scores
● Other outcomes	N/A
● Study design	RCTs
● Include unpublished data?	No

● Restriction by date?	No
● Dosage	N/A
● Minimum sample size	Ten in each treatment arm
● Study setting	Inpatient and outpatient (as long as participants had history of previous self-harm)
Search strategy	**Databases:** CINAHL, EMBASE, MEDLINE, HMIC, PsycBOOKS, PsycEXTRA, PsycINFO **New search:**
Searching other resources	Experts in the field were contacted to identify if any key studies were missed.
Existing reviews	
● Updated	Hawton and colleagues' (2011) updated Cochrane review for self-harm interventions
● Not updated	N/A
General search filter used	See search strategy in Appendix 9
Question specific search filter	See search strategy in Appendix 9
Amendments to filter/ search strategy	See search strategy in Appendix 9
The review strategy	Data from the Cochrane review update will be used for meta-analysis. Studies will be checked for the inclusion criteria.
Additional assessments	1. Exclude non-randomised studies 2. Exclude studies that were designed for people with borderline personality disorder (refer to the NICE guideline).

Harm reduction

Topic	Harm reduction
Review question(s)	For people who self-harm, does the provision of self-management and/or harm minimisation/reduction strategies, compared with no treatment or treatment as usual, improve outcomes?
Sub-question(s)	N/A
Chapter	7 Psychological and psychosocial interventions
Sub-section	7.3 Harm reduction
Topic group	7 – Rory O'Connor, Paul Gill, Stephen Briggs, Andrew Briggs, Alison Wood 8 – Suzanne Kearney, Alison Wood, Paul Gill
Sub-section lead	N/A
Objectives	To review the evidence around harm minimisation/reduction techniques
Criteria for considering studies for the review	
● Intervention	Replacement therapy, positive emotion technique
● Comparator	Treatment as usual
● Types of participants	Participants (aged 8 years old or above) admitted to hospital for treatment of index episode of self-harm). Self-endorsed self-harming behaviour is also included.
● Critical outcomes	Repetition (fatal outcome: completed suicide; non-fatal repetition) Reduction in frequency or severity
● Important, but not critical outcomes	Depression, hopelessness, suicide ideation scores
● Other outcomes	N/A
● Study design	Any study designs (the GDG acknowledged the very limited evidence base in this area, therefore they decided to loosen the normal criteria).
● Include unpublished data?	Will be discussed if there are relevant materials
● Restriction by date?	No

● Dosage	N/A
● Minimum sample size	N/A
● Study setting	Inpatient and outpatient (as long as participants had history of previous self-harm).
Search strategy	**Databases:** CINAHL, EMBASE, MEDLINE, HMIC, PsycBOOKS, PsycEXTRA, PsycINFO
Searching other resources	Experts in the field were contacted to identify if any key studies were missed.
Existing reviews	
● Updated	N/A
● Not updated	N/A
General search filter used	See search strategy in Appendix 9
Question specific search filter	See search strategy in Appendix 9
Amendments to filter/ search strategy	See search strategy in Appendix 9
The review strategy	N/A
Additional assessments	N/A

Training

Topic	Training
Review question(s)	Does the provision of staff training (knowledge, skills based) improve outcomes (for example, staff attitudes, user satisfaction, user engagement with services)?
Sub-question(s)	N/A
Chapter	5 Training
Sub-section	N/A
Topic group	N/A
Sub-section lead	N/A
Objectives	To review the evidence around effectiveness of training
Criteria for considering studies for the review	
● Intervention	Any knowledge, skills-based training
● Comparator	Treatment as usual
● Types of participants	Healthcare professionals
● Critical outcomes	Staff attitudes, staff knowledge, service users' satisfaction, and service users' engagement with services
● Important, but not critical outcomes	N/A
● Other outcomes	N/A
● Study design	RCTs, preferably
● Include unpublished data?	Will be discussed if there are relevant materials
● Restriction by date?	No
● Dosage	N/A
● Minimum sample size	N/A
● Study setting	N/A
Search strategy	**Databases:** CINAHL, EMBASE, MEDLINE, HMIC, PsycBOOKS, PsycEXTRA, PsycINFO

Searching other resources	Keith Hawton's review on staff attitudes
Existing reviews	
● Updated	N/A
● Not updated	N/A
General search filter used	See search strategy in Appendix 9
Question specific search filter	See search strategy in Appendix 9
Amendments to filter/ search strategy	See search strategy in Appendix 9
The review strategy	N/A
Additional assessments	N/A

APPENDIX 9:

SEARCH STRATEGIES FOR THE IDENTIFICATION

OF CLINICAL STUDIES

Available on the CD-ROM.

APPENDIX 10:

CLINICAL STUDY DATA EXTRACTION FORM TEMPLATE

Intervention studies

Methods	Allocation: Follow-up period: N lost to follow-up:
Participants	Setting: Inclusion criteria: Numbers: N participants: N experimental, N control. Profile: N% (n=) female. n% (n=) had diagnosis of X disorder. Source of participants:
Interventions	Experimental: Intervention: Control: Therapist: Type of therapy offered: Experimental: Control: Length of treatment:
Outcomes	Included: Outcome A, B, C, and so on. Excluded:
Notes	

APPENDIX 11:

QUALITY CHECKLIST TEMPLATES FOR

CLINICAL STUDIES AND REVIEWS

Methodology checklist template: randomised controlled trials

Study identification (include author, title, reference, year of publication)					
Guideline topic:			**Review question no:**		
Checklist completed by:					
			Circle one option for each question		
A. Selection bias (systematic differences between the comparison groups)					
A1	An appropriate method of randomisation was used to allocate participants to treatment groups (which would have balanced any confounding factors equally across groups)	Yes	No	Unclear	N/A
A2	There was adequate concealment of allocation (such that investigators, clinicians and participants cannot influence enrolment or treatment allocation)	Yes	No	Unclear	N/A
A3	The groups were comparable at baseline, including all major confounding and prognostic factors	Yes	No	Unclear	N/A
Based on your answers to the above, in your opinion was selection bias present? If so, what is the likely direction of its effect?					
Low risk of bias		Unclear/unknown risk		High risk of bias	
Likely direction of effect:					
B. Performance bias (systematic differences between groups in the care provided, apart from the intervention under investigation)					

B1	The comparison groups received the same care apart from the intervention(s) studied	Yes	No	Unclear	N/A
B2	Participants receiving care were kept 'blind' to treatment allocation	Yes	No	Unclear	N/A
B3	Individuals administering care were kept 'blind' to treatment allocation	Yes	No	Unclear	N/A

Based on your answers to the above, in your opinion was performance bias present? If so, what is the likely direction of its effect?

Low risk of bias	Unclear/unknown risk	High risk of bias

Likely direction of effect:

C. Attrition bias (systematic differences between the comparison groups with respect to loss of participants)					
C1	All groups were followed up for an equal length of time (or analysis was adjusted to allow for differences in length of follow-up)	Yes	No	Unclear	N/A
C2	a. How many participants did not complete treatment in each group?				
	b. The groups were comparable for treatment completion (that is, there were no important or systematic differences between groups in terms of those who did not complete treatment)	Yes	No	Unclear	N/A
C3	a. For how many participants in each group were no outcome data available?				
	b. The groups were comparable with respect to the availability of outcome data (that is, there were no important or systematic differences between groups in terms of those for whom outcome data were not available).	Yes	No	Unclear	N/A

Based on your answers to the above, in your opinion was attrition bias present? If so, what is the likely direction of its effect?

Low risk of bias	Unclear/unknown risk	High risk of bias

Likely direction of effect:

D. Detection bias (bias in how outcomes are ascertained, diagnosed or verified)					
D1	The study had an appropriate length of follow-up	Yes	No	Unclear	N/A
D2	The study used a precise definition of outcome	Yes	No	Unclear	N/A
D3	A valid and reliable method was used to determine the outcome	Yes	No	Unclear	N/A
D4	Investigators were kept 'blind' to participants' exposure to the intervention	Yes	No	Unclear	N/A
D5	Investigators were kept 'blind' to other important confounding and prognostic factors	Yes	No	Unclear	N/A
Based on your answers to the above, in your opinion was detection bias present? If so, what is the likely direction of its effect?					
Low risk of bias		Unclear/unknown risk		High risk of bias	
Likely direction of effect:					

Notes on use of methodology checklist: randomised controlled trials

The studies covered by this checklist are designed to answer questions about the relative effects of interventions such as drugs, psychological therapies, operations or placebos. Such studies can include comparisons of 'test and treat strategies' involving a diagnostic test and subsequent management. The checklist does not cover comparisons of diagnostic test accuracy or questions about prognosis.

This checklist replaces the methodology checklist for randomised controlled trials from *The Guidelines Manual* (NICE, 2009d) (appendix C).

Some of the items on this checklist may need to be filled in individually for different outcomes reported by the study. It is therefore important that the systematic reviewer has a clear idea of what the important outcomes are *before* appraising a study. You are likely to need input from the GDG in defining the important outcomes.

Checklist items are worded so that a 'yes' response always indicates that the study has been designed/conducted in such a way as to minimise the risk of bias for that item. An 'unclear' response to a question may arise when the item is not reported or not clearly reported. 'N/A' should be used when a randomised controlled trial cannot give an answer of 'yes' no matter how well it has been done.

This checklist is designed to assess the internal validity of the study; that is, whether the study provides an unbiased estimate of what it claims to show. Internal validity implies that the differences observed between groups of participants allocated to different interventions may (apart from the possibility of random error) be attributed to the intervention under investigation. Biases are characteristics that are likely to make estimates of effect differ systematically from the truth.

Recording the presence and direction of bias
The checklist contains four sections (A to D), each of which addresses a potential source of bias relating to internal validity. At the end of each section you are asked to give your opinion on whether bias is present and to estimate the likely direction of this bias – that is, whether you think it will have increased or decreased the effect size reported by the study. It will not always be possible to determine the direction of bias, but thinking this through can help greatly in interpreting results.

A: Selection bias
Selection bias may be introduced into a study when there are systematic differences between the participants in the different treatment groups. As a result, the differences in the outcome observed may be explained by pre-existing differences between the groups rather than because of the treatment itself. For example, if the people in one group are in poorer health then they are more likely to have a bad outcome than those in the other group, regardless of the effect of the treatment. The treatment groups should be similar at the start of the study – the only difference between the groups should be the intervention received.

Randomisation
There are two aspects to randomisation:
* generation of the random allocation sequence that results in groups that differ only randomly
* allocation concealment, so that both the participant and the investigator are unaware of which group the next participant will be allocated to when entering the study.

A1. An appropriate method of randomisation was used to allocate participants to treatment groups

If an appropriate method of randomisation has been used, each participant should have an equal chance of ending up in any of the treatment groups. Examples of random allocation sequences include random numbers generated by computer, tables of random numbers, and drawing of lots or envelopes. The allocation sequence should not be related to outcome or prognosis, or be predictable, such as date of birth or admission date.

There are some more complicated ways of allocating people to treatment groups that minimise the differences between groups, such as block randomisation and minimisation. Although these are not truly random, they are usually considered to be adequate for the purpose. If a study does not report the method of randomisation used, this should be scored as 'unclear'.

A2. There was adequate concealment of allocation

If investigators are aware of the allocation group for the next participant being enrolled in the study, there is potential for participants to be enrolled in an order that results in imbalances in important characteristics. For example, a clinician might feel that participants who are more unwell are likely to do better on a new, experimental, treatment and be tempted to enrol such participants when they know they will be allocated to that group. This would result in the participants in the intervention group being, on average, more unwell. Concealment of treatment group may not always be feasible (as in, for example, a comparison of a surgical with a medical intervention), but concealment of allocation up until the point of enrolment in the study should always be possible.

The information presented within the paper should provide some assurance that allocations were not known until at least the point of enrolment. Centralised allocation, computerised allocation systems and the use of coded identical containers are all regarded as adequate methods of concealment. Sealed envelopes can be considered as adequate concealment if the envelopes are serially numbered, sealed and opaque, and allocation is performed by a third party. Poor methods of allocation concealment include alternation, or the use of case record numbers, date of birth or day of the week.

If the method of allocation concealment used is regarded as poor, or relatively easy to subvert, the study must be given a lower quality rating. If a study does not report any concealment approach, this should be scored as 'unclear'.

A3. The groups were comparable at baseline, including all major confounding and prognostic factors

Studies may report the distributions of potential prognostic and confounding factors in the comparison groups, or important differences in the distribution of these factors may be noted.

Formal tests comparing the groups are problematic – failure to detect a difference does not mean that a difference does not exist, and multiple comparisons of factors may falsely detect some differences that are not real.

Clinical input may be required to determine whether all likely confounders have been considered. Confounding factors may differ according to outcome, so you will need to consider potential confounding factors for all of the outcomes that are of interest to your review.

B: Performance bias

Performance bias refers to systematic differences between the comparison groups in the care provided to the participants, other than the intervention under investigation.

This may consist of additional treatment, advice or counselling, rather than a physical intervention, or even simply a belief about the effects of an intervention. If performance bias is present, it can be difficult to attribute any observed effect to the experimental treatment rather than to the other factors.

B1. The comparison groups received the same care apart from the intervention(s) studied

There should be no differences between the treatment groups apart from the intervention received. If some participants received additional treatment (known as 'co-intervention'), this treatment is a potential confounding factor that may compromise the results.

Blinding
Blinding (also known as masking) refers to the process of withholding information about treatment allocation or exposure status from those involved in the study who could potentially be influenced by this information. This can include participants, investigators, those administering care and those involved in data collection and analysis. If people are aware of the treatment allocation or exposure status ('unblinded'), this can bias the results of studies, either intentionally or unintentionally, through the use of other effective co-interventions, decisions about withdrawal, differential reporting of symptoms or influencing concordance with treatment. Blinding of those assessing outcomes is covered in section D on detection bias.

Blinding of participants and carers is not always possible, particularly in studies of non-drug interventions, and so performance bias may be a particular issue in these studies. It is important to think about the likely size and direction of bias caused by failure to blind.

The terms 'single blind', 'double blind' and even 'triple blind' are sometimes used in studies. Unfortunately, they are not always used consistently. Commonly, when a study is described as 'single blind', only the participants are blind to their group allocation. When both participants and investigators are blind to group allocation, the study is often described as 'double blind'. It is preferable to record exactly who was blinded, if reported, to avoid misunderstanding.

B2. Participants receiving care were kept 'blind' to treatment allocation

The knowledge of assignment to a particular treatment group may affect outcomes, such as a study participant's reporting of symptoms, self-use of other known interventions or even dropping out of the study.

B3. Individuals administering care were kept 'blind' to treatment allocation

If individuals who are administering the intervention and/or other care to the participant are aware of treatment allocation, they may treat participants receiving one treatment differently from those receiving the comparison treatment; for example, by offering additional co-interventions.

C: Attrition bias

Attrition refers to the loss of participants during the course of a study. Attrition bias occurs when there are systematic differences between the comparison groups with respect to participants lost, or differences between participants lost to the study and those who remain. Attrition can occur at any point after participants have been allocated to their treatment groups. As such, it includes participants who are excluded after allocation (and may indicate a violation of eligibility criteria), those who do not complete treatment (whether or not they continue measurement) and those who do not complete outcome measurement (regardless of whether or not treatment was completed). Consideration should be given to why participants dropped out, as well as how many. Participants who dropped out of a study may differ in some significant way from those who remained as part of the study throughout. Dropout rates and reasons for dropping out should be similar across all treatment groups. The proportion of participants excluded after allocation should be stated in the study report, and the possibility of attrition bias considered within the analysis; however, these are not always reported.

C1. All groups were followed up for an equal length of time (or analysis was adjusted to allow for differences in length of follow-up)

If the comparison groups are followed for different lengths of time, then more events are likely to occur in the group followed up for longer, distorting the comparison. This may be overcome by adjusting the denominator to take the time into account; for example by using person-years.

C2a. How many participants did not complete treatment in each group?

A very high number of participants dropping out of a study should give concern. The dropout rate may be expected to be higher in studies conducted over a longer period of time. The dropout rate includes people who did not even start treatment; that is, they were excluded from the study after allocation to treatment groups.

C2b. The groups were comparable for treatment completion (that is, there were no important or systematic differences between groups in terms of those who did not complete treatment)

If there are systematic differences between groups in terms of those who did not complete treatment, consider both why participants dropped out and whether any systematic differences in those who dropped out may be related to the outcome under study, such as potential confounders. Systematic differences between groups in terms of those who dropped out may also result in treatment groups that are no longer comparable with respect to potential confounding factors.

C3a. For how many participants in each group were no outcome data available?

A very high number of participants for whom no outcome data were available should give concern.

C3b. The groups were comparable with respect to the availability of outcome data (that is, there were no important or systematic differences between groups in terms of those for whom outcome data were not available)

If there are systematic differences between groups in terms of those for whom no outcome data were available, consider both why the outcome data were not available and whether there are any systematic differences between participants for whom outcome data were and were not available.

D: Detection bias (this section should be completed individually for each important relevant outcome)

The way outcomes are assessed needs to be standardised for the comparison groups; failure to 'blind' people who are assessing outcomes can also lead to bias, particularly with subjective outcomes. Most studies report results for more than one outcome, and it is possible that detection bias may be present in a study for some, but not all, outcomes. It is therefore recommended that this section is completed individually for each important outcome that is relevant to the guideline review question under study. To avoid biasing your review, you should identify the relevant outcomes *before* considering the results of the study. Clinical input may be required to identify the most important outcomes for a review.

D1. The study had an appropriate length of follow-up

The follow-up of participants after treatment should be of an adequate length to identify the outcome of interest. This is particularly important when different outcomes of interest occur early and late after an intervention. For example, after surgical interventions there is usually an early harm because of side effects, with benefits apparent later on. A study that is too short will give an unbalanced assessment of the intervention.

For events occurring later, a short study will give an imprecise estimate of the effect, which may or may not also be biased. For example, a late-occurring side effect will not be detected in the treatment arm if the study is too short.

D2. The study used a precise definition of outcome

and

D3. A valid and reliable method was used to determine the outcome

The outcome under study should be well defined. It should be clear how the investigators determined whether participants experienced, or did not experience, the outcome. The same methods for defining and measuring outcomes should be used for all participants in the study. Often there may be more than one way of measuring an outcome (for example, physical or laboratory tests, questionnaire, reporting of symptoms). The method of measurement should be valid (that is, it measures what it claims to measure) and reliable (that is, it measures something consistently).

D4. Investigators were kept 'blind' to participants' exposure to the intervention

and

D5. Investigators were kept 'blind' to other important confounding and prognostic factors

In this context the 'investigators' are the individuals who are involved in making the decision about whether a participant has experienced the outcome under study. This can include those responsible for taking physical measurements and recording symptoms, even if they are not ultimately responsible for determining the outcome. Investigators can introduce bias through differences in measurement and recording of outcomes, and making biased assessments of a participant's outcome based on the collected data. The degree to which lack of blinding can introduce bias will vary depending on the method of measuring an outcome, but will be greater for more subjective outcomes, such as reporting of pain.

Physical separation of the assessment from the participant (for example, sending samples off to a laboratory) can often be considered as blind if it can be assumed that the laboratory staff are unaware of the treatment assignment.

Methodology checklist template: cohort studies

Study identification (include author, title, reference, year of publication)				
Guideline topic:		**Review question no:**		
Checklist completed by:				
		Circle one option for each question:		
A. Selection bias (systematic differences between the comparison groups)				
A1	The method of allocation to treatment groups was unrelated to potential confounding factors (that is, the reason for participant allocation to treatment groups is not expected to affect the outcome(s) under study)	Yes	No	Unclear	N/A
A2	Were any attempts made within the design or analysis to balance the comparison groups for potential confounders?	Yes	No	Unclear	N/A
A3	The groups were comparable at baseline, including all major confounding and prognostic factors	Yes	No	Unclear	N/A
Based on your answers to the above, in your opinion was selection bias present? If so, what is the likely direction of its effect?				
Low risk of bias		Unclear/unknown risk	High risk of bias	
Likely direction of effect:				
B. Performance bias (systematic differences between groups in the care provided, apart from the intervention under investigation)				
B1	The comparison groups received the same care apart from the intervention(s) studied	Yes	No	Unclear	N/A
B2	Participants receiving care were kept 'blind' to treatment allocation	Yes	No	Unclear	N/A
B3	Individuals administering care were kept 'blind' to treatment allocation	Yes	No	Unclear	N/A

Based on your answers to the above, in your opinion was performance bias present? If so, what is the likely direction of its effect?

Low risk of bias	Unclear/unknown risk	High risk of bias

Likely direction of effect:

C. Attrition bias (systematic differences between the comparison groups with respect to loss of participants)					
C1	All groups were followed up for an equal length of time (or analysis was adjusted to allow for differences in length of follow-up)	Yes	No	Unclear	N/A
C2	a. How many participants did not complete treatment in each group?				
	b. The groups were comparable for treatment completion (that is, there were no important or systematic differences between groups in terms of those who did not complete treatment)	Yes	No	Unclear	N/A
C3	a. For how many participants in each group were no outcome data available?				
	b. The groups were comparable with respect to the availability of outcome data (that is, there were no important or systematic differences between groups in terms of those for whom outcome data were not available)	Yes	No	Unclear	N/A

Based on your answers to the above, in your opinion was attrition bias present? If so, what is the likely direction of its effect?

Low risk of bias	Unclear/unknown risk	High risk of bias

Likely direction of effect:

D. Detection bias (bias in how outcomes are ascertained, diagnosed or verified)					
D1	The study had an appropriate length of follow-up	Yes	No	Unclear	N/A
D2	The study used a precise definition of outcome	Yes	No	Unclear	N/A

D3	A valid and reliable method was used to determine the outcome	Yes	No	Unclear	N/A
D4	Investigators were kept 'blind' to participants' exposure to the intervention	Yes	No	Unclear	N/A
D5	Investigators were kept 'blind' to other important confounding/prognostic factors	Yes	No	Unclear	N/A

Based on your answers to the above, in your opinion was detection bias present? If so, what is the likely direction of its effect?		
Low risk of bias	Unclear/unknown risk	High risk of bias
Likely direction of effect:		

Notes on use of methodology checklist: cohort studies

Cohort studies are designed to answer questions about the relative effects of interventions, such as drugs, psychological therapies, operations or placebos. Such studies can include comparisons of 'test and treat strategies' involving a diagnostic test and subsequent management. This checklist does not cover comparisons of diagnostic test accuracy or questions about prognosis.

This checklist replaces the methodology checklist for cohort studies from *The Guidelines Manual* (NICE, 2009d) (appendix D).

Some of the items on this checklist may need to be filled in individually for different outcomes reported by the study. It is therefore important that the systematic reviewer has a clear idea of what the important outcomes are *before* appraising a study. You are likely to need input from the GDG in defining the important outcomes.

Checklist items are worded so that a 'yes' response always indicates that the study has been designed/conducted in such a way as to minimise the risk of bias for that item. An 'unclear' response to a question may arise when the item is not reported or is not reported clearly. 'N/A' should be used when a cohort study cannot give an answer of 'yes' no matter how well it has been done.

This checklist is designed to assess the internal validity of the study; that is, whether the study provides an unbiased estimate of what it claims to show. Internal validity implies that the differences observed between groups of participants allocated to different interventions may (apart from the possibility of random error) be attributed to the intervention under investigation. Biases are characteristics that are likely to make estimates of effect differ systematically from the truth.

Recording the presence and direction of bias

This checklist contains four sections (A to D), each of which addresses a potential source of bias relating to internal validity. At the end of each section you are asked to give your opinion on whether bias is present, and to estimate the likely direction of this bias – whether you think it will have increased or decreased the effect size reported by the study. It will not always be possible to determine the direction of bias, but thinking this through can help greatly in interpreting results.

A: Selection bias

Selection bias can be introduced into a study when there are systematic differences between the participants in the different treatment groups. As a result, the differences in the outcome observed may be explained by pre-existing differences between the groups rather than because of the treatment itself. For example, if the people in one group are in poorer health, then they are more likely to have a bad outcome than those in the other group, regardless of the effect of the treatment. The treatment groups should be similar at the start of the study – the only difference between the groups should be in terms of the intervention received.

The main difference between randomised trials and non-randomised studies is the potential susceptibility of the latter to selection bias. Randomisation should ensure that, apart from the intervention received, the treatment groups differ only because of random variation. However, care needs to be taken in the design and analysis of non-randomised studies to take account of potential confounding factors. There are two main ways of accounting for potential confounding factors within non-randomised studies. First, participants can be allocated to treatment groups to ensure that the groups are equal with respect to the known confounders. Second, statistical techniques can be used within the analysis to take into account known differences between groups. Neither of these approaches is able to address unknown or unmeasurable confounding factors, and it is important to remember that measurement of known confounders is subject to error. It can rarely, if ever, be assumed that all important factors relevant to prognosis and responsiveness to treatment are known. Hence considerable judgement is needed to assess the internal validity of non-randomised studies; clinical input may be needed to identify potential confounding factors that should be taken into consideration.

A1. The method of allocation to treatment groups was unrelated to potential confounding factors

In non-randomised studies, there will usually be a reason why participants are allocated to the treatment groups (often as a result of clinician and/or patient choice). If this reason is linked to the outcome under study, this can result in confounding by indication (where the decision to treat is influenced by some factor that is related in turn to the treatment outcome). For example, if the participants who are the most ill are selected for the treatment, then the treatment group may experience worse outcomes because of this difference between the groups at baseline. It will not always be possible to determine from the report of a study which factors influenced the allocation of participants to treatment groups.

A2. Were any attempts made within the design or analysis to balance the comparison groups for potential confounders?

This represents an attempt when designing the study to ensure that the groups are similar in terms of known confounding or prognostic factors, in order to optimise comparability between the treatment groups. For example, in a matched design, the controls are deliberately chosen to be equivalent to the treatment group for any potential confounding variables, such as age and sex.

An alternative approach is to use statistical techniques to adjust for known confounding factors in the analysis.

A3. The groups were comparable at baseline, including all major confounding and prognostic factors

Studies may report the distributions of potential prognostic and confounding factors in the comparison groups, or important differences in these factors may be noted.

Formal tests comparing the groups are problematic – failure to detect a difference does not that mean a difference does not exist, and multiple comparisons of factors may falsely detect some differences that are not real.

Clinical input may be needed to determine whether all likely confounders have been considered. Confounding factors may differ according to outcome, so you will need to consider potential confounding factors for each of the outcomes that are of interest to your review.

B: Performance bias

Performance bias refers to systematic differences in the care provided to the participants in the comparison groups, other than the intervention under investigation.

This may consist of additional treatment, advice or counselling, rather than a physical intervention, or even simply a belief about the effects of an intervention. If performance bias is present, it can be difficult to attribute any observed effect to the experimental treatment rather than to the other factors.

Performance bias can be more difficult to determine within non-randomised than within randomised studies, because the latter are likely to have been better planned and executed according to strict treatment protocols that specify standardised interventions and care. It may be particularly difficult to determine performance bias for retrospective studies, where there is usually no control over standardisation.

B1. The comparison groups received the same care apart from the intervention(s) studied

There should be no differences between the treatment groups apart from the intervention received. If some participants received additional treatment (known as 'co-intervention'), this treatment is a potential confounding factor that may compromise the results.

Blinding

Blinding (also known as masking) refers to the process of withholding information about treatment allocation or exposure status from those involved in the study who could potentially be influenced by this information. This can include participants, investigators, those administering care and those involved in data collection and analysis. If people are aware of the treatment allocation or exposure status ('unblinded'), this can bias the results of studies, either intentionally or unintentionally, through the use of other effective co-interventions, decisions about withdrawal, differential reporting of symptoms or influencing concordance with treatment. Blinding of those assessing outcomes is covered in section D on detection bias.

Blinding of participants and carers is not always possible, particularly in studies of non-drug interventions, and so performance bias may be a particular issue in these studies. It is important to think about the likely size and direction of bias caused by failure to blind.

The terms 'single blind', 'double blind' and even 'triple blind' are sometimes used in studies. Unfortunately, they are not always used consistently. Commonly, when a study is described as 'single blind', only the participants are blind to their group allocation. When both participants and investigators are blind to group allocation the study is often described as 'double blind'. It is preferable to record exactly who was blinded, if reported, to avoid misunderstanding.

B2. Participants receiving care were kept 'blind' to treatment allocation

The knowledge of assignment to a particular treatment group may affect outcomes such as a study participant's reporting of symptoms, self-use of other known interventions or even dropping out of the study.

B3. Individuals administering care were kept 'blind' to treatment allocation

If individuals who are administering the intervention and/or other care to the participant are aware of treatment allocation, they may treat participants receiving one treatment differently from those receiving the comparison treatment; for example, by offering additional co-interventions.

C: Attrition bias

Attrition refers to the loss of participants during the course of a study. Attrition bias occurs when there are systematic differences between the comparison groups with respect to participants lost, or differences between the participants lost to the study and those who remain. Attrition can occur at any point after participants have been allocated to their treatment groups. As such, it includes participants who are excluded after allocation (and may indicate a violation of eligibility criteria), those who do not complete treatment (whether or not they continue measurement) and those who do not complete outcome measurement (regardless of whether or not treatment was completed). Consideration should be given to why participants dropped out, as well as how many. Participants who dropped out of a study may differ in some significant way from those who remained as part of the study throughout. Dropout rates and reasons for dropping out should be similar across all treatment groups. The proportion of participants excluded after allocation should be stated in the study report and the possibility of attrition bias considered within the analysis; however, these are not always reported.

C1. All groups were followed up for an equal length of time (or analysis was adjusted to allow for differences in length of follow-up)

If the comparison groups are followed for different lengths of time, then more events are likely to occur in the group followed up for longer, distorting the comparison. This may be overcome by adjusting the denominator to take the time into account; for example by using person-years.

C2a. How many participants did not complete treatment in each group?

A very high number of participants dropping out of a study should give concern. The dropout rate may be expected to be higher in studies conducted over a longer period of time. The dropout rate includes people who did not even start treatment; that is, they were excluded from the study after allocation to treatment groups.

C2b. The groups were comparable for treatment completion (that is, there were no important or systematic differences between groups in terms of those who did not complete treatment)

If there are systematic differences between groups in terms of those who did not complete treatment, consider both why participants dropped out and whether any systematic differences in those who dropped out may be related to the outcome under study, such as potential confounders. Systematic differences between groups in terms of those who dropped out may also result in treatment groups that are no longer comparable with respect to potential confounding factors.

C3a. For how many participants in each group were no outcome data available?

A very high number of participants for whom no outcome data were available should give concern.

C3b. The groups were comparable with respect to the availability of outcome data (that is, there were no important or systematic differences between groups in terms of those for whom outcome data were not available)

If there are systematic differences between groups in terms of those for whom no outcome data were available, consider both why the outcome data were not available and whether there are any systematic differences between participants for whom outcome data were and were not available.

D: Detection bias (this section should be completed individually for each important relevant outcome)

The way outcomes are assessed needs to be standardised for the comparison groups; failure to 'blind' people who are assessing the outcomes can also lead to bias, particularly with subjective outcomes. Most studies report results for more than one outcome, and it is possible that detection bias may be present for some, but not all, outcomes. It is therefore recommended that this section is completed individually for each important outcome that is relevant to the guideline review question under study. To avoid biasing your review, you should identify the relevant outcomes **before** considering the results of the study. Clinical input may be required to identify the most important outcomes for a review.

D1. The study had an appropriate length of follow-up

The follow-up of participants after treatment should be of an adequate length to identify the outcome of interest. This is particularly important when different outcomes of interest occur early and late after an intervention. For example, after surgical interventions there is usually early harm because of side effects, with benefits apparent later on. A study that is too short will give an unbalanced assessment of the intervention.

For events occurring later, a short study will give an imprecise estimate of the effect, which may or may not also be biased. For example, a late-occurring side effect will not be detected in the treatment arm if the study is too short.

D2. The study used a precise definition of outcome

and

D3. A valid and reliable method was used to determine the outcome

The outcome under study should be well defined and it should be clear how the investigators determined whether participants experienced, or did not experience, the outcome. The same methods for defining and measuring outcomes should be used for all participants in the study. Often there may be more than one way of measuring an outcome (for example, physical or laboratory tests, questionnaire, reporting of symptoms). The method of measurement should be valid (that is, it measures what it claims to measure) and reliable (that is, it measures something consistently).

D4. Investigators were kept 'blind' to participants' exposure to the intervention

and

D5. Investigators were kept 'blind' to other important confounding and prognostic factors

In this context the 'investigators' are the individuals who are involved in making the decision about whether a participant has experienced the outcome under study. This can include those responsible for taking physical measurements and recording symptoms, even if they are not ultimately responsible for determining the outcome. Investigators can introduce bias through differences in measurement and recording of outcomes, and making biased assessments of a participant's outcome based on the collected data. The degree to which lack of blinding can introduce bias will vary depending on the method of measuring an outcome, but will be greater for more subjective outcomes, such as reporting of pain.

Physical separation of the assessment from the participant (for example, sending samples off to a laboratory) can often be considered as blind if it can be assumed that the laboratory staff are unaware of the treatment assignment.

Methodology checklist: case-control studies

Study identification Include author, title, reference, year of publication			
Guideline topic:		**Review question no:**	
Checklist completed by:			
Section 1: Internal validity			
		Circle one option for each question	
1.1	The study addresses an appropriate and clearly focused question.	Well covered Adequately addressed Poorly addressed	Not addressed Not reported Not applicable
Selection of participants			
1.2	The cases and controls are taken from comparable populations	Well covered Adequately addressed Poorly addressed	Not addressed Not reported Not applicable
1.3	The same exclusion criteria are used for both cases and controls	Well covered Adequately addressed Poorly addressed	Not addressed Not reported Not applicable
1.4	What was the participation rate for each group (cases and controls)?	Cases: Controls:	
1.5	Participants and non-participants are compared to establish their similarities or differences	Well covered Adequately addressed Poorly addressed	Not addressed Not reported Not applicable

1.6	Cases are clearly defined and differentiated from controls	Well covered Adequately addressed Poorly addressed	Not addressed Not reported Not applicable
1.7	It is clearly established that controls are not cases	Well covered Adequately addressed Poorly addressed	Not addressed Not reported Not applicable
Assessment			
1.8	Measures were taken to prevent knowledge of primary exposure influencing case ascertainment	Well covered Adequately addressed Poorly addressed	Not addressed Not reported Not applicable
1.9	Exposure status is measured in a standard, valid and reliable way	Well covered Adequately addressed Poorly addressed	Not addressed Not reported Not applicable
Confounding factors			
1.10	The main potential confounders are identified and taken into account in the design and analysis	Well covered Adequately addressed Poorly addressed	Not addressed Not reported Not applicable
Statistical analysis			
1.11		Have confidence intervals been provided?	

Section 2: Description of the study **(This information is required for evidence tables to facilitate cross-study comparisons. Please complete all sections for which information is available).** **Please print clearly**	
2.1	How many people participated in the study? *List the numbers of cases and controls separately.*
2.2	What are the main characteristics of the study population? *Include all characteristics used to identify both cases and controls – for example, age, sex, social class, disease status.*
2.3	What environmental or prognostic factor is being investigated?

2.4	What comparisons are made? *Normally only one factor will be compared, but in some cases the extent of exposure may be stratified – for example, non-smokers vs light, moderate or heavy smokers. Note all comparisons here.*
2.5	For how long are participants followed up? *This is the length of time over which participant histories are tracked in the study.*
2.6	What outcome measure(s) is/are used? *List all outcomes that are used to assess the impact of the chosen environmental or prognostic factor.*
2.7	What size of effect is identified? *Effect size should be expressed as an odds ratio. If any other measures are included, note them as well. Include p-values and any confidence intervals that are provided.*
2.8	How was the study funded? *List all sources of funding quoted in the article, whether government, voluntary sector or industry.*
2.9	Does this study help to answer your guideline review question? *Summarise the main conclusions of the study and indicate how it relates to the review question.*

Notes on use of the methodology checklist: case-control studies

Case-control studies are designed to answer questions of the type 'What are the factors that caused this event?'. They involve comparison of individuals who have an outcome with other individuals from the same population who do not have the outcome. These studies start after the outcome of an event, and can be used to assess multiple causes of a single event. They are generally used to assess the causes of a new problem but they may also be useful for the evaluation of population-based interventions such as screening.

The questions in **section 1** are aimed at establishing the internal validity of the study under review – that is, making sure that it has been carried out carefully, and that any link between events and outcomes is clearly established. Each question covers an aspect of methodology that has been shown to make a significant difference to the conclusions of a study.

Case-control studies need to be designed very carefully – the complexity of their design is often not appreciated by investigators, so many poor-quality studies are conducted. The questions in this checklist are designed to identify the main features that should be present in a well-designed study. There are few criteria that should, alone and unsupported, lead to rejection of a study. However, a study that fails to address or report on more than one or two of the questions in the checklist should almost certainly be rejected.

For each question in this section you should choose one of the following categories to indicate how well it has been addressed in the study:

● well covered
● adequately addressed
● poorly addressed
● not addressed (not mentioned, or this aspect of study design was ignored)
● not reported (mentioned, but with insufficient detail to allow assessment to be made)
● not applicable.

1.1 THE STUDY ADDRESSES AN APPROPRIATE AND CLEARLY FOCUSED QUESTION

Unless a clear and well-defined question is specified, it will be difficult to assess how well the study has met its objectives or how relevant it is to the question you are trying to answer.

SELECTION OF PARTICIPANTS

1.2 THE CASES AND CONTROLS ARE TAKEN FROM COMPARABLE POPULATIONS

Study participants may be selected from the target population (all individuals to whom the results of the study could be applied), from the source population (a defined subset of the target population from which participants are selected) or from a pool of eligible people (a clearly defined and counted group selected from the source population). A study that does not include clear definitions of the source population should be rejected.

1.3 THE SAME EXCLUSION CRITERIA ARE USED FOR BOTH CASES AND CONTROLS

All selection and exclusion criteria should be applied equally to cases and controls. Failure to do so may introduce a significant degree of bias into the results of the study.

1.4 WHAT WAS THE PARTICIPATION RATE FOR EACH GROUP (CASES AND CONTROLS)?

Differences between the eligible population and the study participants are important because they may influence the validity of the study. A participation rate can be calculated by dividing the number of study participants by the number of people who are eligible to participate. It is more useful if it is calculated separately for cases and controls. If the participation rate is low or there is a large difference in rate between cases and controls, the study results may be invalid because of differences between participants and non-participants. In these circumstances the study should be downgraded, and rejected if the differences are very large.

1.5 PARTICIPANTS AND NON-PARTICIPANTS ARE COMPARED, TO ESTABLISH THEIR SIMILARITIES OR DIFFERENCES

Even if participation rates are comparable and acceptable, it is still possible that the participants selected to act as cases or controls may differ from other members of the source population in some significant way. A well-conducted case-control study will look at samples of those not participating among the source population to ensure that the participants are a truly representative sample.

1.6 CASES ARE CLEARLY DEFINED AND DIFFERENTIATED FROM CONTROLS

The method of selection of cases is of critical importance to the validity of the study. Investigators have to be certain that cases are truly cases, but must balance this with the need to ensure that the cases admitted into the study are representative of the eligible population. The issues involved in case selection are complex and should ideally be evaluated by someone with a good understanding of the design of case-control studies. If there is no information on how cases were selected it is probably safest to reject the study as a source of evidence.

1.7 IT IS CLEARLY ESTABLISHED THAT CONTROLS ARE NOT CASES

Just as it is important to be sure that cases are true cases, it is important to be sure that controls do not have the outcome under investigation. Controls should be chosen so that information on exposure status can be obtained or assessed in a similar way to that used for the selection of cases. If the methods of control selection are not described, the study should be rejected. If different methods of selection are used for cases and controls, the study should be evaluated by someone with a good understanding of the design of case–control studies.

ASSESSMENT

1.8 MEASURES WERE TAKEN TO PREVENT KNOWLEDGE OF PRIMARY EXPOSURE FROM INFLUENCING CASE ASCERTAINMENT

If there is a possibility that case ascertainment was influenced by knowledge of exposure status, assessment of any association is likely to be biased. A well-conducted study should take this into account in the design of the study.

1.9 EXPOSURE STATUS IS MEASURED IN A STANDARD, VALID AND RELIABLE WAY

The inclusion of evidence from other sources or previous studies that demonstrate the validity and reliability of the assessment methods, or that the measurement method is a recognised procedure, should increase confidence in study quality.

CONFOUNDING FACTORS

1.10 THE MAIN POTENTIAL CONFOUNDERS ARE IDENTIFIED AND TAKEN INTO ACCOUNT IN THE DESIGN AND ANALYSIS

Confounding is the distortion of a link between exposure and outcome by another factor that is associated with both exposure and outcome. The possible presence of confounding factors is one of the principal reasons why observational studies are not more highly rated as a source of evidence. The report of the study should indicate which potential confounders have been considered, and how they have been assessed or accounted for in the analysis. Clinical judgement should be used to consider whether all likely confounders have been taken into account. If the measures used to address the potential effects of confounders are considered inadequate, the study should be downgraded or rejected, depending on how serious the risk of confounding is considered to be. A study that does not address the possibility of confounding should be rejected.

STATISTICAL ANALYSIS

1.11 HAVE CONFIDENCE INTERVALS BEEN PROVIDED?

Confidence intervals are the preferred method for indicating the precision of statistical results, and can be used to differentiate between an inconclusive study and a study that shows no effect. Studies that report a single value with no assessment of precision should be treated with caution.

Section 2 of the checklist asks you to summarise key points about the study that will be added to an evidence table (see appendix K) in the next stage of the process.

Methodology checklist: the QUADAS tool for studies of diagnostic test accuracy

Adapted from: Whiting, P., Rutjes, A. W., Dinnes, J., *et al.* (2004) Development and validation of methods for assessing the quality of diagnostic accuracy studies. *Health Technology Assessment*, 8, 1–234.

Study identification (including author, title, reference, year of publication)				
Guideline topic:		**Review question no:**		
Checklist completed by:				
		Circle one option for each question		
Was the spectrum of participants representative of the patients who will receive the test in practice?	Yes	No	Unclear	N/A
Were selection criteria clearly described?	Yes	No	Unclear	N/A
Was the reference standard likely to classify the target condition correctly?	Yes	No	Unclear	N/A
Was the period between performance of the reference standard and the index test short enough to be reasonably sure that the target condition did not change between the two tests?	Yes	No	Unclear	N/A
Did the whole sample or a random selection of the sample receive verification using the reference standard?	Yes	No	Unclear	N/A
Did participants receive the same reference standard regardless of the index test result?	Yes	No	Unclear	N/A
Was the reference standard independent of the index test? (that is, the index test did not form part of the reference standard)	Yes	No	Unclear	N/A
Was the execution of the index test described in sufficient detail to permit its replication?	Yes	No	Unclear	N/A
Was the execution of the reference standard described in sufficient detail to permit its replication?	Yes	No	Unclear	N/A

Were the index test results interpreted without knowledge of the results of the reference standard?	Yes	No	Unclear	N/A
Were the reference standard results interpreted without knowledge of the results of the index test?	Yes	No	Unclear	N/A
Were the same clinical data available when the test results were interpreted as would be available when the test is used in practice?	Yes	No	Unclear	N/A
Were uninterpretable, indeterminate or intermediate test results reported?	Yes	No	Unclear	N/A
Were withdrawals from the study explained?	Yes	No	Unclear	N/A

Notes on use of methodology checklist: studies of diagnostic test accuracy

This checklist is designed for the evaluation of studies assessing the accuracy of specific diagnostic tests. It does **not** address questions of the usefulness of the test in practice, or how the test compares with alternatives. Such questions should be assessed using the checklists for studies on interventions (see appendices D to F).

The questions in this checklist are aimed at establishing the validity of the study under review – that is, making sure that it has been carried out carefully, and that the conclusions represent an unbiased assessment of the accuracy and reliability of the test being evaluated. Each question covers an aspect of methodology that is thought to make a difference to the reliability of a study.

Checklist items are worded so that a 'yes' response always indicates that the study has been designed and conducted in such a way as to minimise the risk of bias for that item. An 'unclear' response to a question may arise when the answer to an item is not reported, or not reported clearly. 'N/A' should be used when a study of diagnostic test accuracy cannot give an answer of 'yes' no matter how well it has been done.

Was the spectrum of participants representative of the patients who will receive the test in practice?

What is meant by this item

Differences between populations in demographic and clinical features may produce measures of diagnostic accuracy that vary considerably; this is known as spectrum bias. Reported estimates of diagnostic test accuracy may have limited clinical applicability (generalisability) if the spectrum of participants tested is not representative of the patients on whom the test will be used in practice. The spectrum of participants takes into account not only the severity of the underlying target condition but also demographic features and the presence of differential diagnoses and/or comorbidities.

How to score this item

Studies should score 'yes' for this item if you believe, based on the information reported, that the spectrum of participants included in the study was representative of those in whom the test will be used in practice. This judgement should be based on both the method for recruitment and the characteristics of those recruited. Studies that recruited a group of healthy controls and a group known to have the target disorder will be coded as 'no' on this item in nearly all circumstances. Reviewers should pre-specify what spectrum of participants would be acceptable, taking into account factors such as disease prevalence and severity, age and sex. Clinical input may be required from the GDG. If you think that the population studied does not fit into what you specified as acceptable, the study should be scored as 'no'. If there is insufficient information available to make a judgement, this item should be scored as 'unclear'.

Were selection criteria clearly described?

What is meant by this item

This refers to whether studies have reported criteria for entry into the study.

How to score this item

If you think that all relevant information regarding how participants were selected for inclusion in the study has been provided, then this item should be scored as 'yes'. If study selection criteria are not clearly reported, then this item should be scored as 'no'. In situations where selection criteria are partially reported and you feel that you do not have enough information to score this item as 'yes', then it should be scored as 'unclear'.

Was the reference standard likely to classify the target condition correctly?

What is meant by this item

The reference standard is the method used to determine the presence or absence of the target condition. Indicators of diagnostic test accuracy are calculated by comparing the results of the index test with the results of the reference standard. Estimates of test performance are based on the assumption that the index test is being compared with a reference standard that is 100% sensitive and specific. If there are any disagreements between the reference standard and the index test, it is assumed that the index test is incorrect. Thus the use of an inappropriate reference standard can bias estimation of the diagnostic accuracy of the index test.

How to score this item

Making a judgement about the accuracy of the reference standard may not be straightforward. You may need to consult a member of the GDG to determine whether a test is an appropriate reference standard. If a combination of tests is used, you may have to consider carefully whether these were appropriate.

If you believe that the reference standard is likely to classify the target condition correctly, then this item should be scored as 'yes'. If you do not think that the reference standard is likely to have classified the target condition correctly, then this item should be scored as 'no'. If there is insufficient information to make a judgement, then it should be scored as 'unclear'.

Was the period between performance of the reference standard and the index test short enough to be reasonably sure that the target condition did not change between the two tests?

What is meant by this item

Ideally, the results of the index test and the reference standard are collected on the same participants at the same time. If this is not possible and there is a delay, misclassification may occur because of either spontaneous recovery or progression of the disease. This is known as disease progression bias. The length of the period that may cause such bias will vary between conditions. For example, a delay of a few days is unlikely to be a problem for chronic conditions. However, for infectious diseases a delay of only a few days between performance of the index test and the reference standard may be important. This type of bias may also occur in chronic conditions in which the reference standard involves clinical follow-up of several years.

You will have to make judgements about what is considered 'short enough'. You should think about this *before* beginning your review, and define what you consider to be short enough for the specific topic area that you are reviewing. You may need clinical input to decide this.

How to score this item

When to score this item as 'yes' is related to the target condition. For conditions that progress rapidly, a delay of a even few days may be important. For such conditions this item should be scored as 'yes' if the delay between the performance of the index test and the reference standard is very short – a matter of hours or days. However, for chronic conditions, disease status is unlikely to change in a week, a month or even longer. For such conditions, longer delays between performance of the index test and reference standard may be scored as 'yes'. If you think that the period between the performance of the index test and the reference standard was sufficiently long that disease status may have changed between the performance of the two tests, then this item should be scored as 'no'. If insufficient information is provided, it should be scored as 'unclear'.

Did the whole sample or a random selection of the sample receive verification using the reference standard?

What is meant by this item

Partial verification bias (also known as work-up bias, [primary] selection bias or sequential ordering bias) occurs when not all of the study group receive confirmation of the diagnosis by a reference standard. If the results of the index test influence the decision to perform the reference standard, then biased estimates of test performance may arise. If participants are randomly selected to receive the reference standard, the overall diagnostic performance of the test is, in theory, unchanged. However, in most cases this selection is not random, possibly leading to biased estimates of the overall diagnostic accuracy. Partial verification bias generally only occurs in diagnostic cohort studies in which participants are tested using the index test before the reference standard.

How to score this item

If it is clear from the study that all participants (or a random selection) who received the index test went on to receive verification of their disease status using a reference standard, even if this reference standard was not the same for all participants, then this item should be scored as 'yes'. If some of the participants who received the index test did not receive verification of their true disease state (or the selection was not random), then this item should be scored as 'no'. If this information is not reported, this item should be scored as 'unclear'.

Did participants receive the same reference standard regardless of the index test result?

What is meant by this item

Differential verification bias occurs when some of the index test results are verified by a different reference standard. This is a particular problem if these reference standards differ in their definition of the target condition; for example, histopathology of the appendix and natural history for the detection of appendicitis. This usually occurs when participants who test positive on the index test undergo a more accurate, often invasive, reference standard test than those with negative results on the index test. The link (correlation) between a particular (negative) test result and being verified by a less accurate reference standard can lead to biased estimates of test accuracy. Differential verification bias generally only occurs in diagnostic cohort studies in which all participants are tested using the index test before the reference standard is performed.

How to score this item

If it is clear that participants received verification of their true disease status using the same reference standard, then this item should be scored as 'yes'. If some participants received verification using a different reference standard, then this item should be scored as 'no'. If this information is not reported, this item should be scored as 'unclear'.

Was the reference standard independent of the index test? (that is, the index test did not form part of the reference standard)

What is meant by this item

When the result of the index test is used in establishing the final diagnosis, incorporation bias may occur. This incorporation will probably increase the amount of agreement between index test results and the outcome of the reference standard, and hence result in overestimation of the various measures of diagnostic accuracy. For example, a study investigating magnetic resonance imaging for the diagnosis of multiple sclerosis could have a reference standard composed of clinical follow-up, cerebrospinal fluid analysis and investigating magnetic resonance imaging. In this case, the index test forms part of the reference standard. It is important to note that knowledge of the results of the index test does not automatically mean that these results are incorporated in the reference standard. This item will only apply when a composite reference standard is used to verify disease status. In such cases it is essential that a full definition of how disease status is verified and which tests form part of the reference standard is provided.

How to score this item
For studies in which a single reference standard is used, this item will not be relevant and should be scored as 'N/A'. If it is clear that the index test did not form part of the reference standard, then this item should be scored as 'yes'. If it appears that the index test formed part of the reference standard, then this item should be scored as 'no'. If this information is not reported, this item should be scored as 'unclear'.

Was the execution of the index test described in sufficient detail to permit its replication? Was the execution of the reference standard described in sufficient detail to permit its replication?
What is meant by these items
A sufficiently detailed description of the execution of the index test and the reference standard is important for two reasons. First, variation in measures of diagnostic accuracy can sometimes be traced back to differences in the execution of index tests and reference standards. Second, a clear and detailed description (or references) is needed to implement a certain test in another setting. If tests are executed in different ways then this would be expected to have an impact on test performance. The extent to which this would be expected to affect results depends on the type of test being investigated.

How to score these items
If the study reports sufficient details to permit replication of the index test and the reference standard, then these items should be scored as 'yes'. In other cases these items should be scored as 'no'. In situations where details of test performance are partially reported and you consider that you do not have enough information to score these items as 'yes', then they should be scored as 'unclear'.

Were the index test results interpreted without knowledge of the results of the reference standard? Were the reference standard results interpreted without knowledge of the results of the index test?
What is meant by these items
This issue is similar to the blinding of the people who assess outcomes in intervention studies. Interpretation of the results of the index test may be influenced by knowledge of the results of the reference standard, and vice versa. This is known as review bias, and may lead to inflated measures of diagnostic test accuracy. The extent to which this can affect test results will be related to the degree of subjectivity in the interpretation of the test result – the more subjective the interpretation, the more likely

that the interpreter can be influenced by the results of the index test in interpreting the results of the reference standard, and vice versa. It is therefore important to consider the topic area that you are reviewing and to determine whether interpretation of the results of the index test or the reference standard could be influenced by knowledge of the results of the other test.

How to score these items
If the study clearly states that the test results (index test or reference standard) were interpreted blind to the results of the other test, then these items should be scored as 'yes'. If this does not appear to be the case, then they should be scored as 'no'. If this information is not reported, these items should be scored as 'unclear'. If in the topic area that you are reviewing the index test is always performed first, then interpretation of the results of the index test will usually be done without knowledge of the results of the reference standard. Similarly, if the reference standard is always performed first, then the results will be interpreted without knowledge of the results of the index test. In situations where one form of review bias does not apply, the item should be scored as 'N/A'. If interpretation of test results is entirely objective, then test interpretation is not susceptible to review bias and the item should be scored as 'N/A'. Another situation in which this form of bias may not apply is when test results are interpreted in an independent laboratory. In such situations it is unlikely that the person interpreting the test results will have knowledge of the results of the other test (either index test or reference standard).

Were the same clinical data available when the test results were interpreted as would be available when the test is used in practice?
What is meant by this item
The availability of information on clinical data during the interpretation of test results may affect estimates of test performance. In this context, clinical data are defined broadly to include any information relating to the participant that is obtained by direct observation, such as age, sex and symptoms. The knowledge of such factors can influence the diagnostic test result if the test involves an interpretative component. If clinical data will be available when the test is interpreted in practice, then these should also be available when the test is evaluated. However, if the index test is intended to replace other clinical tests, then clinical data should not be available. Thus, before assessing studies for this item it is important to determine what information will be available when test results are interpreted in practice. You should consult the GDG to identify this information.

How to score this item
If clinical data would normally be available when the test results are interpreted in practice and similar data were available when interpreting the index test results in the study, then this item should be scored as 'yes'. Similarly, if clinical data would not be available in practice and these data were not available when the index test results were interpreted, then this item should be scored as 'yes'. If this is not the case, then this item should be scored as 'no'. If this information is not reported, this item should be

scored as 'unclear'. If interpretation of the index test is fully automated, this item may not be relevant and can be scored 'N/A'.

Were uninterpretable, indeterminate or intermediate test results reported?

What is meant by this item

A diagnostic test can produce an uninterpretable, indeterminate or intermediate result with varying frequency, depending on the test. These problems are often not reported in studies on diagnostic test accuracy, the uninterpretable results simply being removed from the analysis. This may lead to the biased assessment of the test characteristics. Whether bias will arise depends on the possible correlation between uninterpretable test results and the true disease status. If uninterpretable results occur randomly and are not related to the true disease status of the individual then, in theory, these should not have any effect on test performance. It is important that uninterpretable results are reported so that the impact on test performance can be considered; however, poor quality of reporting means that this is not always the case.

How to score this item

If it is clear that all test results, including uninterpretable, indeterminate or intermediate results, are reported, then this item should be scored as 'yes'. If the authors do not report any uninterpretable, indeterminate or intermediate results, and if the results are reported for all participants who were described as having been entered into the study, then this item should also be scored as 'yes'. If you think that such results occurred but have not been reported, then this item should be scored as 'no'. If it is not clear whether all study results have been reported, then this item should be scored as 'unclear'.

Were withdrawals from the study explained?

What is meant by this item

This occurs when participants withdraw from the study before the results of both the index test and the reference standard are known. If participants lost to follow-up differ systematically from those who remain, for whatever reason, then estimates of test performance may be biased. Poor quality of reporting of withdrawals may make the impact on estimates of test performance difficult to determine.

How to score this item

If it is clear what happened to all participants who entered the study, for example if a flow diagram of study participants is reported, then this item should be scored as 'yes'. If the authors do not report any withdrawals and if results are available for all participants who were reported to have been entered into the study, then this item should also be scored as 'yes'. If it appears that some of the participants who entered the study did not complete the study (that is, did not receive both the index test and the reference standard), and these participants were not accounted for, then this item should be scored as 'no'. If it is not clear whether all participants who entered the study were accounted for, then this item should be scored as 'unclear'.

APPENDIX 12:
SEARCH STRATEGIES FOR THE IDENTIFICATION
OF HEALTH ECONOMIC EVIDENCE

Available on the CD-ROM.

APPENDIX 13:
METHODOLOGY CHECKLIST FOR
ECONOMIC STUDIES

This checklist is designed to determine whether an economic evaluation provides evidence that is useful to inform the decision-making of the GDG (see Chapter 7). It is not intended to judge the quality of the study per se or the quality of reporting.

Byford, S., Knapp, M., Greenshields, J., *et al.* (2003) Cost-effectiveness of brief cognitive behaviour therapy versus treatment as usual in recurrent deliberate self-harm: a decision-making approach. *Psychological Medicine, 33,* 977–986.		
Section 1: Applicability (relevance to specific guideline review question(s) and the NICE reference case) This checklist should be used first to filter out irrelevant studies.	**Yes/Partially/ No/Unclear/ NA**	**Comments**
Is the patient population appropriate for the guideline?	Yes	
Are the interventions appropriate for the guideline?	Yes	
Is the healthcare system in which the study was conducted sufficiently similar to the current UK NHS context?	Yes	
Are costs measured from the NHS and PSS perspective?	Partially	Voluntary sector, community accommodation, criminal justice system and productivity costs included
Are all health effects on individuals included?	Yes	
Are both costs and health effects discounted at an annual rate of 3.5%?	NA	

Is the value of health effects expressed in terms of QALYs?	Yes	
Are changes in health related quality of life (HRQL) reported directly from patients and/or carers?	Yes	
Is the value of changes in HRQL (that is utilities) obtained from a representative sample of the public?	Unclear	Not specified in article
Overall judgement: Directly applicable		
Other comments:		

Section 2: Study limitations (the level of methodological quality) This checklist should be used once it has been decided that the study is sufficiently applicable to the context of the clinical guideline.	Yes/Partially/ No/Unclear/ NA	Comments
Does the model structure adequately reflect the nature of the health condition under evaluation?	NA	
Is the time horizon sufficiently long to reflect all important differences in costs and outcomes?	Partially	12-month study
Are all important and relevant health outcomes included?	Partially	Unclear whether QALY estimates included suicides
Are the estimates of baseline health outcomes from the best available source?	Yes	
Are the estimates of relative treatment effects from the best available source?	Yes	
Are all important and relevant costs included?	Partially	No costs to patients' family/ carers included (within societal perspective)

Are the estimates of resource use from the best available source?	Yes	
Are the unit costs of resources from the best available source?	Yes	
Is an appropriate incremental analysis presented or can it be calculated from the data?	Yes	
Are all important parameters, whose values are uncertain, subjected to appropriate sensitivity analysis?	Yes	
Is there no potential conflict of interest?	No	
Overall assessment: Minor limitations		
Other comments:		

Byford, S., Harrington, R., Torgerson, D., *et al.* (1999) Cost-effectiveness analysis of a home-based social work intervention for children and adolescents who have deliberately poisoned themselves: results of a randomised controlled trial. *British Journal of Psychiatry, 174*, 56–62.

Section 1: Applicability (relevance to specific guideline review question(s) and the NICE reference case) This checklist should be used first to filter out irrelevant studies.	**Yes/Partially/ No/Unclear/ NA**	**Comments**
Is the patient population appropriate for the guideline?	Yes	
Are the interventions appropriate for the guideline?	Yes	
Is the healthcare system in which the study was conducted sufficiently similar to the current UK NHS context?	Yes	
Are costs measured from the NHS and PSS perspective?	Partially	Educational sector costs included

Are all health effects on individuals included?	Partially	Suicidal Ideation Questionnaire; BHS; Family Assessment Device
Are both costs and health effects discounted at an annual rate of 3.5%?	NA	
Is the value of health effects expressed in terms of QALYs?	No	
Are changes in health related quality of life (HRQL) reported directly from patients and/or carers?	NA	
Is the value of changes in HRQL (that is utilities) obtained from a representative sample of the public?	NA	
Overall judgement: Partially applicable		
Other comments:		

Section 2: Study limitations (the level of methodological quality) This checklist should be used once it has been decided that the study is sufficiently applicable to the context of the clinical guideline.	Yes/Partially/ No/Unclear/ NA	Comments
Does the model structure adequately reflect the nature of the health condition under evaluation?	NA	
Is the time horizon sufficiently long to reflect all important differences in costs and outcomes?	Partially	6-month study
Are all important and relevant health outcomes included?	Partially	
Are the estimates of baseline health outcomes from the best available source?	Yes	
Are the estimates of relative treatment effects from the best available source?	Yes	

Are all important and relevant costs included?	Partially	Educational sector costs included
Are the estimates of resource use from the best available source?	Yes	
Are the unit costs of resources from the best available source?	Yes	
Is an appropriate incremental analysis presented or can it be calculated from the data?	No	No significant differences detected in primary outcomes
Are all important parameters, whose values are uncertain, subjected to appropriate sensitivity analysis?	Partially	One way sensitivity analyses on cost estimates
Is there no potential conflict of interest?	No	
Overall assessment: Minor limitations		
Other comments:		

Green, J. M., Wood, A. J., Kerfoot, M. J., *et al.* (2011). Group therapy for adolescents with repeated self harm: randomised controlled trial with economic evaluation. *British Medical Journal*, *342*, d682.

Section 1: Applicability (relevance to specific guideline review question(s) and the NICE reference case6) This checklist should be used first to filter out irrelevant studies.	**Yes/Partly/ No/Unclear/ NA**	**Comments**
Is the study population appropriate for the guideline?	Yes	Adolescents aged 12 to 17years
Are the interventions appropriate for the guideline?	Yes	Developmental group psychotherapy plus routine care with that of routine care alone

Is the healthcare system in which the study was conducted sufficiently similar to the current UK NHS context?	Yes	
Are costs measured from the NHS and personal social services (PSS) perspective?	Partly	A broad perspective (health, social care, education, and criminal justice sectors)
Are all direct health effects on individuals included?	Partly	QALY and BHS not included
Are both costs and health effects discounted at an annual rate of 3.5%?	NA	12-month time horizon
Is the value of health effects expressed in terms of quality-adjusted life years (QALYs)?	No	
Are changes in health-related quality of life (HRQoL) reported directly from patients and/or carers?	NA	
Is the valuation of changes in HRQoL (utilities) obtained from a representative sample of the general public?	NA	
Overall judgement: Partially applicable		
Other comments:		

Section 2: Study limitations (the level of methodological quality) This checklist should be used once it has been decided that the study is sufficiently applicable to the context of the clinical guideline.	Yes/Partly/ No/Unclear/ NA	Comments
Does the model structure adequately reflect the nature of the health condition under evaluation?	NA	
Is the time horizon sufficiently long to reflect all important differences in costs and outcomes?	Partly	12-month

Are all important and relevant health outcomes included?	Partly	
Are the estimates of baseline health outcomes from the best available source?	Yes	
Are the estimates of relative treatment effects from the best available source?	Yes	
Are all important and relevant costs included?	Yes	
Are the estimates of resource use from the best available source?	Yes	
Are the unit costs of resources from the best available source?	Yes	
Is an appropriate incremental analysis presented or can it be calculated from the data?	Unclear	
Are all important parameters whose values are uncertain subjected to appropriate sensitivity analysis?	Partly	One-way sensitivity analysis done but unclearly reported
Is there no potential conflict of interest?	No	
Overall assessment: Potentially serious limitations		
Other comments:		

Notes on use of methodology checklist: economic evaluations

For all questions:

- answer 'yes' if the study fully meets the criterion
- answer 'partly' if the study largely meets the criterion but differs in some important respect
- answer 'no' if the study deviates substantively from the criterion
- answer 'unclear' if the report provides insufficient information to judge whether the study complies with the criterion
- answer 'NA' ('not applicable') if the criterion is not relevant in a particular instance.

For 'partly' or 'no' responses, use the comments column to explain how the study deviates from the criterion.

SECTION 1: APPLICABILITY

1.1   IS THE STUDY POPULATION APPROPRIATE FOR THE GUIDELINE?

The study population should be defined as precisely as possible and should be in line with that specified in the guideline scope and any related review protocols.

This includes consideration of appropriate subgroups that require special attention. For many interventions, the capacity to benefit will differ for participants with differing characteristics. This should be explored separately for each relevant subgroup as part of the base-case analysis by the provision of estimates of clinical and cost effectiveness. The characteristics of participants in each subgroup should be clearly defined and, ideally, should be identified on the basis of an a priori expectation of differential clinical or cost effectiveness as a result of biologically plausible known mechanisms, social characteristics or other clearly justified factors.

Answer 'yes' if the study population is fully in line with that in the guideline question(s) and if the study differentiates appropriately between important subgroups. Answer 'partly' if the study population is similar to that in the guideline question(s) but: (i) it differs in some important respects; or (ii) the study fails to differentiate between important subgroups. Answer 'no' if the study population is substantively different from that in the guideline question(s).

1.2   ARE THE INTERVENTIONS APPROPRIATE FOR THE GUIDELINE?

All relevant alternatives should be included, as specified in the guideline scope and any related review protocols. These should include routine and best practice in the NHS, existing NICE guidance and other feasible options. Answer 'yes' if the analysis includes all options considered relevant for the guideline, even if it also includes other options that are not relevant. Answer 'partly' if the analysis omits one or more relevant options but still contains comparisons likely to be useful for the guideline. Answer 'no' if the analysis does not contain any relevant comparisons.

1.3   IS THE HEALTHCARE SYSTEM IN WHICH THE STUDY WAS CONDUCTED SUFFICIENTLY SIMILAR TO THE CURRENT UK NHS CONTEXT?

This relates to the overall structure of the healthcare system within which the interventions were delivered. For example, an intervention might be delivered on an inpatient basis in one country whereas in the UK it would be provided in the community. This might significantly influence the use of healthcare resources and costs, thus limiting the applicability of the results to a UK setting. In addition, old UK studies may be severely limited in terms of their relevance to current NHS practice.

Answer 'yes' if the study was conducted within the UK and is sufficiently recent to reflect current NHS practice. For non-UK or older UK studies, a answer 'partly' if differences in the healthcare setting are unlikely to substantively change the cost-effectiveness estimates. Answer 'no' if the healthcare setting is so different that the results are unlikely to be applicable in the current NHS.

1.4   ARE COSTS MEASURED FROM THE NHS AND PERSONAL SOCIAL SERVICES (PSS) PERSPECTIVE?

The decision-making perspective of an economic evaluation determines the range of costs that should be included in the analysis. NICE works in a specific context; in particular, it does not set the budget for the NHS. The objective of NICE is to offer guidance that represents an efficient use of available NHS and PSS resources. For these reasons, the perspective on costs used in the NICE reference case is that of the NHS and PSS. Productivity costs and costs borne by patients and carers that are not reimbursed by the NHS or PSS are not included in the reference case. The reference case also excludes costs to other government bodies, although these may sometimes be presented in additional analyses alongside the reference case.

    Answer 'yes' if the study only includes costs for resource items that would be paid for by the NHS and PSS. Also answer 'yes' if other costs have been included in the study, but the results are presented in such a way that the cost effectiveness can be calculated from an NHS and PSS perspective. Answer 'partly' if the study has taken a wider perspective but the other non-NHS/PSS costs are small in relation to the total expected costs and are unlikely to change the cost-effectiveness results. Answer 'no' if non-NHS/PSS costs are significant and are likely to change the cost-effectiveness results. Some interventions may have a substantial impact on non-health outcomes or costs to other government bodies (for example, treatments to reduce illicit drug misuse may have the effect of reducing drug-related crime). In such situations, if the economic study includes non-health costs in such a way that they cannot be separated out from NHS/PSS costs, answer 'no' but consider retaining the study for critical appraisal. If studies containing non-reference-case costs are retained, use the comments column to note why.

1.5   ARE ALL DIRECT HEALTH EFFECTS ON INDIVIDUALS INCLUDED?

In the NICE reference case, the perspective on outcomes should be all direct health effects, whether for patients or, when relevant, other people principally carers). This is consistent with an objective of maximising health gain from available healthcare resources. Some features of healthcare delivery that are often referred to as 'process characteristics' may ultimately have health consequences; for example, the mode of treatment delivery may have health consequences through its impact on concordance with treatment. Any significant characteristics of healthcare technologies that have a value to people that is independent of any direct effect on health should be noted.

These characteristics include the convenience with which healthcare is provided and the level of information available for patients.

This question should be viewed in terms of what is **excluded** in relation to the NICE reference case; that is, non-health effects.

Answer 'yes' if the measure of health outcome used in the analysis excludes non-health effects (or if such effects can be excluded from the results). Answer 'partly' if the analysis includes some non-health effects but these are small and unlikely to change the cost-effectiveness results. Answer 'no' if the analysis includes significant non-health effects that are likely to change the cost-effectiveness results.

1.6 ARE BOTH COSTS AND HEALTH EFFECTS DISCOUNTED AT AN ANNUAL RATE OF 3.5%?

The need to discount to a present value is widely accepted in economic evaluation, although the specific rate varies across jurisdictions and over time. NICE considers it appropriate to discount costs and health effects at the same rate. The annual rate of 3.5%, based on the recommendations of the UK Treasury for the discounting of costs, applies to both costs and health effects.

Answer 'yes' if both costs and health effects (for example, QALYs) are discounted at 3.5% per year. Answer 'partly' if costs and effects are discounted at a rate similar to 3.5% (for example, costs and effects are both discounted at 3% per year). Answer 'no' if costs and/or health effects are not discounted, or if they are discounted at a rate (or rates) different from 3.5% (for example, 5% for both costs and effects, or 6% for costs and 1.5% for effects). Note in the comments column what discount rates have been used. If all costs and health effects accrue within a short time (roughly a year), answer 'NA'.

1.7 IS THE VALUE OF HEALTH EFFECTS EXPRESSED IN TERMS OF QUALITY ADJUSTED LIFE YEARS?

The QALY is a measure of a person's length of life weighted by a valuation of their HRQoL over that period.

Given its widespread use, the QALY is considered by NICE to be the most appropriate generic measure of health benefit that reflects both mortality and effects on HRQoL. It is recognised that alternative measures exist (such as the healthy-year equivalent), but few economic evaluations have used these methods and their strengths and weaknesses are not fully established.

NICE's position is that an additional QALY should be given the same weight regardless of the other characteristics of the patients receiving the health benefit.

Answer 'yes' if the effectiveness of the intervention is measured using QALYs; answer 'no' if not. There may be circumstances when a QALY cannot be obtained or where the assumptions underlying QALYs are considered inappropriate. In such situations answer 'no', but consider retaining the study for appraisal. Similarly, answer 'no' but retain the study for appraisal if it does not include QALYs but it is still thought to be useful for GDG decision-making: for example, if the clinical evidence indicates that an intervention might be dominant, and estimates of the relative costs of the interventions from a costminimisation study are likely to be useful. When economic evaluations not using QALYs are retained for full critical appraisal, use the comments column to note why.

1.8   ARE CHANGES IN HEALTH-RELATED QUALITY OF LIFE REPORTED DIRECTLY FROM PATIENTS AND/OR CARERS?

In the NICE reference case, information on changes in HRQoL as a result of treatment should be reported directly by patients (and directly by carers when the impact of treatment on the carer's health is also important). When it is not possible to obtain information on changes in patients' HRQoL directly from them, data should be obtained from carers (not from healthcare professionals).

For consistency, the EQ-5D is NICE's preferred measure of HRQoL in adults. However, when EQ-5D data are not available or are inappropriate for the condition or the effects of treatment, other multi-attribute utility questionnaires (for example, the Short Form Six Dimensions, Quality of Well-Being Index or Health Utilities Index) or mapping methods from disease-specific questionnaires may be used to estimate QALYs. For studies not reporting QALYs, a variety of generic or disease-specific methods may be used to measure HRQoL.

Answer 'yes' if changes in patients' HRQoL are estimated by the patients themselves. Answer 'partly' if estimates of patients' HRQoL are provided by carers. Answer 'no' if estimates come from healthcare professionals or researchers. Note in the comments column how HRQoL was measured (EQ-5D, Quality of Well-Being Index, Health Utilities Index and so on). Answer 'NA' if the cost-effectiveness study does not include estimates of HRQoL (for example, studies reporting 'cost per life year gained' or cost-minimisation studies).

1.9   IS THE VALUATION OF CHANGES IN HRQoL (UTILITIES) OBTAINED FROM A REPRESENTATIVE SAMPLE OF THE GENERAL PUBLIC?

The NICE reference case specifies that the valuation of changes in HRQoL (utilities) reported by patients should be based on public preferences elicited using a choice-based method (such as the time trade-off or standard gamble) in a representative sample of the UK population.

Answer 'yes' if HRQoL valuations were obtained using the EQ-5D UK tariff. Answer 'partly' if the valuation methods were comparable to those used for the EQ-5D. Answer 'no' if other valuation methods were used. Answer 'NA' if the study does not apply valuations to HRQoL (for studies not reporting QALYs). In the comments column note the valuation method used (such as time trade-off or standard gamble) and the source of the preferences (such as patients or healthcare professionals).

1.10   OVERALL JUDGEMENT

Classify the applicability of the economic evaluation to the clinical guideline, the current NHS situation and the context for NICE guidance as one of the following:

- **Directly applicable** – the study meets all applicability criteria, or fails to meet one or more applicability criteria but this is unlikely to change the conclusions about cost effectiveness.
- **Partially applicable** – the study fails to meet one or more applicability criteria, and this could change the conclusions about cost effectiveness.
- **Not applicable** – the study fails to meet one or more applicability criteria, and this is likely to change the conclusions about cost effectiveness. Such studies would be excluded from further consideration and there is no need to continue with the rest of the checklist.

SECTION 2: STUDY LIMITATIONS

2.1   DOES THE MODEL STRUCTURE ADEQUATELY REFLECT THE NATURE OF THE HEALTH CONDITION UNDER EVALUATION?

This relates to the choice of model and its structural elements (including cycle length in discrete time models, if appropriate). Model type and its structural aspects should be consistent with a coherent theory of the health condition under evaluation. The selection of treatment pathways, whether health states or branches in a decision tree, should be based on the underlying biological processes of the health issue under study and the potential impact (benefits and adverse consequences) of the intervention(s) of interest.

Answer 'yes' if the model design and assumptions appropriately reflect the health condition and intervention(s) of interest. Answer 'partly' if there are aspects of the model design or assumptions that do not fully reflect the health condition or intervention(s) but that are unlikely to change the cost-effectiveness results. Answer 'no' if the model omits some important aspect of the health condition or intervention(s) and this is likely to change the cost-effectiveness results. Answer 'NA' for economic evaluations based on data from a clinical study which do not extrapolate treatment outcomes or costs beyond the study context or follow-up period.

2.2   IS THE TIME HORIZON SUFFICIENTLY LONG TO REFLECT ALL IMPORTANT DIFFERENCES IN COSTS AND OUTCOMES?

The time horizon is the period of analysis of the study: the length of follow-up for participants in a trial-based evaluation, or the period of time over which the costs and outcomes for a cohort are tracked in a modelling study. This time horizon should always be the same for costs and outcomes, and should be long enough to include all relevant costs and outcomes relating to the intervention. A time horizon shorter than lifetime could be justified if there is no differential mortality effect between options, and the differences in costs and HRQoL relate to a relatively short period (for example, in the case of an acute infection).

Answer 'yes' if the time horizon is sufficient to include all relevant costs and outcomes. Answer 'partly' if the time horizon may omit some relevant costs and outcomes but these are unlikely to change the cost-effectiveness results.

Answer 'no' if the time horizon omits important costs and outcomes and this is likely to change the cost-effectiveness results.

2.3   ARE ALL IMPORTANT AND RELEVANT HEALTH OUTCOMES INCLUDED?

All relevant health outcomes should include direct health effects relating to harms from the intervention (adverse effects) as well as any potential benefits.

Answer 'yes' if the analysis includes all relevant and important harms and benefits. Answer 'partly' if the analysis omits some harms or benefits but these would be unlikely to change the cost-effectiveness results. Answer 'no' if the analysis omits important harms and/or benefits that would be likely to change the cost-effectiveness results.

2.4   ARE THE ESTIMATES OF BASELINE HEALTH OUTCOMES FROM THE BEST AVAILABLE SOURCE?

The estimate of the overall net treatment effect of an intervention is determined by the baseline risk of a particular condition or event and/or the relative effects of the intervention compared with the relevant comparator treatment. The overall net treatment effect may also be determined by other features of the people comprising the population of interest.

The process of assembling evidence for economic evaluations should be systematic – evidence must be identified, quality assessed and, when appropriate, pooled, using explicit criteria and justifiable and reproducible methods. These principles apply to all categories of evidence that are used to estimate clinical and cost effectiveness, evidence for which will typically be drawn from a number of different sources.

The sources and methods for eliciting baseline probabilities should be described clearly. These data can be based on 'natural history' (patient outcomes in the absence of treatment or with routine care), sourced from cohort studies. Baseline probabilities may also be derived from the control arms of experimental studies. Sometimes it may be necessary to rely on expert opinion for particular parameters.

Answer 'yes' if the estimates of baseline health outcomes reflect the best available evidence as identified from a recent well-conducted systematic review of the literature. Answer 'partly' if the estimates are not derived from a systematic review but are likely to reflect outcomes for the relevant group of patients in routine NHS practice (for example, if they are derived from a large UK-relevant cohort study). Answer 'no' if the estimates are unlikely to reflect outcomes for the relevant group in routine NHS practice.

2.5   ARE THE ESTIMATES OF RELATIVE TREATMENT EFFECTS FROM THE BEST AVAILABLE SOURCE?

The objective of the analysis of clinical effectiveness is to produce an unbiased estimate of the mean clinical effectiveness of the interventions being compared.

The NICE reference case indicates that evidence on outcomes should be obtained from a systematic review, defined as the systematic location, inclusion, appraisal and synthesis of evidence to obtain a reliable and valid overview of the data relating to a clearly formulated question.

Synthesis of outcome data through meta-analysis is appropriate provided that there are sufficient relevant and valid data obtained using comparable measures of outcome.

Head-to-head RCTs provide the most valid evidence of relative treatment effect. However, such evidence may not always be available. Therefore, data from non-randomised studies may be required to supplement RCT data. Any potential bias arising from the design of the studies used in the assessment should be explored and documented.

Data from head-to-head RCTs should be presented in the base-case analysis, if available. When head-to-head RCTs exist, evidence from indirect or mixed treatment comparison analyses may be presented if it is considered to add information that is not available from the head-to-head comparison. This indirect or mixed treatment comparison must be fully described and presented as additional to the base-case analysis. (A 'mixed treatment comparison' estimates effect sizes using both head-to-head and indirect comparisons.)

If data from head-to-head RCTs are not available, indirect treatment comparison methods should be used. (An 'indirect comparison' is a synthesis of data from a network of trials that compare the interventions of interest with other comparators.)

When multiple interventions are being assessed that have not been compared within a single RCT, data from a series of pairwise head-to-head RCTs should be presented. Consideration should also be given to presenting a combined analysis using a mixed treatment comparison framework if it is considered to add information that is not available from the head-to-head comparison.

Only indirect or mixed treatment comparison methods that preserve randomisation should be used. The principles of good practice for standard meta-analyses should also be followed in mixed and indirect treatment comparisons.

The methods and assumptions that are used to extrapolate short-term results to final outcomes should be clearly presented and there should be documentation of the reasoning underpinning the choice of survival function.

Evidence for the evaluation of diagnostic technologies should normally incorporate evidence on diagnostic accuracy. It is also important to incorporate the predicted changes in health outcomes and costs resulting from treatment decisions based on the test result. The general principles guiding the assessment of the clinical and cost effectiveness of diagnostic interventions should be the same as for other technologies. However, particular consideration of the methods of analysis may be required, particularly in relation to evidence synthesis. Evidence for the effectiveness of diagnostic technologies should include the costs and outcomes for people whose test results lead to an incorrect diagnosis, as well as for those who are diagnosed correctly.

As for other technologies, RCTs have the potential to capture the pathway of care involving diagnostic technologies, but their feasibility and availability may be limited. Other study designs should be assessed on the basis of their fitness for purpose, taking into consideration the aim of the study (for example, to evaluate outcomes, or to evaluate sensitivity and specificity) and the purpose of the diagnostic technology.

Answer 'yes' if the estimates of treatment effect appropriately reflect all relevant studies of the best available quality, as identified through a recent well-conducted systematic review of the literature. Answer 'partly' if the estimates of treatment effect are not derived from a systematic review but are similar in magnitude to the best available estimates (for example, if the economic evaluation is based on a single large study with treatment effects similar to pooled estimates from all relevant studies). Answer 'no' if the estimates of treatment effect are likely to differ substantively from the best available estimates.

2.6   ARE ALL IMPORTANT AND RELEVANT COSTS INCLUDED?

Costs related to the condition of interest and incurred in additional years of life gained as a result of treatment should be included in the base-case analysis. This should include the costs of handling non-adherence to treatment and treating side effects. Costs that are considered to be unrelated to the condition or intervention of interest should be excluded. If introduction of the intervention requires additional infrastructure to be put in place, consideration should be given to including such costs in the analysis.

Answer 'yes' if all important and relevant resource use and costs are included given the perspective and the research question under consideration. Answer 'partly' if some relevant resource items are omitted but these are unlikely to affect the cost-effectiveness results. Answer 'no' if important resource items are omitted and these are likely to affect the cost-effectiveness results.

2.7   ARE THE ESTIMATES OF RESOURCE USE FROM THE BEST AVAILABLE SOURCE?

It is important to quantify the effect of the interventions on resource use in terms of physical units (for example, days in hospital or visits to a GP) and valuing those effects in monetary terms using appropriate prices and unit costs. Evidence on resource use should be identified systematically. When expert opinion is used as a source of information, any formal methods used to elicit these data should be clearly reported.

Answer 'yes' if the estimates of resource use appropriately reflect all relevant evidence sources of the best available quality, as identified through a recent well-conducted systematic review of the literature. Answer 'partly' if the estimates of resource use are not derived from a systematic review but are similar in magnitude to the best available estimates. Answer 'no' if the estimates of resource use are likely to differ substantively from the best available estimates.

2.8 ARE THE UNIT COSTS OF RESOURCES FROM THE BEST AVAILABLE SOURCE?

Resources should be valued using the prices relevant to the NHS and PSS.

Given the perspective of the NICE reference case it is appropriate for the financial costs relevant to the NHS/PSS to be used as the basis of costing, although these may not always reflect the full social opportunity cost of a given resource. A first point of reference in identifying costs and prices should be any current official listing published by the Department of Health and/or the Welsh Assembly Government.

When the acquisition price paid for a resource differs from the public list price (for example, pharmaceuticals and medical devices sold at reduced prices to NHS institutions), the public list price should be used in the base-case analysis. Sensitivity analysis should assess the implications of variations from this price. Analyses based on price reductions for the NHS will only be considered when the reduced prices are transparent and can be consistently available across the NHS, and if the period for which the specified price is available is guaranteed.

National data based on healthcare resource groups such as the Payment by Results tariff can be used when they are appropriate and available. However, data based on healthcare resource groups may not be appropriate in all circumstances (for example, when the definition of the healthcare resource group is broad, or the mean cost probably does not reflect resource use in relation to the intervention(s) under consideration). In such cases, other sources of evidence, such as micro-costing studies, may be more appropriate. When cost data are taken from the literature, the methods used to identify the sources should be defined. When several alternative sources are available, a justification for the costs chosen should be provided and discrepancies between the sources explained. When appropriate, sensitivity analysis should have been undertaken to assess the implications for results of using alternative data sources.

Answer 'yes' if resources are valued using up-to-date prices relevant to the NHS and PSS. Answer 'partly' if the valuations of some resource items differ from current NHS/PSS unit costs but this is unlikely to change the cost effectiveness results. Answer 'no' if the valuations of some resource items differ substantively from current NHS/PSS unit costs and this is likely to change the cost-effectiveness results.

2.9 IS AN APPROPRIATE INCREMENTAL ANALYSIS PRESENTED OR CAN IT BE CALCULATED FROM THE DATA?

An appropriate incremental analysis is one that compares the expected costs and health outcomes of one intervention with the expected costs and health outcomes of the next-best non-dominated alternative.

Standard decision rules should be followed when combining costs and effects, and should reflect any situation where there is dominance or extended dominance. When there is a trade-off between costs and effects, the results should be presented as an ICER: the ratio of the difference in mean costs to the difference in mean outcomes of a technology compared with the next best alternative. In addition to ICERs, expected net monetary or health benefits can be presented using values placed on a QALY gained of £20,000 and £30,000.

For cost-consequence analyses, appropriate incremental analysis can only be done by selecting one of the consequences as the primary measure of effectiveness.

Answer 'yes' if appropriate incremental results are presented, or if data are presented that allow the reader to calculate the incremental results. Answer 'no' if: (i) simple ratios of costs to effects are presented for each alternative compared with a standard intervention; or (ii) if options subject to simple or extended dominance are not excluded from the incremental analyses.

2.10 ARE ALL IMPORTANT PARAMETERS WHOSE VALUES ARE UNCERTAIN SUBJECTED TO APPROPRIATE SENSITIVITY ANALYSIS?

There are a number of potential selection biases and uncertainties in any evaluation (trial- or model-based) and these should be identified and quantified where possible. There are three types of bias or uncertainty to consider:

- Structural uncertainty – for example in relation to the categorisation of different states of health and the representation of different pathways of care. These structural assumptions should be clearly documented and the evidence and rationale to support them provided. The impact of structural uncertainty on estimates of cost effectiveness should be explored by separate analyses of a representative range of plausible scenarios.
- Source of values to inform parameter estimates – the implications of different estimates of key parameters (such as estimates of relative effectiveness) must be reflected in sensitivity analyses (for example, through the inclusion of alternative scenarios). Inputs must be fully justified, and uncertainty explored by sensitivity analysis using alternative input values.
- Parameter precision – uncertainty around the mean health and cost inputs in the model. Distributions should be assigned to characterise the uncertainty associated with the (precision of) mean parameter values. Probabilistic sensitivity analysis is preferred, as this enables the uncertainty associated with parameters to be simultaneously reflected in the results of the model. In non-linear decision models – when

there is not a straight-line relationship between inputs and outputs of a model (such as Markov models) – probabilistic methods provide the best estimates of mean costs and outcomes. Simple decision trees are usually linear.

The mean value, distribution around the mean, and the source and rationale for the supporting evidence should be clearly described for each parameter included in the model.

Evidence about the extent of correlation between individual parameters should be considered carefully and reflected in the probabilistic analysis. Assumptions made about the correlations should be clearly presented.

Answer 'yes' if an extensive sensitivity analysis was undertaken that explored all key uncertainties in the economic evaluation. Answer 'partly' if the sensitivity analysis failed to explore some important uncertainties in the economic evaluation. Answer 'no' if the sensitivity analysis was very limited and omitted consideration of a number of important uncertainties, or if the range of values or distributions around parameters considered in the sensitivity analysis were not reported.

2.11   IS THERE NO POTENTIAL CONFLICT OF INTEREST?

The BMJ defines competing interests for its authors as follows: 'A competing interest exists when professional judgment concerning a primary interest (such as patients' welfare or the validity of research) may be influenced by a secondary interest (such as financial gain or personal rivalry). It may arise for the authors of a BMJ article when they have a financial interest that may influence, probably without their knowing, their interpretation of their results or those of others.'

Whenever a potential financial conflict of interest is possible, this should be declared.

Answer 'yes' if the authors declare that they have no financial conflicts of interest. Answer 'no' if clear financial conflicts of interest are declared or apparent (for example, from the stated affiliation of the authors). Answer 'unclear' if the article does not indicate whether or not there are financial conflicts of interest.

2.12   OVERALL ASSESSMENT

The overall methodological study quality of the economic evaluation should be classified as one of the following:

- **Minor limitations** – the study meets all quality criteria, or the study fails to meet one or more quality criteria but this is unlikely to change the conclusions about cost effectiveness.
- **Potentially serious limitations** – the study fails to meet one or more quality criteria and this could change the conclusions about cost effectiveness.
- **Very serious limitations** – the study fails to meet one or more quality criteria and this is highly likely to change the conclusions about cost effectiveness. Such studies should usually be excluded from further consideration.

APPENDIX 14: EVIDENCE TABLES FOR ECONOMIC STUDIES

Study ID Country Study type	Intervention details	Study population Study design Data sources	Costs: description and values Outcomes: description and values	Results: cost-effectiveness	Comments
BYFORD2003 UK Cost-effectiveness analysis/ Cost utility analysis	MACT – patients are given a manual and offered up to seven treatment sessions of CBT with a trained therapist over 3 months versus TAU	Patients with history of recurrent deliberate self-harm and no requirement for inpatient psychiatric treatment. Multicentre RCT: MACT (n = 197) TAU (n = 200) Source of clinical effectiveness data: single RCT (Tyrer *et al.*, 2003) Source of resource use: RCT – Client Service Receipt Inventory and patient questionnaire Source of unit costs: UK national sources.	Costs: hospital services, community health services, social services, voluntary sector services, community accommodation, criminal justice system, productivity losses, patient living expenses. Results: total costs per patient MACT: £13,454 (SD £5,313) TAU: £14,288 (SD £7,669) Outcomes: primary outcome was proportion of patients who experienced an episode of self-harm during 12-month follow-up. QALYs were also estimated from EQ-5D utility scores. Results: percentage of patients with a self-harm episode was 7% lower in the MACT group. QALYs were 0.0118 lower in the MACT group.	Cost of a 1% reduction in the percentage of patients with a repeat self-harm episode was −£120 using MACT. Thus, MACT was the dominant strategy. Incremental cost per QALY gained was £66,000 using TAU. CEACs showed >90% probability that MACT was more cost-effective than TAU (using percentage self-harming). Using cost per QALY threshold <£66,000, MACT had higher probability of being cost-effective.	Perspective: societal Currency: UK£ Cost year: 1999/2000 Time horizon: 12 months Discounting: N/A Funded by: UK Medical Research Council

Study ID Country Study type	Intervention details	Study population Study design Data sources	Costs: description and values Outcomes: description and values	Results: cost-effectiveness	Comments
BYFORD1999 UK Cost-effective-ness analysis	Home-based social work intervention (in addition to routine care) – four intensive, family-centred home-based intervention sessions. versus Routine care (routine clinical assessment and psychiatric care – out-patient clinic visits)	Self-poisoned young people (aged 10 to 16 years) who were referred to mental health care teams with diagnosis of self-poisoning RCT: Home-based social work (n = 85) Routine care (n = 77) Data sources: single study based on community sample in Manchester Source of unit costs: UK national sources	Costs: NHS (assessments, intervention sessions, outpatient, inpatient, intensive care, staff – GP, CPN, psychiatrist); education (welfare officers, educational psychologists); social services (social worker, residential care). Outcomes: suicide ideation questionnaire and hopelessness scale; family assessment device – all completed at baseline, 2 and 6 months).	Total mean costs: Intervention: £1,177 (excluding cost of intervention) Intervention: £1,455 (including cost of intervention) Control: £1,751 No statistically significant differences detected between intervention and control in primary outcome measures No synthesis of costs and outcomes performed by authors.	Perspective: societal Currency: UK £ Cost year: 1997/98 Time horizon: 6 months Discounting: NA Funded by: Department of Health, UK

Study ID Country Study type	Intervention details	Study population Study design Data sources	Costs: description and values Outcomes: description and values	Results: cost-effectiveness	Comments
GREEN2011 UK Cost-effectiveness analysis	Manual-based developmental group psychotherapy programme (six weekly sessions followed by a booster of weekly sessions as long as needed, incorporating CBT, DBT and group psychotherapy techniques) plus routine care versus Routine care alone (local child and adolescent mental health services teams provided standard routine care according to their clinical judgment)	Adolescents aged 12 to 17 years with at least two past episodes of self-harm within the previous 12 months Study design: RCT Group therapy (n = 181) Routine care (n = 183) Data sources: Assessment of Treatment In Suicidal Teenagers study in Northwest England Source of resource use: Child and Adolescent Service Use Schedule Sources of unit costs: UK national sources	Costs: NHS (hospital services, community health services, medication), social services (social worker, support worker, school doctor and nurse), education services, voluntary services and criminal justice services. Others: travel cost and productivity loss. Results: total cost per young person over 12 months' follow-up Group therapy: £21,781 (SD £38,794) Routine care: £15,354 (SD £24,981) No statistical significant difference in mean cost detected. Outcomes: primary (frequency of self-harm episodes). Secondary outcomes (severity of self-harm, mood disorder, suicide ideation, global functioning). Measured at baseline, 6 and 12 months. Results: proportion of participants who had not harmed themselves over the preceding 6 months at 12-month follow-up (group therapy: 38.9%; Routine care: 41.9%)	The incremental cost-effectiveness of the group therapy compared to routine care was £2,020 per 1% increase in the proportion of young people not self-harming. The probability of group therapy being cost-effective ranges from 12% to 28% as willingness to pay for outcome improvement increases	Perspective: societal Currency: UK£ Cost year: 2005–06 Time horizon: 12 months Discounting: NA Applicability: partially applicable Quality: potentially serious limitation Funded by: The Health Foundation and sponsored by the University of Manchester

APPENDIX 15:
CLINICAL STUDY CHARACTERISTICS

Available on the CD-ROM.

APPENDIX 16:

CLINICAL EVIDENCE FOREST PLOTS

Available on the CD-ROM.

APPENDIX 17:
GRADE EVIDENCE PROFILES

Available on the CD-ROM.

12   REFERENCES

Adler, P. A. & Adler, P. (2007) The demedicalization of self-injury: from psychopathology to sociological deviance. *Journal of Contemporary Ethnography*, *36*, 537–570.

Afshari, R., Good, A. M., Maxwell, S. R. J., *et al.* (2005) Co-proxamol overdose is associated with a 10-fold excess mortality compared with other paracetamol combination analgesics. *British Journal of Clinical Pharmacology*, *60*, 444–447.

AGREE Collaboration (2003) Development and validation of an international appraisal instrument for assessing the quality of clinical practice guidelines: the AGREE project. *Quality and Safety in Health Care, 12*, 18–23.

Allard, R., Marshall, M. & Plante, M. C. (1992) Intensive follow-up does not decrease the risk of repeat suicide attempts. *Suicide and Life-Threatening Behavior*, 22, 303–314.

Allgulander, C. & Fisher, L. D. (1990) Clinical predictors of completed suicide and repeated self-poisoning in 8895 self-poisoning patients. *European Archives of Psychiatry & Neurological Sciences*, *239*, 270–276.

Ansel, E. L. & McGee, R. K. (1971) Attitudes towards suicide attempters. *Bulletin of Suicidology*, *8*, 22–28.

Appleby, L., Morriss, R., Gask, M., *et al.* (2000) An educational intervention for front-line health professionals in the assessment and management of suicidal patients (The STORM Project). *Psychological Medicine*, *30*, 805–812.

Arnold, L. (1995) *Women and Self-injury: a Survey of 76 Women.* Bristol: Bristol Crisis Service for Women.

Babiker, G. & Arnold, L. (1997) *The Language of Injury: Comprehending Self-mutilation*. Leicester: British Psychological Society.

Bailey, S. (1994) Critical care nurses' and doctors' attitudes to parasuicide patients. *The Australian Journal of Advanced Nursing*, *11*, 11–16.

Baker, D. & Fortune, S. (2008) Understanding self-harm and suicide websites: a qualitative interview study of young adult website users. *Crisis*, *29*, 118–122.

Barbui, C., Esposito, E. & Cipriani, A. (2009) Selective serotonin reuptake inhibitors and risk of suicide: a systematic review of observational studies. *Canadian Medical Association Journal*, *180*, 291–297.

Barr, W., Leitner, M. & Thomas, J. (2004) Do older people who self-harm receive the hospital care they need? *Quality in Ageing and Older Adults*, *5*, 10–19.

Bateman, A. & Fonagy, P. (2009) Randomized controlled trial of outpatient mentalization-based treatment versus structured clinical management for borderline personality disorder. *American Journal of Psychiatry*, *166*, 1355–1364.

Battaglia, J., Wolff, T. K., Wagner-Johnson, D. S., *et al.* (1999) Structured diagnostic assessment and depot fluphenazine treatment of multiple suicide attempters in the emergency department. *International Clinical Psychopharmacology*, *14*, 361–372.

References

Beautrais, A. (2010) Postcard intervention for repeat self-harm: randomised controlled trial. *British Journal of Psychiatry*, *197*, 55–60.

Beck, A. T. & Steer, R. A. (1987) *Manual for Beck Depression Inventory*. San Antonio, TX: Psychological Corporation.

Beck, A. T. & Steer, R. A. (1989b) Clinical predictors of eventual suicide: a 5- to 10-year prospective study of suicide attempters. *Journal of Affective Disorders*, 17, 203–209.

Beck, A. T., Weissman, A., Lester, D., *et al.* (1974a) The measurement of pessimism: the Hopelessness Scale. *Journal of Consulting and Clinical Psychology*, *42*, 861–865.

Beck, A. T., Schuyler, D. & Herman, I. (1974b) Development of suicidal intent scales. In *The Prediction of Suicide* (eds A. T. Beck, H. L. P. Resnik & D. J. Lettieri). Bowie, MD: Charles Press.

Beck, A., Kovacs, M. & Weissman, A. (1979) Assessment of suicidal intention: the Scale for Suicide Ideation. *Journal of Consulting and Clinical Psychology*, *47*, 343–352.

Beck, A. T., Steer, R. A., Kovacs, M., *et al.* (1985) Hopelessness and eventual suicide: a 10-year prospective study of patients hospitalized with suicidal ideation. *American Journal of Psychiatry*, *142*, 559–563.

Beck, A. T., Brown, G. & Steer, R. A. (1989a) Prediction of eventual suicide in psychiatric inpatients by clinical ratings of hopelessness. *Journal of Consulting and Clinical Psychology*, *57*, 309–310.

Beck, A. T., Brown G. K. & Steer, R. A. (1997) Psychometric characteristics of the Scale for Suicide Ideation with psychiatric outpatients. *Behaviour Research Therapy*, 11, 1039–1046.

Beck, A., Brown, G., Steer, R. *et al.* (1999) Suicide ideation at its worst point: a predictor of eventual suicide in psychiatric outpatients. *Suicide and Life-Threatening Behavior*, *29*, 1–9.

Bennewith, O., Stocks, N., Gunnell, D., *et al.* (2002) General practice based intervention to prevent repeat episodes of deliberate self-harm: cluster randomised controlled trial. *British Medical Journal*, *324*, 1254–1257.

Bennewith, O., Gunnell, D., Peters, T., *et al.* (2004) Variations in the hospital management of self-harm in adults in England: observational study. *British Medical Journal*, *7448*, 1108–1109.

Bergen, H., Hawton, K., Waters, K., *et al.* (2010a) Epidemiology and trends in non-fatal self-harm in three centres in England: 2000–2007. *British Journal of Psychiatry*, *197*, 493–498.

Bergen, H., Hawton, K., Waters, K., *et al.* (2010b) Psychosocial assessment and repetition of self-harm: the significance of single and multiple repeat episode analyses. *Journal of Affective Disorders*, *127*, 257–265.

Berlin, J. A. (2001) Does blinding of readers affect the results of meta-analyses? *Lancet*, *350*, 185–186.

Berlim, M. T., Perizzolo, J., Lejderman, F., *et al.* (2007) Does a brief training on suicide prevention among general hospital personnel impact their baseline attitudes towards suicidal behaviour? *Journal of Affective Disorders*, *100*, 233–239.

Bille-Brahe, U. & Jessen, G. (1994) Repeated suicidal behavior: a two-year follow-up. *Crisis*, *15*, 77–82.

Birch, S., Cole, S., Hunt, K., *et al.* (2011) Self-harm and the positive risk taking approach. Can being able to think about the possibility of harm reduce the frequency of actual harm? *Journal of Mental Health, 20,* 203–303.

Bisconer, S. & Gross, D. (2007) Assessment of suicide risk in a psychiatric hospital. *Professional Psychology: Research and Practice, 38,* 143–149.

Bjornaas, M. A., Jacobsen, D., Haldorsen, T., *et al.* (2009) Mortality and causes of death after hospital-treated self-poisoning in Oslo: a 20-year follow-up mortality and causes of death after self-poisoning. *Clinical Toxicology, 47,* 116–123.

Blake, D. R. & Mitchell, J. R (1978) Self-poisoning: management of patients in Nottingham, 1976. *British Medical Journal, 1,* 1032.

Bolger, S., O'Connor, P., Malone, K., *et al.* (2004) Adolescents with suicidal behaviour: attendance at A&E at six month follow up. *Irish Journal of Psychiatric Medicine, 21,* 78–84.

Bolton, J., Pagura, J., Enns, M., *et al.* (2010) A population-based longitudinal study of risk factors for suicide attempts in major depressive disorder. *Journal of Psychiatric Research, 44,* 817–826.

Bosman, M. & Meijel, B. (2008) Perspectives of mental health professionals and patients on self-injury in psychiatry: a literature review. *Archives of Psychiatric Nursing, 22,* 180–189.

Botega, N., Silva, S., Reginato, D., *et al.* (2007) Maintained attitudinal changes in nursing personnel after a brief training on suicide prevention. *Suicide and Life Threatening Behaviour, 37,* 145–153.

Boyle, A., Jones, P. & Lloyd, S. (2006). The association between domestic violence and self-harm in emergency medicine patients. *Emergency Medicine Journal, 23,* 604–607.

Brent, D. A., Kolko, D. J., Wartella, M. E. *et al.* (1993) Adolescent psychiatric inpatients' risk of suicide attempt at 6-month follow-up. *Journal of the American Academy of Child and Adolescent Psychiatry, 32,* 95–105.

Brezo, J., Paris, J. & Turecki, G. (2005) Personality traits as correlates of suicidal ideation, suicide attempts, and suicide completions: a systematic review. *Acta Psychiatric Scandinavica, 113,* 180–206.

Briggs, A., Sculpher, M. & Claxton, K. (2006) Making decision models probabilistic. In *Decision Modelling for Health Economic Evaluation* (eds A. Briggs, M. Sculpher & K. Claxton). New York: Oxford University Press.

Brophy, M. (2006) *Truth Hurts: Report of the National Inquiry into Self-harm Among Young People.* London, Mental Health Foundation.

Brown, G. K., Ten Have, T., Henriques, G. R., *et al.* (2005) Cognitive therapy for the prevention of suicide attempts: a randomized controlled trial. *Journal of the American Medical Association, 294,* 563–570.

Buglass, D. & Horton, J. (1974) The repetition of parasuicide: a comparison of three cohorts. *British Journal of Psychiatry, 125,* 168–174.

Burgess, S., Hawton, K. & Loveday, G. (1998) Adolescents who take overdoses: outcome in terms of changes in psychopathology and the adolescents' attitudes to care and to their overdose. *Journal of Adolescence, 21,* 209–218.

Byford, S., Harrington, R., Torgerson, D., *et al.* (1999) Cost-effectiveness analysis of a home-based social work intervention for children and adolescents who have deliberately poisoned themselves. *British Journal of Psychiatry, 174,* 56–62.

Byford, S., Knapp, M., Greenshields, J., *et al.* (2003) Cost-effectiveness of brief cognitive behaviour therapy versus treatment as usual in recurrent deliberate self-harm: decision-making approach. *Psychological Medicine, 33,* 977–986.

Byford, S., Barrett, B., Harrington, V., *et al.* (2009) Lifetime and current costs of supporting young adults who deliberately poisoned themselves in childhood and adolescence. *Journal of Mental Health, 18,* 297–306.

Byrne, S., Morgan, S., Fitzpatrick, C., *et al.* (2008) Deliberate self-harm in children and adolescents: a qualitative study exploring the needs of parents and carers. *Clinical Child Psychology and Psychiatry, 13,* 493–504.

Bywaters, P. & Rolfe, A. (2002) *Look Beyond the Scars: Understanding and Responding to Self-injury and Self-harm.* London: NCH Action for Children.

Camgan, J. T. (1994) The psychosocial needs of patients who have attempted suicide by overdose. *Journal of Advanced Nursing, 20,* 635–642.

Cardell, R. & Pitula C. R. (1999) Suicidal inpatients' perceptions of therapeutic and nontherapeutic aspects of constant observation. *Psychiatric Services, 50,* 1066–1070.

Carlborg, A., Jokinen, J., Nordstrom, A., *et al.* (2010) Attempted suicide predicts suicide risk in schizophrenia spectrum psychosis. *Nordic Journal of Psychiatry, 64,* 68–72.

Carter, G. L., Clover, K. A., Bryant, J. L., *et al.* (2002) Can the Edinburgh Risk of Repetition Scale predict repetition of deliberate self-poisoning in an Australian clinical setting? *Suicide and Life-Threatening Behavior, 32,* 230–239.

Carter, G. L., Clover, K., Whyte, I. M., *et al.* (2005) Postcards from the EDge project: randomised controlled trial of an intervention using postcards to reduce repetition of hospital treated deliberate self poisoning. *British Medical Journal, 331,* 805–809.

Carter, G. L., Clover, K., Whyte, I. M., *et al.* (2007) Postcards from the EDge: 24-month outcomes of a randomised controlled trial for hospital-treatment self-poisoning. *British Journal of Psychiatry, 191,* 548–553.

Carter, G. L., Willcox, C. H., Lewin, T. J., *et al.* (2010) Hunter DBT project: randomized controlled trial of dialectical behaviour therapy in women with borderline personality disorder. *Australian and New Zealand Journal of Psychiatry, 44,* 162–173.

Cedereke, M. & Öjehagen, A. (2007) Formal and informal help during the year after a suicide attempt: a one-year follow-up. *International Journal of Social Psychiatry, 53,* 419–428.

Cedereke, M., Monti, K. & Ojehagen A. (2002) Telephone contact with patients in the year after a suicide attempt: does it affect treatment attendance and outcome? A randomised controlled study. *European Psychiatry, 17,* 82–91.

Centre for Reviews and Dissemination (2007) *NHS Economic Evaluation Database Handbook.* York: Centre for Reviews and Dissemination, University of York.

Available at: http://www.york.ac.uk/inst/crd/pdf/nhseed-handb07.pdf (accessed 5 October 2011).

Chan, S. W., Chien, W. & Tso, S. (2009) Evaluating nurses' knowledge, attitude and competency after an education programme on suicide prevention. *Nurse Education Today*, *29*, 763–769.

Chandrasekaran, R. & Gnanaselane, J. (2008) Predictors of repeat suicidal attempts after first-ever attempt: a two-year follow-up study. *Hong Kong Journal of Psychiatry*, 18, 131–135.

Chen, V. C. H. (2010) Non-fatal repetition of self-harm: population-based prospective cohort study in Taiwan. *British Journal of Psychiatry*, *196*, 31–35.

Chen, V. C., Tan, H. K., Chen, C. Y., *et al.* (2011) Mortality and suicide after self-harm: community cohort study in Taiwan. *British Journal of Psychiatry*, *198*, 31–36.

Chitsabesan, P., Harrington, R., Harrington, V., *et al.* (2003) Predicting repeat self-harm in children: how accurate can we expect to be? *European Child and Adolescent Psychiatry*, *12*, 23–29.

Christiansen, E. & Jensen, B. F. (2007) Risk repetition of suicide attempt, suicide or all deaths after an episode of attempted suicide: a register-based survival analysis. *Australian and New Zealand Journal of Psychiatry*, *41*, 257–265.

Cipriani, A., Pretty, H., Hawton, K., *et al.* (2005) Lithium in the prevention of suicidal behavior and all-cause mortality in patients with mood disorders: a systematic review of randomized trials. *American Journal of Psychiatry*, *162*, 1805–1819.

Clarke, T., Sherr, L. & Watts, C. (2000) *Young People and Self-harm; Pathways in Care.* Essex: Public Health Research Report No. 140.

Clarke, T., Baker, P., Watts, C. J., *et al.* (2002) Self-harm in adults: a randomised controlled trial of nurse-led case management versus routine care only. *Journal of Mental Health*, *11*, 167–176.

Clarkin, J. F., Levy, K. N., Lenzenweger, M. F., *et al.* (2007) Evaluating three treatments for BPD: a multivariate study. *American Journal of Psychiatry*, *164*, 922–928.

Cochrane Collaboration (2011) *Review Manager (RevMan)* [computer program]. Version 5.0.25 for Windows. Oxford, England. The Cochrane Collaboration.

Cohen, F. & Lazarus, R. S. (1979). Coping with the stresses of illness. In *Health Psychology: A Handbook* (eds G. C. Stone, F. C. Cohen & N. E. Adler), pp. 217–254. London: Jossey-Bass.

Colman, I., Newman, S. C., Schopflocher, D., *et al.* (2004) A multivariate study of predictors of repeat parasuicide. *Acta Psychiatrica Scandinavica*, *109*, 306–312.

Cooke, E. & James, V. (2009) A self-harm training needs assessment of school nurses. *Journal of Child Health Care*, *13*, 260–274.

Cooper, J., Kapur, N., Webb, R., *et al.* (2005) Suicide after deliberate self-harm: a 4-year cohort study. *American Journal of Psychiatry*, *162*, 297–303.

Cooper, J., Husain, N., Webb, R., *et al.* (2006a) Self-harm in the UK: differences between South Asians and Whites in rates, characteristics, provision of service and repetition. *Social Psychiatry and Psychiatric Epidemiology*, *41*, 782–788.

Cooper, J., Kapur, N., Dunning, J., *et al.* (2006b) A clinical tool for assessing risk after self-harm. *Annals of Emergency Medicine, 48*, 459–466.

Cooper, J., Kapur, N. & Mackway-Jones, K. (2007) A comparison between clinicians' assessment and the Manchester Self-Harm Rule: a cohort study. *Emergency Medicine Journal, 24*, 720–721.

Cooper, J., Husain, N., Webb, R., *et al.* (2008) Erratum: Self-harm in the UK: differences between South Asians and Whites in rates, characteristics, provision of service and repetition. *Social Psychiatry and Psychiatric Epidemiology, 43*, 1024.

Cooper, J., Murphy, E. & Webb, R. (2010) Ethnic differences in self-harm, rates, characteristics and service provision: three-city cohort study. *British Journal of Psychiatry, 197*, 212–218.

Corcoran, J., Kelleher, M. J., Keeley, H. S., *et al.* (1997) A preliminary statistical model for identifying repeaters of parasuicide. *Archives of Suicide Research, 3*, 65–74.

Corcoran, J., Mewse, A. & Babiker, G. (2007) The role of women's self-injury support-groups: a grounded theory. *Journal of Community & Applied Social Psychology, 17*, 35–52.

Cotgrove, A., Zirinsky, L., Black, D., *et al.* (1995) Secondary prevention of attempted suicide in adolescence. *Journal of Adolescence, 18*, 569–577.

Craigen, L. & Foster, V. (2009) "It was like a partnership of the two of us against the cutting": investigating the counselling experiences of young adult women who self-injure. *Journal of Mental Health Counselling, 31*, 76–94.

Crawford, M. J., Turnbull, G. & Wessely, S. (1998) Deliberate self harm assessment by accident and emergency staff – an intervention study. *Journal of Accident & Emergency Medicine, 15*, 18–22.

Crawford, M. J., Patton, R., Touquet, R., *et al.* (2004) Screening and referral for brief intervention of alcohol-misusing patients in an emergency department: a pragmatic randomised controlled trial, *The Lancet, 364*, 1334–1339.

Crawford, M. J., Csipke, E., Brown, A., *et al.* (2010) The effect of referral for brief intervention for alcohol misuse on repetition of deliberate self-harm: an exploratory randomized controlled trial. *Psychological Medicine, 40*, 1821–1828.

Crockwell, L. & Burford G. (1995) What makes the difference? Adolescent females' stories about their suicide attempts. *Journal of Child and Youth Care, 10*, 1–14.

Cull, J. G. & Gill, W. S. (1988) *Suicide Probability Scale (SPS) Manual*. Los Angeles: Western Psychological Services.

Curtis, C. (2006) Sexual abuse and subsequent suicidal behaviour: exacerbating factors and implications for recovery. *Journal of Child Sexual Abuse, 15*, 1–21.

Curtis, L. (2009) *Unit Costs of Health and Social Care*. Canterbury: Personal Social Services Research Unit, University of Kent.

Curtis, L. (2010) *Unit Costs of Health and Social Care 2010*. Canterbury: Personal Social Services Research Unit, University of Kent.

David, A. S., Hotopf, M., Moran, P., *et al.* (2010) Mentally disordered or lacking capacity? Lessons for management of serious deliberate self harm. *British Medical Journal, 341*, c4489.

De Leo, D. & Heller, T. S. (2004) Who are the kids who self-harm? An Australian self report school survey. *Medical Journal of Australia*, *181*, 140–144.

De Leo, D., Scocco, P., Marietta, P., *et al.* (1999) Physical illness and parasuicide: evidence from the European Parasuicide Study Interview Schedule. (EPSIS/WHO-EURO). *International Journal of Psychiatry in Medicine*, *29*, 149–163.

Dennis, M., Beach, M., Evans, A., *et al.* (1997) An examination of the accident and emergency management of deliberate self-harm. *Journal of Accident and Emergency Medicine*, *14*, 311–315.

Dennis, M., Wakefield, P., Molloy, C., *et al.* (2005) Self-harm in older people with depression: comparison of social factors, life events and symptoms. *British Journal of Psychiatry*, *186*, 538–539.

Dennis, M. S., Wakefield, P., Molloy, C., *et al.* (2007) A study of self-harm in older people: mental disorder, social factors and motives. *Aging and Mental Health*, *11*, 520–525.

Department of Health (1999) *National Service Framework for Mental Health*. London: Department of Health.

Department of Health (2006) *Our Health, Our Care, Our Say: A New Direction for Community Services*. London: Her Majesty's Stationary Office.

Department of Health (2007) *Best Practice in Managing Risk – Principles and Evidence for Best Practice in The Assessment and Management of Risk to Self and Others in Mental Health Services*. London: Department of Health.

Dieserud, G., Loeb, M. & Ekeberg, O. (2000) Suicidal behavior in the municipality of Baerum, Norway: a 12-year prospective study of parasuicide and suicide. *Suicide and Life-Threatening Behavior*, *30*, 61–73.

Dieserud, G., Roysamb, E., Braverman, M., *et al.* (2003) Predicating repetition of suicide attempt: a prospective study of 50 suicide attempters. *Archives of Suicide Research*, *7*, 1–15.

Dimigen, C., Del Priore, C., Butler, S., *et al.* (1999) 'Psychiatric disorder among children at time of entering local authority care: questionnaire survey'. *British Medical Journal, 319*, 7211.

Doering, S. H., Horz, S., Rentrop, M., *et al.* (2010) Transference-focused psychotherapy versus treatment by community psychotherapists for borderline personality disorder: randomised controlled trial. *British Journal of Psychiatry*, *196*, 389–395.

Donaldson, D., Spirito, A. & Esposito-Smythers, C. (2005) Treatment for adolescents following a suicide attempt: results of a pilot trial. *Journal of the American Academy of Child & Adolescent Psychiatry*, *44*, 113–120.

Dorer, C., Feehan, C., Vostanis, P., *et al.* (1999) The overdose process: adolescents' experience of taking an overdose and their contact with services. *Journal of Adolescence*, *22*, 413–417.

Dower, J., Donald, M., Kelly, B., *et al.* (2000) *Pathways to Care for Young People who Present for Non-fatal Deliberate Self-harm*. Queensland: School of Population Health, University of Queensland.

Draper, B. (1996) Attempted suicide in old age. *International Journal of Geriatric Psychiatry*, *11*, 577–587.

References

Dubois, L., Walter, M., Bleton, L., *et al.* (1999) Comparative assessment and a prospective protocol support for specific youth suicide attempters: analysis of the initial psychiatric diagnosis, patient compliance and recurrence rate for a year (preliminary results). [Evaluation comparative et prospective d'un protocole de prise en charge specifique de jeunes suicidants: analyse du diagnostic psychiatrique initial, de l'observance therapeutique et du taux de recidive a un an (resultats preliminaires).] *Annales Medico-Psychologiques, 157*, 557–561.

Duperouzel, H. & Fish, R. (2007) Why couldn't I stop her? Self injury: the views of staff and clients in a medium secure unit. *British Journal of Learning Disabilities, 36*, 59–65.

Eccles, M., Freemantle, N. & Mason, J. (1998) North of England evidence based guideline development project: methods of developing guidelines for efficient drug use in primary care. *British Medical Journal, 316*, 1232–1235.

Evans, E., Hawton, K. & Rodham, K. (2005) Suicidal phenomena and abuse in adolescents: a review of epidemiological studies. *Child Abuse and Neglect, 29*, 45–58.

Evans, K., Tyrer, P., Catalan, J., *et al.* (1999b) Manual-assisted cognitive-behaviour therapy (MACT): a randomized controlled trial of a brief intervention with bibliotherapy in the treatment of recurrent deliberate self-harm. *Psychological Medicine, 29*, 19–25.

Evans, M. O., Morgan, H. G., Hayward, A., *et al.* (1999a) Crisis telephone consultation for deliberate self-harm patients: effects on repetition. *British Journal of Psychiatry, 175*, 23–27.

Fergusson, D., Doucette, S., Glass, K. C., *et al.* (2005) Association between suicide attempts and selective serotonin reuptake inhibitors: systematic review of randomised controlled trials. *British Medical Journal, 330*, 396–399.

Field, P. A. & Morse, J. M. (1991) *Nursing Research: the Application of Qualitative Approaches.* Beckenham, Kent: Croom Helm.

Fish, R. & Duperouzel, H. (2008) 'Just another day dealing with wounds': self-injury and staff-client relationships. *Learning Disability Practice, 11*, 12–15.

Fleischmann, A., Bertolote, J. M., Wasserman, D., *et al.* (2008) Effectiveness of brief intervention and contact for suicide attempters: a randomized controlled trial in five countries. *Bulletin of the World Health Organisation, 86*, 703–709.

Fliege, H., Lee, J.-R., Grimm, A., *et al.* (2009) Risk factors and correlates of deliberate self-harm behaviour: a systematic review. *Journal of Psychosomatic Review, 66*, 477–493.

Fortune, S., Sinclair, J. & Hawton, K. (2008) Adolescents' views on preventing self-harm. *Social Psychiatry and Psychiatric Epidemiology, 43*, 96–104.

Friedman, T., Newton, C., Coggan, C., *et al.* (2006) Predictors of A&E staff attitudes to self-harm patients who use self-laceration: Influence of previous training and experience. *Journal of Psychosomatic Research, 60*, 273.

Furukawa, T. A., Barbui, C., Cipriani, A., *et al.* (2006) Imputing missing standard deviations in meta-analyses can provide accurate results. *Journal of Clinical Epidemiology, 59*, 7–10.

Gairin, I., House, A. & Owens, D. (2003) Attendance at the accident and emergency department in the year before suicide: retrospective study. *British Journal of Psychiatry*, *183*, 28–33.

Galfavy, H. C., Oquendo, M. A. & Mann, J. J. (2008) Evaluation of clinical prognostic models for suicide attempts after a major depressive episode. *Acta Psychiatrica Scandinavica*, *117*, 244–252.

Gask, L., Dixon, C., Morriss, R., *et al.* (2006) Evaluating STORM skills training for managing people at risk of suicide. *Journal of Advanced Nursing*, *54*, 739–750.

Gask, L., Lever-Green, G. & Hays, R. (2008) Dissemination and implementation of suicide prevention training in one Scottish region. *BMC Health Services Research*, *8*, 1–13.

Gates, B. (2003) Self-injurious Behaviour. In *Learning Disabilities: Toward Inclusion* (4th edn) (ed. B. Gates). London: Churchill Livingstone.

General Medical Council (2009) *Confidentiality.* London: General Medical Council. Available at: http://www.gmc-uk.org/static/documents/content/Confidentiality_0910.pdf (accessed 5 October 2011).

Gibb, S. J., Beautrais, A. L. & Surgenor, L. J. (2010) Health-care staff attitudes towards self-harm patients. *Australian and New Zealand Journal of Psychiatry*, *44*, 713–720.

Gibbons, J. S., Butler, J., Urwin, P., *et al.* (1978) Evaluation of a social work service for self-poisoning patients. *British Journal of Psychiatry*, *133*, 111–118.

Glassman, L. H., Weierich, M. R., Hooley, J. M., *et al.* (2007). Child maltreatment, non-suicidal self-injury and the mediating role of self-criticism. *Behaviour, Research & Therapy*, *45*, 2483–2490.

Gordon, K. H., Selby, E. A., Anestis, M. D., *et al.* (2010) The reinforcing properties of repeated deliberate self-harm. *Archives of Suicide Research*, *14*, 329–341.

GRADE Working Group (2004) Grading quality of evidence and strength of recommendations. *British Medical Journal*, *328*, 1490–1497.

Gratz, K. (2003) Risk factors for and functions of deliberate self-harm: an empirical and conceptual review. *Clinical Psychology*, *10*, 192–205.

Gratz, K. L. & Gunderson, J. G. (2006) Preliminary data on an acceptance-based emotion regulation group intervention for deliberate self-harm among women with borderline personality disorder. *Behavior Therapy*, *37*, 25–35.

Green, J., Wood, A., Kerfoot, M., *et al.* (2011) Group therapy treatment for adolescents with repeated self-harm: a randomised controlled trial with economic evaluation. *British Medical Journal*, *342*, d682.

Groholt, B., Ekeberg, O. & Haldorsen, T. (2006) Adolescent suicide attempters: what predicts future suicidal acts? *Suicide and Life-Threatening Behavior*, *36*, 638–650.

Gunnell, D., Hawton, K., Ho, D., *et al.* (2008) Hospital admissions for self-harm after discharge from psychiatric inpatient care: cohort study, *British Medical Journal*, *337*, 1–7.

Guthrie, E., Kapur, N., Kway-Jones, K., *et al.* (2001) Randomised controlled trial of brief psychological intervention after deliberate self poisoning. *British Medical Journal*, *323*, 135–138.

Hallahan, B., Hibbeln, R. J., Davis, J. M., *et al.* (2007) Omega-3 fatty acid supplementation in patients with recurrent self-harm: single-centre double-blind randomised controlled trial. *British Journal of Psychiatry, 190,* 118–122.

Hamilton, M. (1960) A rating scale for depression. *Journal of Neurology, Neurosurgery, and Psychiatry, 23,* 56–62.

Harrington, R., Kerfoot, M., Dyer, E., *et al.* (1998) Randomized trial of a home-based family intervention for children who have deliberately poisoned themselves. *Journal of the American Academy of Child & Adolescent Psychiatry, 37,* 512–518.

Harris, J. (2000) Self-harm: cutting the bad out of me. *Qualitative Health Research, 10,* 164–173.

Harriss, L. & Hawton, K. (2005a) Suicidal intent in deliberate self-harm and the risk of suicide: the predictive power of the Suicide Intent Scale. *Journal of Affective Disorders,* 86, 225–233.

Harriss, L., Hawton, K. & Zahl, D. (2005b) Value of measuring suicidal intent in the assessment of people attending hospital following self-poisoning or self-injury. *British Journal of Psychiatry, 186,* 60–66.

Haukka, J., Arffman, M., Partonen, T., *et al.* (2009) Antidepressant use and mortality in Finland: A register-linkage study from a nationwide cohort. *European Journal of Clinical Pharmacology, 65,* 715–720.

Haw, C. & Hawton, K. (2008) Life problems and deliberate self-harm: associations with gender, age, suicidal intent, psychiatric and personality disorder. *Journal of Affective Disorders, 109,* 139–148.

Haw, C., Hawton, K., Houston, K., *et al.* (2001) Psychiatric and personality disorders in deliberate self-harm patients. *British Journal of Psychiatry, 178,* 48–54.

Haw, C., Bergen, H., Casey, D., *et al.* (2007) Repetition of deliberate self-harm: a study of the characteristics and subsequent deaths in patients presenting to a general hospital according to extent of repetition. *Suicide and Life-Threatening Behavior, 37,* 379–396.

Hawton, K. (2002) United Kingdom legislation on pack sizes of analgesics: background, rationale, and effects on suicide and deliberate self-harm. *Suicide and Life-Threatening Behavior, 32,* 223–229.

Hawton, K. & Fagg, J. (1988) Suicide and other causes of death following attempted suicide. *British Journal of Psychiatry, 152,* 359–366.

Hawton, K. & Fagg, J. (1992) Deliberate self-poisoning and self-injury in adolescents. a study of characteristics and trends in Oxford, 1976–89. *British Journal of Psychiatry, 161,* 816–823.

Hawton, K. & Fagg, J. (1995) Repetition of attempted suicide: the performance of the Edinburgh predictive scales in patients in Oxford. *Archives of Suicide Research, 1,* 261–272.

Hawton, K. & Harriss, L. (2006) Deliberate self-harm in people aged 60 years and over: characteristics and outcome of a 20-year cohort. *International Journal of Geriatric Psychiatry, 21,* 578–581.

Hawton, K. & Harriss, L. (2008a) The changing gender ratio in occurrence of deliberate self-harm across the lifecycle. *Crisis, 29,* 4–10.

Hawton, K. & Harriss, L. (2008b) Deliberate self-harm by under-15-year-olds: characteristics, trends and outcome. *Journal of Child Psychology & Psychiatry & Allied Disciplines, 49*, 441–448.

Hawton, K. & Rodham, K. (2006) *By Their Own Hand: Deliberate Self-Harm and Suicidal Ideas in Adolescents.* London: Jessica Kingsley.

Hawton, K., Gath, D. & Smith, E. (1979) Management of attempted suicide in Oxford. *British Medical Journal, 2*, 1040–1042.

Hawton, K., Bancroft, J., Catalan, J., *et al.* (1981) Domiciliary and out-patient treatment of self-poisoning patients by medical and non-medical staff. *Psychological Medicine, 11*, 169–177.

Hawton, K., McKeown, S., Day, A., *et al.* (1987) Evaluation of out-patient counselling compared with general practitioner care following overdoses. *Psychological Medicine, 17*, 751–761.

Hawton, K., Fagg, J., Simkin, S., *et al.* (1997) Trends in deliberate self-harm in Oxford, 1985–1995. Implications for clinical services and the prevention of suicide. University Department of Psychiatry, Warneford Hospital, Oxford. *British Journal of Psychiatry, 171*, 556–560.

Hawton, K., Rodham, K., Evans, E., *et al.* (2002) Deliberate self-harm in adolescents: sclf report survey in schools in England. *British Medical Journal, 325*, 1207–1211.

Hawton, K., Harriss, L., Hall, S., *et al.* (2003a) Deliberate self-harm in Oxford, 1990–2000: a time of change in patient characteristics. *Psychological Medicine, 33*, 987–995.

Hawton, K., Zahl, D. & Weatherall, R. (2003b) Suicide following deliberate self-harm: long term follow-up of patients who presented to a general hospital. *British Journal of Psychiatry, 182*, 537–542.

Hawton, K., Bergen, H., Cassey, D., *et al.* (2007) Self-harm in England: a tale of three cities: multicentre study of self-harm. *Social Psychiatry and Psychiatric Epidemiology, 42*, 513–521.

Hawton, K., Bergen, H., Simkin, S., *et al.* (2009) Effect of withdrawal of co-proxamol on prescribing and deaths from drug poisoning in England and Wales: time series analysis. *British Medical Journal, 338*, 2270.

Hawton, K., Bergen, H., Simkin, S., *et al.* (2010) Toxicity of antidepressants: rates of suicide relative to prescribing and non-fatal overdose. *British Journal of Psychiatry, 196*, 354–358.

Hawton, K. K. E., Townsend, E., Arensman, E., *et al.* (2011) Psychosocial and pharmacological treatments for deliberate self harm. *Cochrane Database of Systematic Reviews* published online 21 January 2009, DOI: 10.1002/14651858.CD001764.

Hazell, P. L., Martin, G., McGill, K., *et al.* (2009) Group therapy for repeated deliberate self-harming adolescents: failure of replication of a randomized trial. *Journal of the American Academy of Child and Adolescent Psychiatry, 48*, 662–670.

Heath, N., Toste, J., Nedecheva, T., *et al.* (2008) An examination of nonsuicidal self-injury among college students. *Journal of Mental Health Counseling, 30*, 137–156.

Hickey, L., Hawton, K., Fagg, J., *et al.* (2001) Deliberate self-harm patients who leave the accident and emergency department without a psychiatric assessment: a neglected population at risk of suicide. *Journal of Psychosomatic Research, 50,* 87–93.

Higgins, J. P. T. & Thompson, S. G. (2002) Quantifying heterogeneity in a meta-analysis. *Statistics in Medicine, 21,* 1539–1558.

Higgins, J. P. T. & Green, S. (eds) (2009) *Cochrane Handbook for Systematic Reviews of Interventions.* Version 5.0.2 [updated September 2009]. The Cochrane Collaboration, 2009. Available from: www.cochrane-handbook.org

Hirsch, S., Walsh, C. & Draper, R. (1982) Parasuicide: a review of treatment interventions. *Journal of Affective Disorders, 4,* 299–311.

Hjelmeland, H., Hawton, K., Nordvik, H., *et al.* (2002) Why people engage in parasuicide: a cross-cultural study of intentions. *Suicide and Life-Threatening Behavior, 32,* 380–393.

HMSO (1983) *The Mental Health Act 1983.* London: the Stationery Office. Available from: http://www.opsi.gov.uk/acts/acts1983/pdf/ukpga_19830020_en.pdf

HMSO (1989) *The Children Act 1989.* London: The Stationery Office. Available from: http://www.opsi.gov.uk/acts/acts1989/Ukpga_19890041_en_1.htm

HMSO (2004) *The Children Act 2004.* London: The Stationery Office. Available from: http://www.opsi.gov.uk/acts/acts2004/pdf/ukpga_20040031_en.pdf

HMSO (2005) *The Mental Capacity Act 2005.* London: the Stationery Office. Available from: http://www.opsi.gov.uk/acts/acts2005/ukpga_20050009_en_1

HMSO (2007a) *The Mental Health Act 2007.* London: The Stationery Office. Available from: http://www.opsi.gov.uk/acts/acts2007/pdf/ukpga_20070012_en.pdf

HMSO (2007b) *The Mental Capacity Act Code of Practice.* London: The Stationary Office. Available from: http://www.dh.gov.uk/en/Publicationsandstatistics/Publications/PublicationsPolicyAndGuidance/DH_084597

HMSO (2008) Code of Practice: Mental Health Act 1983 amended 2008. London: The Stationary Office. Available from: http://www.dh.gov.uk/cn/Publicationsandstatistics/Publications/PublicationsPolicyAndGuidance/DH_084597

Holdsworth, N., Belshaw, D. & Murray, S. (2001) Developing A&E nursing responses to people who deliberately self-harm: the provision and evaluation of a series of reflective workshops. *Journal of Psychiatric Mental Health Nursing, 8,* 449–458.

Holley, H. L., Fick, G. & Love, E. J. (1998) Suicide following an inpatient hospitalization for a suicide attempt: a Canadian follow-up study. *Social Psychiatry and Psychiatric Epidemiology, 33,* 543–551.

Holma, K., Melartin, T., Haukka, J., *et al.* (2010) Incidence and predictors of suicide attempts in DSM-IV major depressive disorder: a five-year prospective study. *American Journal of Psychiatry, 167,* 801–808.

Hood, A. (2006) *Improving Outcomes for Suicidal Individuals.* PhD. Thesis, University of Auckland, Department of Psychology, Auckland.

Hopkins, C. (2002) But what about the really ill, poorly people? (An ethnographic study into what it means to nurses on medical admissions units to have people who have harmed themselves as patients). *Journal of Psychiatric and Mental Health Nursing, 9,* 147–154.

Horne, O. & Csipke, E. (2009) From feeling too little and too much, to feeling more and less? A nonparadoxical theory of the functions of self-harm. *Qualitative Health Research*, *5*, 655–667.

Horrocks, J., Price, S., House, A., *et al.* (2003) Self-injury attendances in the accident and emergency department: clinical database study. *British Journal of Psychiatry*, *183*, 34–39.

Horrocks, J., Hughes, J., Martin, C., *et al.* (2005) *Patient Experiences of Hospital Care Following Self-harm – A Qualitative Study*. University of Leeds: Academic Unit of Psychiatry and Behavioural Sciences.

Huband, N. & Tantam, D. (2004) Repeated self-wounding: women's recollection of pathways to cutting and of the value of different interventions. *Psychology and Psychotherapy: Theory, Research and Practice*, *77*, 413–428.

Hulten, A., Jiang, G. X., Wasserman, D., *et al.* (2001) Repetition of attempted suicide among teenagers in Europe: Frequency, timing and risk factors. *European Child and Adolescent Psychiatry*, *10*, 161–169.

Hume, M. & Platt, S. (2007) Appropriate interventions for the prevention and management of self-harm: a qualitative exploration of service-users' views. *BMC Public Health*, *7*, 1–9.

Hunter, C. & Cooper, J. (unpublished) *A qualitative investigation into the lived experience of psychosocial assessment following self-harm.* Ph. D. University of Manchester.

Husain, M. I., Waheed, W. & Husain, N. (2006) Self-harm in British South Asian women: psychosocial correlates and strategies for prevention. *Annals of General Psychiatry*, *5*, 7.

Jadad, A. R., Moore, R. A., Carroll, D., *et al.* (1996) Assessing the quality of reports of randomised clinical trials: is blinding necessary? *Controlled Clinical Trials*, *17*, 1–12.

James, M. & Warner, S. (2005) Coping with their lives – women, learning disabilities, self-harm and the secure unit: a Q-methodological study. *British Journal of Learning Disabilities*, *33*, 120–127.

Jeffery, D. & Warm, A. (2002) A study of service providers' understanding of self-harm. *Journal of Mental Health*, *11*, 295–303.

Johnsson, F., Ojehagen, A. & Traskman-Bendz, L. (1996) A 5-year follow-up study of suicide attempts. *Acta Psychiatrica Scandinavica*, *93*, 151–157.

Johnston, A., Cooper, J., Webb, R., *et al.* (2006) Individual- and area-level predictors of self-harm repetition. *British Journal of Psychiatry*, *189*, 416–421.

Kapur, N., House, A., Creed, F., *et al.* (1998) Management of deliberate self poisoning in adults in four teaching hospitals. *British Medical Journal*, *316*, 831–832.

Kapur, N., House, A., Creed, F., *et al.* (1999) General hospital services for deliberate self-poisoning: an ex pensive road to nowhere? *Postgraduate Medical Journal*, *75*, 599–602.

Kapur, N., House, A., Dodgson, K., *et al.* (2002) Does the general hospital management of deliberate self-poisoning make a difference to outcome? A cohort study. *British Medical Journal*, *325*, 866–867.

Kapur, N., House, A., May, C., *et al.* (2003) Service provision and outcome for deliberate self-poisoning in adults. *Social Psychiatry and Psychiatric Epidemiology, 38,* 390–395.

Kapur, N., Cooper, J., Rodway, C., *et al.* (2005) Predicting the risk of repetition after self-harm: cohort study. *British Medical Journal, 330,* 394–395.

Kapur, N., Cooper, J., King-Hele, S., *et al.* (2006) The repetition of suicidal behavior: a multicenter cohort study. *Journal of Clinical Psychiatry, 67,* 1599–1609.

Kapur, N., Murphy, E., Cooper, J., *et al.* (2008) Psychosocial assessment following self-harm: results from the multi-centre monitoring of self-harm project. *Journal of Affective Disorders, 106,* 285–293.

Kapur, N., Cooper, J., Bennewith O., *et al.* (2010a) Postcards, green cards and telephone calls: therapeutic contact with individuals following self-harm. *British Journal of Psychiatry, 197,* 5–7.

Kapur, N., Clements, C., Bateman, N., *et al.* (2010b) Advance directives and suicidal behaviour. *British Medical Journal, 341,* c4557.

Keene, J. (2005) A cross sectional study of assessed need and multiple service use among a self harm population: informing the development of inter-agency integrated care. *International Journal of Integrated Care, 5,* 1–6.

Kibler, J. (2009) Self-injury in the schools: an exploratory analysis of Midwest school counsellors' knowledge and experience. *North American Journal of Psychology, 11,* 309–322.

Kim, Y. S., Koh, Y. J., Leventhal, B. (2005) School bullying and suicidal risk in Korean middle school students. *Pediatrics, 115,* 357–363.

King, M., Semlyen, J., Tai, S. S., *et al.* (2008). A systematic review of mental disorder, suicide and deliberate self-harm in lesbian, gay and bisexual people. *BioMed Central Psychiatry, 8,* 70.

Klomek, A. B., Marrocco, F., Kleinman., M., *et al.* (2007) Bullying, depression, and suicidality in adolescents. *Journal of the American Academy of Child & Adolescent Psychiatry, 46,* 40–49.

Klomek, A. B., Sourander, A., Niemelä, S., *et al.* (2009) Childhood bullying behaviours as a risk for severe suicide attempts and completed suicides. *Journal of the American Academy of Child & Adolescent Psychiatry, 46,* 40–49.

Klomek, A. B., Sourander, A. & Gould, M. (2010) The association of suicide and bullying in childhood to young adulthood: a review of cross-sectional and longitudinal research findings. *Canadian Journal of Psychiatry, 55,* 282–288.

Klonsky, D., Moyer, A. (2008) Childhood sexual abuse and non-suicidal self-injury: meta-analysis. *British Journal of Psychiatry, 192,* 166–170.

Kokaliari, E. & Berzoff, J. (2008) Nonsuicidal self-injury among nonclinical college women: lessons from Foucault. *Affilia: Journal of Women & Social Work, 23,* 259–269.

Kool, N., van Meijel, B. & Bosman, M. (2009) Behavioral change in patients with severe self-injurious behavior: a patient's perspective. *Archives of Psychiatric Nursing, 23,* 25–31.

Koons, C. R., Robins, C. J., Tweed, J. L., *et al.* (2001) Efficacy of dialectical behavior therapy in women veterans with borderline personality disorder. *Behavior Therapy*, *32*, 371–390.

Krarup, G., Nielsen, B., Rask, P., *et al.* (1991) Childhood experiences and repeated suicidal behavior. Acta Psychiatrica Scandinavica, 83, 16–19.

Kreitman, N. (ed.) (1977) *Parasuicide*. London: Wiley.

Kreitman, N. & Chowdhury, N. (1973) Distress behaviour: a study of selected Samaritan clients and parasuicides ('attempted suicide' patients): Part II: attitudes and choice of action. *British Journal of Psychiatry*, *123*, 9–14.

Kreitman, N. & Foster, J. (1991) The construction and selection of predictive scales, with special reference to parasuicide. *British Journal of Psychiatry*, *159*, 185–192.

Lamprecht, H. C., Pakrasi, S., Gash, A., *et al.* (2005) Deliberate self-harm in older people revisited International. *Journal of Geriatric Psychiatry*, *20*, 1090–1096.

Lauterbach, E., Felber, W., Müller-Oerlinghausen, B., *et al.* (2008) Adjunctive lithium treatment in the prevention of suicidal behaviour in depressive disorders: a randomised, placebo-controlled, 1-year trial. *Acta Psychiatrica Scandinavica*, *118*, 469–479.

Law, G. U., Rostill-Brookes, H. & Goodman, D. (2009) Public stigma in health and non-healthcare students: attributions, emotions and willingness to help with adolescent self-harm. *International Journal of Nursing Studies*, *46*, 309–322.

Lesniak, R. G. (2010) The lived experience of adolescent females who self-injure by cutting. *Advanced Emergency Nursing Journal*, *32*, 137–147.

Lewis, S. P. & Darcy, A. S. (2010) Self-harm reasons, goal achievement, and prediction of future self-harm intent. *The Journal of Nervous and Mental Disease*, *198*, 362–369.

Liberman, R. P. & Eckman, T. (1981) Behavior therapy versus insight-oriented therapy for repeated suicide attempters. *Archives of General Psychiatry*, *38*, 1126–1130.

Lilley, R., Owens, D., Horrocks, J., *et al.* (2008a) Methods of self-harm: a multi-centre comparison of episodes of poisoning and injury. *British Journal of Psychiatry*, 192, 440–445.

Lilley, R., Owens, D., Horrocks, J., *et al.* (2008b) Hospital care and repetition following self-harm: multicentre comparison of self-poisoning and self-injury. *British Journal of Psychiatry*, *192*, 440–445.

Lindgren, B.-M., Astrom, S. & Graneheim, U. H. (2010) Help to ransom: parents of self-harming adults describe their lived experience of professional care and caregivers. *International Journal of Qualitative Studies of Health and Well-being*, *5*, 1–10.

Linehan, M. M. (1981) The *Suicidal Behaviours Questionnaire (SBQ)*. Unpublished instrument, University of Washington, Seattle.

Linehan, M. M. (1993) *Cognitive-Behavioural Treatment of Borderline Personality Disorder.* New York: Guilford.

Linehan, M. M., Goodstein, J. L., Nielsen, S. L., *et al.* (1983) Reasons for staying alive when you are thinking of killing yourself: the reasons for living inventory. *Journal of Consulting and Clinical Psychology*, *51*, 276–286.

Linehan, M. M., Armstrong, H. E., Suarez, A., *et al.* (1991) Cognitive-behavioral treatment of chronically parasuicidal borderline patients. *Archives of General Psychiatry, 48,* 1060–1064.

Linehan, M. M., Schmidt, H., Dimeff, L. A., *et al.* (1999) Dialectical behavior therapy for patients with borderline personality disorder and drug-dependence. *American Journal on Addictions, 8,* 279–292.

Linehan, M. M., Dimeff, L. A., Reynolds, S. K., *et al.* (2002) Dialectical behavior therapy versus comprehensive validation therapy plus 12-step for the treatment of opioid dependent women meeting criteria for borderline personality disorder. *Drug and Alcohol Dependence, 67,* 13–26.

Linehan, M. M., Comtois, K. A., Murray, A. M., *et al.* (2006) Two-year randomized controlled trial and follow-up of dialectical behavior therapy vs therapy by experts for suicidal behaviors and borderline personality disorder. *Archives of General Psychiatry, 63,* 757–766.

Livesey, A. (2009) Self-harm in adolescent in-patients. *Psychiatric Bulletin, 33,* 10–12.

Long, M. & Jenkins, M. (2010) Counsellors' perspectives on self-harm and the role of the therapeutic relationship for working with clients who self-harm. *Counselling and Psychotherapy Research, 10,* 192–200.

Lonnqvist, J. & Ostamo, A. (1991) Suicide following the first suicide attempt. a five-year follow-up using a survival analysis. *Psychiatria Fennica, 22,* 171–179.

Lonnqvist, J. & Suokas-Muje, J. (1986) Staff's attitudes toward patients who attempt suicide. *Crisis, 7,* 47–53.

Mackay, N. & Barrowclough, C. (2005) Accident and emergency staff's perceptions of deliberate self-harm: attributions, emotions and willingness to help. *British Journal of Clinical Psychology, 44,* 255–267.

MacLeod, A. K., Pankhania, B., Lee, M., *et al.* (1997) Parasuicide, depression and anticipation of positive and negative future experiences. *Psychological Medicine, 27,* 973–977.

Madge, N., Hewitt, A., Hawton, K., *et al.* (2008) Deliberate self-harm within an international community sample of young people: comparative findings from the Child & Adolescent Self-harm in Europe (CASE) Study. *Journal of Child Psychology and Psychiatry, 49,* 667–677.

Mann, T. (1996) *Clinical Guidelines: Using Clinical Guidelines to Improve Patient Care Within the NHS.* London: Department of Health.

May, V. (2001) Attitudes to patients who present with suicidal behaviour. *Emergency Nurse, 9,* 26–32.

McAllister, M. & Walsh, K. (2003) CARE: a framework for mental health practice. *Journal of Psychiatric and Mental Health Nursing, 10,* 39–48.

McAllister, M., Moyle, W., Billet, S., *et al.* (2009) 'I can actually talk to them now': qualitative results of an educational intervention for emergency nurses caring for clients who self-injure. *Journal of Clinical Nursing, 18,* 2838–2845.

McAuliffe, N. & Perry, L. (2007) Making it safer: a health centre's strategy for suicide prevention. *Psychiatric Quarterly, 78,* 295–307.

McAuliffe, C., Corcoran, P., Keeley, H., *et al.* (2006) Problem-solving ability and repetition of deliberate self-harm: a multicentre study. *Psychological Medicine*, *36*, 45–55.

McAuliffe, C., Corcoran, P., Hickey, P., *et al.* (2008) Optional thinking ability among hospital-treated deliberate self-harm patients: a 1-year follow-up study. *British Journal of Clinical Psychology*, *47*, 43–58.

McDonald, G., O''Brien, L. & Jackson, D. (2007) Guilt and shame: experiences of parents of self-harming adolescents. *Journal of Child Health Care*, *11*, 298–310.

McHale, J. & Felton, A. (2010) Self-harm: what's the problem? A literature review of the factors affecting attitudes towards self-harm. *Journal of Psychiatric and Mental Health Nursing*, *17*, 732–740.

McLean, J., Maxwell, M., Platt, S., *et al.* (2008) *Risk and Protective Factors for Suicide and Suicidal Behaviour: a literature review*. ISBN 978 0 7559 7304 0 (Web-only publication). Edinburgh: Scottish Government Social Research. Available from: http://www.scotland.gov.uk/Publications/2008/11/28141444/0

McLeavey, B., Daly, R., Ludgate, J., *et al.* (1994) Interpersonal problem-solving skills training in the treatment of self-poisoning patients. *Suicide and Life-Threatening Behavior*, *24*, 382–394.

McMain, S. F., Links, P. S., Gnam, W. H., *et al.* (2009) A randomized trial of dialectical behavior therapy versus general psychiatric management for borderline personality disorder. *American Journal of Psychiatry*, *166*, 1365–1374.

McManus, S., Meltzer, H., Brugha, T., *et al.* (2009) *Adult Psychiatric Morbidity in England, 2007: Results of a Household Survey*. London: National Centre for Social Research.

Meltzer, H., Harrington, R., Goodman, R., *et al.* (2001) *Children and Adolescents Who Try to Harm, Hurt or Kill Themselves: a Report of Further Analysis from the National Survey of the Mental Health of Children and Adolescents in Great Britain in 1999*. London: Office for National Statistics.

Meltzer, H., Lader, D., Corbin, T., *et al.* (2002) *Non-Fatal Suicidal Behaviour Among Adults aged 16 to 74 in Great Britain*. London: The Stationery Office.

Meltzer, H. Y., Alphs, L., Green, A. I., *et al.* (2003) Clozapine treatment for suicidality in schizophrenia: International Suicide Prevention Trial (InterSePT). *Archives of General Psychiatry*, *60*, 82–91.

Meltzer, H., Vostanis, P., Ford, T., *et al.* (2011) Victims of bullying in childhood and suicide attempts in adulthood. *European Psychiatry*, DOI: 10.1016/j.eurpsy.2010.11.006 (E-published ahead of print 8 February 2011).

Merrill, J., Milner, G., Owens, J., *et al.* (1992) Alcohol and attempted suicide. *British Journal of Addictions*, *87*, 83–89.

Miranda, R., Scott, M., Hicks, R., *et al.* (2008) Suicide attempt characteristics, diagnoses, and future attempts: comparing multiple attempters to single attempters and ideators. *Journal of the American Academy of Child & Adolescent Psychiatry*, *47*, 32–40.

Montgomery, S., Montgomery, D., Jayanthi-Rani, S., *et al.* (1979) Maintenance therapy in repeat suicidal behaviour: a placebo controlled trial. In: *Proceedings of the 10th International Congress for Suicide Prevention and Crisis Intervention.* Ottawa, Canada, pp. 227–229.

Montgomery, S. A., Roy, D. & Montgomery, D. B. (1983) The prevention of recurrent suicidal acts. *British Journal of Clinical Pharmacology, 15*, 183–188.

Morgan, H. G., Burns-Cox, C. J., Pocock, H., *et al.*, (1975) Deliberate self-harm: clinical and socioeconomic characteristics of 368 patients. *British Journal of Psychiatry, 127*, 564–574.

Morgan, H. G., Jones, E. M. & Owen, J. H. (1993) Secondary prevention of non-fatal deliberate self-harm. The green card study. *British Journal of Psychiatry, 163*, 111–112.

Morgan, S. (2004) *Positive Risk-Taking: an Idea Whose Time Has Come.* Brighton: Pavilion Publishing.

Morgan, S. (2007) *Working with Risk – Trainer's Manual.* Brighton: Pavilion Publishing.

Morriss, R., Gask, L., Battersby, L., *et al.* (1999) Teaching front-line health and voluntary workers to assess and manage suicidal patients. *Journal of Affective Disorders, 52*, 77–83.

Morriss, R., Gask, L., Webb, R., *et al.* (2005) The effects on suicide rates of an educational intervention for front-line health professionals with suicidal patients (the STORM Project). *Psychological Medicine, 35*, 957–960.

Moyer, M. & Nelson, K. (2007) Investigating and understanding self-mutilation: the student voice. *Professional School Counselling, 11*, 42–48.

Murphy, E., Dickson, S., Donaldson, I., *et al.* (2007) *Self-harm in Manchester: 1st September 2003 to 31st August 2005.* Manchester: University of Manchester.

Murphy, E., Kapur, N., Webb, R., *et al.* (2011) Risk factors for repetition and suicide following self-harm in older adults: multicentre cohort study. *British Journal of Psychiatry.* Published online ahead of print 8 December, 2011; DOI: 10.1192/bjp.bp.111.094177.

Nada-Raja, S., Morrison, D. & Skegg, K. (2003) A population-based study of help-seeking for self-harm in young adults. *Australian and New Zealand Journal of Psychiatry, 37*, 600–605.

National Institute for Mental Health in England (2003) *Personality Disorder: No Longer a Diagnosis of Exclusion.* Leeds: NIMHE.

National Self Harm Network (2000) *Cutting the Risk: Self-harm, Self-care and Risk-Reduction.* Nottingham: The National Self Harm Network. Available at: http://harm-ed.com/attachments/Cutting_the_Risk.pdf (accessed 7 October 2011).

NCCMH (2004) *Self-harm: the Short-term Physical and Psychological Management and Secondary Prevention of Self-harm in Primary and Secondary Care.* Leicester & London: The British Psychological Society and the Royal College of Psychiatrists. [Full guideline].

NCCMH (2009) *Borderline Personality Disorder: Treatment and Management.* Leicester & London: The British Psychological Society and the Royal College of Psychiatrists. [Full guideline].

NHS Information Centre (2009) *Hospital Episode Statistics HES (Admitted Patient Care) England 2008/09.* London: NHS Information Centre for Health and Social Care. Available from: www.hesonline.nhs.uk

NICE (2004a) *Self-harm: the Short-term Physical and Psychological Management and Secondary Prevention of Self-harm in Primary and Secondary Care.* NICE Clinical Guideline 16. London: NICE.

NICE (2004b; amended 2007) *Depression: Management of Depression in Primary and Secondary Care.* NICE Clinical Guideline 23. London: NICE.

NICE (2004c; amended 2007) *Anxiety: Management of Anxiety (Panic Disorder, with or without Agoraphobia, and Generalised Anxiety Disorder) in Adults in Primary, Secondary and Community Care.* NICE Clinical Guideline 22 (amended). London: NICE.

NICE (2004d) *Eating Disorders: Core Interventions in the Treatment and Management of Anorexia Nervosa, Bulimia Nervosa and Related Eating Disorders.* NICE Clinical Guideline 9. London: NICE.

NICE (2005a) *Depression in Children and Young People: Identification and Management in Primary, Community and Secondary Care.* NICE Clinical Guideline 28. London: NICE.

NICE (2005b) *Obsessive-compulsive Disorder: Core Interventions in the Treatment of Obsessive-compulsive Disorder and Body Dysmorphic Disorder.* NICE Clinical Guideline 31. London: NICE.

NICE (2005c) *Post-traumatic Stress Disorder (PTSD): the Management of PTSD in Adults and Children in Primary and Secondary Care.* NICE Clinical Guideline 26. London: NICE.

NICE (2005d) *Violence: the Short-term Management of Disturbed/Violent Behaviour in Inpatient Settings and Emergency Departments.* NICE Clinical Guideline 25. London: NICE.

NICE (2006) *Bipolar Disorder: the Management of Bipolar Disorder in Adults, Children and Adolescents, in Primary and Secondary Care.* NICE Clinical Guideline 38. London: NICE.

NICE (2007a) *Drug Misuse: Psychosocial Interventions.* NICE Clinical Guideline 51. London: NICE.

NICE (2007b) *Drug Misuse: Opioid Detoxification.* NICE Clinical Guideline 51. London: NICE.

NICE (2008) *Social Value Judgements: Principles for the Development of NICE Guidance* (2nd edition). London: NICE.

NICE (2009a) *Depression: the Treatment and Management of Depression in Adults* NICE Clinical Guideline 90. London: NICE.

NICE (2009b) *Schizophrenia: Core Interventions in the Treatment and Management of Schizophrenia in Primary and Secondary Care.* NICE Clinical Guideline 82. London: NICE.

NICE (2009c) *Depression in Adults with a Chronic Physical Health Problem: Treatment and Management.* NICE Clinical Guideline 91. London: NICE.

NICE (2009d) *The Guidelines Manual.* London: NICE.

NICE (2009e) *Borderline Personality Disorder: Treatment and Management.* Clinical Guideline 78. London: NICE.

NICE (2009f) *Antisocial Personality Disorder: Treatment, Management and Prevention.* NICE Clinical Guideline 77. London: NICE.

NICE (2011a) *Generalised Anxiety Disorder and Panic Disorder (with or without Agoraphobia) in Adults: Management in Primary, Secondary and Community Care.* NICE Clinical Guideline 113. London: NICE.

NICE (2011b) *Alcohol-use Disorders: Diagnosis, Assessment and Management of Harmful Drinking and Alcohol Dependence.* NICE Clinical Guideline 115. London: NICE.

Niméus, A., Träskman-Bendz, L. & Alsen. M. (1997) Hopelessness and suicidal behavior. *Journal of Affective Disorders, 42,* 2–3.

Niméus, A., Alsén, M. & Träskman-Bendz, L. (2000) The Suicide Assessment Scale: an instrument assessing suicide risk of suicide attempters. *European Psychiatry, 15,* 416–423.

Niméus, A., Alsén, M. & Träskman-Bendz, L. (2002) High suicide intent scores indicate future suicide. *Archives of Suicide Research, 6,* 211–219.

Nimeus, A., Hjalmarsson, S. F., Sunnqvist, C., *et al.* (2006) Evaluation of a modified interview version and of a self-rating version of the suicide assessment scale. *European Psychiatry, 21,* 471–477.

Nock, M. K., Borges, G., Bromet, E. J., *et al.* (2008). Cross-national prevalence and risk factors for suicidal ideation, plans and attempts. *British Journal of Psychiatry, 192,* 98–105.

Nordentoft, M., Breum, L., Munck, L. K., *et al.* (1993) High mortality by natural and unnatural causes: a 10 year follow up study of patients admitted to a poisoning treatment centre after suicide attempts. *British Medical Journal, 306,* 1637–1641.

Nordstrom, P., Asberg, M., Berg-Wistedt, A., *et al.* (1995) Attempted suicide predicts suicide risk in mood disorders. *Acta Psychiatrica Scandinavica, 92,* 345–350.

Novakovic, M., Ille, T. & Maric-Tiosavljevic, D. (2006) Forms of parasuicide in young people in Bosnia. *Psychiatria Danubina, 18,* 39–47.

O'Connor, R. C., Rasmussen, S., Miles, J., *et al.* (2009a) Self-harm in adolescents: self-report survey in schools in Scotland. *British Journal of Psychiatry, 194,* 68–72.

O'Connor, R. C., Rasmussen, S. & Hawton, K. (2009b) Predicting deliberate self-harm in adolescents: a six month prospective study. *Suicide and Life-Threatening Behavior, 39,* 364–375.

O'Connor, R.C., Rasmussen, S. & Hawton, K. (2010) Predicting depression, anxiety and self-harm in adolescents: the role of perfectionism and acute life stress. *Behaviour Research and Therapy, 48,* 52–59.

O'Connor, R. C., Ryan, C., Masterton, G., *et al.* (2011a) *The Role of Psychological Factors in Predicting Short-term Outcome Following Suicidal Behaviour.* Final Report CZG/2/449 to Chief Scientist Office, Scotland.

O'Connor, R. C., Rasmussen, S. & Beautrais, A. (2011b) Recognition of suicide risk, crisis helplines and psychosocial interventions: a selective review. In *International Handbook of Suicide Prevention: Research, Policy and Practice* (eds R. C. O'Connor, S. Platt & J Gordon). Chichester: WileyBlackwell.

O'Donovan, A. (2007) Pragmatism rules: the intervention and prevention strategies used by psychiatric nurses working with non-suicidal self-harming individuals. *Journal of Psychiatric and Mental Health Nursing, 14,* 64–71.

Oldershaw, A., Richards, C., Simic, M., *et al.* (2008) Parents' perspectives on adolescent self-harm: qualitative study. *British Journal of Psychiatry, 193,* 140–144.

Oquendo, M. A., Galfalvy, H., Russo, S., *et al.* (2004) Prospective study of clinical predictors of suicidal acts after a major depressive episode in patients with major depressive disorder or bipolar disorder. *American Journal of Psychiatry, 161,* 1433–1441.

Osman, A., Kopper, B., Linehan, M., *et al.* (1999) Validation of the Adult Suicidal Ideation Questionnaire and the Reasons for Living Inventory in an adult psychiatric inpatient sample. *Psychological Assessment, 11,* 115–123.

Osman, A., Bagge, C., Gutierrez, P., *et al.* (2001) The Suicidal Behaviors Questionnaire – Revised (SBQ-R): validation with clinical and nonclinical samples. *Assessment, 8,* 443–454.

Ougrin, D., Zundel, T., Ng, A., *et al.* (2011) Trial of Therapeutic Assessment in London (TOTAL): randomised controlled trial of therapeutic assessment versus standard psychosocial assessment in adolescents presenting with self-harm. *Archives of Disease in Childhood, 96,* 148–153.

Owens, D., Dennis, M., Read, S., *et al.* (1994) Outcome of deliberate self-poisoning: An examination of risk factors for repetition. *British Journal of Psychiatry, 165,* 797–801.

Owens D., Horrocks, J. & House, A. (2002) Fatal and non-fatal repetition of self-harm: systematic review. *British Journal of Psychiatry, 181,* 193–199.

Pallikkathayil, L. & Morgan, S. (1988) Emergency department nurses' encounters with suicide attempters: a qualitative investigation. *Scholarly Inquiry for Nursing Practice, 2,* 237–253.

Palmer, L., Strevens, P., & Blackwell, H. (2006) *Better Services for People who Self-harm: Data Summary - Wave 1 Baseline Data.* London, Royal College of Psychiatrists.

Patsiokas, A. T. & Clum, G. A. (1985) Effects of psychotherapeutic strategies in the treatment of suicide attempters. *Psychotherapy: Theory, Research and Practice, 22,* 281–290.

Patterson, P., Whittington, R. & Bogg, J. (2007) Testing the effectiveness of an educational intervention aimed at changing attitudes to self-harm. *Journal of Psychiatric and Mental Health Nursing, 14,* 100–105.

Pembroke, L. R. (1994) *Self-harm: Perspectives from Personal Experience.* London: Survivors Speak Out.

Pembroke, L. R. (2007) Harm minimisation: limiting the damage of self injury. In *Beyond Fear and Control. Working with Young People who Self-harm* (eds H. Spandler & S. Warner). Ross-on-Wye: PCCS Books.

Pengelly, N. & Ford B. (2005) *Alternatives to Self Harm: service user handbook and guidelines.* Selby and York Primary Care Trust.

Pengelly, N., Ford, B., Blenkiron, P., *et al.* (2008) Harm minimisation after repeated self-harm: development of a trust handbook. *Psychiatric Bulletin, 32,* 60–63.

405

Petrie, K. & Brook, R. (1992) Sense of coherence, self-esteem, depression and hopelessness as correlates of reattempting suicide. *British Journal of Clinical Psychology*, *31*, 293–300.

Pfaff, J. J., Acres, J. G. & McKelvey, R. S. (2001) Training general practitioners to recognise and respond to psychological distress and suicidal ideation in young people. *The Medical Journal of Australia*, *174*, 222–226.

Piacentini, J., Rotherum-Borus, M. J., Gillis, J. R., *et al.* (1995) Demographic predictors of treatment attendance among suicide attempters. *Journal of Consulting & Clinical Psychology*, *63*, 469–473.

Pitula, C. R. & Cardell, R. (1996) Suicidal inpatients' experience of constant observation. *Psychiatric Services*, *47*, 649–651.

Platt, S. & Salter, D. (1987) A comparative investigation of health workers' attitudes towards parasuicide. *Social Psychiatry and Psychiatric Epidemiology*, *22*, 202–208.

Polk, E. & Liss, M. (2009) Exploring the motivations behind self-harm. *Counselling Psychology Quarterly*, *22*, 233–241.

Preuss, U. W., Schuckit, M. A., Smith, T. L., *et al.* (2003) Predictors and correlates of suicide attempts over 5 years in 1,237 alcohol-dependent men and women. *American Journal of Psychiatry*, *160*, 56–63.

Ramon, S., Bancroft, J. & Skrimshire, A. (1975) Attitudes towards self-poisoning among physicians and nurses in a general hospital. *British Journal of Psychiatry*, *127*, 257–264.

Ray, E. (2007) A multidimensional analysis of self-mutilation in college students. *Dissertation Abstracts International: Section B: The Sciences and Engineering*, *68* (9-B), 6331. ISBN: 9780549171522

Redley, M. (2010) The clinical assessment of patients admitted to hospital following an episode of self-harm: a qualitative study. *Sociology of Health and Illness*, *32*, 470–485.

Reece, J. (2005) The language of cutting: initial reflections on a study of the experiences of self-injury in a group of women and nurses. *Issues in Mental Health Nursing*, *26*, 561–574.

Reynolds, W. M. (1991) *Adult Suicide Ideation Questionnaire: Professional Manual.* Odessa, FL: Psychological Assessment Resources, Inc.

Richardson, J. & Lelliott, P. (2003) Mental health of looked after children. *Advances in Psychiatric Treatment*, 9, 249–256.

Rissanen, M. L., Kylma, J. & Laukkanen, E. (2009) Descriptions of self-mutilation among Finnish adolescents: a qualitative descriptive inquiry. *Issues in Mental Health Nursing*, *29*, 145–163.

Roberts-Dobie, S. & Donatelle, R. J. (2007) School counsellors and student self-injury. *Journal of School Health*, *77*, 257–264.

Rogers, J. (2003) Sexual abuse and suicide: why we may not know what we think we know. *Archives of Suicide Research*, *7*, 83–91.

Ross, S. & Heath, N. (2002) A study of the frequency of self-mutilation in a community sample of adolescents. *Journal of Youth and Adolescence*, *31*, 67–77.

Royal College of Psychiatrists (2007) *Evaluating the Benefits and Challenges of the 'Better Services for People who Self-Harm' Programme.* London: Royal College of Psychiatrists.

Runeson, B., Tidemalm, D., Dahlin, M. *et al.* (2010) Method of attempted suicide as predictor of subsequent successful suicide: national long term cohort study. *British Medical Journal, 341*, 3222.

Russell, G., Moss, D. & Miller, J. (2010) Appalling and appealing: a qualitative study of the character of men's self-harm. *Psychology & Psychotherapy: Theory, Research & Practice, 83*, 91–109.

Rygnestad, T. (1997) Mortality after deliberate self-poisoning. a prospective follow-up study of 587 persons observed for 5279 person years: risk factors and causes of death. *Social Psychiatry and Psychiatric Epidemiology, 32*, 443–450.

Salkovskis, P. M., Atha, C. & Storer, D. (1990) Cognitive-behavioural problem solving in the treatment of patients who repeatedly attempt suicide. A controlled trial. *British Journal of Psychiatry, 157*, 871–876.

Samuelsson, M. & Asberg, M. (2002) Training program in suicide prevention for psychiatric nursing personnel enhance attitudes to attempted suicide patients. *International Journal of Nursing Studies, 39*, 115–121.

Sansone, R. A., Chu, J. & Wiederman, M. W. (2007) Self-inflicted bodily harm among victims of intimate-partner violence. *Clinical Psychology & Psychotherapy, 14*, 352–357.

Santos, J., Saraiva, C. & Sousa, L. (2009) The role of expressed emotion, self-concept, coping, and depression in parasuicidal behaviour: a follow-up study. *Archives of Suicide Research, 13*, 358–367.

Saunders, L. & Broad, B. (1997) *The Health Needs of Young People Leaving Care.* Leicester: De Montfort University.

Saunders, K. E. A., Hawton, K., Fortune, S., *et al.* (2011) Attitudes and knowledge of clinical staff regarding people who self-harm: a systematic review. *Journal of Affective Disorders*, (accepted 22 August 2011, available online 16 September 2011; DOI: 10.1016/j.jad.2011.08.024).

Schoppmann, S., Schrock, R., Schnepp, W., *et al.* (2007) "Then I just showed her my arms..." Bodily sensations in moments of alienation related to self injurious behaviour. A hermeneutic phenomenological study. *Journal of Psychiatric and Mental Health Nursing, 14*, 587–597.

Schunemann, H. J., Best, D., Vist, G. *et al.* for the GRADE Working Group (2003) Letters, numbers, symbols and words: how to communicate grades of evidence and recommendations. *Canadian Medical Association Journal, 169*, 677–680.

Scoliers, G., Portzky, G., van Heeringen, K., *et al.* (2009) Sociodemographic and psychopathological risk factors for repetition of attempted suicide: a 5-year follow-up study. *Archives of Suicide Research, 13*, 201–213.

Shaw, S. N. (2006) Certainty, revision, and ambivalence: a qualitative investigation into women's journeys to stop self-injuring. *Women & Therapy, 29*, 153–177.

Shepherd, G., Boardman, J. & Slade, M. (2008) *Making Recovery a Reality.* London: Sainsbury Centre for Mental Health.

References

Sidley, G. L., Calam, R., Wells, A., *et al.* (1999) The prediction of parasuicide repetition in a high-risk group. *British Journal of Clinical Psychology, 38*, 375–386.

Simm, R., Roen, K. & Daiches, A. (2008) Educational professionals' experiences of self-harm in primary school children: 'You don't really believe, unless you see it'. *Oxford Review of Education, 34*, 253–269.

Sinclair, J. & Green, J. (2005) Understanding resolution of deliberate self-harm: qualitative interview study of patients' experiences. *British Medical Journal, 330*, 1112.

Sinclair, J. M., Gray, A. & Hawton, K. (2006) Systematic review of resource utilization in the hospital management of deliberate self-harm. *Psychological Medicine, 36*, 1681–1693.

Sinclair, J. M. A., Gray, A., Rivero-Arias, O., *et al.* (2010a) Healthcare and social services resource use and costs of self-harm patients. *Social Psychiatry and Psychiatry Epidemiology, 46*, 263–271.

Sinclair, J. M. A., Hawton, K. & Gray, A. (2010b) Six year follow-up of a clinical sample of self-harm patients. *Journal of Affective Disorders, 121*, 247–252.

Skegg, K. (2005) Self-harm. *Lancet, 366*, 1471–1483.

Skegg, K., Nada-Raja, S., Dickson, N., *et al.* (2003) Sexual Orientation and Self-Harm in Men and Women. *American Journal of Psychiatry, 160*, 541–546.

Skogman, K., Alsen, M. & Ojehagen, A. (2004) Sex differences in risk factors for suicide after attempted suicide – a follow-up study of 1052 suicide attempters. *Social Psychiatry and Psychiatric Epidemiology, 39*, 113–120.

Slee, N., Garnefski, N., van der Leeden, R., *et al.* (2008) Cognitive-behavioural intervention for self-harm: randomised controlled trial. *British Journal of Psychiatry, 192*, 202–211.

Smith, S. E. (2002) Perceptions of service provision for clients who self-injure in the absence of expressed suicidal intent. *Journal of Psychiatric and Mental Health Nursing, 9*, 595–601.

Sokero, T. P., Melartin, T. K., Rytsala, H. J., *et al.* (2005) Prospective study of risk factors for attempted suicide among patients with DSM-IV major depressive disorder. *British Journal of Psychiatry, 186*, 314–318.

Soloff, P. H. & Fabio, A. (2008) Prospective predictors of suicide attempts in borderline personality disorder at one, two, and two-to-five year follow-up. *Journal of Personality Disorders, 22*, 123–134.

Spirito, A., Boergers, J., Donaldson, D., *et al.* (2002) An intervention trial to improve adherence to community treatment by adolescents after a suicide attempt. *Journal of Child and Adolescent Psychiatry, 41*, 435–442.

Spirito, A., Valeri, S., Boergers, J., *et al.* (2003) Predictors of continued suicidal behaviour in adolescents following a suicide attempt. *Journal of Clinical Child and Adolescent Psychology, 32*, 284–289.

Stanley, B., Träskman-Bendz, L. & Stanley M. (1986) The suicide assessment scale: a scale evaluating change in suicidal behaviour. *Psychopharmacology Bulletin, 1*, 200–205.

408

Stanley, N., Riordan, D. & Alaszewski, H. (2005) The mental health of looked after children: matching response to need. *Health and Social Care in the Community*, *13*, 239–248.

Statham, D. J., Heath, A. C., Madden, P. A., *et al.* (1998) Suicidal behaviour: an epidemiological and genetic study. *Psychological Medicine*, *28*, 839–855.

Steele, M. & Doey, T. (2007) Suicidal behaviour in children and adolescents. Part 1: etiology and risk factors. *The Canadian Journal of Psychiatry*, *52*, 21S–34S.

Stewart, C. D., Quinn, A, Plever, S., *et al.* (2009) Comparing cognitive behavior therapy, problem solving therapy, and treatment as usual in a high risk population. *Suicide and Life-Threatening Behavior*, *39*, 538–547.

Suokas, J. & Lonnqvist, J. (1991) Outcome of attempted suicide and psychiatric consultation: risk factors and suicide mortality during a five-year follow-up. *Acta Psychiatrica Scandinavica*, *84*, 545–549.

Suokas, J., Suominen, K., Isometsa, E., *et al.* (2001) Long-term risk factors for suicide mortality after attempted suicide – findings of a 14-year follow-up study. *Acta Psychiatrica Scandinavica*, *104*, 117–121.

Sutton, J. (2007) *Healing the Hurt Within: Understand Self-injury and Self-harm, and Heal the Emotional Wounds* (revised and updated 3rd edition). Oxford: How To Books.

Taylor, B. (2003) Exploring the perspectives of men who self-harm. *Learning in Health and Social Care*, *2*, 83–91.

Taylor, C., Cooper, J. & Appleby, L. (1999) Is suicide risk taken seriously in heavy drinkers who harm themselves? *Acta Psychiatrica Scandinavica*, *100*, 309–311.

Taylor, T., Hawton, K., Fortune, S., *et al.* (2009) Attitudes towards clinical services among people who self-harm: Systematic review. *British Journal of Psychiatry*, *194*, 104–110.

Thompson, A., Powis, J. & Carradice, A. (2008) Community psychiatric nurses' experience of working with people who engage in deliberate self-harm. *International Journal of Mental Health Nursing*, *17*, 153–161.

Torhorst, A., Möller, H. J., Bürk, F., *et al.* (1987) The psychiatric management of parasuicide patients: a controlled clinical study comparing different strategies of outpatient treatment. *Crisis*, *8*, 53–61.

Torhorst, A., Möller, H. J., Kurz, A., *et al.* (1988) Comparing a 3-month and a 12-month-outpatient aftercare program for parasuicide repeaters. In *Current Issues of Suicidology* (eds H. J. Möller, A. Schmidtke & R. Welz), pp. 419–424. Berlin, Germany: Springer-Verlag.

Treloar, A. J. C. & Lewis, A. J. (2008a) Professional attitudes towards deliberate self-harm in patients with borderline personality disorder. *Australian and New Zealand Journal of Psychiatry*, *42*, 578–584.

Treloar, A. J. C. & Lewis, A. J. (2008b) Targeted clinical education for staff attitudes towards deliberate self-harm in borderline personality disorder: randomized controlled trial. *Australian and New Zealand Journal of Psychiatry*, *42*, 981–988.

Turnbull, G. & Chalder, T. (1997) Effects of education on attitudes to deliberate self-harm. *Psychiatric Bulletin, 21,* 334–335.

Turner, R. M. (2000) Naturalistic evaluation of dialectical behavior therapy-oriented treatment for borderline personality disorder. *Cognitive and Behavioral Practice, 7,* 413–419.

Tyrer, P., Thompson, S., Schmidt, U., *et al.* (2003) Randomized controlled trial of brief cognitive behaviour therapy versus treatment as usual in recurrent deliberate self-harm: the POPMACT study. *Psychological Medicine, 33,* 969–976.

Vaiva, G., Ducrocq, F., Meyer, P., *et al.* (2006) Effect of telephone contact on further suicide attempts in patients discharged from an emergency department: randomised controlled study. *British Medical Journal, 332,* 1241–1245.

Van Aaist, J., Shotts, S., Vitsky, J., *et al.* (1992) Long-term follow-up of unsuccessful violent suicide attempts: risk factors for subsequent attempts. *The Journal of Trauma, 33,* 457–464.

van den Bosch, L. M. C., Verheul, R., Schippers, G. M., *et al.* (2002) Dialectical behavior therapy of borderline patients with and without substance use problems: implementation and long-term effects. *Addictive Behaviors, 27,* 911–923.

van der Sande, R., van Rooijen, L., Buskens, E., *et al.* (1997) Intensive in-patient and community intervention versus routine care after attempted suicide. A randomised controlled intervention study. *British Journal of Psychiatry, 171,* 35–41.

van Heeringen, C., Jannes, S., Buylaert, W., *et al.* (1995) The management of non-compliance with referral to out-patient after-care among attempted suicide patients: a controlled intervention study. *Psychological Medicine, 25,* 963–970.

Verkes, R. J, Van der Mast, R. C., Hengeveld, M. W., *et al.* (1998) Reduction by paroxetine of suicidal behavior in patients with repeated suicide attempts but not major depression. *American Journal of Psychiatry, 55,* 543–547.

Waern, M., Sjöström, T., Marlow, T., *et al.* (2010) Does the Suicide Assessment Scale predict risk of repetition? A prospective study of suicide attempters at a hospital emergency department. *European Psychiatry, 25,* 421–426.

Walker, B. L. & Osgood, N. J. (1996) Preventing suicide and depression: a training program for long-term care staff. *OMEGA – Journal of Death and Dying, 42,* 55–69.

Wang, A. G. & Mortensen, G. (2006) Core features of repeated suicidal behaviour: a long term follow-up after suicide attempts in a low-suicide-incidence population. *Social Psychiatry and Psychiatric Epidemiology, 41,* 103–107.

Waterhouse, J. & Platt, S. (1990) General hospital admission in the management of parasuicide. A randomised controlled trial. *British Journal of Psychiatry, 156,* 236–242.

Weinberg, I., Gunderson, J. G., Hennen, J., *et al.* (2006) Manual assisted cognitive treatment for deliberate self-harm in borderline personality disorder patients. *Journal of Personality Disorders, 20,* 482–492.

Welu, T. (1977) A follow-up program for suicide attempters: evaluation of effectiveness. *Suicide and Life-Threatening Behavior, 7,* 17–30.

Wheatley, M. & Austin-Payne, H. (2009) Nursing staff knowledge and attitudes towards deliberate self-harm in adults and adolescents in an inpatient setting. *Behavioural and Cognitive Psychotherapy, 37,* 293–309.

Whitehead, L. (2002) *Therapeutic Aspects of the Psychosocial Assessment Following Overdose*. Oxford Brookes University: School of Health Care.

Whiting, P., Rutjes, A. W., Dinnes, J., *et al.* (2004) Development and validation of methods for assessing the quality of diagnostic accuracy studies. *Health Technology Assessment*, *8*, 1–234.

Whitlock, J., Eells, G., Cummings, N., *et al.* (2009) Nonsuicidal self-harm in college populations: mental health provider assessment of prevalence and need. *Journal of College Student Psychotherapy*, *23*, 172–183.

Wisely, J., Hare, D. & Fernandez–Ford, L. (2002) A study of the topography and nature of self–injurious behaviour in people with learning disabilities. *Journal of Learning Disabilities*, *6*, 61–71.

Wittouck, C., De Munck, S., Portzky, G., *et al.* (2010) A comparative follow-up study of aftercare and compliance of suicide attempters following standardized psychosocial assessment. *Archives of Suicide Research*, *14*, 135–145.

Wong, J. P. S., Stewart, S. M., Claassen, C., *et al.* (2008) Repeat suicide attempts in Hong Kong community adolescents. *Social Science and Medicine*, *66*, 232–241.

Wood, A., Trainor, G., Rothwell, J., *et al.* (2001) Randomized trial of group therapy for repeated deliberate self-harm in adolescents. *Journal of the American Academy of Child and Adolescent Psychiatry*, *40*, 1246–1253.

World Health Organization (2011) Suicide rates per 100,000 by country, year and sex [webpage]. Available at: http://www.who.int/mental_health/prevention/suicide_rates/en/index.html (accessed September 2011).

Yeo, H. M. & Yeo, W. W. (1993) Repeat deliberate self-harm: a link with childhood sexual abuse? *Archives of Emergency Medicine*, *10*, 161–166.

Zahl, D. L. & Hawton, K. (2004) Repetition of deliberate self-harm and subsequent suicide risk: long-term follow-up study of 11 583 patients. *British Journal of Psychiatry*, *185*, 70–75.

13   ABBREVIATIONS

A&E	accident and emergency department
ASIQ	Adult Suicide Ideation Questionnaire
BDI	Beck Depression Inventory
BHS	Beck Hopelessness Scale
BMJ	British Medical Journal
CAMHS	child and adolescent mental health services
CASE	Child and Adolescent Self-Harm in Europe
CBT	cognitive behavioural therapy
CDSR	Cochrane Database of Systematic Reviews
CEAC	cost-effectiveness acceptability curves
CENTRAL	Cochrane Central Register of Controlled Trials
CFI	case fatality index
CI	confidence interval
CINAHL	Cumulative Index to Nursing and Allied Health Literature
CMHT	community mental health team
CPA	care programme approach
CPN	community psychiatric nurse
DBT	dialectical behaviour therapy
df	degrees of freedom
DHA	docosahexaenoic acid
DSM (-III, -IV, -R)	*Diagnostic and Statistical Manual of Mental Disorders* of the American Psychiatric Association (3rd edition, 4th edition, Revision)
DSH	deliberate self-harm
EMBASE	Excerpta Medical Database
EPA	eicosapentaenoic acid
EQ-5D	European Quality of Life - 5 Dimensions
ERRS	Edinburgh Risk of Repetition Scale
FN	false negative
FP	false positive
FTI	fatal toxicity index
FU1	1 months' follow-up
FU2	6 months' follow-up
GCA	Global Clinical Assessment

GDG	Guideline Development Group
GHQ (-12)	General Health Questionnaire (12 items)
GP	general practitioner
GRADE	Grades of Recommendations: Assessment, Development and Evaluation
HAM-D	Hamilton Depression Rating Scale
HDRS	Hamilton Depression Rating Scale
HMIC	Health Management Information Consortium
HMSO	Her Majesty's Stationary Office
HRQoL	health-related quality of life
HTA	Health Technology Assessment
ICER	incremental cost-effectiveness ratio
IPEO	Instrument for Psychosocial Evaluation and Care of Suicide Attempters
IPSST	interpersonal problem-solving skills training
ITT	intention to treat
IV	inverse variance
K	total number of studies
MACT	manual-assisted cognitive behavioural therapy
MD	mean difference
MDD	major depressive disorder
MEDLINE	Medical Literature Analysis and Retrieval System Online
M-H	Mantel-Haenszel Test
MSHR	Manchester Self-Harm Rule
n/a *or* N/A *or* NA	not applicable
n	number of participants
N	total number of participants
NCCMH	National Collaborating Centre for Mental Health
NHS	National Health Service
NICE	National Institute for Health and Clinical Excellence
NPV	negative predictive value
OR	odds ratio
PICO	patient, intervention, comparison and outcome
PPV	positive predictive value
PSS	personal social services
PsycINFO	Psychological Information Database
PsycNET	a collection of databases from the APA's full-text database, including PsycINFO, PsycEXTRA and PsycBOOKS

QALY	quality of life year
RCT	randomised controlled trial
RFL	Reasons for Living Inventory
RR	relative risk/risk ratio
SBAQ	Suicide Behaviours and Attitudes Questionnaire
SBQ-R	Suicide Behaviours Questionnaire – Revised
SCL-90	Symptom Checklist (-90 items)
SD	standard deviation
s/h	self-harm
SIRI (-2)	Suicide Intervention Response Inventory (2nd version)
SIS	Suicide Intent Scale
SMD	standardised mean difference
SPS	Suicide Probability Scale
SSI (–C, –W)	Scale for Suicide Ideation (– Current, at Worst Point)
SSRI	selective serotonin reuptake inhibitor
STORM	Skills Training On Risk Management
SUAS	Suicide Assessment Scale
TAU	treatment as usual
TCA	tricyclic antidepressant
TN	true negative
TP	true positive